The Comedy of Charlie Chaplin

Artistry in Motion

Dan Kamin

THE SCARECROW PRESS, INC.
Lanham, Maryland • Toronto • Plymouth, UK
2008

SCARECROW PRESS, INC.

Published in the United States of America
by Scarecrow Press, Inc.
A wholly owned subsidiary of The Rowman & Littlefield Publishing Group, Inc.
4501 Forbes Boulevard, Suite 200, Lanham, Maryland 20706
www.scarecrowpress.com

Estover Road
Plymouth PL6 7PY
United Kingdom

British Library Cataloguing in Publication Information Available

Library of Congress Cataloging-in-Publication Data

Kamin, Dan, 1946–
The comedy of Charlie Chaplin : artistry in motion / Dan Kamin.
p. cm.
Includes bibliographical references and index.
ISBN-13: 978-0-8108-6142-8 (hardback : alk. paper)
ISBN-10: 0-8108-6142-9 (hardback : alk. paper)
1. Chaplin, Charlie, 1889–1977—Criticism and interpretation. I. Title.
PN2287.C5K35 2008
791.4302'8092—dc22
2008018036

∞™ The paper used in this publication meets the minimum requirements of American National Standard for Information Sciences—Permanence of Paper for Printed Library Materials, ANSI/NISO Z39.48-1992.
Manufactured in the United States of America.

For the women in my life,
Carol and Hester.
Without you,
even Charlie Chaplin couldn't cheer me up.

Contents

Acknowledgments

This book is only the latest of my attempts to get Charlie Chaplin out of my system. There are a number of people who must share the blame for my failure. Frank Scheide and Hooman Mehran, coeditors of *The Chaplin Revue* book series, have repeatedly ensnared me into participating in their dubious literary enterprises. I do so only out of pity, since these unfortunates suffer from an even more virulent form of the disease than I do. Then there are the people I think of as the Chaplin mafia, including Bonnie McCourt, Lisa Stein, Bruce Lawton, Alice Artzt, Shunichi Ohkubo, Ono Hiroyuki, David Totheroh, and Louise Burton, to name a few, all of whom have enabled me through their misguided acts of kindness.

Speaking of enablers, Kate Guyonvarch of Association Chaplin in Paris has been all too willing to offer her time and resources, knowing full well what the result would be. She, Josephine Chaplin, and the association allowed me—indeed, encouraged me—to print many of the pictures in this book, no doubt hoping to lure new victims. Cecilia Cenciarelli of Progetto Chaplin has cheerfully provided materials from the Chaplin Archive, housed at the Cineteca Bologna—and why not? The very existence of these organizations attests to the global nature of the crisis.

Two generations of Scarecrow Press editors must share a portion of the blame as well, though theirs was a hopeless task. Had it been possible to edit Chaplin out of my life, Carol Fryday would surely have done it by now. That our marriage has survived not only Chaplin, but her careful editorial scrutiny of this manuscript, is, like a Chaplin film, a miracle of love and laughter.

A Note to the Reader

This was supposed to be a revised edition of a book called *Charlie Chaplin's One-Man Show*, but it soon became apparent that the book, like almost everything Charlie Chaplin touches in his films, was turning into something else in front of my eyes. It was becoming a new book—based on the old one, to be sure, but so different that it needed a new title.

When I wrote the original in the early 1980s, I was cranking 8mm and 16mm prints through small film editors and projecting them onto my living room wall, or taking notes in darkened movie theatres. While there was a certain pioneering charm about having to study the films this way, it wasn't easy to do. With Chaplin's complete output now available on DVD I've been able to examine the films much more closely. In the process I've discovered many gems—gags, scenes, and sometimes whole films—that I overlooked or gave short shrift the first time. I've also been able to draw on a wealth of new material that has come out over the past two decades. So many books on Chaplin have been published that there are now books *about* the books on Chaplin. Significant primary source material, such as the Chaplin studio records and many of his outtakes, has also come to light, so that there is more information available than ever before about the man and his art.

But the main reason my old book ended up morphing into this new one is that my ideas have evolved considerably, due in no small part to the doors that opened to me after that first one came out. I was invited to give many presentations on Chaplin at film festivals and colleges, and became involved with a number of intriguing theatrical projects, including plays about Chaplin at Harvard's American Repertory Theatre and Canada's Shaw Festival. Symphony orchestras began asking me to create live "silent movies" on stage. Hollywood beckoned as well: I devised the physical comedy sequences for *Benny and Joon* with Johnny Depp, and helped to re-create Chaplin's art for the movie *Chaplin*. Obviously, there could be no better way of putting my ideas about Chaplin to the test than training Robert Downey Jr. for the title role in *Chaplin*, and I've described that experience in a postscript, "Teaching Charlie Chaplin How to Walk."

One of the unexpected pleasures of the first book was that it ushered me into a worldwide circle of Chaplin authors, scholars, aficionados, and even family members. Many of these people have become treasured friends. If this new book pleases them, I could ask for no higher praise—although a few favorable reviews would also be nice.

INTRODUCTION

The Surprising Art of Charlie Chaplin

Charlie Chaplin first strolled onto a movie screen early in 1914, one of many actors featured in the short, crude knockabout comedies produced by Mack Sennett's Keystone Film Company. The public immediately took notice of him, and he obliged by cranking out films at the phenomenal rate of almost one a week. No later commentator ever pronounced any these films a work of genius, yet they rocketed him to fame. By the end of the year the Essanay Company hired him away from Keystone at nearly ten times his original salary, and boasted in a trade journal that

MILLIONS ARE
LAUGHING WITH
CHARLES CHAPLIN
THE WORLD'S GREATEST COMEDIAN
IS NOW WITH
ESSANAY[1]

It wasn't hype, for manifestations of Chaplin's popularity were everywhere. Theater owners began sponsoring Chaplin look-alike contests to capitalize on the craze, and the first in a long line of Chaplin impersonators began to appear on the vaudeville stage and in films. Tin Pan Alley and European music publishers, quick to exploit what even Chaplin thought must be a temporary fad, published more than twenty songs about him in 1915 alone. The titles and illustrated covers reveal what the public found so appealing—"That Charlie Chaplin Walk," "Charlie Chaplin Waddle," and "Charlie Chaplin's Frolics." Lines of chorus girls, doing the now famous walk, sang "Those Charlie Chaplin Feet" in Broadway revues. There was a thriving market for Chaplin novelties of all types, including squirt rings, lapel pins, pennants, statuettes, and 10-cent "costume kits." Jokes, cartoons, and poems about him proliferated in newspapers and magazines:

> This is a very curious world,
> So many things are happ'nin';
> For all the girls
> Wear Pickford curls,
> And boys play Charlie Chaplin.[2]

One of the 1915 songs about Chaplin. Even such a simplified representation as this crude cartoon image was instantly recognizable.

The Chaplin craze hit Britain just as hard, as reflected in this comic postcard from 1916.

All this fuss can seem a bit puzzling if one looks at these early films in living rooms or college classrooms. It's only when they're projected on large screens in front of large audiences—especially audiences that include children—that they demonstrate their undiminished power to delight.

Seeing one that way planted the seed for this book.

The occasion was a museum screening of silent comedy shorts, among which were *The Masquerader*, a Chaplin Keystone from 1914, and Buster Keaton's *Cops*, a 1922 gem often singled out as Keaton's finest short. It seemed unfair to juxtapose the mature Keaton with the novice Chaplin, and I was certain that the audience would respond more strongly to *Cops*.

But I was in for a surprise. While *Cops* drew appreciative intermittent laughter from the audience, *The Masquerader* had them giggling, chuckling, and roaring throughout. Apparently, something was operating beyond the rudimentary story and gags of the Chaplin film, which involved Chaplin being fired from his job as a screen actor, then returning the next day dressed up as a woman and "vamping" the film director. The audience was evidently responding the way a 1914 audience would have. Somehow, Chaplin's mere presence was winning them over. We cared about how this fellow felt, and were fascinated with the things he was doing. A palpable warmth crept over the auditorium. In contrast, the Keaton film, though wonderfully ingenious and chock full of amazing acrobatic stunts, seemed chilly, cerebral, and a bit remote, much like his screen character. The children particularly seemed to move in and out of Keaton's brilliant dark comedy, whereas they were riveted to the Chaplin film.

So what did this modern audience find so compelling about *The Masquerader*? The answer had to be *the way he moved*. Chaplin's art begins and ends with movement.

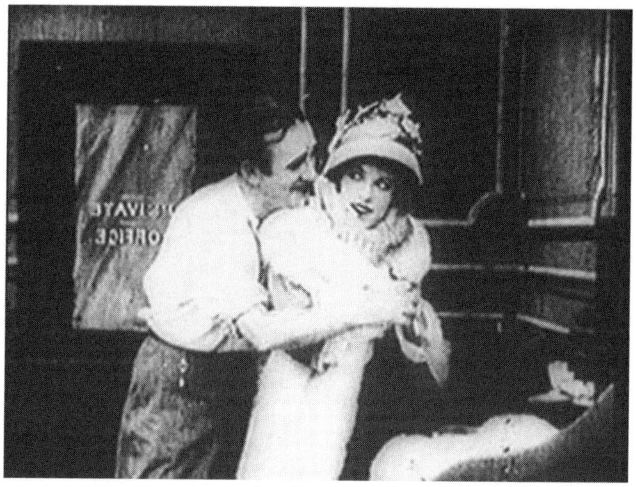

Charlie turns on the charm in *The Masquerader*.

Chaplin isn't just *pretending* to be a woman, he *becomes* a woman—and a very attractive one at that. The effect is at once startling, unnerving, and very funny.

It wasn't the first time I'd been surprised by a Chaplin film. The first time was when I was in college and saw my first Chaplin film, *The Gold Rush*. This was no fledgling ten-minute quickie like *The Masquerader*, but a full-length feature, considered by many to be Chaplin's masterpiece. I'd rarely heard laughter that loud or sustained in a movie theatre. And the film was more than funny; it was full of suspenseful thrill sequences and moments of unexpected poignancy. Chaplin was amazing to watch, a comic dervish, his movements as polished and graceful as those of a dancer. The audience cheered and applauded.

I left the theatre in a daze. How could a silent movie from 1925 pack that much of a punch? What was the secret behind its strange power? And where had Chaplin *been* when I was growing up? To find out, I went to the library, where I discovered numerous books on Chaplin. It was certainly interesting to read about his rise from obscurity to worldwide fame, the fabulous wealth he earned, the juicy scandals that dogged him, and how he managed to get himself banished from America. This explained some of what I wanted to know—but not his *art*. Chaplin himself said little on the subject in his lengthy 1964 autobiography.

There were some excellent critical works that traced the evolution of his character and the plots of his films, described celebrated gags and sequences, and recounted

This British postcard accurately depicts Charlie's characteristic gestures. The note on the other side says "He could get the job of king if he tried for it . . . Everybody is Charlie mad on this side. Sing songs about him & crack jokes."

the public and critical reception to his work. The authors were uniformly lavish in their praise, some of them rising to rhapsodic heights. Yet the core quality that made the films so compelling remained elusive. That's because it's difficult to describe movement, and Chaplin's art is, first and foremost, an art of movement. He is the consummate mime.[3] Authors Raoul Sobel and David Francis hit the nail on the head in *Chaplin, Genesis of a Clown*, when they said that mime

> was Chaplin's supreme gift. No amount of intelligence, perception, emotion and ideas could have taken its place, for without the ability to translate them into gesture and movement, the "Little Fellow" would have remained a dead letter, a character Chaplin might have dreamed about but never have realized.[4]

Chaplin on the first issue of a popular American film magazine, 1915. Charlie's looking at himself and laughing, just like everyone else.

To deepen my understanding of Chaplin's art I began to study mime.[5] I learned to dissect movement and think about it analytically, eventually embarking on a career as a mime artist and comedian. I kept on watching the Chaplin films, mostly for pleasure, but also in the hope that someday they would yield up their secrets. Eventually they did, and that's when I knew I had to write this book. It's the book I wanted to *read* about Chaplin.

The book is divided into three sections. Part I, "That Charlie Chaplin Walk," recounts Chaplin's theatrical background, examines how and why he moves the way he does on the screen, and considers how he adapted his stage technique to the film medium. A close look at his only solo film, the celebrated *One A.M.*, demonstrates how he puts it all together.

Part II, "Charlie Chaplin's Frolics," examines how Chaplin's physical virtuosity led him to create the timeless visual comedy that brought silent films to their peak. Chapter 5, "Gagman," deals with his defining comic motif, his magical transformation gags. Chapter 6, "Cast of Characters," looks at the evolution of Chaplin's character and the characters who surround him. Chapter 7, "Shall We Dance?" explores his unparalleled achievement in conjuring comedy from the fundamental physical laws of movement.

Part III, "March of the Movies," deals with Chaplin's dilemma as a silent comedian in the sound era. After 1928 he faced the problem of integrating antithetical elements—sound and movement, verbal and visual comedy. Each of his sound films represents a different experiment, and he never repeated himself. Considering them individually reveals the sometimes surprising ways that Chaplin remained true to his silent roots, while at the same time reinventing himself to keep his art viable.

We have ample documentation that Chaplin was irresistibly funny on stage. Though we can never witness those performances, we're fortunate that his stage skills blossomed in the film medium, and that the films will survive to work their magic on future generations—or at least some members of future generations.

Though Chaplin was without question the funniest man in the world in 1915 and for years afterward, no one holds that title forever. The public no longer flocks to his films in droves, and they never will again. His historical moment has passed.

His fame as a cultural phenomenon is likely to endure, however, since, more than any other artist of his time, Chaplin's life and art were intertwined with the signal events and preoccupations of the twentieth century, including:

- *The rise of the film industry.* Chaplin helped to popularize film and legitimize it as an art form. In 1918 he became one of the founding members of United Artists.
- *The cult of celebrity.* Chaplin was the prototype, attracting crowds in the tens of thousands when he traveled. His image was used to sell millions of magazines, toys, song sheets, and every imaginable kind of novelty item.
- *The World Wars.* He made comedies about both of them while they were still raging.
- *The public appetite for scandal.* He tested the limits of public tolerance with a busy sex life that became fodder for the tabloid press.
- *Art and politics.* The left-wing content of his later films, along with his outspoken activism, made him a target of McCarthy-era politicians and the FBI, who ultimately goaded him into exile in 1952.
- *Politics and art.* Twenty years later, with the Vietnam War raging, Chaplin was invited home to receive an honorary lifetime achievement Oscar. The occasion allowed the film industry and the media to laud Chaplin's filmic achievements, and, by implication, deliver a stinging rebuke to the repressive policies of the then-current regime.
- *Triumph of the underdog.* Three years later, in 1975, the child of the London slums was knighted. He died on Christmas Day 1977, bringing to a close a rags-to-riches saga that would be totally unbelievable—if it weren't true.

Yet, in the end, Chaplin's films transcend even the amazing story of his life, not just because of what they

Another British postcard reflects Chaplin's characteristic mix of humor and sentiment.

Chaplin on the first issue of a popular British film magazine, 1919.

say but because of the way they say it. Charlie Chaplin speaks the primal language of movement, and he speaks it better than anyone else in the history of motion pictures. He creates a swirling comic world and fills it with magical surprises and choreographic comedy that are a wonder to behold. He establishes an intimate rapport with his audience, and through his physical eloquence he demonstrates, with bracing clarity, how deeply we can understand what goes through another person's head—and his heart. That's why his films retain the power to mesmerize an audience today, just as they mesmerized audiences the world over in 1914.

To discover Charlie Chaplin is like encountering a beloved, long-lost friend. The reunion is so joyous that no words are necessary. It is enough to laugh, and to know that we are not alone.

Notes

1. *Motion Picture News*, 1915, cited in Gerald McDonald, *The Picture History of Charlie Chaplin* (Franklin Square, NY: Nostalgia Press, 1965), n.p.

2. *Motion Picture Magazine*, May 1916, cited in Raoul Sobel and David Francis, *Chaplin, Genesis of a Clown* (London: Quartet Books, 1977), 137.

3. A word on the word *mime*, since I use it throughout the book. When I wrote my first book in the early 1980s, mime, as popularized by Marcel Marceau and practiced by street mimes across the country, was in the process of wearing out its welcome. Within the next few years the public turned against it with a vengeance. Mimes became the butt of innumerable cartoons and jokes, such as, "If you shoot a mime, do you need a silencer?" Mime jokes became the "safe" ethnic jokes of their time, and most mimes gave up their striped shirts and white-face makeup and found other avenues of expression.

Unfortunately, the baby was thrown out with the bathwater, because the word *mime* was at one time a rather arcane but useful theatrical term. Derived from the ancient Greek word *mimos*, meaning "to imitate," mime came to mean body language, the use of posture, movement, and gestures to convey information. That's the way it's used in this book. But for most people the word now connotes bad art: the cloyingly cute guy annoying people in the park.

This sudden downturn in popularity was to be expected, for historically, that's what mime has always done—it appears on the world stage, struts its stuff for a while, and then gets unceremoniously hooted off, only to reappear in a new guise. It did this three times in the twentieth century. Silent film represented the pinnacle of popularity of mime as a discrete art form, dominating world entertainment for almost two decades. When the public embraced sound films, silent films were instantly rendered obsolete. A couple of decades later mime resurfaced in the form of silent sketches on the television variety shows of Red Skelton, Sid Caesar, and others—performers who had grown up on silent films and prided themselves on their ability to act out stories in pantomime, another word for mime. As those shows ran their course the white-faced mimes, led by Marceau, took center stage, dazzling audiences with amazing optical illusions created with movement.

But even as the public was tiring of white-faced performers, mime was morphing into new forms. French master teacher Jacques Lecoq modernized the ancient mask tradition and trained the popular group Mummenschanz, and Julie Taymore, who made mime and masks the centerpiece of her Broadway hit *The Lion King*. Michael Jackson derived his famous moonwalk from Marceau's walking-against-the-wind sketch, and soon break-dancers were incorporating that and other illusion mime movements into their acrobatic urban dance form. And then there's entertainment juggernaut Cirque du Soleil, a mimelike, animal-free reinvention of the circus. What *is* Cirque du Soleil, if not the illegitimate offspring of P. T. Barnum and Marcel Marceau?

4. Sobel and Francis, *Chaplin*, 134.

5. My teacher was Jewel Walker, who had studied with Etienne Decroux, considered the father of modern mime. Decroux invented the illusions popularized by his student Marcel Marceau.

PART ONE

That Charlie Chaplin Walk, 1915. This photo became Chaplin's most iconic image, endlessly reproduced in magazines and newspapers, and used as the basis for statuettes, toys, and dozens of other novelty items.

CHAPTER ONE

On the Boards

"I never lost sight of my ultimate aim to become an actor."[1]

Charlie Chaplin was born in 1889 to two music hall performers, Charles and Hannah Chaplin. Charles was a headliner throughout the 1890s, so successful that at least eight of his signature comic songs were published. He smiles jauntily from the illustrated covers, waving gaily or tipping his hat to the viewer.

Offstage, life was not as cheery. The young couple separated during Charlie's second year, and Hannah, who had worked intermittently as a singer, actress, and dancer in the halls, now found herself trying to support Charlie and his older half-brother, Sydney, on her meager earnings as a performer.

In his autobiography Chaplin relates in vivid detail how his performing career began at the age of five. During one of her engagements Hannah's voice failed her on stage. The manager, having seen Charlie entertaining her friends in the wings, led him onto the stage. Feeling quite at ease, Charlie sang a popular cockney character song, and the audience began throwing coins. He stopped abruptly, announcing that he would resume singing once he had gathered up the money. The audience laughed. The manager hurried out to help him gather up the money and Charlie became alarmed, thinking the man wanted it for himself. Another laugh. Reassured that the money was his, he danced and did a few imitations, including one of his mother singing. Then he did something that astounded the crowd.

> In repeating the chorus, in all innocence, I imitated Mother's voice cracking and was surprised at the impact it had on the audience. There was laughter and cheers, then more money throwing; and when Mother came on the stage to carry me off, her presence evoked tremendous applause. That night was my first appearance on the stage and Mother's last.[2]

The whole scene sounds suspiciously like something out of one of Chaplin's later pictures, so readers might be forgiven if they're a bit skeptical.[3] But true or not, there can be no better evocation of the birth of Chaplin as an artist. Nothing is unusual about a cute boy singer, but by breaking out of his role to gather up his loot, he injected an endearing bit of spontaneity into the occasion. Then he topped himself by imitating the humiliating failure of his mother's voice. The audacity and casual cruelty of this impersonation delighted the audience, which was no doubt also impressed by Chaplin's precocious skill as a mimic.

The other intriguing thing about the anecdote is that it reveals that the young Charlie already had a repertoire of song, dance, and mimicry skills. Throughout his life Chaplin would entertain people with snatches of old songs and dead-on imitations of the entertainers he had seen in his youth. Chaplin always credited his mother for his talent at mime and mimicry. He loved to recount how they would sit by the window for hours, Hannah imitating and making astute observations about passersby. He learned the rudiments of his craft at her knee. He also learned that performing meant rewards and attention from others. After Hannah taught him a humorous poem, "Miss Priscilla's Cat," that she had copied down from a shop window, he became a school celebrity by reciting it for all the classes.

As Hannah's performing career spluttered, she tried to make ends meet with piecemeal sewing jobs. Charlie helped by dancing for pennies to barrel organs outside pubs and finding assorted other odd jobs to earn money. Chaplin's father was legally liable for supporting the boys, but he resisted, and Hannah was forced repeatedly to take legal action; Chaplin Senior got into trouble several times with the authorities and was at one point arrested for nonsupport.

The family was in desperate straits, leading a vagabond existence in and out of dismal apartments and the dreaded workhouse.[4] Hannah's mental health began to deteriorate alarmingly. In his autobiography Chaplin attributes this, at least in part, to malnutrition. When he was ten she was committed to a mental hospital for the first time and the boys were sent to live with Chaplin Senior for a couple of months.

Although he recalled seeing his father perform once on the stage, up to that point he barely knew him. Chaplin describes the reunion in a way that reveals his budding mime artistry:

> He fascinated me. At meals I watched every move he made, the way he ate, the way he held his knife as though it were a pen when cutting his meat. And for years I copied him.[5]

Unfortunately for the boys, both Chaplin Senior and his mistress were alcoholics, and neither of them welcomed the prospect of raising two more boys—they already had a four-year-old son of their own. The two months were an ordeal for all concerned, ending when Hannah was discharged from the asylum. She gathered up the boys, and the trio found another small apartment.

Life began to improve. Sydney found work, Charlie went back to school, and Chaplin Senior finally coughed up some much-needed cash. More importantly, perhaps reacting to Hannah's fragile mental condition, he arranged for Charlie to join the Eight Lancashire Lads, a clog-dancing act. This would relieve Hannah of Charlie's care and provide her some desperately needed income—and get Charles Senior off the hook.

Thus, Charlie Chaplin began his professional career at the age of nine. He toured with the Lancashire Lads for the next year and a half, on a grueling schedule of rehearsing and performing two or three shows a day and attending school in whatever town they might be. During this time Charlie was exposed to the great pool of artistic talent on the music hall stage, and he eagerly lapped it up, watching enraptured from the wings. Inevitably he began aping some of the other performers, such as the popular actor Bransby Williams, who movingly portrayed various Dickens characters. Chaplin's impersonation must have been good, for he was given a chance to do the act one night as part of the Lancashire Lads' turn.

In his autobiography Chaplin, who wasn't much given to making fun of himself in print, amusingly describes the ensuing disaster. Playing Williams as the old man from *The Old Curiosity Shop*, he wore an oversized bald wig fringed with hair. This, along with the hunched-over posture he adopted, made him look like a giant beetle creeping across the stage, and the audience giggled. This time the laughter was unwelcome. He was unable to change the audience's mood, for his voice was choked with such heartfelt emotion that he was inaudible. Before long he was unceremoniously hooted off. This humiliating experience evidently didn't discourage him for long, for soon he and another boy in the troupe were dreaming up a comedy act, to be called the Millionaire Tramps.[6]

During the Christmas season of 1900 the troupe appeared in the pantomime *Cinderella*[7] at the London Hippodrome. Chaplin played a cat, wearing a mask with a mechanical winking eye. During one performance he improvised some of the kind of risqué comic business that later audiences would love in his films. He walked up to a dog and sniffed its behind, then turned to the audience and winked. He sniffed the dog some more, then trotted to the proscenium, sniffed it, and lifted his leg. The manager, understandably alarmed by these off-color antics, made sure there were no repetitions, and Charlie continued in the role without the improvisation for another three months.[8] During the run he also had the opportunity work with the star of the show, the great Spanish clown Marceline, whose droll comic style he admired.

The following year Chaplin Senior died of alcohol-related illness, leaving the family completely on their own. Sydney, who had earlier been trained to work at sea, went out on several voyages, returning with precious funds. Charlie was in and out of school and various odd jobs.

Just after Charlie turned fourteen, Hannah relapsed into incoherence and was once more committed, this time for eight months. Charlie was left on his own, lying to the authorities so that he wouldn't be sent back to the workhouse. Deeply ashamed, he skulked in and out of the little apartment, avoiding the landlady and others, eating when he could and occasionally sleeping on the streets.

Then his luck changed. Sydney returned from the sea determined to make good on the stage—but it was Charlie who got the opportunity first. Bravely presenting himself to a theatrical agency, he was immediately hired to play in a production of *Sherlock Holmes*, written by Sir Arthur Conan Doyle and the American actor William Gillette. Holmes would be portrayed by the popular actor H. A. Saintsbury, and Chaplin would play Billy, the cockney page boy. First, however, he appeared in the role of a cockney newsboy in Saintsbury's short-lived play *Jim, A Romance of Cockayne*.[9]

While Charlie had rehearsed his short dancing routines rigorously with the Lancashire Lads, rehearsing a full-length play with dialogue was another matter altogether—and a revelation. Saintsbury, sensing the boy's talent, was patient and encouraging during the rehearsals of both plays. He introduced Chaplin to the actor's craft, toning down his tendency to mug and move his head too much.

Jim was an old-fashioned melodrama—evidently a little *too* old-fashioned, given its short run. But Saintsbury's tutelage was to prove invaluable to Chaplin, who accords him full credit in his autobiography. Saintsbury was a matinee idol of Victorian theatre, an established master of the form. While Chaplin would often parody the excesses of melodramatic actors in his films, he witnessed—and respected—their dramatic power.

He demonstrates this delightfully in a scene in *The Pawnshop*, made in 1916. A geezer—clearly a thespian of the old school—comes in to pawn his wedding ring. Behind the counter a skeptical Charlie mocks his florid gestures, but before long is reduced to sobs by the man's sad tale. Wiping away his tears, Charlie purchases the ring—whereupon the old fraud peels off change from an enormous wad of bills, nods briskly, and strides out. Charlie blinks and slaps himself in the face with the back of his hand. He has been bamboozled by the old pro's hammy but effective acting.

When *Jim* opened, Charlie received his first notices, and they were full of praise even though the show itself was panned. The good notices continued as he toured with Saintsbury in *Sherlock Holmes*, then with other *Holmes* companies, on and off, for the next two and a half years.

Getting this work marked the end of a life of destitution for the Chaplin brothers, which was fortunate, for the fog of madness now permanently settled in around poor Hannah. She was again committed to the lunatic asylum, and would live in such institutions until the Chaplin boys were able to bring her to America in 1921. There she lived out her remaining days in addled comfort.

The desperate poverty of Chaplin's childhood left an indelible mark, as we know from his films. He was obsessed with money and remained frugal to the point of parsimony even after becoming rich. During his long engagement with the *Holmes* companies he supplemented his quite sufficient income with photography and other schemes.

Although shy, Chaplin occasionally entertained the other actors in the company with his impersonations, continuing the practice begun in his early years. He would delight his friends with impromptu performances throughout his life; his ability to entertain fellow professionals no doubt greatly increased his confidence in his abilities. He would need all the confidence he could get when it came time to generate original material for his films.

The highlight of Chaplin's time on the legitimate stage was his being invited, in 1905, to play Billy at the Duke of York's Theatre in the West End of London. This time, coauthor William Gillette himself played the title role. Gillette performed in a much more naturalistic "American" fashion. Chaplin watched him carefully and no doubt profited from the experience of working with him; mostly, though, he watched the beautiful leading lady, Marie Doro. The sixteen-year-old Charlie was hopelessly smitten. Not so smitten, however, that he didn't fully enjoy his new status and privileges as a West End actor. These included courtesy access to other plays and an invitation to attend the funeral of the noted actor Sir Henry Irving.

Alas, it was not to last for long, for the theatre was booked for a Christmas revival of *Peter Pan*, and the engagement closed after a couple of months. Gillette returned to America. A final provincial tour of the play with yet another company lasted three more months, marking the end of Charlie's career in the legitimate theatre.

Although he was reluctant to do so, Charlie now returned to the music hall. Syd had become enthusiastic about the possibilities of comedy following several successful appearances in shipboard entertainments. As Charlie had earlier helped Syd find work in the *Sherlock Holmes* companies, now Syd helped Charlie land an engagement in a new comedy sketch, *Repairs*. The show, featuring incompetent workmen causing slapstick mayhem, sounds like the prototype for any number of Chaplin films. Charlie played the part of a dim-witted plumber's assistant. Told by the plumber to hang up his hat, he asks where. Instructed to hammer a nail into a wall and hang the hat on it, he manages to make a mess, knocking first through a door panel, then a water pipe.

During their break the workers get drunk on beer and do a wild "sand dance" on the sawdust produced by the carpenter. The two posed photos that survive of the sketch were presumably taken after this point, for the stage is a mess and Charlie is front and center, his nose reddened. In one shot he stares blankly ahead as his boss angrily brandishes the offending hat; his head tilts slightly to one side, giving a quizzical look, his arms hang limply at his sides, and his legs protrude from comically short trousers. In the second photo he kneels, about to chop or hammer a piece of wood; this time his head is tilted sharply in the opposite direction. In both shots Syd, who played a labor agitator, perches precariously atop a ladder in the upstage area, sporting the kind of walrus mustache he was to wear in many films.

Charlie left *Repairs* after a couple of months to take a job with another music hall sketch, *Casey's Circus*. This burlesque revue was a sequel to the very popular *Casey's Court*.[10] The premise will be familiar to anyone who has ever seen a Little Rascals comedy: A group of street urchins puts on an amateur show. The *Court* troupe put on a music hall–type entertainment, featuring much singing and dancing, while *Casey's Circus* had the urchins putting on a circus climaxed by a parody of the popular spectacle *Dick Turpin's Ride to York*, which involved a great deal of frenetic action. Charlie was the principal player among the urchins, and the well-known comic actor Will Murray played Mrs. Casey.[11] Murray rehearsed him in the several roles he played during the half-hour piece, including Dick, and later claimed to have taught him how to turn corners in his distinctive way for the role.

But Chaplin made an ever bigger impression with his portrayal of the immensely popular "Doctor" Walford Bodie, the "magnetic healer, bloodless surgeon and electric wizard," a genuine phenomenon of the age who attracted thousands with demonstrations of his healing powers, a combination of hypnosis, massage, and the dramatic application of static electricity. Chaplin had seen the elegant Bodie offstage, at Irving's funeral, but had never seen him perform. Nevertheless, when made up Chaplin looked remarkably like the real Bodie, impressive and imposing. He had photographs taken of himself in character, and reprints one in his autobiography. Chaplin described his performance on the opening night to an interviewer in 1915:

> Once in the glare of the footlights, I dropped into the part, determined to play it, play it well, and hold the audience. . . . I advanced slowly, impressively, feeling the gaze of the crowd, and, with a carefully studied gesture, hung my cane—I held it by the wrong end! Instead of hanging on my arm, as I expected, it clattered on the stage. Startled, I stooped to pick it up, and my high silk hat fell from my head. I grasped it, put it on quickly, and, paper wadding falling out, I found my whole head buried in its black depths.
>
> A great burst of laughter came from the audience. When, pushing the hat back, I went desperately on with my serious lines, the crowd roared, held its sides, shrieked with mirth till it gasped. The more serious I was, the funnier it struck the audience. I came off at last, pursued by howls of laughter and wild applause, which called me back again. I had made the hit of the evening.[12]

This description captures what would become a central element of Chaplin's comic style, his serious demeanor in the midst of slapstick action. That combination seemed to be a forte with English comedians, and with Chaplin's next mentor, Fred Karno, in particular.

Sydney preceded Charlie into the Karno company, joining in 1906. It took awhile for him to persuade Karno to see his brother, and after the year-and-a-half run of *Casey's Circus* ended Charlie was "between engagements" for about seven months. All of his projects during this interval failed; he wrote an unproduced comic sketch, appeared as the lead in a play that closed in a week, and had a disastrous and humiliating one-night appearance as a Jewish comedian.

Karno, by then the undisputed king of music hall comedy, had produced an unending series of inventive comedy sketches, beginning with *Hilarity* in 1895 and continuing with such hits as *Jail Birds*, *London Suburbia*, *The Dandy Thieves*, and his longest running success, *Mumming Birds*. *Repairs* was in the mold of such shows, but evidently not as good, for it closed shortly after Chaplin's departure. By the time Chaplin joined Karno in 1908 there were at least ten Karno companies touring England and other parts of the world.

The brilliance of the former circus acrobat lay in his largely wordless slapstick sketches. Often set to music, these sketches spotlighted troupes trained to incredible precision. As Chaplin later stated:

> Each man working for Karno had to have perfect timing and had to know the peculiarities of everyone else in the cast so that we could, collectively, achieve a cast tempo.
>
> It took about a year for an actor to get the repertoire of a dozen shows down pat. Karno required us to know a number of parts so that the players could be interchanged. When one left the company it was like taking a screw or a pin out of a very delicate piece of machinery.[13]

In his later writing Chaplin ignores the creative contributions of many of his collaborators and colleagues, but he speaks proudly of his days with Fred Karno. Karno applied the kind of precision to comedy acting that Charlie had learned in the dance routines he'd performed with the Lancashire Lads. His "fun factory" (where the troupe rehearsed) was the training ground for many comedians who went on to successful careers.

To his already impressive set of physical skills Chaplin now added the distinctive Karno brand of acrobatic comedy. Karno's technical perfectionism and endless rehearsals became Chaplin's credo as a filmmaker. Karno also insisted on surprising moments of seriousness or incongruous tenderness during his skits. For example, after knocking an adversary out cold, a comedian might gently slide something soft under his head to cushion it. This, of course, was a comic vein that Chaplin mined extensively in his films.

During his years with Karno Chaplin also picked up many of the quirky mannerisms that were to make his film appearances so distinctive. For example, from Fred Kitchen he learned the trick of tossing a cigarette behind him and kicking it backward, along with an array of other kicks and falls. Kitchen later claimed credit for his splay-footed shuffle as well.[14]

Though at first skeptical of Chaplin's youth and shyness, Karno recognized his mime talent. His tryout role was in a sketch called *The Football March*, playing opposite one of Karno's chief comedians, Harry Weldon. Chaplin played the comic villain who attempts to bribe goalkeeper Weldon into throwing the big game.

In his autobiography Chaplin describes his performance in detail, and it sounds much like the comic business he performed as "Doctor" Bodie. Again, he's in formal clothes, sporting a cane and cape. He enters dramatically, back to the audience, then turns suddenly around to reveal a bright red nose. Drunks—especially rich drunks—are a staple of music hall comedy, and Chaplin gets a big laugh. He builds upon it by tripping over a dumbbell, then entangles his cane with a punching bag; struggling to release the cane, he smacks himself with the bag. Trying to strike the bag back, he is smacked in the ear by his cane. Suddenly his pants drop, and he grabs for the button on the stage floor. But it's not the button. "Those confounded rabbits," he says disgustedly.

Weldon, waiting in the wings for his entrance cue, is puzzled by all the laughter in a role that previously had served only to set off his own entrance. He enters and Chaplin drags him into the flow of improvisation, saying, "Quick! I'm undone! A pin!"

His performance was a hit with the audience, and, more importantly, with Karno, who hired him on the spot. It also earned him the enmity of Weldon, who mistreated him during the run and bad-mouthed him ever after.

The next part Chaplin played, the "Inebriated Swell" in *Mumming Birds*, was to become his signature role in the Karno company—and a signature role for him in films as well. Subtitled "An Up-To-Date Musical Travesty on the Modern Music Hall," *Mumming Birds* featured a bill of very bad variety acts on a stage-within-the-stage—a stage framed by two tiers of box seats occupied by other members of the company playing spectators.[15] The false spectators, notably the swell, become all too involved with the acts.

Chaplin brought a boisterous physicality to the genteel inebriate, enlivening the role with his characteristic fierce concentration. Stan Laurel, who performed with Chaplin for years in the company, elaborates on how compelling he was as a performer:

> He even made those of us in the cast break up time after time. . . . He had those eyes that absolutely forced you to look at them. He had the damnedest way of looking at an audience. He had the damnedest way of looking at *you*, onstage. . . . They're very dark, the deepest kind of blue, and intense, just like him. And they can dominate anyone they look at. That's a part of the secret of his great success—eyes that make you believe in him whatever he does.[16]

The show begins as the wealthy drunk is ushered to his box. Led in by a pretty usherette, he smiles and bows to her. Totally sozzled, and possibly a bit infatuated by her as well, he takes off one of his gloves and hands it to her, along with a tip. Then he absentmindedly tries to tug the same glove off again, pulling to no avail on his bare fingers. She gently corrects him and exits. He produces a cigarette and tries to light it by holding the tip to an electric lightbulb, thus introducing one of the most pervasive gag devices of his films, treating one object (lightbulb) as if it is another (gaslight). He's about to smash the bulb in frustration when he notices that a fat boy, sitting in the box on the opposite side of the stage, is holding out a lit match to him. Utterly misjudging the distance between them, the drunk leans towards the boy, cigarette in mouth—and tumbles spectacularly out of his box. Such comic misjudgments were to become characteristic of Chaplin's many drunk acts on film.

At this point the curtain opens on the stage-within-the-stage, and the acts commence. The drunk chases an awful singer offstage, groans at a ham actor doing a recitation of "The Trail of the Yukon," imagines a pretty soubrette is singing "You Naughty, Naughty Man" directly to him, and, finally, accepts the challenge of "Marconi AIi, the Terrible Turk, the Greatest Wrestler Ever to Appear Before the British Public" to wrestle him for a handsome purse. The drunk simply tickles the scrawny Ali silly, until he falls helplessly to the mat. This leads to a general melee of food throwing, yelling, and clothes ripping that ends the act.

Chaplin's great success in this role prompted Karno to offer him the important goalkeeper role in a London production of *The Football Match*. Like his mother before him, Chaplin suffered an attack of laryngitis, and after two unsuccessful performances he was unceremoniously put back into a *Mumming Birds* company.

However, he would eventually play this and most of the other leading roles in the Karno repertoire, including another aristocratic bumbler, Archibald Binks, in *Skating*, a brand new sketch cowritten by Syd. This obviously suggested the setting for Chaplin's later film *The Rink* (1916), and gave him the opportunity to polish the spectacular skating skills he would put to good use in that film and *Modern Times* (1936).

Another role provided him with a theme he often returned to in films. In *Jimmy the Fearless, or the Boy 'ero,* Chaplin played a boy whose parents scold him roundly at dinner for his obsession with penny-dreadful thrillers. After dinner, Jimmy reads himself to sleep on a chair in the living room. The scene shifts, and Jimmy performs a series of amazing feats of derring-do. He fights a duel, rescues a fair maiden, and is just about to save his parents from being evicted when he's rudely interrupted by his father, who shakes him awake and chases him offstage with a belt. This transition from a heroic or romantic dream to dreary reality would become a feature of many Chaplin films, including *His Prehistoric Past* (1914), *The Bank* (1915), *Shoulder Arms* (1918), *Sunnyside* (1919), *The Idle Class* (1921), *The Kid* (1921), *The Gold Rush* (1925), *Modern Times*, and *Limelight* (1952).

Doughboy Charlie wakes from his dream of conquest to find himself still in boot camp. *Shoulder Arms.*

Late in 1910, after nearly three years in the company, Chaplin was given the opportunity to tour America as the lead comedian in a new Karno act, *The Wow-Wows, or A Night in a Secret Society*. It dealt with the bizarre initiation rites suffered by a new recruit, again named Archibald Binks. Perhaps because he had read about the mysterious and sinister activities of the Ku Klux Klan, Karno believed Americans to be obsessed with the subject of secret societies, and assumed the show would be a smash.[17]

The New York debut was not auspicious. Although Chaplin received good notices as Binks, the pun-filled sketch did not. Reviewers and audiences were put off by a torrent of unfunny verbal humor from a company known for robust physical comedy, and it began to look as though the troupe would have to slink back to England in defeat. Luckily, they were able to pull out the old Karno standby *Mumming Birds*, retitled *A Night in an English Music Hall* for American audiences. This did the trick, and they crisscrossed the country for the better part of two years. For repeat engagements they dusted off a similar show called *A Night in a London Club*, featuring club members performing an amateur variety show. Both of these shows also billed Chaplin as the ubiquitous Binks, evidently Karno's preferred name for toff characters.

Six months into the tour a reviewer in Butte, Montana, summed up the American reaction to Chaplin in *A Night in an English Music Hall*:

> The art of pantomime is recognized in theatredom as one of the most difficult known to the profession. It means that the actor must make known his intentions solely by signs and his general actions. . . . Seated in one of the music boxes is a decidedly hilarious person who evidently is suffering from too many exciting libations and consequently he insists on participating in each and every act in a manner that is so funny that the audience out in front can't help laughing enthusiastically. He scarcely says more than three words during the entire course of the act, yet so funny are his actions that he proves himself one of the best pantomime artists ever seen here.[18]

The review was written a couple of days after Chaplin's twenty-second birthday. The troupe continued on its grueling schedule of a town a week, two or three performances a day, for another fourteen months, then returned wearily to England in the summer of 1912. Chaplin was put to work at once by Karno, but it was a lonely and restless summer for him. Sydney had married, so the brothers were never again to be roommates.

Chaplin found that England paled compared to America, with its wide-open stretches of land and its promise of opportunities unbound by the rigid British class system. He leaped at the opportunity to return in the fall with another Karno troupe. This time Karno was determined to make a success of *The Wow-Wows*, and Chaplin and the company obligingly beefed up the show with new physical business. They played it successfully for six months, through March 1913, then trotted out *A Night in an English Music Hall* for a few weeks, and ended the tour with six months of *A Night in a London Club*.

When the company performed the revamped *Wow-Wows* in Butte in December 1912,[19] Chaplin was not only singled out by name in the review, but given raves for his prior performances as well.

> Archie is here. His coming to the Empress theatre is a most interesting event for Archie's presence there means a thoroughly good time for all patrons. . . .
>
> Archie is really Charles Chaplin and he is the leading comedian in the big act produced by Fred Karno and known as *The Wow Wows*, or "*A Night in a Secret Society*." The latter part of the title begins to throw some light on Archie and what he does. Many patrons immediately will recall on reading it that Mr. Chaplin made a tremendous hit here as Archie in *A Night in a London Music Hall* and Archie in *A Night in an English Club*. The way he used to fall out of the box in that London Music hall sketch and the funny pantomime work he did in the other production—well Archie certainly was one great big scream.
>
> This time Mr. Chaplin has a new departure. Instead of pantomime work he has a speaking part as well and thus the question that often was asked as to what kind of a speaking actor he would be has been answered and most satisfactory at that.[20]

What is notable here is that the reviewer saw the shows not as unrelated sketches, but as the unfolding adventures of the Archie/Chaplin character. Soon enough, audiences around the world would see his films that way as well, eagerly anticipating each new installment of the saga. But they would have to wait much longer than the citizens of Butte—a full quarter century—before hearing him speak.

The pioneering comedy filmmaker Mack Sennett had seen Chaplin perform during one of his tours, and was struck not only by how funny he was, but by his easy, graceful style of movement.[21] He hired him in 1913 for his recently formed Keystone Film Company. Chaplin's long years on the road were at an end, and his cinematic journey was about to begin.

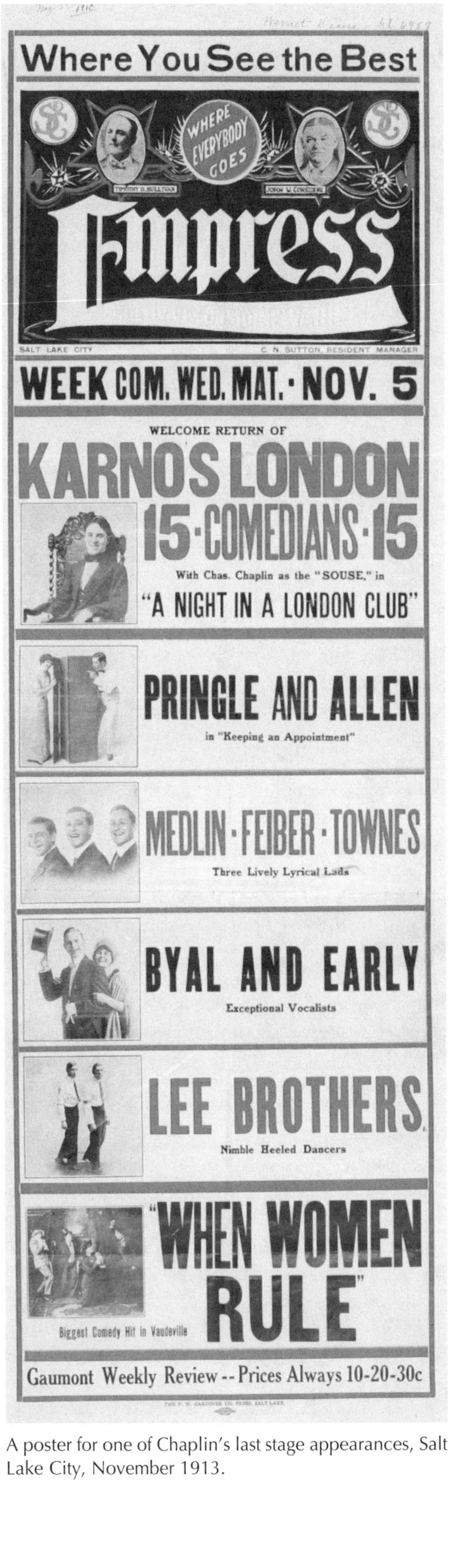

A poster for one of Chaplin's last stage appearances, Salt Lake City, November 1913.

Notes

1. Charles Chaplin, *My Autobiography* (New York: Simon & Schuster, 1964), 76.

2. Chaplin, *My Autobiography*, 21.

3. Many of Chaplin's biographers are skeptical as well, and one of the postmortem pleasures he left us is watching the spectacle of them bickering over the reliability of his autobiography and other writings. David Robinson, the first to be given access to Chaplin's papers, threw down the gauntlet in 1985 with *Chaplin, His Life and Art* (New York: McGraw-Hill, 1985), declaring the autobiography to be a truthful and accurate account. Kenneth Lynn (*Charlie Chaplin and His Times* [New York: Simon & Schuster, 1997]) and "A. J" Marriot (*Chaplin—Stage by Stage* [Herts, UK: Marriot Publishing, 2005]) beg to differ, and offer lively rebuttals to Robinson's view. Speculation will undoubtedly continue.

Without question, Chaplin made false or contradictory statements to interviewers. He initially claimed, for example, to have been born in Fontainebleau, France, a fiction that was repeated by writers for years. That whopper was on him, but other fabrications may have been at least partially the work of overzealous reporters trying to capture Chaplin's elusive comic spirit. Chaplin himself wearied of the banality of many of the questions he was asked—and the apparent impossibility of not being misquoted. Recognizing that newspaper and magazine copy was essentially just a way to stoke public interest with free advertising, he may have concluded that the truth shouldn't be allowed to get in the way of a good story.

Adding to the confusion, Chaplin employed various ghostwriters to produce articles and one travel book, *My Trip Abroad*, published in 1922. An earlier ghostwritten account became quite controversial. In 1915 Rose Wilder Lane interviewed Chaplin for a serialized autobiography, which ran in thirty installments in the *San Francisco Bulletin*. Lane arranged for the series to be published as a hardcover book, *Charlie Chaplin's Own Story*, in 1916. When sent a predistribution copy Chaplin promptly threatened legal action unless the book was destroyed. Copies survived, however, to be treasured by collectors and bedevil generations of future writers on Chaplin.

In Robinson's view the work is a complete fiction, and indeed parts of it are ridiculous, recasting Chaplin's boyhood as a Dickensian melodrama. But since it is clearly based on Wilder's interviews, dismissing it altogether may be throwing the biographical baby out with the bathwater. For better or worse, I have included an extract from the book later in this chapter, because it provides the only known description of another of Chaplin's early performances.

Which brings us back to this performance: Chaplin's account of taking his mother's place on the stage has the ring of truth, for he repeated the story to several early interviewers, omitting the telling detail about imitating his mother's voice cracking. We'll never know if he fabricated that part for his autobiography. If it didn't happen, it should have.

4. A charity institution for orphans and the poor.

5. Chaplin, *My Autobiography*, 35.

6. While this may seem to be prescient, one must remember that such characters were a staple of music hall comedy.

7. In America the words *mime* and *pantomime* have been used more or less interchangeably, but in England *pantomime* refers specifically to a family theatrical entertainment presented during the Christmas holidays, involving music, dance, and spectacular transformation effects.

8. "A. J" Marriot points out that Chaplin told a very different story in his 1933 travel narrative "A Comedian Sees the World," which was serialized in *Woman's Home Companion* from September 1933 through January 1934. In the earlier version the pantomime is *Puss in Boots*, not *Cinderella*, and Chaplin is dressed as a dog, not a cat. Marriot further claims that the Lancashire Lads did not even appear in *Cinderella*, so Chaplin was evidently employed on his own—or, more likely, as a "loan out" from the troupe. Despite the discrepancies, both versions feature Chaplin doing the same typically Chaplinesque business, so again, the essentials of the story ring true.

Marriot exhaustively researched Chaplin's stage career for his book *Chaplin—Stage by Stage*, attempting to set the historical record straight by reproducing playbills, reviews, photos, and other documentation. He takes gleeful pleasure in correcting what he sees as the mistakes, or deliberate misstatements, made by Chaplin and Robinson.

9. The term *Cockayne* was a nickname for London.

10. The *Court* of the title referred to the courtyard of a block of flats. Dan Lipton, the writer of these shows, later claimed that he actually based them on seeing Charlie and a friend at play, and Marriot presents evidence that this was indeed the case. In 1903 Lipton's flat in Walcot Gardens overlooked a courtyard where Charlie and his friend would play at being vaudevillians. At the time Charlie lived two blocks away, on Pownall Terrace, in the last home he would share with his mother.

11. A convention of British pantomime was that grotesque female roles, such as Cinderella's stepsisters, be played by male comedians.

12. Charlie Chaplin, *Charlie Chaplin's Own Story* (Indianapolis, IN: Bobbs-Merrill, 1916), 174–75. This is the "spurious" autobiography, discussed above. In the full account Chaplin (or his ghostwriter, Lane) claims that he really intended his portrayal to be serious and that the mishaps were just that, and not carefully worked-out bits of business. This, of course, strains credulity. The likelier story is that Chaplin described the act to Lane (or perhaps even acted it out for her), and that she embellished upon it. The comic business itself is so detailed and characteristic that it is likely to have been what actually transpired in the routine.

From other sources quoted by Marriot we know that the act continued with a parody of Bodie's "electrical healing" powers, during which a troupe member planted in the audience was miraculously "cured."

13. Cited in John McCabe, *Charlie Chaplin* (New York: Doubleday, 1978), 28–29. The original interview appeared in *Variety* in January 1942.

14. After Chaplin became famous many comedians claimed credit for one or another of his characteristic movements. According to Fred Karno, the Tramp walk was originally created by Karno player Walter Groves for a sketch called *The GPO* (General Post Office), then passed on to Kitchen when he took on the role, and thence to Chaplin. Chaplin himself was never forthcoming on the subject. For Karno's comment see Patrice Blouin, Christian Delage, and Sam Stourdzé, *Chaplin in Pictures* (Paris: NBC Editions, 2005), n.p.

15. Such elaborate settings were typical of Karno shows. Perhaps his most elaborate was for the *Wontdetainia* (based on the recent introduction of giant luxury liners such as the ill-fated Lusitania). The huge ship set filled the stage and could rock both back and forth and to and fro. To create the astonishing illusion that the ship was sailing across the stage, it was assembled section by section in the wings.

16. McCabe, *Charlie Chaplin*, 34.

17. Newspaper ads for the show, reprinted in Marriot's book (187) show cartoons of the terrified Binks surrounded by robed and hooded figures.

18. "Pantomime Star at the Majestic," unsigned article in the *Butte Inter Mountain*, April 18, 1911; reprinted in Charles Chaplin, *My Life in Pictures* (New York: Grosset & Dunlap, 1975), 66.

19. The company was popular in Butte, returning five times. For the rest of his life Chaplin would extol the beauty and dignified elegance of the boomtown's prostitutes.

20. Cited by Marriot, *Chaplin*, 184–85. The review is from the *Butte Miner* of December 8, 1912 (Marriot misprints the year in his book). I have relied throughout this chapter on Marriot's pioneering research into Chaplin's early career.

21. Sennett gave himself full credit for discovering and hiring Chaplin for Keystone, but so did other members of the company. See David Robinson, *Chaplin, His Life and Art* (London: Penguin, 2001), 105–106. This extensively revised edition supercedes previous editions of Robinson's work.

CHAPTER TWO

Fooling for the Flickers

"Pantomime to me is an expression of poetry, comic poetry."[1]

By the time Chaplin entered the film world at age twenty-four, he was a thoroughly seasoned professional with thirteen years of stage experience behind him—two as a dancer, three as an actor, and eight as a music hall comedian, six of them with the foremost comedy and pantomime troupe of the era. We know from reviews and the accounts of his contemporaries that Chaplin's brilliance as a mime set him apart almost from the outset. Before he made a single film he was already making a name for himself as a mime comedian in America. When he left his Karno troupe late in 1913, it disbanded, unable to obtain further bookings without him. Audiences and managers wanted Chaplin, and many of his early film reviewers were familiar with his stage work.

Chaplin was the first mime of genius whose work outlasted live performance, enabling future audiences to experience his art more or less directly. I say "more or less" because we can never experience the films the way his original audiences experienced them, any more than we can travel back in time to see him on stage. The context has shifted in too many ways. For one thing, by the time Chaplin was becoming a major star, toward the end of 1914, the world had embarked upon a war that seemed to threaten civilization itself:

> Is it the man, or is it his work, or is his personality the embodiment of a world-thought? Does a war-sick universe turn from the horrors of wholesale slaughter to the rib-tickling situation of a man hit on the head by a mallet in the hands of this gentle little Englishman . . . who looks out on the world with the naïve wonder of a little child?[2]

Many other factors make it difficult to see Chaplin's early films in context. The first audiences saw the films in movie theaters, whereas we're far more likely to see them in our homes, in classrooms, or in museums. Fashions have changed dramatically—not only in clothing, but in the very idea of what constitutes the proper shape and weight of a human body. Changes in the way we dress and look are accompanied by more subtle changes in the way we hold ourselves and move. The very way we think and relate to each other changes. And of course our humor changes. Jokes wear out their welcome and are replaced by new ones. We strike fashionable new comic attitudes.

Art forms reflect these changes, provide a historical record of them, and accelerate the introduction of new ones. For centuries people looked to characters in books and on the stage as role models, but such characters were never as universally available, nor as visually appealing, as film actors, who by the teens had become godlike, iconic figures, affecting culture in ways both superficial and profound. It's difficult to trace stylistic changes in stage acting because the old forms are folded into new ones over generations, but we can instantly see what's different when we view an old film. Given the extent of the intervening cultural changes, it becomes something of a miracle that any film, play, song, or book survives its epoch—and, of course, very few do.

For a contemporary audience, films from the midteens inevitably look quaint. We are, after all, peeking into a vanished world nearly a century old. Clothing—especially women's—is old-fashioned, and film technology is outmoded. The stories unfold in stark black and white, without sound.[3] These early films are occasionally intriguing, sometimes mildly interesting, and often maddeningly boring. Most comedies of the period have lost all trace of humor, and it's often hard to fathom what was ever *supposed* to be funny about them.

But Chaplin looked quaint from the outset. That word, along with *peculiar*, *odd*, and *eccentric*, pops up repeatedly in his early reviews. Looking quaint was an asset. It set him apart and reinforced his particular kind of humor. The Karno quality of gravity—serious, sober attention in the midst of violent slapstick—was recognized at once by perceptive critics, as was his investigation of the comic possibilities of virtually all his action on the screen:

> His odd little tricks of manner and his refusal to do the most simple things in an ordinary way are essential features of his method, which thus far has defied successful imitation.[4]

> Chaplin possesses that indefinable something which makes you laugh heartily and without restraint at what in others would be commonplace actions.[5]

To understand "that indefinable something" that allowed Chaplin to make commonplace actions funny, we'll take a close look at his body, how he dresses it, and the way he moves it.

Chaplin was a relatively small man—5 feet, 6½ inches tall—and oddly proportioned. In his own description, "[M]y head's too big for my body, my arms are too short for my body, and my hands are too small for my arms."[6] In *The Pilgrim*, made in 1923 when Chaplin was thirty-four, a wanted poster describes convict Charlie thus:

> May be disguised. 30 to 35 years of age. About five feet four inches in height. Weight about 125 pounds. Pale face. Black bushy hair sometimes parted in the middle. Small black moustache. Blue eyes. Small hands, large feet. Extremely nervous. Walks with feet turned out.

The weight and the age are accurate, but the description drops a couple of inches from his height; Chaplin wanted his audience to think of him as small to enlist their sympathy. Both descriptions mention that he has an oddly proportioned body. Nevertheless, possibly influenced by his grace of movement, Somerset Maugham described him as having "a neat figure, admirably proportioned; his hands and feet are well-shaped and small."[7] The writer Max Eastman rhapsodized about how

> the trim grace and veritable perfection of his build and carriage, which is that of the prince of tumblers, tap dancers, tightrope walkers—the prince of agility and poise—harmonize with the classic perfection of his head to make a unitary impression of great beauty. He seems to possess, above all, complete and exquisite integration.[8]

When Chaplin dons a bathing suit in *The Cure* and *The Adventurer* (both from 1917) we can see that, at age twenty-eight, he is in excellent physical condition, without an ounce of fat on him. At the same time, he has none of the muscle-bound look of the physical culturist, like his friend Douglas Fairbanks, or Buster Keaton, who performed an even more strenuous form of physical comedy. Chaplin's development seems admirably suited to move his small frame, while at the same time preserving maximum flexibility.

One of the most striking things about Chaplin's Tramp character is his assumption of a regal posture. The shabby but genteel Tramp almost always holds his head perfectly upright. This is an unusual posture for anyone, much less the misfit outsider he usually portrayed; most people crane their heads slightly forward. Chaplin had become the "millionaire tramp" of his earlier imaginings, and the look was reinforced by the high wing-collar shirts he almost always wears, usually with inappropriate long ties.

Aristocrats and others born to wealth expect the world to meet their needs without much effort on their parts, and Chaplin exploits this sense of privilege in the way he deals with the other people in his films. In his very first appearance, in a short film called *Making a Living* (1914), he's a well-dressed but insolvent con man looking for a job at a newspaper. He extols his virtues to a editor, slapping the man's knee hard to emphasize his points; when the man pulls his knee away, Chaplin, somewhat annoyed, pulls it back and leans on it with his elbow. The man's knee, after all, is there for his convenience. This characteristic became funnier once Chaplin assumed his Tramp costume. Sitting on a park bench with a pretty girl, he'll pull her toward him with the hook of his cane, as casually as one might reach for a salt shaker. Simply his due, he seems to say.

In his first few films Chaplin occasionally mimicked the gestures of the Keystone players around him, such as Ford Sterling, who played the kind of "Dutch" (German) character comedian then popular on the vaudeville stage. Sterling substituted a scowling face and broad gestures for the broad German accent of his stage counterparts; for example, he was forever hopping up and down to indicate surprise or frustration, his knees pumping out to the sides, or thrusting his head forward pugnaciously to face down an adversary. But Chaplin soon found a more congenial gestural vocabulary; it suited him better, for example, to pull his head *backward* over his trunk, to communicate haughty disdain, rather than thrusting it forward like Sterling. He also came to realize what expressions worked best for him onscreen. He experimented with many moods and facial contortions in his early films that disappear in his later ones.

As Stan Laurel noted, Chaplin's eyes helped him achieve his extraordinary rapport with audiences on the stage, and this was certainly true on film as well. One of the most striking things about Chaplin's film performances was that he seemed to relate to the world outside his films—he was aware that there was an audience out there watching him, and he looked directly at the camera to acknowledge it. From his long experience on the variety stage Chaplin understood the importance of connecting with the audience. In his autobiography, contrary to what Laurel said, Chaplin wrote that he never had the "come-hither" quality needed by great stage comedians. Perhaps not, but he certainly had it as a film actor.

Thus, when he pulls a particularly good one on someone, he looks at the camera and laughs right along with us. Chaplin's silent laugh is infectious and striking. One recent writer accurately, if unkindly, called Chaplin's mouth "a pinched aperture stuffed with equine incisors."[9] But those big teeth give him a radiant smile that lights up the screen. He often coyly covers it with his hand: the naughty child caught doing something he shouldn't. These conspiratorial laughs are powerful invitations for

The joke is on the diners, the laugh is for us. *The Rink.*

us to share his point of view in a scene—in fact, we *have* to share his point of view to enjoy his often violent behavior toward the various rivals, bullies, and other characters that bedevil him.

Chaplin was by no means the only player on the Keystone lot to address the camera. The comic or distressed take was a standard carryover from the stage during the period, and villains frequently shot the audience their best "curses, foiled again" expressions. Mabel Normand, the most popular comedienne of the silent era, frequently gazed toward the camera in silent entreaty. The rotund and popular comedian Fatty Arbuckle often looked at the camera, particularly when playing the part of a shy, elephantine maiden. He even made jokes about the camera's existence, directing it to tilt discreetly upward while he was changing his pants, for example.

After the teens the practice of looking at the camera faded, but a few notable comic actors continued to employ it. In the Laurel and Hardy films both Ollie and comic villain James Findlayson direct numerous exasperated looks at the lens. And Groucho, of course, shoots many verbal asides at the camera and wiggles his eyebrows salaciously at us. These moments stand out as comic bits because all the other actors are trapped in their filmic reality, unaware that there's an audience out there watching.

With Chaplin the technique goes beyond a comic bit. No film actor has ever reached through the lens as effectively as he does. The difference lies is the subtlety and frequency with which he uses the device. He doesn't just laugh into the camera to engage us—he keeps *glancing* at it, rarely playing a scene without stealing looks towards the lens. Even when he's not focusing directly on it, he presents his face to it, in effect inviting us to look into those eyes that Stan Laurel found so hypnotic. This theatrical strategy makes us a constant witness to his flickering emotions.

In addition, when Charlie looks out at us directly he seems to linger and savor the moment. His looks are like classical asides in theatre, offering us a bit of privileged information on the action. It becomes such a subliminal part of his performances that we hardly notice he's doing it, yet we never lose the feeling that he is conscious of us. For this reason, even when he's doing the most idiotic or violent things, he never appears to be simply stupid or nasty, because on one level he's out here with us, the audience, sharing our enjoyment at his antics.[10] As his films grow longer and the plots and characters become more realistic, Chaplin tones down this aspect of his performing style somewhat, and it ceases to become a gag in and of itself. But he never loses it entirely, even in his talking

Looking at the camera. *A Dog's Life.*

Charlie bows to us after saving the day. *The Pawnshop.*

pictures, and properly so, for it is a defining aspect of his acting technique, illuminating all his performances.

With the easy intimacy he establishes with his looks at the camera, Chaplin is able to ensure our complicity in some quite risqué behavior as well, such as the outrageous way he flirts with women. Scenes of him slinging his leg onto a girl's lap, or "accidentally" pulling her skirt up with the crook of his cane, seem bold even today. In 1914 and 1915 the effect was shocking and, in the eyes of some, obscene.[11]

Chaplin's eye contact with the camera is one of the key elements of his performing technique, and its importance can hardly be overstated. He consistently sets up his scenes so that the audience can watch the actions between the characters and at the same time engage in a continuous one-on-one "dialogue" with him. His acting thus takes on a presentational, highly stylized quality, a self-consciousness that reaches an exuberant comic peak in the series of films Chaplin made for the Mutual Film Corporation in 1916–1917. In these films the dialogue with the film audience sometimes becomes so overt that it upstages the scene he's playing. For example, in both *The Pawnshop* and *The Cure* melodramatic moments are mocked when Charlie suddenly turns to the camera for quick theatrical bows, arms akimbo. Breaking the reality of his film *becomes* the joke.

The bold makeup Chaplin employs as the Tramp is a comic mask that effectively augments his bold playing style. It is, in effect, clown white, setting him apart from the other players, whose faces appear gray by comparison. His eyebrows are drawn higher and heavier than his natural brows, and his eyes are heavily outlined in black. The square "toothbrush" mustache is a virtual bull's-eye, drawing our eye even in long shots. Far from obscuring his features, the mustache highlights the shape of his nose and the expressions of his mouth. His head, already proportionally large for his body, is made larger still by his shock of dark, curly, tousled hair. Chaplin must have sensed immediately how effectively his hair enhanced his appearance onscreen, for he allowed it to grow out over the first few months, and styled it carefully to frame his strongly patterned face. That tousled head of hair reinforces his head movements, such as his frequent gesture of shaking his head after a fall, and nicely counterpoints his carefully trimmed mustache. His derby hat completes the image, neatly recapitulating the shape of his little mustache. The effect is graphically powerful, at once comical and strangely appealing.

One has only to look at a picture of Chaplin out of makeup to see how much of a construction his screen self is. The difference in appearance is striking. In addition, he holds his head differently when he's not in character, often presenting his forehead to the camera, giving him an intellectual look, in contrast to the instinct-driven

Chaplin and Edna Purviance in *The Cure.*

Chaplin, 1921. Collection of Jewel and Marj Walker.

Chaplin in *Easy Street.*

Tramp, whose face is presented more full-on and openly. Even photos of Chaplin in costume, but minus his mustache, are a bit jarring; one has to search for the Tramp image, just as people who met him offscreen searched in vain for the impish Tramp in the earnest, solemn young man before them. Most intriguingly, photos of Chaplin in full mufti, but between scenes or behind the camera, also seem unlike the familiar figure. Clearly, the character is not just a matter of the costume and makeup, but comes to life only when Chaplin inhabits him physically, assuming his characteristic postural, attitudinal, and gestural quirks, including that unique dialogue with the camera.

On the other hand, there exists a rehearsal film of the scene in *City Lights* (1931) in which Chaplin ogles a statue of a nude woman in a store window while pretending he's studying a smaller statue of a man on horseback. Chaplin wears a bulky black sweater with sporty white trim, white slacks, and white shoes. Only the familiar derby and cane cue us as to his identity—that and his movement. It is most disconcerting to see the Tramp emerge from this dapper-looking gentleman, yet there he is, unmistakably.[12] The performance is virtually identical to the way he does it in the film, but the facial expressions look different; they seem more exaggerated without the familiar mustache and stark makeup to set them off. It's strange to watch, as though we're seeing the image of the puppeteer overlapping the puppet. Marilyn Monroe could conjure her screen character up in much the same way—it is said that she could walk down the street unnoticed if she didn't assume her sexpot persona.

If Chaplin beckons us into his filmic world with his eyes and the movements of his head, he uses his trunk to engage us on an emotional level, eliciting trust, sympathy, and empathy for his character. He also uses it to clearly communicate his emotional state and define his relationship to other characters.

This large claim is not as outlandish as it may at first appear. We're accustomed to reading emotions in the face and hands, but the trunk is just as expressive, if in less obvious ways. An inflated or deflated chest acts as a barometer of our emotional state. For example, we hold our breath and tense our chest when we're in danger. We speak "from the heart"—and we move from there as well. Our "gut-level" feelings are in our bellies, and those bellies are unprotected by bone and therefore vulnerable to attack, both physical and emotional. Consequently, how we present our trunks says a lot about how we feel about ourselves and others. To take a simple example, if someone crosses his or her arms when speaking, we sense he or she has something to hide. Presenting the trunk openly, on the other hand, indicates a defenseless or trusting attitude.

Chaplin often has something to hide from the other characters in his films, but he has nothing to hide from us, and he wants us to know it. For that reason he consistently opens his trunk to the camera, and he draws our attention to it by wearing a snug coat. The coat also accentuates the narrowness of his chest and his all-too-evident frailty, made even more evident by the contrasting oversize baggy pants and big shoes.

In a 1918 magazine article Chaplin analyzed the rationale behind appearing small and vulnerable:

> Everyone knows that the little fellow in trouble always gets the sympathy of the mob . . . . I always accentuate my helplessness by drawing my shoulders in, drooping my lip pathetically and looking frightened. It is all part of the art of pantomime, of course.[13]

In most of his early films Chaplin does not overtly play for sympathy, but he often draws his shoulders up and in, which makes him look as though his head is emerging, turtle-style, from his trunk. This gives him an endearing, vulnerable look. However, the description above hardly scratches the surface of the subtle ways in which Chaplin uses his trunk to enlist our sympathy. For one thing, he positions it very carefully in relation to the camera. Two people engaged in conversation tend to face each other square on. If a third person joins them, they automatically turn their trunks to include him. In his films, Chaplin treats the camera as that third person, consistently playing scenes so that he includes us. He almost *never* crosses his arms over his chest; on

Framing his trunk. *The Pilgrim.*

the contrary, he'll sometimes frame it by making an "L" shape with his arms, one hand on the side of his face, the other supporting his elbow, a position later adopted by Jack Benny.

The tight coat also makes us immediately aware of the slightest postural change, and Chaplin uses the heightened visibility to convey an amazing array of emotions and attitudes. He deflates his chest, lets his shoulders droop, and draws his arms backward when he's feeling helpless. He ripples his trunk sinuously and rolls his shoulders in an ecstasy of bashful excitement when he's flirting. He inhales deeply and elevates his upper chest when he's feeling cocky or brave, though such moments are invariably short-lived for Charlie. For example, in *Shoulder Arms* he pumps up his chest and bravely volunteers for a dangerous mission, only to be told, "You may Never return!" You can practically hear the hiss of air as his chest deflates like a punctured balloon.

The way he uses his arms complements Chaplin's emotionally expressive trunk. This becomes apparent when we look at the way he executes a common gesture, putting his hands on his hips. Instead of jamming his fists into his waist, as most men would do, he often bends his hands softly at the wrists, holding the backs against his sides. He frequently cradles his waist, with his thumbs in front and his palms in back, in effect caressing his trunk. These are decidedly feminine gestures. Even when he places his hands on his hips in the ordinary way, Chaplin holds them a bit high up—perhaps as a consequence of having those too-short arms—which lends him a childlike quality. Chaplin thus "borrows" typically female or childlike gestures to make himself endearing and sympathetic. As one observer put it,

> [S]o much of his physical beauty results from Chaplin allowing his forcefully masculine self the freedom of feminine grace.[14]

Chaplin is indeed forcefully masculine, particularly in his Keystone films; it seems the whole series is about flirting with women, fighting with men, and getting drunk as often as possible. The occasional feminine grace note counterbalances all that bad behavior, and he cultivated such moments. The Tramp becomes uncommonly adept at cooking, for example, although he often employs such unconventional methods as cracking eggs with a hammer (*The Vagabond*, 1916). He is also preoccupied with grooming, and forever brushing off his clothing and buffing his fingernails, or pretending to clean them with the tip of his cane. He's never without a handy straight or hairpin, and exhibits a hairdresser's flair with women's hair.[15]

One of the reasons his films have such extraordinarily warmth is another "feminine" attribute he allows himself, the way he touches everything and everyone around him. Physically, he sets the stage by the way he relaxes his arms and hands, often drawing his arms slightly back at the shoulders and letting them dangle loosely at his sides. His hands are also held loosely, making them look soft and fleshy. Their smallness accents the delicacy of his touch. Occasionally he wears sleeves that are a bit too long, making his hands look even smaller and reinforcing his look of a kid playing grown-up.

Chaplin touches the other characters in his films frequently, and with an easy intimacy. There is a heartbreaking moment in *The Vagabond* when he's been disappointed in love; he's bidding his girl goodbye, and his hands hold her tenderly for a farewell moment, then flutter over her back like butterflies. When not battling with men he occasionally touches them with the same tender regard, to great comic effect, such as when he kisses the forehead of someone he's just flattened, or puts a pillow under the victim's head. He treats objects the same way, holding them delicately, like a magician handles props, enchanted by their possibilities.

Chaplin subtly conveys emotional content in the way he touches himself as well. In both *City Lights* and *Modern Times* Charlie refers to himself by patting his chest with the palm of his hand. This gesture lends him a sincere, heartfelt quality that he wouldn't have if he'd touched his chest with, say, his thumb, as James Cagney might have, or the tip of his forefinger, or simply pointed without touching himself at all. Similarly, when he touches his face he often does it with the soft palm rather than the more "intellectual" fingertips. One of the great sensual pleasures of Chaplin's films is the way he embraces the physical world with his caressing touch.

Referring to himself. *Modern Times.*

Obviously, we are dealing here with movement qualities that were to a great extent developed by Chaplin instinctually, based on his physique and the natural movement impulses ingrained in him from childhood. But there can be no question that Chaplin augmented his natural gift with conscious craft. "I had talent as a kid," he said. "All it needed was polish. I've been riding on that ever since . . . . Success is good for people."[16]

Stage performers develop their technique in front of the audience, but working on film presented Chaplin with exciting new possibilities. He was able to hone his expressive craft by watching his alter ego onscreen in a way he could never watch himself onstage. He could sit unnoticed in the audience, watching them watch him, sensing what was working and what wasn't, eavesdropping on their conversations. His films provide us with a living diary of his metamorphosis from stage to film artist, and watching them in order we can see how he developed the legendary rapport with audiences that made him such a phenomenon. We can witness his canny body language evolving.

The physical expression of emotions constitutes a universal, wordless language, and audiences from every culture understood and identified with Chaplin's depiction of feelings. They found his acting to be novel, funny, and true to life. His character seemed so compelling and believable that he hardly seemed to be acting at all, despite his stylized gestures and quaint appearance. The public enjoyed the unusually rich palette of emotions this comedian silently paraded before them, and laughed at the way he would make quicksilver changes from one to another. In short, to see a Chaplin film was to get a privileged glimpse into a fascinating character's inner world. Like all great actors, he was able to use exterior action to show interior thought; he was thought incarnate, and by the mid-1920s he was commonly considered to be the greatest actor in the world.

Such transparent acting was especially rare during the teens, a period when many film actors played with gestures that today seem broad and hammy. But Chaplin brought from the stage a rich repertoire of subtle and quirky ways to show character and emotion through movement, and he used them to add intriguing new dimensions to his character.

For example, he found from the outset that tilting his pelvis back into a "swayback" position gave him a good comic attitude and enriched the personality of his character. The posture was fussy, like his small, carefully trimmed mustache; it summoned up the studied elegance and posture of a ballet dancer, made ridiculous by Charlie's outsized trousers and shoes, and it made him look like a small child playing at being grown-up—children often lock their knees to feel stronger, which has the effect of automatically tilting the pelvis back.

This pelvic tilt also augments Chaplin's "female" gracefulness with a quite explicit parody of female sexuality. A pulled-back pelvis is a provocative, alluring posture adopted by the women of many different eras. When Chaplin began making films, women had only recently stopped wearing bustles to enhance their natural curves. His adoption of this bustle-like posture further stresses his feminine aspect, countering his "forcefully masculine" character and behavior. In his early films Charlie aggressively pursues every pretty woman he sees; adopting this female posture softens his advances and makes them seem more comical than sexual.

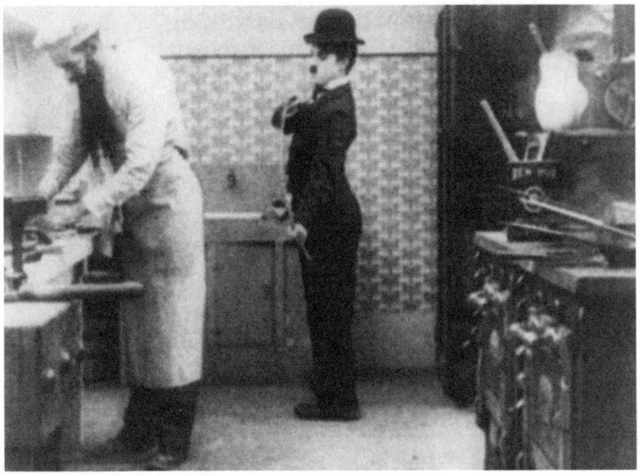

Charlie's stance. *The Rink.*

The tilted-back pelvis, of course, also draws our attention to his posterior, a prime comic object in his films. Part of the comedy results from his solicitous treatment of it, rubbing it after he's had a particularly hard fall—or a particularly stiff drink. The posteriors of others are also comic objects, convenient targets for the comic violence that is Charlie's other chief preoccupation. Watching characters kick the living daylights out of each other was obviously irresistibly funny to audiences of the time, and Chaplin's films, like most Keystone films, are filled with battered butts. In his autobiography Chaplin quotes an early, perceptive admirer—a judge, no less—on the deeper meaning of this practice:

> What I like about your comedy is your knowledge of fundamentals—you know that the most undignified part of a man's anatomy is his arse, and your comedies prove it. When you kick a portly gentleman there, you strip him of all his dignity. Even the impressiveness of a Presidential inauguration would collapse if you came up behind the President and kicked him in the rear. There's no doubt about it: the arse is the seat of self-consciousness.[17]

You don't see much arse kicking in contemporary movies. Styles have changed, and butt kicking is no longer a surefire laugh, except with children, who still find it hilarious.

Chaplin found other, more inventive ways to use his posterior expressively. For example, when a sadistic masseur lunges for Charlie in *The Cure*, Charlie insultingly "twitches" his rear at the man, a nice variant on the more common, but less atavistic, gestures of thumbing the nose, biting the thumb, or flipping the bird. The affront is even more pointed in *City Lights*, when he accidentally sits squarely on the nose of a statue being dedicated for a new city monument, effectively insulting the pompous officials, the passive crowd, and vacuous ceremonial expressions of civic pride.

The tilted-back pelvis reinforces Charlie's fastidiousness, adding to the impression made by his regal head position, fussy mustache, shabby though always neat dress clothing, and incessant grooming behavior. A character this fastidious is able to get away with jokes about subjects that in other hands would be disgusting. Thus, in *The Vagabond* he picks up an expectoration, thinking it's a coin; in *The Immigrant* (1917) he features a sequence of explicit seasickness and vomiting jokes; in both *Easy Street* (1916) and *The Cure* he mistakes innocent liquids that have dribbled upon him for urine, and he gets "real" baby urine on his hands in both *The Kid* and *The Great Dictator* (1940).

Chaplin loves pushing the envelope of good taste with such bathroom humor. Sitting in a café in *A Dog's Life* (1918) he sobs uncontrollably at a singer's sad song. A fat woman sitting on the tier above him sobs as well, falling onto her siphon bottle and spraying seltzer onto the floor beside his dog. Instead of leaping to the obvious conclusion, Charlie assumes that the dog, too, is moved by the song, and wipes its eyes. Even more boldly, in *Modern Times* jailbird Charlie ducks under the table to tie his shoe as a prison attendant dumps some viscous slop on his plate; when he sits up and sees the mess, he immediately looks up toward the ceiling—such a disgusting concoction could only have been dropped by a passing bird.

Charlie's manifest disgust as he deals with these indignities, along with the clever ways the gags are staged, cancels out our own distaste. Even Chaplin's more refined critics, some of whom were offended by his work, had to acknowledge that at least as far as his audience was concerned, he rose above his material. In 1916 Ben Hecht, future author of *The Front Page* and other American comic classics, wrote that Chaplin appeared onscreen

> amid the roars and wild elation of idiots, prostitutes, crass, common churls . . . converted into a natural and mutual simplicity. The stuffy, maddening "bathos" that clings to the mob like a stink is dispelled, wiped off the air. Charlie Chaplin is before them, Charles Chaplin with the wit of a vulgar buffoon, and the soul of a world artist. . . . He is absurd; unmanly; tawdry; cheap; artificial. And yet behind his crudities, his obscenities, his inartistic and outrageous contortions, his "divinity" shines. He is the Mob-God.[18]

Chaplin's posture also suggests the stance of a ballet dancer, and the contrast between his art and classical ballet is illuminating. Like a dancer, he holds his head regally, elevates his trunk, tilts his pelvis back, spreads his feet apart, and wears clothing that evokes a world of wealth and privilege. But in his case that world is out of reach, for his clothes are shabby, and his baggy trousers conceal rather than reveal the lower extremities that might allow him to take flight. Like a dancer, his gestures are somewhat florid and mechanical looking, but Charlie's gestures are miles from the standardized, artificial vocabulary of ballet. His touch is intimate and real, not ethereal and symbolic. Rather than walking on his toes—a technically improbable feat that makes dancers look otherworldly—Charlie trudges along flat-footed in his oversize shoes. The Tramp aspires to the gravity-free, fairyland existence of the ballet world, but, as Chaplin once said, his feet won't let him. He is earthbound, both physically and emotionally, and much of the comedy derives from the tension between his inner and outer worlds. Again and again, the Tramp's innate drive toward grace and beauty is confounded by the harsh reality of his circumstances.

Whatever the complexities embodied in the Tramp, people found him and his ways irresistible. His shoes and funny walk generated the first wave of excitement. Surely one of the reasons for his immediate success was that *everybody* could do that walk:

> Among the happy youths of the slums, or the dandies of clubdom or college, an imitation of . . . Chaplin . . . is considered the last word in humor. To be Chaplinesque is to be funny; to waddle a few steps, and then look naively at your audience, is a recognized form to which successful comedy is trending. . . . The world has Chaplinitis.[19]

Comic postcard, 1916. Collection of Lisa Stein.

Chaplin's first onscreen imitator was Mabel Normand, performing under his direction in one of his best Keystones, *Mabel's Married Life* (1914). Alone in the their apartment Mabel despairs of her ineffectual spouse. Addressing the camera directly, she points to her shoe, puts her hand on her head, and rolls her eyes, as though to say, "Can you believe those stupid shoes?" Then she mocks his eccentric walk, scrunching her face into a scowl and doing a cross between a hop and a waddle. It's a rough but perfectly clear approximation.

The fact is that *anyone* could do a recognizable approximation, but actually moving like Chaplin was another matter. His walk is far more complex and subtle than the stiff, side-to-side duck waddle assumed by Mabel and most of his other imitators. Given the peculiarities of his posture and costume, he walks surprisingly lightly, with a pleasing economy of movement. If he wants to tilt from side to side, he moves from the hip joint, not the waist, as Mabel does; it is much more elegant and structurally sound to move from the hip joint. And he only does that occasionally, to communicate some specific emotion, such as when he shakes himself out of his funk at the end of *The Tramp* (1915) His knees pump up and down, and he tilts from side to side as he strolls jauntily off. But those are extreme moments. What makes his "everyday" walk notable—and comic—is that this shabby, big-shoed tramp is walking as elegantly as a dancer. He manages the apparent weight of those big shoes with ease, and there is a stillness at his center of gravity that lends his slight frame a satisfying sense of stability.

Charlie's walk is difficult to imitate because of a quality that's difficult to mimic, the extraordinary relaxation of his body. His is not the indolent relaxation of the couch potato, but the relaxation-in-motion of an athlete, his body energized and ready for action even when at rest. It probably derives, to a great extent, from the drunk roles Chaplin played with Karno for so many years. Drunks have to be relaxed to stagger around convincingly. But whether drunk or sober, relaxation is the indispensable background to Chaplin's eloquence, the canvas upon which his mimetic art is drawn. It is one of his most appealing qualities as a performer, and without it his movements wouldn't have the fluid quality that makes them so sensual and appealing to watch. Relaxation also complements and counterbalances the slapstick action sequences that fill his films. Max Eastman's description of how he moved offscreen—"the prince of agility and poise"—is equally true of his movements onscreen. By comparison, most of us hold ourselves stiffly and walk with physical tension that restricts our flow of movement.

Surely this, in addition to his comic qualities, was why people felt like *being* Chaplin. It was *instructive* to pretend to be him. He didn't seem to suffer from the tension-inducing inhibitions and that constrained most people. True, he was an eccentric, a loner, a nutcase, but he was also admirable—charming, funny, idiosyncratic, emotional, independent. And he moved like a dancer trapped in a comic ballet. Is it any wonder the public demanded to see more, and to know more? He gladly obliged, cranking out films, submitting to interviews for eager fan magazines, and posing for hundreds of photos for his avid fans.

Those photos are fascinating, because Chaplin had a particular talent for striking memorable poses. Many of them became iconic, reproduced endlessly to promote his films and sell offshoot products. But Chaplin's skill at posing for still photos offers another clue to the appeal of his movement, a peculiar quality of stillness in the midst of motion. Watching Chaplin move is almost like watching a flip book; one sees the stillness and motion at the same time.

Sometimes Chaplin juxtaposes stillness and motion for a gag. In *The Adventurer* and *The Vagabond*, Charlie abruptly freezes out of a full run, his face to a wall, to become invisible to his pursuers. In *Shoulder Arms* he spins an ingenious variation, disguising himself in a tree costume to infiltrate enemy lines. While the idea of a tree costume as camouflage is ridiculous, like many of Charlie's dodges it proves surprisingly effective—he fools not only the German soldiers, but, in one startling instance, us as well. In *The Gold Rush* he literally freezes, becoming stiff as a board from the cold to hoodwink a kindly prospector into offering him food and shelter.

Chaplin's ability to pose for photos and his freeze gags are natural outgrowths of an extremely crisp movement

Fooling the audience. Charlie as a tree, standing on a tree stump, center. *Shoulder Arms*.

style that gives him a puppetlike quality. He turns this tendency into a wonderful gag when he pretends to be a mechanical fun-house figure to elude police in *The Circus* (1928). But its main effect is to impose upon his performances a geometrical precision that is totally consistent with his presentational style. Of course, filmic movement is itself an illusion, created by many still photographs flashing upon the screen each second. But that fact doesn't lend the movements of other screen actors a precise and geometrical quality,[20] nor does it account for Chaplin's satisfying movement style on the screen.

The secret lies in the extraordinary articulation of his body. His movement is hypnotic to watch both because it flows so well and because it is so selective. Quite often, only one part of Chaplin's body moves at a time. When he shakes his head, for example, recovering from a blow or a fall, his head is the only thing that moves, and it moves like a washing machine agitator, rapidly rotating left and right, rather than wobbling around. Far from making him look stiff, such machinelike precision is highly amusing, directing the eye of the viewer, in exactly the same way a magician directs our eye to what *he* wants us to see.

It is Chaplin's body control and taste for geometrical movements that enable him to turn ordinary movements like shaking his head into trademark comic gestures. For example, a commonplace shrug of the shoulders "causes" his arms to fly straight out to the sides as his hands flip up. Then he drops his arms abruptly, in the supremely resigned manner of a bored aristocrat. Or he lifts his hat straight up off his head, or tips it from the back as though it's a hinged lid. Or he kicks someone so that his leg, in a piston motion, extends parallel to the ground. He doesn't just *stop* when rushing into a room, he *skids* to a stop, one leg hopping and the other extending out to the side, as though to brake his momentum. Watching him round a corner at a full run is like watching a car going into a skid: He halts his forward momentum by skip-hopping on one leg and rotating his body on its axis, while at the same time clamping his hat down on his head and extending the other leg out sideways for balance. The turn completed, he charges off in the new direction, his head bent backward from the momentum. With such distinctive comic gestures, many of which were easy to imitate by fans young and old, Chaplin cemented his fame.[21]

All of these are examples, of course, of his "refusal to do the most simple things in an ordinary way." Chaplin himself was fully aware of this characteristic of his movement: "[I]n pantomime the technique of movement is so mechanical."[22] When he started making films Chaplin

Chaplin in a characteristic pose.

immediately understood that in the absence of sound, movement alone defines both character and comedy. His more perceptive critics understood it as well.

> Once in every century or so a man is born who is able to color and influence his world. . . . And now in these laughter-loving days Charles Chaplin is doing it with pantomime and personality—a finished actor, a master of his art, a comedian who has compelled the world to laugh with him and to love him.[23]

Paradoxically, the mechanical quality of his movement doesn't dehumanize Charlie as a character, but rather becomes the source of the comical eccentricity his early reviewers noted. While Chaplin obviously derived much of his technique from the numerous precision comedy sketches he learned with the Karno company, other Karno alumni were not as successful in film. Chaplin grasped almost immediately how to adapt his performances to the new medium, and within a few short months he took over the creative process as well, writing and directing his own films. Once he was a creator and not merely a comic actor being told what to do, his gags could emanate from his performing technique. For example, performing with mechanical precision led him to create numerous gags in which a person is made to seem like a thing, the culmination of which occurs in *Modern Times* when Charlie literally becomes a cog in the industrial machinery.[24] An additional bonus Chaplin derived from his stylized playing was that it effectively set off his more poignant moments. Juxtaposed with his furious comic geometry, naturalistic scenes of sadness or tenderness in his films take on a startling intensity.

His puppetlike qualities are further reinforced by his costume and makeup. The distinctive dark shape of the costume and the strongly patterned face make him into a human caricature. Only the image of Mickey Mouse, years later, would rival Chaplin's as a comic icon, but Chaplin's image is much more complex. For one thing, the costume lends to Chaplin's small frame a peculiar integrity. Photos of him in ordinary street clothing reveal his unusual proportions, while the comic costume somehow makes everything harmonize. His overly large head, made still larger by his penumbra of hair and his hat, is balanced by his overly large pants and shoes. His incongruously regal deportment highlights the paradoxical juxtaposition of elegance and shabbiness inherent in the costume, only one of several contradictions it embodies: large versus small, rich versus poor, youth versus age. With regard to the latter, the critic Parker Tyler points out that Chaplin's costume makes him look like an adult as seen from the vantage point of a small child: Looking up, the child sees enormous legs and feet, a tapered trunk, and a huge head looking down at him.

The evocative implications of the costume and character are barely explored in the plots and gags of the Keystone films, but they were immediately apparent to audiences:

> Chaplin has created an entirely new variety of screen comedian—a weird figure in whom one may recognize elements of the dude, the tramp, the acrobat, and, flavoring all, the "silly ass" of whom the drunken swell in "Mumming Birds" was so perfect a type. This extraordinary character wanders through the recent Keystone releases—there is no other word to describe the Chaplin touch—and indulges in escapades which are side-splitting in their weird absurdity and their amazing suddenness.[25]

Other Keystone characters occasionally mock his clothing, but in the world of the Keystone films the costume doesn't usually set Charlie apart because he's of a different social class so much as because he's a "weird figure," distinctive and silly, the dude tramp. His costume is clownish, yet realistic enough to allow him credibility as a character.

Comparing Chaplin's costume with Chester Conklin's is instructive. Conklin, or "Walrus" as he was called because of the huge, drooping mustache that covers his mouth, wears clothing very similar to Charlie's, including baggy pants, a long tie, and a jacket with too-long sleeves.[26] Like Charlie, he often holds his shoulders high as well. But Conklin's body is normally proportioned, so the clothes simply look ill-fitting rather than animating any child-adult dichotomy about him. The big mustache and outsized clothes are funny on his scrawny frame, but the effect is one-dimensional. Conklin usually plays

Chaplin and Chester Conklin in *Dough and Dynamite.*

a slow-witted working-class character, without the behavioral complexities that make Charlie so intriguing. Whether dressed as a cop or as a baker, he looks and behaves like a slovenly idiot: his stomach protruding, his hat askew. Charlie, by contrast, always looks neatly put together, even fussy. His morning suit, along with his wing-collared shirt, bowler, and dandy's cane point him toward the upper class, but the misfit garments and big shoes give him away, along with that long tie—a gentleman would wear an ascot with morning clothes. Chaplin would spend a quarter century exploring the contradictions inherent in his costume.

But even at the outset the graphic power of the costume on the screen made an enormous impact, setting Chaplin immediately apart on the crowded movie screens of 1914. Just as everyone could imitate Charlie's signature walk, everyone could draw him, and the image was quickly translated into toys, statuettes, and newspaper cartoons. Stills of Chaplin from even his earliest films reveal the magnetic power of his silhouette to draw attention away from the other characters, who were, for the most part, conventionally attired in well-fitting clothes. The exceptions were Conklin and Sennett himself, who tended to dress and act like a country bumpkin, in ridiculously undersized clothing.

Happily, Chaplin's appearance and movement were complemented by the film technology of the period. Because many early silent films survive only in mutilated and degraded form, a legend has grown that that's how they always looked. In fact, the original films featured stunningly clear photography. The film stock was higher contrast than the panchromatic stock introduced in the late 1920s, and this made Chaplin's heavy makeup look quite natural onscreen. Only in his films of the 1930s did his makeup become evident as makeup.

Even more important than the high-contrast quality of early film to Chaplin's work was the fact that comedies were expected to be shown speeded up. Comedy filmmakers were quick to capitalize on the possibilities for faster-than-life motion. Mack Sennett exploited the technique very effectively in the trademark chase scenes that fill his films, often featuring careening lines of people and cars full of Keystone Kops. Chaplin's performing style made him a happy addition to Sennett's world. His precise movement seemed even more so when seen faster than life, and his unique gestures set him apart from the more conventional actors around him. Chaplin explains:

> There was a lot Keystone taught me and a lot I taught Keystone. In those days they knew little about technique, stagecraft or movement, which I brought to them from the theatre. They also knew little about natural pantomime. In blocking a scene, a director would have three or four actors blatantly stand in a straight line facing the camera, and, with the broadest gestures, one would pantomime "I-want-to-marry-your-daughter" by pointing to himself, then to his ring finger, then to the girl. Their miming dealt little with subtlety or effectiveness, so I stood out in contrast.[27]

In fact, the miming of the Keystone players wasn't quite as broad as Chaplin says, and his own wasn't all that subtle, at least initially. In *Mabel's Married Life*, which Chaplin directed, after Mabel parodies his walk she points to her ring, makes a praying gesture, and throws up her hands in dismay. The gestures Chaplin brought with him from the stage were necessarily broad, for they were designed to play in large houses. What set him apart was that, although his gestures were broad, they were interesting and even compelling to watch because of their formal qualities.

Chaplin's rapid advancement as a filmmaker and the development of his character is accurately tracked in many books about him. What is not often noted, however, is that his gestural vocabulary is virtually complete from his earliest Keystone films; many of the most endearing comic moments and sequences from his later comic masterpieces are seen in virtually identical form in the Keystones. However, in the earlier films they have less impact, because Chaplin's storytelling, directorial, and editing skills were still rudimentary. "All I need to make a film," he famously told Sennett, "is a park, a policeman and a pretty girl."[28] In fact, that's all he often *got*, along with the occasional café set. Editing within a given scene was virtually nonexistent; the plots are mostly variants of the usual Keystone formula of rivals fighting over women, ending in a chase and, as often as not, a dunking in the lake or a fall into the ocean off the pier. Yet watching these films is like watching a butterfly emerging from a cocoon; it's not always pleasant to see, but it's fascinating. And occasionally a whole film takes flight, such as the eleven-minute gem *The New Janitor*.

As his popularity, salary, and artistic independence grew exponentially during his first years in Hollywood, Chaplin faced the urgent need to come up with new material. He would make fifty films in his first two years, stimulated by success and inspired by increasing production budgets. Luckily for him, his growth as a filmmaker coincided with his growth as a mime. As his stories grew more complex and subtle, so did his mimetic acting. For example, an early scene in *Easy Street* finds Charlie trying to decide whether to apply for a policeman's job. He musters up his courage, elevates his chest, and pulls

Charlie agonizes over whether to become a policeman. *Easy Street.*

his shoulders back—but wavers, midstride, as he tries to enter the police station; we see the exact moment that his fear overcomes his courage. He agonizes, approaching the door and retreating several times before finally finding the courage to take the plunge. It is a brilliantly played little scene, totally physicalizing the internal process of making a decision.

Chaplin's mime skills became so sophisticated that he could manipulate the audience's perception of his size and weight. We can see this particularly in the twelve Mutual films he made in 1916–17. In all but the solo *One A.M.*, the gigantic Eric Campbell, who was nearly a foot taller than Charlie, is his main antagonist. However, the physical relationship between the two varies according to Chaplin's dramatic needs in each film. In *Easy Street*, for example, after Charlie becomes a policeman, he is terrorized by Eric, the toughest thug on the ironically named slum street. Campbell here seems like a creature of folklore. Massive, immovable, seemingly indestructible, he doesn't even blink as Charlie's whales away at him with his nightstick. Charlie prevails only with quicksilver evasions and tricky ruses—and the handy application of a gas street lamp and iron stove as weapons. Chaplin has come a long way from his Keystone days, when looking small and acting coy were simply dodges to take the edge off his aggressive behavior. Now his small stature becomes central to plots that feature him as a fragile soul, the lonely, wandering Tramp of legend.

On the other hand, in *The Adventurer* the two trade blows throughout the film, and nothing is made of their size difference. Once again Charlie's attitude toward Eric determines their physical relationship. In this case they are on equal terms, both poseurs in the land of the rich; Charlie is an escaped convict, and Eric is cowardly and gauche. Eric is outraged at Charlie's success with the pretty heiress, Edna Purviance, but Charlie is not in the slightest intimidated by him; he parries his hostility and physical assaults as easily as he eludes the clumsy efforts of the police to capture him.

Complementing these size changes is Chaplin's manipulation of his apparent weight. By and large in the films he appears light when he is victimized and heavy when he becomes the aggressor, sometimes in the same film: In *The Cure* Charlie torments gouty Eric Campbell, but is intimidated by the bulky masseur played by Henry Bergman. As the massage scene begins Charlie stands casually in the dressing room, hand in pocket. Bergman comes in to look him over, flipping him front to back as easily as if Charlie is a cardboard cutout. He then sits him down on a cot and pushes him over with a flick of his hand. Charlie's knees remain up as he goes over backward, making the backward movement look completely involuntary on his part—as though there isn't *time* to unbend his legs in the face of such overwhelming force. Establishing Bergman's great strength sets us up for a

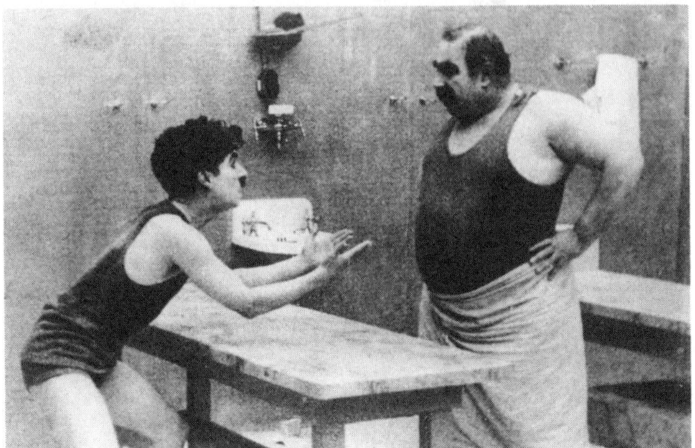
A massage becomes a wrestling match. Charlie and Henry Bergman in *The Cure.*

Charlie twitches his posterior at Bergman.

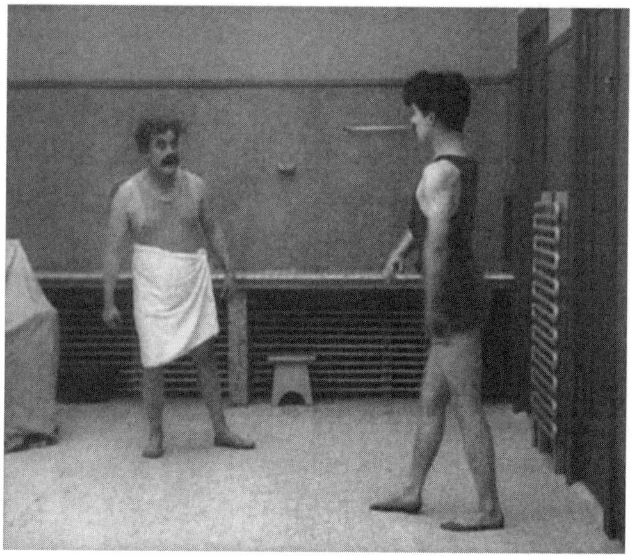

. . . and turns to vanquish one last enemy.

brief "fear" scene as Charlie watches him maul a victim, painfully bending the poor man's heels over his head. Finally, Bergman beckons Charlie over for the inevitable confrontation—which Charlie promptly turns into a wrestling match. Naturally, Charlie defeats Bergman with his superior agility.

The wrestling scene affords a fine opportunity to see Chaplin's physical virtuosity, since he wears a bathing suit throughout. He makes the most of his visibility with several effective postural changes. He assumes a "tough-guy" wrestler pose, his spine curved in a semicircle and arms held threateningly outstretched; a spinal undulation brings his pelvis back to its characteristic cocked position—and straight back into the hot radiator; we see

After defeating Bergman Charlie feels confident . . .

the steam rise off the pipes. He jumps instantly away, arching his entire back and rubbing his behind, and then resumes his original position. Once he has vanquished Bergman and dispatched another attendant he struts around in triumph, head and upper chest elevated, pelvis pulled back, elbows out, knees pumping up and down—the cock-of-the-walk.

Chaplin's skill at manipulating our sense of his body's size and weight is extended to the way he handles objects. In *His Musical Career* (1914) Charlie is the assistant piano mover to another of Chaplin's favorite comic foils, Mack Swain (Swain was to replace Eric Campbell after the latter's untimely death in an auto accident in 1917). Almost all the gags in this film are gags of weight, as puny Charlie does much of the heavy lifting. Chaplin's simulation of weight in the prop piano is effective, as is his comic inability to unbend after carrying it all around the living room for the indecisive owners. In *The Pawnshop* Charlie deftly adds weight to a doughnut Edna has baked. He takes it in his left hand, which immediately pulls his entire arm straight downward. The weight further translates into his trunk, which sags sideways and pulls him off balance. He then "presses" it like a dumbbell. Finally he tosses it onto a plate, which shatters. Sense of weight is again used to comic effect in *The Pilgrim*, when Charlie as a bogus minister compares the weight of the collection boxes that have been circulated on opposite sides of the church; he smiles warmly at the congregants who have filled their box, and glares coldly at the ones who didn't.

On a sloping surface one's own body weight becomes a force to be reckoned with, and Chaplin explores the comic possibilities in the first half of *The Immigrant*,

Edna's doughnut is heavier than Charlie expected. *The Pawnshop.*

Chaplin and Mack Swain in the tilting cabin of *The Gold Rush.*

which takes place on the voyage to America. For ten minutes the boat rocks almost continually, giving the viewer a visceral sense of the motion that inspires many of the gags. Chaplin skillfully varies the degree of rocking from scene to scene, so that the viewer doesn't become as seasick as the passengers. The exterior ship set, which shows the sea in the background in several shots, is able to tilt somewhat, but in most of the shots the camera, which is mounted on a pendulum device, augments the degree of the tilt or simulates it altogether. In one of the early establishing shots Chaplin helps the illusion along by shuffling sideways on one foot in the direction of the tilt, his other leg extended in his standard "skidding" position, and then reversing direction. The artifice is almost undetectable until one looks away from Charlie and notices that none of the other passengers is reacting to the motion of the boat—except by moaning in agony or heading for the rail.

No such fakery is necessary for the ship's interior dining hall scene. This smaller set, constructed in the studio, seesaws spectacularly, leading to a boisterous comedy of slipping and sliding. A portly woman, played by the versatile Henry Bergman, enters and loses her footing, sliding back and forth across the floor on her back (the floor was wet down to facilitate the scene). Charlie enters and she rolls onto her stomach, tripping him up. He slides back and forth on top of her as she rolls back and forth across the floor. Finally, they untangle, and she struggles to a seat. Charlie has managed to regain his feet and retrieve his hat and cane. His back to us, he glides smoothly back and forth across the cabin, his legs spread, holding his pants tightly at the waistband as though to steady himself. It's an uproarious and intricately choreographed sequence, made all the more impressive by its having been captured in a single uninterrupted shot. There follows a second, equally delightful sequence in which Charlie "shares" a sliding soup bowl with the passenger across the table.

Chaplin used another tilting set for the thrill climax of *The Gold Rush.* Prospectors Charlie and Mack Swain wake up, ignorant of the fact that their cabin has been blown to a precarious perch, extending halfway over the edge of a cliff. As long as they are on opposite sides of the cabin it maintains its precarious balance, but when they both walk to the side overhanging the cliff, it suddenly begins to tilt dramatically. While Swain terrorizes Charlie with his superior size and bulk in other parts of the film, for this scene they are both equally terrified, and they apparently weigh the same as well. No viewer will notice the discrepancy in this exciting sequence.

The skills to manipulate the audience's perception of one's weight and size, or to lend weight to objects, indicates a high order of what might be called "pure" mime skills, in the modern sense of the ability to conjure invisible props. Chaplin demonstrates his ability to do that in many scenes. Taking off an imaginary glove in Karno's *Mumming Birds* sketch is probably only one of many such tricks Chaplin learned from his mentor. Other examples from the films include eating an imaginary meal for Paulette Goddard in *Modern Times*; catching and killing flies in *The Vagabond*; performing an invisible flea circus act in *Limelight* and the recently discovered film fragment *The Professor*;[29] showing his brood of children by indicating their heights in comically precise ascending order in *The Pawnshop* and *A Dog's Life*; and referring to a shapely woman by tracing her outline in *Modern Times* and *The Great Dictator*.

The last couple of instances demonstrate the visceral yet hard to describe appeal of Chaplin's performances. While showing the heights of children or tracing the shape of a beautiful woman may sound like clichés in print, when we see these actions on film, Chaplin's handling is so original that the cliché never comes to mind. On the contrary, such moments stand out like diamonds gleaming brightly in a field. The difference lies in the subtle shadings of mime technique, the unexpected rhythms and shapes that make the movements so pleasurable to watch.

Going hand in hand with Chaplin's ability to conjure props is his ability to conjure characters, instantly transforming himself another person by changing his posture and movement. Thus, Chaplin plays both David and Goliath for a silent sermon in *The Pilgrim*, and demonstrates an amorous encounter between a fat man and a pretty girl at the end of *Modern Times*.

The latter film casts Chaplin as an entertainer, a role he often played in private as well. According to numerous accounts Chaplin was a consummate party entertainer. He and George Gershwin were the prized party guests of the 1920s. Just as Gershwin would inevitably sit down at the piano, Chaplin would invariably take the floor and begin telling stories. Soon these stories would be elaborated into hysterical bits, and the guests, naturally, would gather around, enthralled. Late in life Chaplin admitted, "It was always hard for me to make friends. I was shy and inarticulate. Doug Fairbanks was my only real friend, and I was a showpiece for him at parties."[30] Shy he may have been, but he did informal performances all his life, often for audiences of one. The stories would sometimes take the form of outrageous imitations of celebrities like Eleanora Duse, John Barrymore, Jimmy Walker, or Howard Hawks in revealing situations.[31] His exquisite mime always served as illustration—Chaplin, it seems, wasn't capable of talking about something without acting it out—and at other times the mime would take over altogether, as when he would recount a recent fishing trip, or offer a passionate discourse on slavery, or reflect upon the Crucifixion and the character of Jesus.[32] He would switch from role to role, portraying objects and animals as well as human characters.

Chaplin also had more polished party turns. Wedging his cane against the floor, he would walk up a wall, or he would portray both the bullfighter and the bull in a comic story of the bullring. For one charity performance he did a dance with invisible balloons. Another piece had him as an art connoisseur in a museum, studying a wall of paintings, the first of which is about three feet off the ground. They get progressively taller, and so does Chaplin as he strains to see them.[33]

Minister Charlie and his dubious congregation.

David . . .

. . . and Goliath. *The Pilgrim*.

Max Eastman drew Chaplin out of his shell with elaborate party games, including a speech-making challenge in which guests drew a subject out of one hat and a character from another, and then delivered an impromptu speech in character. Eastman also introduced Chaplin to complicated variations on the game of charades and an elaborate drama game in which pairs of people hastily created a one-act play. The David and Goliath sermon, which is a high point of *The Pilgrim*, came out of one of these sessions. While most of these flights of impromptu invention were never recorded, there are tantalizing glimpses of Chaplin at play in newsreel footage and home movies.[34]

Such games and social performing served Chaplin in several ways. He was able to blow off steam by performing for and with sympathetic friends, losing a bit of the self-consciousness that goes with the territory of being a celebrity. At the same time, it was a way of generating new material and trying it out on captive audiences; one writer described an evening with Chaplin and Paulette Goddard at the Trocadero nightclub during the production of *Modern Times*. Chaplin couldn't resist jumping up and launching into the gibberish song that climaxes the film, with its accompanying mime routine of the fat man and pretty girl.[35]

Although Chaplin's gift for mime was recognized from the start of his performing career, the physical skills he brought with him from the stage, formidable as they were, weren't enough to make him into a great *film* mime. The work of indisputably great clowns and mimes almost invariably loses its essential appeal and humor on film, because the aesthetic divide between stage and screen is great. Chaplin was one of the few who bridged that divide. It was not only his great talent as a mime, but his ability to conceive and direct scenes specifically for the film medium, that gave his work its lasting value. He had to become as good behind the camera as he was in front of it.

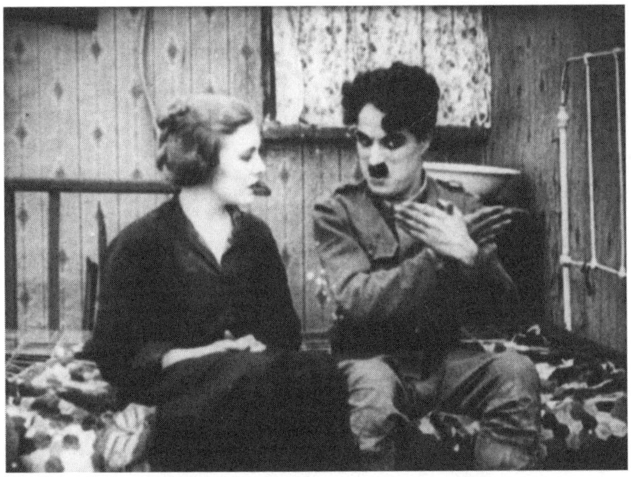

Charlie pantomimes an eagle to show French girl Edna that he is an American soldier. *Shoulder Arms.*

Notes

1. Charlie Chaplin, cited in Richard Meryman, "Chaplin: Ageless Master's Anatomy of Comedy," *Life*, March 10, 1967, 89.

2. Charles A. McGuirk, "Chaplinitis," *Motion Picture Magazine*, July 1915, 122. The most enthusiastic audience for the Keystone films were the soldiers themselves, and cartoonists often pictured Chaplin's character at war. His popularity among soldiers was so great that the British and Canadian military authorities in 1916 actually forbade the men to trim their mustaches down in the Chaplin manner, fearing that it would affect discipline.

The Chaplin Keystones remained popular throughout the war years and beyond. They were reissued with new titles, combined and reedited to create "new" Chaplin films, and "updated" with dreadful, pun-laden subtitles that are thuddingly unfunny today.

3. Silent films, of course, were never shown silently, but always with live musical accompaniment. Until very recently, reissues of Chaplin's early films seldom had properly scored and synchronized music. Instead, generic "honky-tonk" music was laid down indiscriminately. This seriously detracts from their appeal. Chaplin's 1915–1917 films for Essanay and Mutual have been released in restored versions with decent soundtracks, but as of this writing his 1914 Keystone films have not, making them difficult to evaluate properly. For a thorough examination of this issue see Ted Okuda and David Maska, *Charlie Chaplin at Keystone and Essanay: Dawn of the Tramp* (Lincoln, NE: iUniverse, 2005).

4. *New York Dramatic Mirror* (1914), cited in Gerald D. McDonald, Michael Conway, and Mark Ricci, eds., *The Films of Charlie Chaplin* (New York: Citadel Press, 1965), 69.

5. Maxson F. Judell, *Madison (WI) State Journal*, May 15, 1915, cited in McDonald et al., *The Films of Charlie Chaplin*, 119.

6. Chaplin, cited by John McCabe, *Charlie Chaplin* (Garden City, NY: Doubleday, 1978), 235–36.

7. Maugham, cited by Peter Cotes and Thelma Niklaus, *The Little Fellow* (New York: Citadel Press, 1965), 11.

8. Max Eastman, *Great Companions* (New York: Farrar, Straus and Cudahy, 1959), 213.

9. Matthew Sweet, "The Other Chaplin," *Independent on Sunday* [London], October 19, 2003, 19.

10. Walter Kerr eloquently discusses Chaplin's filmic detachment in his perceptive book *The Silent Clowns* (New York: Knopf, 1975).

11. It is interesting to note that as Chaplin's sex life became the subject of tabloid headlines, his screen character became less sexually aggressive.

12. This can be seen in *Unknown Chaplin*, the stunning three-hour documentary by Kevin Brownlow and David Gill.

13. Charlie Chaplin, "What People Laugh At," *American*, November 1918, cited by Donald McCaffrey in *Focus on Chaplin* (Englewood Cliffs, NJ: Prentice-Hall, 1971), 51. The quotation is from one of Chaplin's ghostwritten articles, though it was probably based on interviews with him.

14. Joseph Morgenstern, "The Custard Pie of Creation," *Newsweek*, June 6, 1966, 92.

15. In real life Chaplin cut his own hair, and he loved cutting the hair of his leading ladies and family members.

16. Chaplin, cited by Morgenstern, "The Custard Pie of Creation," 92-3.

17. Chaplin, *My Autobiography* (New York: Simon & Schuster, 1964), 217.

18. *The Little Review*, 1916.

19. McGuirk, "Chaplinitis," 121.

20. Danny Kaye is one of the few screen comedians who has the sort of brisk, precise movements that were Chaplin's trademark. Happily, Kaye also had quicksilver vocal talents that complemented his physical skills. Unfortunately, few of his films were worthy of his formidable gifts.

21. See chapter 7, "The Dancer," for a fuller exploration of Chaplin's comic choreography.

22. Chaplin, *My Autobiography*, 326.

23. McGuirk, "Chaplinitis," 122.

24. Chaplin became the best example of comedy theorist Henri Bergson's dictum that comedy emanates from human beings acting in mechanical ways.

25. *Kinematograph Weekly*, 1914, cited in McDonald et al., *The Films of Charlie Chaplin*, 32.

26. Conklin claimed that Chaplin used one of his jackets the day he assembled his Tramp costume.

27. Chaplin, *My Autobiography*, 152.

28. Chaplin, *My Autobiography*, 159.

29. This fascinating film features Chaplin as the surly Professor Bosco, a character most unlike the Tramp. A self-contained, five-minute fragment in which the professor's fleas escape in a doss-house is all that survives of the film, and it features some of Chaplin's finest mime work. This scene is examined in detail in chapter 14 and can be seen in *Unknown Chaplin*.

30. Cited by Candice Bergen, "I Thought They Might Hiss," *Life*, April 21, 1972, 90.

31. David Raksin, Chaplin's musical assistant on *Modern Times*, recounted one that sounded hilarious: Chaplin imitated the way several recent presidents would look at the moment of sexual climax. Author interview, 1985.

32. Chaplin astounded and alarmed his friends for many years by claiming that he would play Jesus Christ in a film.

33. Interestingly, many of Chaplin's party performances seem close to the kind of stage mime sketches Marcel Marceau became famous for years later.

34. *Unknown Chaplin* contains several wonderful examples, including a prototype of the globe dance from *The Great Dictator* shot in the 1920s, years before the advent of Adolf Hitler, at a party at Pickfair, the mansion of Mary Pickford and Douglas Fairbanks.

35. R. J. Minney, *Chaplin—The Immortal Tramp* (London: George Newnes, 1954), 143. This was unusual, for Chaplin generally avoided calling attention to himself in public. He quickly stopped when the other diners began gathering around him.

CHAPTER THREE

Shoot the Mime

"My technique is the outcome of thinking for myself . . . it is not borrowed from what others are doing."[1]

Although Chaplin denied credit to many of his film collaborators, he wrote of Mack Sennett with the same respect and gratitude he always accorded Fred Karno, his stage mentor. And with good reason, for the Keystone film world Chaplin entered late in 1913 provided him with the foundation for all his later work. But first he needed to master the elements of that world—and the film medium—to suit his own emerging purposes.

Chaplin and others present at the time have recorded his bewilderment at the technology of filmmaking when he arrived at Keystone. Used to the straightforward rehearsal-performance routines of his stage years, he couldn't at first grasp the role of editing in the film process, which made it possible (and practical) to shoot scenes out of sequence. Evidently he learned quickly, for he was both directing and writing his own films within three months. At the outset it was Chaplin's performances that set him apart, but once he begin directing and writing, his films were also technically equal or superior to the other work being done there at the time. Within the next couple of years Chaplin would utilize the medium with far greater sophistication than Sennett ever attained.

Chaplin recognized that his intimate and natural style of mime acting was far more effective on the screen than the cruder gesticulating of the Keystone troupe. Nevertheless, it must have come as a pleasant surprise to him to see how film actually enhanced his performances. Everything about the new medium seemed to work to his advantage. The stark black-and-white images made his new costume and makeup stand out, decisively setting him apart from the other characters. And the absolute silence of film, along with its sped-up action, seemed curiously well suited to his performing style.

The screen world was much more silent than the stage world of Fred Karno. Even when playing the largely wordless drunk, Chaplin played him in sketches that featured live music, singing, and occasional bits of dialogue. In the complete silence of film Chaplin blossomed, and it is to his great credit that in his mature silent films, sound is never missed.[2]

A special bonus Chaplin got from the silence was the unreality it imposed on the silent screen world, an unreality made even more so by the faster-than-life action. A convention of Sennett's film world was that no one could be injured, despite the falls from rooftops, plunges from cliffs, or assaults they endured from bricks, knives, guns, and pitchforks. Bodies in the Keystone films were treated as indestructible objects. Since Chaplin's stage work was strongly acrobatic, this was a natural transition for him to make. "The Little Limey," as he was at first disparagingly called on the lot, earned the company's respect by demonstrating his sophisticated techniques for falling without injury. Indeed, one marvels at some of those falls down stairways and on sidewalks and asphalt roads.

It is hard for a modern viewer to appreciate the importance of sped-up action in Chaplin's art, since the device has, for the most part, been misused since the silent era. After the 1950s filmmakers fastened on the idea of using undercranking, as it was originally called,[3] for a nostalgic or cutely comic "retro" effect, finding easy humor in a clichéd and patronizing view of what silent movies looked like. TV variety shows of the 1950s often spoofed silent movies as well; Buster Keaton was a willing participant in several of these parodies. The practice was revived by filmmakers during the 1960s and 1970s, notably in *Tom Jones* and the Beatles' movies. Woody Allen used it with some success in *Sleeper* (1973), his most visual comedy; scenes of slipping on a giant banana peel, or reeling drunkenly after being awakened from suspended animation, are well enough conceived and executed to justify the device. But in his next film, *Love and Death* (1975), undercranking becomes a facile evasion in what is primarily a verbal film, covering up uninspired visual gags. Allen veered away from visual comedy after this.

Undercranking was ubiquitous in the silent film era. Cameras were hand cranked and projectors had rheostats. Each film originally had its projection speed indicated on musical cue sheets given to the music director and projectionist, and sometimes printed on the film's leader as well. Proper projection speed was a matter of some controversy even then, but we do know that the best silent films seldom used undercranking as a gag in and of itself. Instead, it was used as an accent, to move the action along briskly. In the silent-screen world we can absorb visual information quickly. Natural speed—particularly for nonaction scenes in which characters are speaking to each other—simply slows down the pace unnecessarily. In general, dramas were expected to be shown at a speed only slightly faster than life, except for chase and fight sequences, which were sped up (a convention that continued well into the sound era). Silent comedies, however, with their greater emphasis on action sequences and physical comedy, were shown faster, whizzing by at up to 30 percent faster than life, or even more in some cases.

Undercranking was particularly important for Chaplin, and served him in several respects. First and foremost, it underscored the mechanical precision of his movement, discussed at length in the last chapter. For Chaplin, as well as for the other slapstick comedians, it also made the knockabout comedy—essentially a comedy of force and pain—less "real," and hence comfortably removed from life. The audience knew that no one was really being hurt in these films, though the actors supplied an array of exaggerated comic expressions of pain and discomfort to accompany the falls, blows, and burns they suffered. Undercranking also made the comic fight scenes and stunts both safer to execute and more convincing to watch. When films slowed down to real-life speed in the sound era, much of this kind of action comedy passed into the realm of animated cartoons, where it remains today.

Fast motion enhances not only Chaplin's acrobatic tumbles but also his balletic qualities and physical resilience. Part of Chaplin's resistance to making sound films must surely have been that he knew that, at the quotidian pace of real life, he would appear sluggish in comparison to the way he looked in his silent films. In addition, he was entering his forties, no longer the lithe acrobat of the Mutuals made fifteen years earlier. Chaplin solved this problem, in part, by building into all of his sound films opportunities for undercranked scenes.

In his silent films Chaplin sets a pace and then varies the undercranking subtly from scene to scene.[4] The whirring sound of the hand-cranked camera told Chaplin how much his actions would be sped up, and he adjusted his performance accordingly (like the other silent comedians, Chaplin missed the clicking sound of the silent camera in the sound era). When the camera slowed up, he could slow up. While the pace of undercranking varies widely in his films, it is safe to say that before *The Great Dictator* in 1940 we *never* see Chaplin move at natural speed.[5]

Sped-up action also augments the amazing stunt work in Buster Keaton's short films, but in his features he came to prefer a slower speed. Keaton didn't want the sense of an unreal, springier world that came with undercranking, for two reasons. First, his characters were more naturalistic than Chaplin's, so he wanted them to have the gravity of dramatic characters. Second, the palpable reality of large objects was critical to his films. He wanted the audience to *feel* the heaviness of the trains in *The General*, the ship in *The Navigator*, the house that falls on him in *Steamboat Bill, Jr*. Only by sensing the mass of these objects can we fully experience the exhilarating thrill of danger that infuses his films. Still, undercranking enhances his amazing acrobatics and makes his signature running movement—he rockets along more like a projectile than a human being—a pleasure to behold.

Because Chaplin uses sped-up action constantly we are seldom aware that he's doing it at all. Instead, it becomes a subliminal enhancement to his performances, increasing the excitement in his chase scenes, making him look even more graceful on roller skates in *The Rink* and *Modern Times*, and accelerating the motion of the revolving door in *The Cure* that spins him around uncontrollably every time he enters. Only rarely does the speed become a gag in and of itself, such as when that pesky revolving door spits him across the lobby and up the stairs; with the aid of undercranking, Chaplin is able to achieve the illusion that he is falling *up* stairs. But such moments are exceptions, and usually the effect is used as an accent, much as music provides a background that underscores a movie's emotional content.

Speed manipulation was only one kind of trick photography, of course. The early pioneer of film trickery was Georges Méliès, a stage magician who saw film as an extension of his illusionary art. For a time his films fascinated the world public with their amazing slow-motion effects; scenes of objects vanishing, appearing, and transposing; and people who seemed to float, fly, and change size. Sennett exploited such effects for his comic chases and slapstick mayhem, and other comic filmmakers commonly used blatant trick photography throughout the 1920s. The films of Larry Semon, for example, are filled with animated objects and other impossible gags. Keaton said that Semon's comedies probably got more laughs from audiences than anyone's, but they were eminently forgettable. Today they are hardly watchable. Perhaps because today's audiences are more film wise, or perhaps because of proliferation of that kind of humor in animated films, the tricks in Semon and Sennett films have little intrinsic interest for modern viewers.

As the silent era continued, the better silent-film comedians seldom used overt trick photography. Buster Keaton and Harold Lloyd understood, no less than Chaplin, that the audiences wanted to believe in the physical skill they demonstrated in their performances, and in their willingness to risk real danger. Thus, they all developed ways to persuade the film audience of the authenticity of what they were watching.

Films of the 1910s used minimal editing within scenes, and directors shot very little "coverage" as we think of it today—that is, shooting a master wide shot, then coming in for closer shots from various angles, all of which are edited together to create a seamless "invisible" editing in which the cutting is pervasive and unobtrusive. By the early 1920s filmic storytelling had evolved significantly, due in no small part to the innovations in cinematography and editing of D. W. Griffith (under whom Mack Sennett served his apprenticeship). The better comics reaped a special benefit from shooting certain scenes without Griffith-style cross-cutting, and they all developed a preference for sustained long shots to capture their more spectacular stunts. Thus, when Chaplin falls backward off a ten-foot ladder in *The Pawnshop*, there are no convenient cutaways that would allow him to fake the fall. There are cutaways *leading* to the fall that help to build the suspense, but for the payoff shot the ladder simply teeters back and forth a couple of times and topples. The audience clearly sees him take the fall, land, spring up, and check his watch. There are no stunt doubles, nor does the street upon which he tumbles have pads to cushion his fall.

For Keaton and Lloyd sustained long shots were equally critical, if not more so, since they used thrill sequences more often than Chaplin. They were careful to film them in such a way that we can see there's no stunt

A backward fall. *The Pawnshop.*

doubling. That's one of the reasons their thrill sequences are *more* thrilling than those in modern thrillers; audiences regularly burst into applause when seeing them.

Today's audiences witness far riskier-*appearing* stunts in films, but the palpable sense of danger has all but vanished. For one thing, no major star would be allowed to risk life and limb—not to mention the investors' money—shooting a risky scene. So the impression of risk must be accomplished by other means, namely, moving cameras, special effects, stunt doubles, computer graphics, and rapid-fire editing. Action shots in contemporary movies seldom last more than a few seconds, so the physical integrity of a performance is lost in all the razzle-dazzle. This makes it possible for nondancers in films like *Chicago*—as well as performers in music videos—to give the impression that they can dance. Bravura, silent-film-style stunt comedy is now largely the province of action and martial arts films; indeed, Jackie Chan models many of his sequences on Buster Keaton's. But while the computerized special effects and cabling that enable contemporary action stars to do their stunts are impressive, we're rarely left with the feeling of awe and admiration that we have after witnessing a Chaplin, Keaton, or Lloyd film.

Chaplin occasionally used special effects, but like Keaton, who used trick photography with consummate skill in *The Playhouse* and *Sherlock, Jr.*, he found ingenious ways to disguise the fact by fusing the special effect with physical skill. For instance, in *Pay Day* (1922) Charlie is a bricklayer on a scaffold. He is thrown bricks from below, which he catches in the crook of his leg, on the back of his heel, and in other unlikely ways. It's a film trick achieved by running the film backward. In reality, he removes the bricks from the wall, places them on his leg, and lets them drop. But this is easier said than done! Chaplin had to conceive his movement so that the reversed film didn't give the trick away. Sennett employed such trickery in a much cruder way, as a self-consciously filmic joke: for example, someone would jump backward from a swimming pool onto a diving board. Chaplin gets a better payoff than the easy laugh; the casual viewer of *Pay Day* is impressed by the sequence as yet another demonstration of Chaplin's astonishing skills. The film trick has been rendered invisible.[6]

Chaplin liked this particular device, which allowed him to solve the brain-teaser problem of integrating backward action sequences into his films, and he used it several times. In *The Bond*, made a few years earlier in 1918, ribbons wind themselves around him and leading lady Edna Purviance, demonstrating "the bond of love." In this instance no attempt is made to disguise the effect; the entire short propaganda film, an early commercial urging the audience to buy war bonds, is highly stylized, with stark black background and cutout crescent moon. In its striking graphic simplicity it anticipates contemporary television commercials. He used the reverse action effect more subtly in the balloon dance in *The Great Dictator*: The dictator, standing behind his desk, suddenly "jumps" onto the top without apparent effort. Once again, we know there's a trick involved, but it's so skillfully executed, and so skillfully edited into the overall sequence, that we can't be sure whether it is accomplished by reverse action or whether he's being lifted by an invisible cable. In fact, the sequence begins with Chaplin scampering up a curtain, obviously accomplished with some kind of cable; doing the same trick with different methods is a standard magician's gambit to fool the audience. He utilizes the device again to do an impressive stunt in *Limelight* (discussed in chapter 14).

One of his most ingenious uses of the trick was left on the cutting room floor. In an outtake from *Behind the Screen* (1916), shown in the documentary *Unknown Chaplin*, prop man Charlie walks past an actor practicing with a huge axe, which slices into the floor perilously close to his foot. Without missing a beat Charlie steps over the axe and walks on. The illusion is undetectable, and Chaplin evidently intended it as a running gag, for he shot dozens of variations. It's funny and harrowing, but for reasons that are now unclear in the end the gag itself was axed.

Chaplin uses a different kind of film trickery for the literal cliffhanger sequence that climaxes *The Gold Rush*. Exterior shots of a miniature cabin teetering on a cliff, and, at one point, a miniature Charlie hanging out of it, are intercut with interior shots of Charlie and Mack

Miniature cabin, puppet Charlie. *The Gold Rush.*

Swain desperately struggling to get out of the cabin before it plummets into the abyss. This sequence rivals the thrill climaxes in Keaton and Lloyd films, even though no dangerous stunts are actually being performed. The interior tilting cabin set is obviously real, and the comedy of slipping and sliding played out in it compels our belief in the cabin's vertiginous perch. The action, the effective model work, and, above all, the rhythm of the editing merge the elements into an exciting and very convincing whole.

In Chaplin's first couple of years, critics often felt called upon to criticize his temerity in being a one-man show—writing, editing, directing, and starring in his own movies. "Oh, for a Chaplin author!" went the cry.[7] These criticisms were drowned out by the gales of laughter and applause that greeted his silent masterworks of the late teens and twenties, and Chaplin's art for a time seemed unassailable. Critics and learned writers during this period almost seemed to be vying with each other to heap extravagant praise upon him. But when he resisted the coming of sound with two essentially silent pictures in the 1930s, Chaplin became an anachronism, albeit a affectionately remembered one. While he was still generally well reviewed, and his new films were seen as important events, no longer were they greeted with virtually unanimous acclaim. Beginning with *Modern Times* in 1936, critics began taking pot shots Chaplin's latest presumption, adding explicit social commentary to his films. Most were simply bemused, but to the critic for the *New Republic*, Otis Ferguson, *Modern Times*—if not Chaplin's character—seemed as anachronistic as his filmic silence.

> Chaplin himself is not dated, never will be; he is a reservoir of humor, master of an infinite array of dodges, agile in both mind and body; he is not only a character but a

> complex character, with the perfect ability to make evident all the shades of his odd and charming feelings; not only a touching character, but a first class buffoon and I guess the master of our time in dumb show. But this does not make him a first-class picture maker. He may personally surmount his period, but as director-producer he can't carry his whole show with him, and I'll take bets that if he keeps on refusing to learn any more than he learned when the movies themselves were just learning, each successive picture he makes will seem, on release, to fall short of what went before. The general reaction to this one anyway is the wonder that these primitive formulas can be so genuinely comic and endearing.[8]

Ferguson would have won his bet. Chaplin's remaining five films, while they had their champions, were to one degree or another savaged by critics. Never again would he bask in undiluted critical acclaim. Later critics even found some of his formerly celebrated films overrated. In his last sentence Ferguson put his finger on what would become an increasingly bothersome critical paradox about Chaplin: Why does his primitive filmmaking still *work*? Shouldn't we know better? A later commentator put it even more bluntly:

> How could someone so woefully ignorant of the very basics of his medium produce some of the greatest films (not novels or plays or music hall turns but *films*) ever made? Will none of the critics tell us that?[9]

The most frequently cited criticism of Chaplin as a director is that his films are more stagy than cinematic. This criticism ignores the fact that, despite their vaunted staginess, Chaplin's films could *not* effectively be reproduced on stage. The full figure onscreen might be fifteen feet high, making possible a subtlety in performance that would be lost on the stage. His long shots work well in part due to that starkly effective makeup, which allows Chaplin, by and large, to dispense with close-ups, saving them for moments of high intensity such as the fabled ending of *City Lights*.

Nevertheless, the criticism is true to some extent. Chaplin's camera is often immobile, or moves just slightly, and he frequently frames shots widely. Individual shots often go on for much longer than shots in other movies. Add to this his apparently cavalier disregard for some basic elements of movie craft, such as continuity in his editing, and you have Ferguson's vision of a stubborn curmudgeon of cinema. Yet when seen in relation to the importance of mime in his films these "flaws" become virtues.[10] For Chaplin, his own movement on the screen is the essential subject of his films. "I am the unusual and I do not need camera angles,"[11] he said.

Chaplin's idiosyncratic attitude toward film craft was frustrating to his loyal cameraman, Rollie Totheroh, and to several of his assistant directors, a number of whom wrote acidly about their experiences.[12] His critical reputation as a director fell to its nadir when his films were rereleased and reevaluated in the 1960s and 1970s. Many critics of the time, who were busily celebrating the self-conscious, flashy cinematic techniques then in vogue, found the recently rediscovered silent masterworks of Keaton more "cinematic," and Keaton's comic antihero startlingly undated. The Chaplin-Keaton debate had begun.

Chaplin's filmmaking was considered crude by comparison. But Chaplin genuinely felt that if his own performance was up to snuff, other details of the film became unimportant. Robert Parrish, who played the bratty newsboy in *City Lights*, visited the studio while Chaplin was viewing rushes from *Monsieur Verdoux*. One take caught an electrician in the shot. The very fact that Parrish *noticed* the electrician was proof to Chaplin that his performance hadn't worked.

In the 1960s, when classic film was rediscovered and celebrated as a serious art form, film was declared, first by the French and then everyone else, to be a director's medium. The director, it was asserted, was the guiding spirit and true author of a film. Up to that time few directors' names were known to the general public; actors reigned supreme in the public mind. Suddenly, superstar directors like Alfred Hitchcock, newly elevated in public esteem, could maintain, with characteristic dry wit, that actors were cattle, so many chess pieces to move around. But when one has the supreme cinema actor and movement artist of the century, *and* he's one of the superstar directors himself, it's difficult to argue that fancy camera movement and flashy editing ought to be the focus of interest.

This is not to say that Chaplin directorial virtues went unnoticed. With renewed scrutiny some critics found subtleties in his films. Though it's difficult to take one's eyes off him for even a moment, when one does, the films reveal some unexpected directorial riches. In some cases this takes the form of nice little character bits and minor gags going on in the background, some of which might not be spotted except on a large screen. For example, there is a shot of the assembly line in *Modern Times* that shows about ten workers behind Charlie, toiling away at meaningless operations on the metal nut plates that speed by.

But more often it was his crudities that were mentioned. Anyone who watches the films carefully can pick out glaring gaps in the continuity. In *The Vagabond*, for

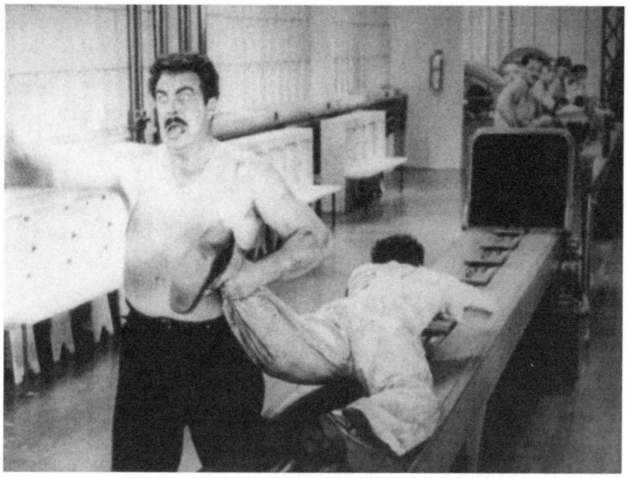

Charlie on the assembly line in *Modern Times*. Note the workers in background.

example, Charlie is being chased around and through a bar; he loses his hat in one exterior shot, and it reappears as he runs through the bar's interior. In *The Rink* he decisively buttons his vest up crookedly, then strides into the next room with it correctly buttoned. Since the films center so much on Charlie's body, cuts from long to mid-range shots or close-ups often find him in new positions, or with his hair looking noticeably different. These gaps are understandable given the breakneck speed with which Chaplin cranked out his early films, and they largely disappear in the films he made after 1918.

Yet even the famous final scene in *City Lights* contains a significant discontinuity. The scene cuts between two heartrending close-ups of Charlie and the blind girl, her sight now restored. The truth of their relationship dawns on her as she sees the Tramp—her benefactor—for the first time. Charlie holds a rose she has given him, and bites his forefinger shyly, as he does in *The Bank*, *The Circus*, and several earlier films. That is, he bites his forefinger in *his* close-ups. In the shots of her, taken from over his shoulder, his hand is held lower. His hand position changes in each shot of the sequence, and it's easy to see why—if he'd held his finger in his mouth for the reverse shots of her, the rose would have blocked her face and ruined the perfect composition. So Chaplin allowed the discontinuity to stand. He must have figured, who's going to notice? And, for that matter, who's going to quibble with the scene James Agee eulogized as "the greatest piece of acting and the highest moment in movies"?[13]

The films of Keaton and Lloyd don't contain such blatant continuity gaps, and this is probably because both men were team players to a much greater extent than Chaplin. They made more silent features, more quickly, and they relied on their production teams to notice and correct such details during the shooting and editing process. Chaplin, absolute monarch at his studio, dismissed such matters as too trivial to dwell upon. He was also ungenerous about crediting his production team. Both Keaton and Lloyd always referred to their films as team efforts and fully credited their collaborators. They also allowed other comic players significant costarring roles. In his silent period Chaplin rarely did—Mack Swain's wonderfully crazed prospector in *The Gold Rush* and Harry Myers's alcoholic millionaire in *City Lights* are notable exceptions. He became more generous in his sound films, sharing the spotlight with Jack Oakie in *The Great Dictator*, Martha Raye in *Monsieur Verdoux*, and Keaton himself in *Limelight*.

The public didn't mind, of course, since they were coming to see *him*. Nor did the public or the critics notice his continuity gaps. Which brings us around again to the purpose of Chaplin the director, which is to properly showcase the remarkable performances of Chaplin the actor. In this respect his directing is not merely adequate—it's brilliant.

> [W]ith more experience I found that the placing of a camera was not only psychological but articulated a scene; in fact, it was the basis of cinematic style. . . . Placement of camera is cinematic inflection. There is no set rule that a close-up gives more emphasis than a long shot. A close-up is a question of feeling; in some instances a long shot can effect great emphasis.[14]

One can see why Chaplin had to direct himself by comparing his first directorial effort, *Caught in the Rain*, with the films preceding it.[15] The standard Keystone action and plot are still there—the story is cobbled together from his previous "park" and "hotel" comedies—but the pace suddenly slows up. Director Chaplin allows actor Chaplin the breathing space to explore the possibilities of each scene. This is most noticeable in the first sequence, in which Chaplin flirts with a woman in a park. The various gags develop in a leisurely fashion, and Chaplin cuts the sequence together in a pleasing manner, smoothly integrating three different settings: the woman on the park bench, her husband at a refreshment stand off to her left, and Charlie at a water fountain off to her right. He has placed the woman in a fulcrum position between the two men, who will clash with each other here and throughout the rest of the film.

Charlie initiates contact with the woman by waving from the fountain. She laughs when he squirts himself trying to get a drink, and he takes this as an invitation and promptly joins her on the bench. Although she repeatedly rebuffs him, he persists in making advances as the woman's outraged husband looks on from the refreshment stand. Chaplin pursues his flirtation with several nicely performed gags, including sitting on a thorny rose and then offering the crushed flower to her (she tosses it away angrily), then swinging his legs onto her lap. Griffith-style intercutting between the three settings, along with the inclusion of several dialogue subtitles, allows Chaplin to build the scene with considerable filmic sophistication. For the action on the park bench, instead of relying on a single long take, as was customary at Keystone, Chaplin inserts a medium shot of him kissing her hand, which calls attention to the unwanted intimacy of the gesture. This is the moment that spurs the husband to action, and he rushes over to scold his wife and knock Charlie down.

On the other hand, later in the film, Chaplin chooses to film the drunken Charlie undressing for bed in his hotel room without cutaways. Cuts wouldn't have been meaningful in this solo scene; instead, Chaplin opts to let it play out for a whole minute. He later uses this approach to great effect in his solo film *One A.M.* (1916). The furious action in *One A.M.* allows him to get away with even longer takes, but he is careful to ensure against filmic monotony with judicious titles and cutaway shots.

Between those two films Chaplin's directorial style developed by fits and starts, influenced, beyond question, by his various technical collaborators. During his time with Essanay he experimented with moving cameras and special effects of various kinds, but because his movement style expressively incorporates every part of his body, as we've noted, he developed a marked preference for the stage-like full-figure framing. After all, those funny feet were his fortune, along with his signature gestures, acrobatic ability, and movement style.

This did not mean that Chaplin set up his camera and let it run as though filming a stage play. Anyone who has ever seen an archival, single-camera video of a stage production knows that an unrelieved, static shot deadens drama after a very short time, and such documents are tedious to watch. Chaplin understood that shooting himself full-figure wasn't enough to make good films. In fact, his framing varies greatly from shot to shot. Much as a still photographer carefully frames his photos for maximum effect, Chaplin learned to frame shots as tightly as possible to include the action, yet minimize the need for camera movement—or, more accurately, to make sure that the camera movement didn't compete with his own movement.

> My own camera setup is based on facilitating choreography for the actor's movements. When a camera is placed on the floor or moves about the player's nostrils, it is the camera that is giving the performance and not the actor. The camera should not obtrude.[16]

Chaplin's camera tracks and pans effectively when the occasion warrants. As we've seen, he learned at the outset to use fluid montage to tell his stories. Yet he always gravitated back to shots that show the uninterrupted movement of the actors across the screen space. As he grew more adept at staging ensemble scenes Chaplin began to pull the camera even further back, confident that he would stand out. He knew audiences wanted to see his performance whole and uninterrupted.

By the time of his Mutual films he had a firm grasp on cinematic technique, and he consistently shot, framed, and cut in a way that effectively reinforces the overall group choreography, along with his own movements. During that period cameraman-cinematographer Rollie Totheroh became his invaluable alter ego behind the camera. Rollie would remain with Chaplin for the rest of his American career, shooting and lighting almost all of his subsequent films.

In a poignant little group scene from *The Immigrant*, Chaplin demonstrates how effectively he can frame and cut to showcase both his individual performance and the work of the ensemble. The immigrants, weary from their long voyage, lounge listlessly on deck. A subtitle announces "The arrival in the Land of Liberty," and one of them notices the Statue of Liberty. They all surge toward the railing, gazing reverently at the statue. A medium shot of Charlie and Edna shows how moved they are by the sight, but the mood is abruptly shattered (in a smooth cut to a wider shot) by a customs official who brusquely ropes the group off. This wide shot is superbly staged; as the group of twenty or so immigrants are penned in by the official, a sort of surging motion in the group brings Charlie, Edna, and her ailing mother to the foreground. In the next cut, another medium shot, Charlie gazes down at the rope squeezing against his chest, then meaningfully up at the Statue. He makes a wry expression: "Land of Liberty" indeed. Other customs officials arrive (in another wide shot), and one of them pushes the group back further. Charlie surreptitiously kicks him in the behind, and it's one of the most satisfying kicks in all cinema. The official whirls around, but Charlie plays innocent.

The sequence is edited seamlessly. Charlie's costume and white makeup make him stand out, as usual, but now he is equally set off by the group's positioning and movement. That surge forward tacitly makes him their representative, and he rises to the occasion with his

The Land of Liberty. *The Immigrant.*

Everything in view makes Charlie's dilemma tangible. *Easy Street.*

sneaky kick. Each shot builds the emotional impact of the whole; a remarkable amount of information is conveyed, with crystal clarity, in a very short time. There are no close-ups; the two medium shots show Charlie, with four or five of the other actors, from the waist up. But in the context of this film, and Chaplin's work generally, they bring us unusually close to his face, and the effect is a dramatic increase in intimacy. The first of them punctuates the touching moment when he sees the statue and is moved nearly to tears, and the second his indignation at being penned in. They blend smoothly with the longer shots that contain the scene's expositional and comic moments. This beautiful little scene, poignant and funny, expertly blends staged action with filmic technique.

In the twelve films he made for Mutual one can watch Chaplin attain mastery of all the essential elements of his craft. The Tramp enters a more complex filmic world, inhabited by a richer and more interesting cast of characters, and far more elaborate props and settings. Chaplin had grown as a mime, a storyteller, a comedian, and a filmmaker. His directing of the other actors is sure, and the action starts to look more like choreography than standard film directing; he learns to extend the graceful quality of his personal movement style into the movements of his ensemble cast.[17]

Even scenes that focus on him exclusively in the Mutual series take on a new depth. When Charlie walks back and forth in front of that police station in *Easy Street*, trying to decide whether to go in, there are no cuts that break up the action; they would only interrupt his eloquent way of communicating his thoughts with every part of his body. Instead, Chaplin shoots the scene full-figure and in a single take, and the camera pans gently back and forth with Charlie as he vacillates.

Several subtle directorial devices serve to further clarify the action. The cop in the doorway never takes his eyes off Charlie, despite the fact that Charlie never directly acknowledges him. The cop is framed in the doorway, which in turn is framed squarely in the center of the film frame. A single step leads to the doorway—a big step, as we discover, for Charlie. The sign, prominently displayed next to the doorway, reads

POLICEMAN
WANTED
AT ONCE

The smaller size of "at once" lends a desperate, pleading tone—perhaps they'd even accept a vagrant like Charlie? Literally everything in view helps to make Charlie's dilemma tangible. The sign beckons to him, and the door stands invitingly open, if only he can overcome the obstacles presented by the step, the cop, and his own faltering courage.

But the stakes are even higher than Charlie imagines. Even as he delicately agonizes over whether to become a cop, the rest of the force is being beaten to a pulp by a vicious gang on Easy Street. Before long he'll be there too, fighting for his life. Chaplin the director has greatly enhanced the performance of Chaplin the actor.

During his American stage career Chaplin repeated just three sketches over a period of four years. With film stardom he had to feed the voracious public appetite for his films. If he didn't keep cranking, that appetite would diminish, and with it the fabulous fortune he was making. The tremendous pressure proved to be an incentive for him to move to new levels in his art, and the results speak for themselves. While his earlier work was sufficient to earn him world acclaim, with the Mutual series he laid claim to cinematic immortality as well, for these films have stood the test of time. In the heady atmosphere of success he found ever-better ways to present his performances, coming up with one memorable gag, sequence, and film after another.

Later in *Easy Street*, for example, after vanquishing the villain, he sits down on a backless chair for a self-congratulatory smoke—and tumbles over backward. Shot square-on from the front, his upper body abruptly disappears from view as he falls backward, and his legs flail in the air. Any other angle would have reduced the surprise and the impact of the gag. *The Vagabond* begins with the familiar feet strolling toward us, seen through the bottom of a saloon's swinging doors. It's a witty, teasing entrance, as iconic as the lonely walk down the road that ends several of his classic films. One can imagine the pleasure and anticipation of the audience in 1916, watching those familiar funny feet and waiting for him to push through the doors and make them laugh once again.

In the Mutuals, Chaplin's filmmaking and mimetic skills fully support each other. Again and again he strikes the tricky balance between shooting long takes and cutting away so that the scenes don't become static. Audiences leave the theatre knowing that they've witnessed a performance of extraordinary physical skill, even if they're largely unaware of the level of filmic sophistication necessary to create that impression. Further, the display of skill is fully integrated with the film, not a tangential stunt or non sequitur; it illuminates Chaplin's character and deepens the comic and dramatic values of the film.

This is the essential achievement of Chaplin's art, and it explains the paradox, noted by Ferguson and others, of how Chaplin's apparently old-fashioned filmmaking "can be so genuinely comic and endearing." Fashions may change, but some old things are simply too good to discard.

Notes

1. Charles Chaplin, *My Autobiography* (New York: Simon & Schuster, 1964), 255.

2. In *The Silent Clowns* Walter Kerr persuasively argues that silent comedies generally hold up better than silent dramas for modern audiences. Silent comedies seem to thrive in the limitations of the medium, while silent dramas are apt to seem like sound movies with something missing. It is instructive in this regard to compare the silent and sound versions of Hitchcock's *Blackmail*, both from 1929. While the silent version is elegant, we get far more information about the characters and their motivations through the dialogue in the sound version.

3. The term *undercranking* dates from the days of hand-cranked cameras. Cranking the film through the camera at a slower speed than it would later be projected resulted in faster-than-life action.

4. As mentioned, there is considerable disagreement over how fast silent films were originally projected, and how fast they should be projected today. The controversy particularly dogs current releases of Chaplin's silent films. Some of these films run too fast at sound speed, so they must be slowed down. Luckily, contemporary DVD technology makes this possible—but it's a judgment call. Some of the best available commercial copies of the Essanay and Mutual films slow them down too much, diminishing or destroying their humor. This issue is considered in greater detail in chapter 12.

5. The exception being when he breaks his long cinematic silence to sing at the end of *Modern Times*.

6. The sequence is discussed in more detail in chapter 7.

7. Julian Johnson, *Photoplay*, 1915. Cited in Gerald D. McDonald, Michael Conway, and Mark Ricci, eds., *The Films of Charlie Chaplin* (New York: Bonanza Books, 1965), 108. Johnson was one of a chorus of critics who lauded Chaplin's aspirations toward doing more substantial work. This topic is explored in depth by Charles Maland in his indispensable *Chaplin and American Culture* (Princeton, NJ: Princeton University Press, 1989).

8. Otis Ferguson, "Hallelujah, Bum Again," *New Republic*, February 19, 1936.

9. Graham Petrie, "So Much and Yet So Little: A Survey of Books on Chaplin," *Film Quarterly* (Spring 1973), cited in Richard Dyer MacCann, *The Silent Comedians* (Metuchen, NJ: Scarecrow Press, 1993), 118. In this astringent little piece Petrie deplores how writers on Chaplin don't analyze his films in terms of film theory as much as they simply describe scenes from them. Then he goes on to criticize blatant inaccuracies in the descriptions and shortcomings in the critical analysis. One wonders what Petrie would have made of the many fine critical books that have come out since he wrote his article, including several works already cited, and excellent studies by John Kimber (*The Art of Charlie Chaplin* [Sheffield, England: Sheffield Academic Press, 2000]) and Julian Smith (*Chaplin* [Boston: Twayne, 1984]), among others.

Gerald D. McDonald put his finger on the central problem of writing about Chaplin in the excellent opening essay to *The Films of Charlie Chaplin*, a 1965 book that opened the floodgates of Chaplin studies in postmodern times: "To see a Chaplin comedy, then to try to tell what you have seen, is a difficult thing to do" (16). True, but it is a worthwhile thing to do as well, for only by observing and then carefully describing the actions can one begin to fathom the intricacies of Chaplin's artistry. One of the first to do so was Gilbert Seldes, who wrote a detailed description of the action of *The Pawnshop* in his pioneering book *The Seven Lively Arts* (New York: Harper & Row, 1924). There is obviously much more to come, for Chaplin's art has proven to be both irresistible and inexhaustible.

10. Gerald Mast offers a concise, eloquent, and comprehensive defense of Chaplin's directing technique in *The Comic Mind* (Indianapolis, IN: Bobbs-Merrill, 1973) 65–67.

11. Chaplin, cited by Theodore Huff, *Charlie Chaplin* (New York: Henry Schuman, 1951), 297.

12. See especially Taves, Brian, "Charlie Dearest," *Film Comment* (April 1988). This article recounts the horrible experiences Robert Florey had as associate director of *Monsieur Verdoux*. Florey actually wrote several books about Chaplin, an idolatrous one in 1927 and a much less flattering portrait in 1952, along with a detailed account of his clashes with Chaplin on *Monsieur Verdoux* in a 1948 work, *Hollywood d'Hier et d'Aujourn'hui* (Paris: Éditions Prisma, 1948). Unfortunately, to date none of these have been translated from the French. See also comments by Eddie Sutherland, who assisted Chaplin on *The Gold Rush*, in Kevin Brownlow's *The Parade's Gone By* (New York: Knopf, 1968).

13. James Agee, "Comedy's Greatest Era," *Life*, September 5, 1949, 77.

14. Chaplin, My *Autobiography*, 151.

15. David Robinson, in *Chaplin, His Life and Art* (London: Penguin, 2001), presents evidence that *Twenty Minutes of Love*, made a few weeks earlier, might have been Chaplin's first directorial effort. If it was, he learned very quickly, for *Caught in the Rain* is better in every way.

16. Chaplin, My *Autobiography*, 255.

17. The choreographic aspect of Chaplin's directing style is examined in detail in chapter 7.

CHAPTER FOUR

Drunk Again

"One more film like that and it will be goodbye Charlie."[1]

One A.M., Chaplin's fourth film in his series for Mutual, is his only solo film—except for a brief appearance by Albert Austin as a cab driver, Chaplin sustains the entire twenty-six minutes himself, substituting inanimate props for human characters.[2] In its relative simplicity it offers a fine opportunity to examine Chaplin's movement and directing technique apart from his more complex ensemble productions of this period.

The film represented a departure from Chaplin's prior stage and film experience. With the exception of a few boyhood solo burlesque turns with the *Casey's Circus* troupe, he had always worked as part of an ensemble. Although many of his film routines have the appearance of solo performances, they almost always involve other characters, if only in peripheral roles. For example, in *The Pawnshop* our eyes are glued on Charlie as he "evaluates" an alarm clock by systematically dissecting it. But the clock's hopeful owner (Albert Austin again) looks on as well, and his puzzlement as Charlie destroys the clock, and then outrage when Charlie rejects it, anchors the scene dramatically. *One A.M.* is also notable in that it marks the debut of Rollie Totheroh as Chaplin's chief cameraman and cinematographer.

Chaplin is reported to have made his "goodbye Charlie" remark when the film first came out, but in his last book he evidently looked back on it with some pride, calling it "a pure exercise in mime and technical virtuosity, with no plot or secondary characters."[3] Actually, it does have a plot, albeit a simple one: Charlie arrives home and goes to bed. But the simplest actions—opening the door, lighting a cigarette, going upstairs—become extremely complicated because Charlie is roaring drunk. *One A.M.* is Chaplin's most thorough exploration of the altered state of awareness of the "inebriated swell" he had played for so long on the stage. Although he abandons his Tramp character for this film, wearing well-fitting evening clothes, he does retain three of the Tramp's visual characteristics: his curly, unkempt hair (usually when Chaplin played the toff, as in *The Idle Class* and *A Night in the Show*, he slicked his hair down); his mustache; and oversize shoes—though, unlike the Tramp's battered brogans, these are elegant, high-topped affairs, with fashionably pointed toes and substantial heels.[4]

The film begins with Charlie's arrival in a cab. He peers through the window and smiles, evidently glad to be home. Charlie's eyes are unfocused and they waver, but his facial expressions are restrained, suggesting his attempt to maintain his control and dignity. He will need all he can muster, for every task proves formidable, beginning with opening the cab door.

As Austin patiently waits, his hand outstretched for the fare, Charlie reaches through the window and feels around for the door handle at the back of the door, but it is at the front. Characteristically, he neglects to check for an inside handle. That would be too simple. Instead, he sticks his head out the window, sees the handle, and reaches for it again—but the window frame blocks his arm. He slaps the frame in frustration. "They should build these handles nearer the door," says the film's first subtitle. There are eleven such titles in *One A.M.*, all of them quoting his unspoken thoughts for our benefit—he isn't mouthing words or speaking to anyone else. These "thought balloons" clarify the action with humorous comments, but primarily serve to cover what would

otherwise be awkward cuts in the action, as in this case; when we return to Charlie the camera has been repositioned slightly, revealing that Chaplin has inserted a second take. Because they are used to cover cuts rather than to provide essential information, the titles, like the film's several close-ups, occasionally seem superfluous.

Charlie moves forward in the cab, slapping both sides of the offending door frame. He is now framed in the door's large open window and rests his arms against the lower edge for a moment, giving the camera a sickly smile. He holds a handkerchief and cigarette in his dangling left hand and rests his chin on his right. Looking down, he does a subtle double-take action, craning his head further down as he sees the handle directly below him. He looks up, smiles at the camera in a self-deprecating way, and reaches down awkwardly to twist it open. As he opens the door in the perfectly matched long shot that follows, we see that the cab does indeed have an inside handle, which Charlie has ignored.

Chaplin has introduced in these first moments two of his character's biggest problems dealing with reality. First, he doesn't rationally assess his situation—one usually opens a car door with the inside handle. Second, when his actions fail to bring about the desired result, he doesn't learn from his mistakes, but rather obsessively repeats them. While this is a definition of insanity, Charlie isn't insane, just wooly-brained from drink. The repetition offers Chaplin a chance to spin endless variations on his comedy of dim-witted drunken ineptitude.

Charlie emerges from the cab, his right hand still absently holding onto the outside door handle. He looks at the meter and the outstretched hand of the cabbie. Forgetting that his arm is still hooked around the window frame, he reaches awkwardly into his pants pocket for the cab fare, and then notices that he's become "stuck" to the door. Another subtitle, "I never did like taxis," reinforces Charlie's frustration.[5] He kicks the door away, but it swings back to hook his arm again; Charlie doesn't notice because his attention has momentarily wandered—as the door swings back he transfers the handkerchief into his right hand and wipes his mouth with it. This is a good illustration of the pleasurable paradox of Chaplin's many performances as a drunk: While Charlie the character is mentally and physically impaired by the liquor, Chaplin the actor is executing the comedy of errors with consummate skill and split-second comic timing.

Charlie now tries to put the hanky into his pants pocket, but since the door is again between his hand and his pocket, he succeeds only in sliding the handkerchief ineffectually against the door, and ends up dropping it onto the ground. He irrationally reaches down through the door window for it, instead of simply closing the door, but he still can't reach it. Trying to outwit the door, he pushes it away from him and dives toward the elusive rag, but it swings back and once again he gets caught hanging in the frame. Charlie's trouble retrieving his handkerchief recapitulates his earlier dilemma with the door handle, except that instead of his elbow or shoulder being caught by the door frame, now it's his whole upper body. The gag has grown in scale, and concludes in a satisfying way when Charlie pushes the door away again, harder, just managing to grab the handkerchief before the door knocks him back into the cab. He's back where he started.

Charlie emerges, a bit dazed, pulls some change out of his pocket and looks at the cab meter to determine his fare. Austin, his eyes tactfully averted, still holds his cupped hand out expectantly. But the numbers on the meter begin to whirl and change as Charlie studies them. He turns to the camera, blinks, and leans against the cab to wait them out. These whirling numbers indicate either Charlie's inability to focus, or, more tellingly, that he's whiled away his evening playing slot machines. Either way, the numbers come up zero, so he merely drops his lit cigarette into Austin's hand and pockets his change. Austin winces, shakes the cigarette off, and angrily demands his fare. Charlie gives him a coin and dismisses him with a wave of the hand. Austin looks down at the coin with irritation—the rich lush is not much of tipper. By the time he looks up, Charlie is in trouble again; he closes the door and tries to walk away, but is abruptly spun back against the door because his cape has been caught in it. Austin looks on with some concern—probably more for his cab than the cheapskate—as Charlie tries to pull free, bracing his foot on the cab's front spare tire. Charlie twists the door handle open and falls backwards into a somersault on the grassy curbside. He gives the door a hard kick, making Austin wince again. Staggering to his feet, he retrieves his top hat, and gives Austin (and us) a brief smile and nod as he turns and wanders off. Austin glares after him.

It has taken Charlie a full three minutes to get out the cab and pay the fare. The sequence is shot and cut in the following way:

1. Medium long shot of the cab pulling up to the curb.
2. Medium shot tightly framing Charlie in the back seat and the driver in the open front seat; the car is stopped in this shot, resulting in a slight jump cut from the previous shot, in which the car was still moving. Charlie tries to find the outside handle.
3. Title: "They should build these handles nearer the door."
4. Medium shot similar to shot 2, but with the camera at a different angle. Charlie slaps the door frame, moves forward in the cab, sees the handle through the large door window, and opens the door.
5. Charlie emerges from the cab in a full-figure shot, gets "stuck" on the door frame.
6. Title: "I never did like taxis."
7. A continuation of shot 5 with a few seconds of action missing. Business with handkerchief, ending with Charlie knocked back into the cab.
8. Charlie emerges from the cab in a medium shot. Business reading meter and "paying" driver with burning cigarette.
9. Medium long shot that seems to continue shot 7. Charlie pays driver, tries to leave, but cape gets caught in door. He pulls free, falling in the process. He rises unsteadily and exits.

The sequence uses three basic camera setups: two medium shots that show Charlie's struggles with the door handle and the meter, and a wider shot that frames him full-figure to showcase his battles with the open door. With the exception of the jump cut after the cab pulls up, all seven shots are perfectly matched on Chaplin's movement, blending to create a seamless illusion of continuous action. Individual shots run for up to fifty seconds. The camera frames each segment of the action perfectly, and, except for a slight pan downward when Charlie falls onto the grass, it remains stationary.

I've described the action and how it's filmed in this much detail to illustrate Chaplin's approach to conjuring physical comedy from the ordinary tasks of life. The framing, cutting, and the length of individual shots attest to Chaplin's method of filming in such a way that his physical skill, not the cutting, is the evident heart and soul of his comedy. The scene wouldn't be as effective in a single long take; the medium shots add variety, allow us to savor Charlie's flickering facial changes, and clearly show the whirling meter numbers from his addled point of view. Had Chaplin followed more conventional practice by showing, for example, a close up of Austin glaring at Charlie, or an extreme close-up of the meter, we would lose some of the film's relentless focus on the drunk, as obsessive in its way as the drunk's obsessive attempts to deal with reality.

The presence of cabbie Albert Austin in every shot adds subtle dramatic tension to the scene, his outstretched hand a constant reminder to the drunk to get on with it. But the drunk doesn't care, because he's drunk, and he's rich. Other people are there to serve him, or, in this case, to act as convenient ashtrays. By playing his drunk as callous rather than sympathetic, Chaplin makes it clear that he deserves all the abuse he's about to bring down upon himself. In effect, he's simultaneously both the hero and villain of his film. Austin's contemptuous expression at the end prepares us for the painful excursion we're about to take into the private world of this privileged souse.

Chaplin's drunken walk is just as distinctive and compelling to watch as his Tramp walk. As he makes his way up the porch steps to his front door, he can't walk a straight line; instead, he staggers in a perfect S-curve. Finding the door locked, he turns toward the camera and walks to the front of the porch to check his pockets for the key, reinforcing the action with another title—"Where's my key?"[6]—then revolves back toward the door to check under the welcome mat. Revolving again toward the camera, he returns to the front of the porch to check his pockets again.

The turns and S-curves impose a choreographic quality to the drunk's pattern of movement that somewhat belies his drunkenness, and his trajectory is highlighted by the way the scene plays out a single long shot, interrupted only by the subtitle, rather than being assembled from a variety of different shots.

Unable to find his key, Charlie decides to break into his home through a window, managing to stick his foot into a goldfish bowl as he climbs through backwards. He then offers us another example of the kind of tortured logic that got him so hopelessly entangled with the car window frame: Discovering his key in his vest pocket, he crawls back outside through the window—again dousing his foot—to open the door properly. This kind of obtuse thinking would become central to the work of Laurel and Hardy ten years later, notably in their 1932 Academy Award–winning short, *The Music Box*. In that comic gem, after painstakingly hefting a piano up endless flights of steps, they are told that there's a road that leads up the hill. They didn't *have* to carry the piano up the steps, after all. So they start *down* the steps with it . . .

The drunk's already impaired sense of balance is further tested by a small rug as he enters the house through the door. With the aid of concealed wires, the rug slides as Charlie steps onto it. After a series of slides and revolutions on the rug, he finally releases the doorknob he has been holding and falls, propelling the rug into the house. Another title—"I must have a skate on!"—covers a slight change of the rug position so that Charlie can rise on it and fall against a coat tree. He tries to steady himself holding onto the tree, resulting in some even more dramatic "skating." After another couple of twists and falls on the pesky rug, he kicks free of it, rises, walks forward, and takes a really spectacular fall on another rug, both legs flying upward as he apparently crashes down on his rear end.

Close examination reveals Chaplin's technique for falling without injury. Usually he cushions his fall by catching himself with his arms or hands, but in this case his arms fly above his head, so he has to do all the work with his legs. As one leg flies into the air, the other immediately straightens to join it parallel to the floor, and he lands on the flat backs of both legs to absorb the force of the fall. When he lands both legs immediately fly up in the air and he goes over onto his back, sitting up again as his legs come down. With undercranking, the subterfuge is undetectable; it looks like both Charlie's legs fly up and he lands squarely on his butt. Chaplin uses his mechanical movement technique to advantage during his falls. Whenever he lands and his legs fly up, as they come down they seem to "lever" his trunk upward into a sitting position. This mechanical-toy action distinguishes his portrayal from the limp flailing of a real drunk, and also makes it clear that he's not really hurt. He may be clumsy and stupid, his perception of reality may be askew, but this drunk remains lithe, energetic, and apparently indestructible.

Falling is a main motif in *One A.M.*—more so than in any other Chaplin film. He falls no fewer than thirty-six times, well over once per minute. Undoubtedly this is the "technical virtuosity" Chaplin refers to, and it is impressive. Indeed, it's hard to see how he manages to do some of these falls without injury.[7] Each is slightly different from the others, carefully motivated by his action, and they build to an amazing series of falls down the twin staircases. But Chaplin's facility with falling may have led him somewhat astray. For some observers, even his inventive variations become a bit wearing. Chaplin uses fewer falls to greater effect in other films in the series, notably *The Cure*, in which he again plays his inebriated swell character. But the falls in that film are grounded in a more ambitious plot, and each one furthers the story of the drunk's systematic transformation of a stately health spa into a drunken dance hall. Two telling spills neatly bookend the film: At the beginning a drunken Charlie accidentally steps into the "health spring," outraging the invalids who are sipping the healthful but foul-tasting waters; and at the end a newly sober Charlie swears off the demon rum, but falls into the well, which has been liberally laced with Charlie's alcohol.

When Charlie takes his flying fall on the rug in *One A.M.*, he lands between a tiger rug and a stuffed bobcat. Somehow he contrives to land so that his hand ends up in the tiger's mouth. A medium cutaway, perfectly matched on action, shows Charlie's discovery of his alarming new predicament. In his confused mental state the tiger appears all too real. He jerks his hand free

and edges away, but his other hand (in a rare close-up) touches the paw and snout of the bobcat, which Charlie finds is looking right up at him. Caught between the beasts, he looks at us in dismay, conveying his fear with his stiffly held legs and feet. It gradually dawns on him that maybe the immobile creatures aren't alive. Warily, he nudges the bobcat with his foot and pats it on the snout. Next comes a brilliant touch. Standing, his hands casually in his pockets, confident now that the cats are unreal, he kicks the bobcat on the rump, which causes it to whirl and "bite" him on the ankle. We share his startled reaction that the animal has come to life.

After repeating the gag with a variation in which he tries to mollify the beast, Charlie moves toward a round table in the center of the living room to get a drink. His unsteady walk and his steady focus on the liquor bottle combine to distract us from the fact that his right hand is secretly attaching his cape to the table. This sets up another sustained sequence as Charlie, glass in hand, walks

around the table toward the liquor decanter—but since his cape is caught the tabletop revolves with him, and the decanter stays tantalizingly out of reach. This prompts an amusing title: "That's the fastest round of drinks I ever saw." After circling the table several times in both directions, Charlie notices that his cape is caught. Smiling toward the camera, he drops the cape from his shoulders. Then comes another brilliant variation. Looking at the decanter to distract us from his careful placement of his foot into his cape, he begins circling the table again, and this time his foot drags his cape, which causes the table to revolve as before. After circumnavigating it a couple of times Charlie falls, and the table (in the same shot) revolves exactly one and one-half times, bringing the decanter to rest precisely where he's sitting. A title asks, "What detained you?"

The table routine demonstrates Chaplin's great ability to make highly choreographed material appear spontaneous. His concentration on his apparent task is so intense that we don't notice—on first viewing—the preparatory movements of attaching his cape to the table or catching his foot in his cape. The scene is shot in one continuous two-minute take, preserving Chaplin's performance without cutaways. How he gets the table to revolve at the end so that the decanter stops right next to him is anyone's guess.

Chaplin braces a hand on the table to rise, suggesting his increasing need for something to stabilize his world. From this point on in the film he will use the table, banisters, and walls repeatedly for support and guidance.

Even when he's not falling or using objects to steady himself, Chaplin never lets us forget that he's drunk. What is so persuasive about how he plays the role is his deep understanding of the mechanics of movement. He knows that the act of standing up is a tenuous affair for anyone, for our weight is not distributed evenly, like that of a piece of furniture, on four flat-bottomed surfaces. Instead, it is borne unsteadily at three points on each foot: where the bone comes through at the base of the heel, at the ball of the foot, and opposite that at the base of the small toe. Standing "still" is an illusion that doesn't exist in real life. We balance the wildly different shapes of our body—our spherical head, rectangular trunk, cubic pelvis, and the tapering cylinders of our extremities—on the two narrow platforms of our feet. Standing is in fact a continuous process of falling and catching ourselves.

Chaplin exaggerates this inherent instability ever so slightly, which is what makes his drunk so convincing. He's not trying to stagger; he's trying to stand still. In effect, he does a little dance with gravity that we can all relate to, for we all do the same dance—only we're better at it. Preventing ourselves from falling is inbred in us, one of our most basic physical skills, mastered early and practiced over a lifetime. But given Charlie's inebriated state, the slightest miscalculation of momentum or unexpected disturbance in his precarious world throws off his fragile equilibrium, and he topples, quite believably.

Having gotten the decanter within reach, Charlie next tries to mix himself a drink. But he aims the seltzer bottle in the wrong direction because he confuses the squirting spout with the lever, and misses his small wineglass entirely. Thinking that perhaps the glass is too small, he picks up the decorative canister that held the seltzer, and misses it with a squirt of seltzer as well. Then he tries pouring liquor from the decanter bottle into the canister, but since the canister is made of an open meshwork, the liquor pours right through it onto his feet. He gives up on the liquor for the moment and lights a cigarette, but then blows on the cigarette and shakes it as though extinguishing a match; he tosses the lit cigarette towards a nearby cuspidor, and misses.[8] A moment later the match burns his fingers. Retrieving his cigarette from the floor, he tosses it towards the cuspidor again, but once again he overshoots. He staggers backward while trying to bend over forward to pick up the cigarette, then crawls forward and picks it up. A title informs us that "This *has* been done!"—meaning that surely someone, somewhere, has accomplished the difficult feat. Charlie pulls the cuspidor toward him, rises, and elaborately positions the cigarette directly above it. Posing decoratively, like a circus acrobat about to perform a great stunt, he drops the cigarette into the cuspidor and looks up with a self-satisfied smirk.

Although this sequence uses small objects, it is shot entirely in a long shot. Chaplin's movement makes his actions and intentions abundantly clear. However, he comes in for a closer shot for his next attempt to light a cigarette. This time he strikes a match on the bottom of his top hat, looks at the match for a moment to make sure it's lit, then shakes it out, entirely forgetting to light the cigarette. He is puzzled when he can't draw on the cigarette. For this gag the close up is important so that we see the unlit cigarette. Chaplin retains the cigarette and periodically tries to light it during the violent comic action to come.

Walking back toward the front door (and taking another rug-slide in stride), Charlie tries to hang his cape on the coat tree in the corner. But the peg slants downward, yet another object that confounds him. Charlie holds onto the cape with both hands, his arms and body movement reinforcing the action as the cape slides ineffectually off the peg. Putting it back on, he tries to go up the steps at the right, but slips on another of those small rugs and falls flat on his face onto the stairs. He moves to the center of the room and, without looking back, absently "hangs" the cape where he assumes the coat tree is standing. Since the tree remains in the corner, the cape merely drops to the floor. This gag of misjudging distance appears in many of Chaplin's films, a carryover from his days with Karno.

Charlie still thirsts for that drink. Taking no chances that the decanter will mysteriously move on its own again, he dives toward the table and grabs the bottle. On his knees, he pours a drink, tilts his head back, and gargles in a characteristically idiosyncratic gesture. Getting up off his knees, Charlie walks behind the table and checks his vest pockets for matches, but gets distracted when he sees a stuffed ostrich. He flips his top hat onto its head with a flourish. Following yet another skirmish with the stuffed bobcat, which again seems to go for his ankle, Charlie kicks it away and falls in front of the stairway on the left side of the living room. A close-up of his exasperated face is followed by a title: "Good night!" He's ready for bed.

What follows is a remarkable series of assaults on the stairs as Charlie tries to make his way to bed.[9] On his first attempt, he works his way unsteadily up the steps, but when he reaches the top he falls on his face and slides back to the bottom. He gets up and immediately tries again, his arms outstretched like a tightrope walker, his right hand delicately touching the banister. As he gets higher he falters, stepping backward as if drawn by an invisible force. He gamely presses on but simply can't overcome the inertial pull backward, and walks backward down the stairs. Without breaking his momentum he spins around and moves smoothly toward the table for another drink. Having established this backward inertia, like a man irresistibly drawn toward the edge of a cliff,

even the slight motion of tilting the glass to his mouth causes him to fall over backward. He holds onto the glass and decanter as he goes over, however, and doesn't spill a precious drop. After putting the decanter and glass on the floor and carefully checking his nose for injury, he rises and tries unsuccessfully to strike another match. Going up the stairs again, he staggers into the wall, then falls across the banister, balancing on it as he slides on his belly all the way down before hitting the floor and rolling. Chaplin breaks his momentum slightly on the way down by holding onto the stuffed ostrich for a moment, and he cushions his fall with a thickly padded rug. Nevertheless, it's a spectacular and harrowing stunt, and he pours himself a well-earned drink from the decanter, which he's left conveniently on the floor within easy reach.

Charlie rises, straightening his hair and coat as best he can, but he has trouble standing up straight because of the way his back now involuntarily arches backward. He rubs his aching back and rear end and has another go at the stairs. As he ascends, the backward pull once again gets the better of him; he bends over at what appears to be an impossible angle, and we're waiting for him to tumble over backward at any moment. Instead he falls on his face again and slides down on his stomach, revolving as he reaches the bottom so he's sitting on the floor facing the camera. He sighs deeply.

He rises and this time *runs* up the stairs, actually reaching the landing before falling and somersaulting backward onto the stairs for another slide down on his belly. Unruffled, he strikes a match on his shoe, but accidentally blows it out with a burp. This seems to disorient him further, if that's possible; he forgets that he hasn't lit the cigarette, shakes out the already extinguished match, and tries to draw on his unlit cigarette.

Charlie notices mountain-climbing equipment against the wall. He swings the backpack on, loops a safety rope around himself (attaching the other end to a piano), dons an alpine hat complete with jaunty feather, and grabs a long pole and pick. Now he wedges the pole against each step as he hooks the pick onto the stair rails, working his way gradually up. Unfortunately, when he gets to the top he falls and somersaults down the stairs yet again. "If I knew how to yodel I'd make it!" reads the most amusing title in the film.

Charlie divests himself of his gear and, turning back to the stairs, climbs up by hanging onto the banister with both arms. Finally, he makes it all the way to the landing, only to be knocked in the jaw by the huge pendulum swinging along the upstairs balcony wall.[10] The blow makes him somersault onto the stairs and down. After checking his tender jaw and nose for injuries he announces, "I'll take another route."

Walking across to the other staircase, he ascends smoothly but walks quickly back down when he sees the stuffed bear at the top. Fortifying himself with another drink and checking his vest pockets, he discovers that he has (as another title informs us) "No more matches." Charlie spies the chandelier and mistakes the electric light for a gaslight, as he had in *Mumming Birds* years before. To reach it he gets onto the table and crawls, walks, and runs, but the tabletop revolves under him, becoming a treadmill as he perseveres like Sisyphus in his futile quest. Occasionally he stops, and the table spins him around like a merry-go-round. The dizzying two-and-a-half minute sequence is interrupted only by a medium shot of Charlie grimly pursuing the chandelier, and one punning title, "Light exercise." Finally, he falls, and the table spins him off onto the floor. Both Charlie and the cigarette he's still stubbornly holding look much the worse for wear.

Undaunted, he makes another attempt on the staircase, but now he's really staggering. He reaches the top and falls, this time rolling himself up in the carpet on the way down (revealing the thick foam pads on the steps that make such stunt work possible). At the bottom, Charlie's head and arms emerge, and he pours himself another drink from the conveniently placed decanter. We're beginning to understand why this man needs to drink.

Choosing another route, Charlie climbs up the coat tree to avoid the steps altogether. He sways precariously at the top, as he would two films later atop a ladder in *The Pawnshop*, and makes it to the landing, but gets smacked again by the pendulum, which swings across the door opening. As he falls down the right staircase he dislodges the stuffed bear from the corner, which tumbles down with Charlie, so terrifying him that he scampers up

the coat tree in a flash. After being socked three more times by the pendulum, Charlie finally manages to crawl through the upstairs door.

The entire staircase sequence is a triumph of theme and variations, consisting of ten failed attempts before he finally makes it to the top for good on his eleventh. Along the way, Chaplin manages to recapitulate most of the other routines in the film with rugs, stuffed animals, table, drinks, and cigarettes. Earlier, incomplete prints of the film seemed to have many awkward cuts, but with the sequence restored the awkwardness vanishes and most cuts dovetail smoothly into each other.[11] Each of Charlie's attempts is captured in a single sustained take, and some takes include several attempts. This highlights the variations he spins and proves unequivocally that Chaplin is actually executing the stunts, rather than constructing them in the editing room via shorter, safer takes. One gets the impression that if he could have, he would have used even longer sustained takes.

Throughout the sequence Chaplin's astonishing acrobatic prowess on the steps is juxtaposed with his more delicate business with the cigarette and liquor, which, though shot mostly in long shots, is just as clear, since Chaplin is as good at clarifying subtle actions as he is at taking spectacular falls.

Once upstairs, Charlie walks nervously through a room filled with more stuffed animals and trophy heads, and then into his bedroom for the climax of the film—his struggle with the Murphy bed. Although this sequence is nearly as long and even more intricate than the preceding stairs sequence, it takes place in a much smaller area, using only eight shots and one subtitle, as compared with twenty-three shots and three subtitles for the stairs sequence.

1. Charlie finally manages to light his cigarette, staggering after he strikes the match on his shoe and leaving his hat on the floor. He drops the match into the hat and looks around.
2. Subtitle: "Where's that bed?"
3. He looks behind a drape, and finally notices the switch panel on the back wall. He presses a switch and the bed revolves out of the side wall, sweeping him along with it for six complete revolutions, whereupon it throws him onto the floor. He gets up and pushes the switch to stop it. He tries pushing the switch again, and again the bed sweeps him with it in the opposite direction for three more revolutions before he manages to turn it off.
4. A waist-up close-up shows Charlie studying the bed as he leans against the back wall.

5. Charlie steps forward to drop some ashes into his hat, walks in front of the bed, and again presses the switch. The bed abruptly drops to the floor, trapping Charlie underneath (he grasps at a support under the bed to cushion this fall). Emerging from the tail end, he sits down and notices that his hat is trapped under a leg of the bed (dropping his ashes brought our attention to the hat's position earlier). After trying unsuccessfully to lift the bed up to free his hat, he pulls the hat upward by its brim, managing to tear it apart. He sits back down on the bed and drops his cigarette from his mouth; stooping to pick it up, he is unaware that the bed is folding back up into the wall. He stands and puts the cigarette back into his mouth, then sits and falls backward onto the floor. He pushes the switch and the bed lowers again, once more trapping him underneath. This time he manages to raise it about thirty degrees off the floor before emerging from the end. He tries to push it down to the floor, but it bounces and hits him on the chin. He gets on the bed to try to bounce it down, riding it like a buck-

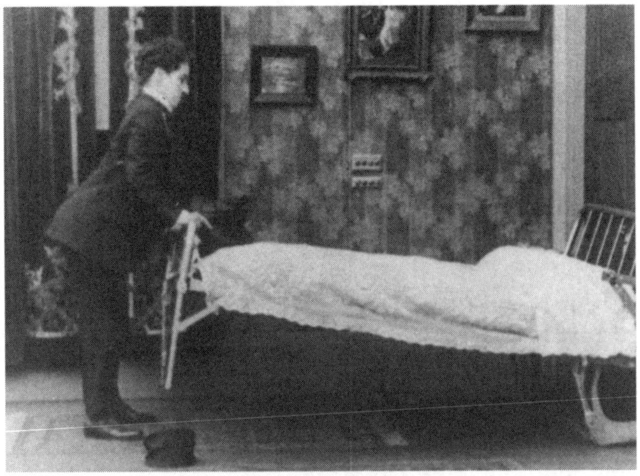

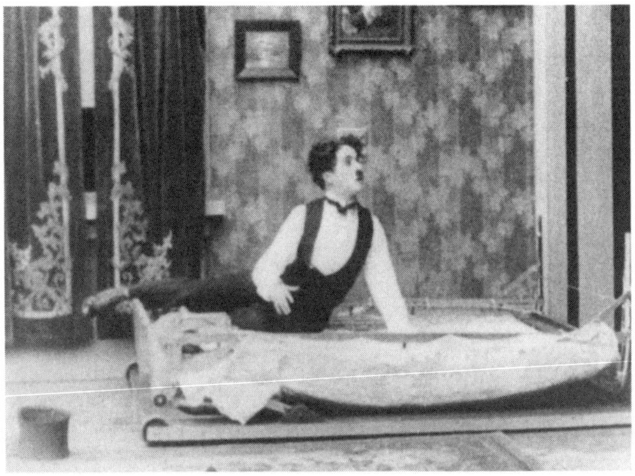

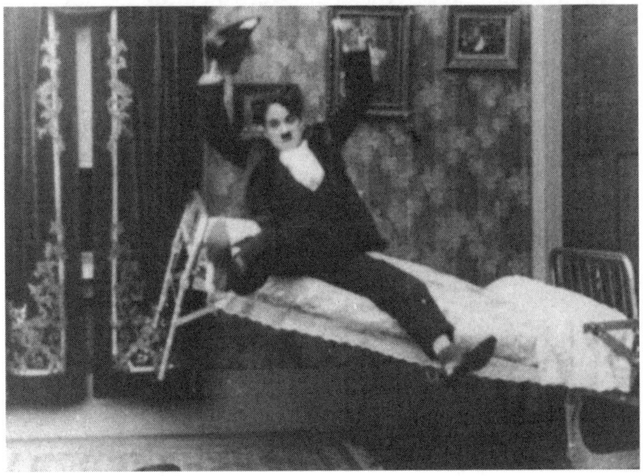

ing bronco, but it bucks him off. Finally, he dives onto it, and is immediately folded into the wall as the bed retracts. His head and arm are visible at the upper corner as he struggles to get out.

6. A medium close-up shows Charlie struggling to free himself.
7. The bed comes down, and Charlie sits on the edge, putting his hat brim onto his head. He gets up for a moment, turning quickly to dive onto the bed as it rises. He forces it down, sitting down on it to keep it in place. After hanging his coat over the tail of the bed he accidentally spits his cigarette onto the floor, but every time he gets up to retrieve it the bed starts to go up, and he has to dive at it again. Finally he misses and the bed folds up in the wall. As he stands facing it in frustration it suddenly juts out of the wall bottom first, and Charlie falls onto the springs on the underside, which is now uppermost.

   He tries to squeeze under so he doesn't have to sleep on the hard springs, but soon gives up, fluffs his coat as a pillow and lies down on the underside. But now the bed rises into the wall, causing Charlie to do a backward somersault onto the floor. He gets up, walks to the bed, gestures "forget it," and lies down on the floor, whereupon the bed falls on top of him.
8. Charlie emerges from the tail and looks back over the bed.
9. Crawling out the rest of the way, Charlie warily grips the bed rail as he rises, leaps onto the bed, and falls with the mattress through the frame, which rises into the wall. Getting up again, Charlie doesn't notice the frame has descended around him, and he trips over it as he walks forward. It's the last and funniest fall in the film. Gathering up his coat and the tattered remains of his hat, he walks away, defeated.

The bed sequence is a tour de force that demonstrates one of Chaplin's great strengths as a comedian, his ability to milk a single situation or prop for all it's worth.

The marvelous bed was designed by Chaplin's technical director, Ed Brewer, and the way it moves is truly amazing—it spins, comes out of the wall from either end, bounces, comes apart. But Chaplin's movement is even more amazing. As he spins around in it at the beginning of the sequence, for example, he manages to react differently for each of the nine passes, pushing against it, being swept along, rotating against the flow of the movement, and so on. Charlie's reasonable actions as he struggles to free himself make for a beautiful bit of seemingly effortless comic choreography. The bed also introduces a new wrinkle to the film: This time it's not Charlie's drunken condition that's causing his problems; rather, as he engages in mortal combat with the infernal device, it becomes apparent that the bed is out to get him.

Although the sequence is divided into nine shots, almost all the action occurs in what appears to be a single wide shot, interrupted by three brief cutaways to medium shots and one subtitle. The cutaways, totaling less than fifteen seconds of the six-minute routine, seamlessly integrate to punctuate pauses in the frenetic action. Although it's hard to be certain, the action in the five long shots appears to come from only two separate takes, but there may be more; it may have been necessary to stop the action in order to reset the bed prop for its various movements. Nevertheless, the illusion that we're watching an uninterrupted performance is perfect, illustrating the success of Chaplin's method of framing his action as tightly as possible, letting individual shots run as long as possible, and unobtrusively cutting to include his best takes.

If one has a quibble with this sequence it would be that the bed, ingenious as it is, is a trick prop, and Chaplin as a rule prefers to make the viewer see ordinary objects in a new way through the unusual way he handles them, as he does earlier in the film with the stuffed animals and table. Not that he is averse to the idea of trick props when the occasion warrants. The factory in *Modern Times* is one giant trick prop, in which he's fed by one machine and eaten by another, and as late as *Limelight* Chaplin uses a trick costume that allows his leg to shorten. However, generally he prefers to let his comedy emanate from movement rather than trick props, however ingenious.

In *One A.M.* he mixes the two kinds of props. All Charlie wants are a few of the basic comforts of home. He'd like to have one last drink, a final smoke, and a night's sleep in a warm bed. He pursues these simple pleasures with obsessive determination, for his long night of dissipation has left him befuddled and accident prone. His self-imposed difficulties are compounded by disturbing encounters with the taxi meter, the pendulum, and the bed; drunk or sober, such things shouldn't exist in a rational universe. But Charlie's universe is anything but rational. It's a mad place where stuffed animals are real, and one can tumble down the steps ten times in a row without breaking a single bone.

Most comic films made in 1916 or before no longer work as entertainment. Chaplin's still do, and *One A.M.* demonstrates why. In it's apparent simplicity we see the clockwork mechanics of a great physical comedian, still ticking away after all these years.

After his humiliating defeat by the bed, Charlie goes into the bathroom for a drink of water. Instead, he ends up accidentally giving himself a cold shower. Resignedly, he climbs into the tub, covers himself with the wet bath mat, drapes his coat over the end of the tub as a pillow, and, with a sudden downward tilt of his head, falls asleep.

Notes

1. Chaplin, cited by Theodore Huff, *Charlie Chaplin* (New York: Henry Schuman, 1951), 71.

2. The version of the film I'm describing in this chapter is the most complete one currently available, released in the Image Entertainment DVD collection *The Chaplin Mutual Comedies: Restored 90th Anniversary Edition*. Chaplin's Mutual comedies, his most celebrated early films, have been in continual circulation since they were made, appearing in the theatrical, nontheatrical, television, and home movie markets. The ongoing popularity of the films encouraged the various copyright holders and distributors—Chaplin was not among them—to update them for current market needs, giving them continued commercial viability and exposure, but compromising Chaplin's original vision. Some of the changes were to remove the logos of previous distributors from the subtitle cards. A significant compromise occurred when musical soundtracks were added by the Van Beuren Corporation in 1932; available technology left the company no choice but to trim the image on three sides to make room for the optical soundtrack and conform to the new aspect ratio of sound films, resulting in some awkward framing. Until recently, when letterboxing and other technology allowed preservation of a more complete image, TV screens would further trim the image, sometimes resulting in the feet or head of characters being cut off by the screen.

The current DVD edition comes close to the originals, but still is not definitive. Collector-scholars have tracked the various changes and discrepancies among existing prints, so there will no doubt be further improvements to come.

3. Charles Chaplin, *My Life in Pictures* (New York: Grosset & Dunlap, 1975), 130–31.

4. Audiences of the time wouldn't have seen this characterization as a major departure, as Chaplin played the rich drunk

in several earlier films. In addition, elements of the "insolent aristocrat" he plays here are very much part of his portrayal of the Tramp. For the best examination of this issue, see John Kimber, *The Art of Charlie Chaplin* (Sheffield, UK: Sheffield Academic Press), 2000.

5. This subtitle is somewhat puzzling, since it's inserted within what is almost certainly the same take, meaning that Chaplin didn't need it to cover a jump cut between two different takes. Like most of the other subtitles in the film, it doesn't provide necessary information, nor is it a particularly funny line. The likelihood is that he used it to trim down his performance slightly. Other prints of the film don't include the title, but have a gap in the action where the title was, suggesting that it was part of the original release version.

6. This subtitle is missing from the otherwise definitive Image Entertainment copy of the film, and there is a slight gap in the action indicating where the missing subtitle was. I include it here because it's in most other prints I've seen, and is consistent with the other titles.

7. It's tempting to read his "one more film like that and it will be goodbye Charlie" comment as referring to how dangerous the film was to make. More likely Chaplin simply saw the film as a bit thin.

8. A cuspidor, or spittoon, was a kind of ashtray into which men would spit their excess tobacco juice.

9. Interestingly, he does a similar series of falls down stairs in his first self-directed film, *Caught in the Rain*, which indicates that Chaplin probably learned his stair-falling skills—and possibly much of the stair routine he does in *One A.M.*—as part of the Karno troupe.

Chaplin never wasted material. The last Karno routine he learned (it is not certain whether he ever actually performed it), in the summer before his second American tour, was *The Hydro*, about a health spa; eventually his brother Sydney starred in it. Chaplin, of course, would resurrect the health spa setting in *The Cure*, which also features gags with a staircase. We don't know whether *The Hydro* featured a man with a bandaged, gouty foot, but both *Caught in the Rain* and *The Cure* do.

10. The pendulum, like the fare-spinning taxi meter and the demonic Murphy bed to come, is an "impossible" prop, but it fits perfectly in this dreamlike house, a surrealistic vision before the term was coined. With its garish striped wallpaper, rotating tables, slippery floors, and profusion of animal trophies, the house reflects the idle and pointless life of its dissipated bachelor owner. Even the sinister electrical Murphy bed is pointless—there's no reason for a Murphy bed to be electric, but it is, because he can afford it. That the cutting-edge technology runs amok is poetic justice.

11. The expanded table and staircase sequences in this print add about seven minutes to most previously available versions of the film. It's likely that some of the film's distributors tried to improve upon Chaplin by cutting down much of the repeated business, and this probably accounts for the different versions. But the expanded length, in my view, greatly improves the film. It makes the drunk's obsessive behavior—the central gag of the film—even crazier. It also showcases Chaplin's ability to come up with seemingly endless variations on a simple theme, and makes his performance even more outstanding, since the restored footage contains some of his most impressive feats.

PART TWO

Charlie Chaplin's Frolics, 1915. The exceptional artwork on this sheet music captures the many facets of Charlie's jaunty appeal.

CHAPTER FIVE

Gagman

"It doesn't matter how serious the story is—it all amounts to a bit of business or a gag. In the end, everything is a gag."[1]

In *The Gold Rush* Chaplin impales two long bread rolls on forks and has them do a dance on the tabletop.[2] The gag is at once ingenious, graceful, and—there is no other word—magical.

When people see a seemingly impossible magic trick, they first gasp, and then they laugh. This kind of laughter is different than the laugh in response to a joke. It is a laughter of delight that stems from the surprise of having one's perceptions about reality playfully contradicted.

Similar laughter of delight occurs when we watch someone doing something inherently difficult, such as virtuoso banjo playing, with apparent ease. The dancing of Fred Astaire, the acrobatics of Buster Keaton, and the juggling of W. C. Fields all seem impossibly skillful, the more so because of the casual way they perform their feats.

Dancing the "Oceana Roll." *The Gold Rush.*

Chaplin elicits both kinds of laughter in his most characteristic gags, which are gags of confusion—their underlying structure is a confusion of one thing with another, such as when he makes those rolls and forks behave like legs and feet. These kinds of gags have been called "transformation gags," "metamorphosis gags," and, perhaps most tellingly, "visual puns." Just as a verbal pun confuses the meanings of similar sounding words—"hair today, gone tomorrow"—Chaplin's visual puns confuse the functions of similar looking objects or movements. Chaplin is unique in his ability to conceive and execute such material. While by no means the only kind of gag he employs, close examination of his films reveals the frequency with which they occur, and the many variations of them that percolate through his films. Virtually all of his greatest comic sequences have at their heart a transformation gag. They are central to his achievement.

The casual viewer doesn't have to think about such subtleties to enjoy the humor, of course, nor were Chaplin's original reviewers and biographers prone to notice, much less comment upon, such arcane matters as the structural underpinnings of his comedy. They preferred to discuss Chaplin's character and the plots of his films. Like the hypnotic power of his movement on the screen, his gags were considered simply a manifestation of his genius—hilarious to watch, but impossible to define or explain.[3]

Yet it becomes clear when we examine them how Chaplin's transformation gags lend a satisfying sense of unity and a distinctive visual "flavor" to the films, akin to the way that characteristic harmonies allow us to identify a passage by Gershwin, Mozart, or The Beatles, even if we're hearing it for the first time. Chaplin's work was so distinctive that a word, *Chaplinesque*, was coined to describe it in the early 1920s, and the word appeared in dictionaries for many years. While the dictionary definition was a tautology—"like Chaplin"—everyone knew what it meant, for it summed up the elements that made his films so appealing: the shabby-elegant costume, the distinctive blend of pathos and comedy, and the comedy itself. Especially the comedy. That's what the public was paying to see. Because later generations came to think of silent film as a primitive affair, consisting of crude pie-in-the-face comedy, the high order of visual thinking in Chaplin's comic sequences comes as a surprise to audiences new to the films.

Chaplin spun a surprising number of variations on the idea of transformation. While the eight categories that follow are somewhat permeable, looking at the gags in this way allows us to appreciate how deeply Chaplin's comedy is based on transformation, and to see how his comic thinking evolved throughout his career.

1. Object/Object

The most common and obvious of Chaplin's transformation gags is when Charlie uses one object as if it is another. These object transformations reach an exuberant peak in the Mutual series. For example, in *The Vagabond*, strolling violinist Charlie sets out to rescue Edna from her gypsy captors. Deciding that a thick branch will be a more effective weapon than his violin bow, he strides toward the encampment. When he encounters one of the ruffians midway across a wooden bridge, Charlie *immediately* whips the stick over the side of the bridge, as though he's fishing.

Now this transformation is not particularly imaginative, since a fishing pole is basically a stick with a string attached. The objects are too similar for the transformation to be startling. What makes the sequence funny is Charlie's instantaneous change of intention—stick as weapon becomes stick as fishing pole. The ruse is so deftly performed that it seems an instinctive act of camouflage on Charlie's part, and we're not surprised that the gypsy falls for it.

More imaginative is Charlie's transformation of a roll of dough into a lei and a wooden spoon into a ukulele, to give Edna a kitchen serenade in *The Pawnshop*. The next moment the dough becomes a rope to lasso his rival around the neck, and shortly thereafter gobs of it serve as snowballs that he hurls at a fellow employee.

Among all Chaplin's films, *The Pawnshop* stands out for the sheer quantity of its object transformations. The film is a virtual catalogue of ways to use one thing as if it is another. The scene in which Charlie dissects an alarm clock, treating it as if it is a heart (listening with a stethoscope), a mouth (pulling a tooth with pliers), a jewel (looking at it through a jeweler's loupe, which is actually the mouthpiece off a candlestick telephone), a can of sardines (opening it with a can opener and being repelled by the odor), yard goods (measuring and cutting the mainspring as though it's a ribbon) and so on, has often been described, and is justly famous. At the end of the sequence Charlie "winds" the now empty clock case with the key, which causes the dismantled pieces to wriggle around on the counter (via an unseen magnet). While it's a nice climax to the scene, this sort of impossible gag, which Chaplin experimented with in *One A.M.*, the film immediately preceding *The Pawnshop*, is far more typical of lesser comedies of the teens and twenties, and Chaplin seldom ventured into such territory again. How much more inventive and satisfying when, in the same film, he dries the dishes by passing them through a clothes wringer, passing a cup through twice, and then passing his own hands through to dry them. The wringer is later used to flatten a wad of dough for Charlie's pie making.

A kitchen serenade. *The Pawnshop.*

As far back as 1914, in *Dough and Dynamite*, Charlie uses dough as bracelets, handcuffs, quicksand, and, inevitably, projectiles. From his earliest films, in fact, we can watch Chaplin experimenting with unusual ways of handling objects. He also used transformations to test the boundaries of taste, using tablecloths and the occasional lady's skirt to blow his nose. "Mr. Chaplin is funny with a funniness which transcends his dirt and his vulgarity," read a 1915 review.[4]

But despite the occasional critical objection, Chaplin had no intention of giving up the earthy humor his audiences loved. Instead, he found a way to make it acceptable to his more refined viewers by using subtle transformation gags to allude to unpleasant realities. Thus, in both *The Cure* and *Easy Street* Chaplin *thinks* he has been urinated upon—in one case by a toy dog, in the second by a baby—but the audience has clearly seen that he has inadvertently spilled more innocent liquids—water in one film, milk in the other—onto his lap. We have the pleasure of seeing his disgust without being ourselves disgusted. Contrast this to the approach taken by Max Linder, the French comedian popular in the 1910s. In *Max's Hat* (1913), Max has trouble arriving at his destination with his hat intact. After going through several hats, he finally arrives and puts it down, only to have a dog urinate (onscreen) into it, and the host drench himself trying it on. It is certainly startling to see this in a movie, but it's funny only in the coarsest sense.

Chaplin, on the other hand, became a master at handling such unsavory material. In the rural countryside of *The Vagabond*, waiting for the rescued Edna to return to enjoy his painstakingly prepared alfresco breakfast, he casually mimes a routine in which he keeps flies away by catching them in the air, placing them into his pocket, and crushing them with a blow from his fist, thus neatly killing and disposing of them with one blow.[5] His "hygienic" method of fly extermination is made funny rather than gross by the fact that the flies are all mimed, and by the imaginative transformation of his fist into a swatter and his pocket into a trash can.

Chaplin brilliantly extends the fly gag to comically underscore his feelings during the ensuing breakfast scene. Charlie catches another fly just as Edna returns with the well-dressed artist she has just met in the woods. Charlie shakes the artist's hand, unthinkingly squashing the fly between their palms. This reinforces the wariness we see on Charlie's face as he greets the unwelcome guest, and sure enough, we watch "his romance fading" as Edna and the artist talk over breakfast. Charlie expresses his dismay by catching another fly and intentionally flicking it into the man's eye. The action is perfectly staged, with the artist sitting at screen right, his back to the camera, Charlie opposite him, and Edna in the middle. We don't need to see the artist's face; watching Edna's enraptured eyes fastened upon him, and Charlie's annoyed expression as he sizes up the situation, tells us all we need to know. We're with Charlie all the way as he flicks the fly across the screen into the artist's eye.

Earlier in the film Charlie had used a sock as a washcloth to clean Edna's face, ears, and nose. The rustic comedy of manners is ironically concluded when, meeting Edna's long-lost, wealthy mother, Charlie shakes her hand with his elbow held chest high, mocking the regal way she proffers her hand, and then sniffs distastefully at the perfumed smell it leaves on his fingers.

As these transformations define Charlie's relationship with the upper-class world of *The Vagabond*, his mock elegance in his own world is shown by his careful table setting for breakfast. Turning over a washtub, he spreads a checkered shirt over it for a tablecloth, and deftly rolls its sleeves into the kind of peaked napkins one would find at a fancy restaurant. During the meal he primly tucks the end of the "napkin" into his collar, and proceeds to flick flies.

Chaplin reworked the idea of an elegant meal in unlikely surroundings for the famous New Year's Eve dinner in *The Gold Rush*. Penniless prospector Charlie has gone to a great deal of trouble to prepare a lavish meal for his love, Georgia, and two other dance hall girls. He has festooned his rough cabin with seasonal decorations, thoughtfully provided beautifully wrapped party favors, and even trimmed a newspaper to simulate a lace tablecloth. The dinner is a great success, and the girls demand a speech. Charlie, too overcome for words, obliges by dancing the "Oceana Roll." He is so sweetly innocent, so utterly charming during this scene, and his dance is such a surprising and virtuoso display of visual poetry, that *we* fall in love with him,[6] which makes it all the more poignant when we discover that his moment of triumph is but a dream; he awakens to the harsh reality that he has been stood up by the unfeeling trio.

Charlie's roll dance is an elaborate non sequitur that very effectively deepens the romantic subplot of the film. Most of his transformation gags make their satirical or ironic points in a more offhand manner. Thus, Charlie strides with great authority to open the combination lock safe in *The Bank*, only to emerge carrying his janitor's bucket and mop. Similarly, he opens the safe in *The Pawnshop* for his bag lunch. In *Work* (1915) the lady of the house immediately puts her valuables in a safe after meeting scruffy paperhangers Charlie and his boss—whereupon they collect *their* valuables and ostentatiously safety-pin them into Charlie's pocket.

One of the most brilliant transformations occurs in *The Kid*, and Chaplin sets it up with a grubby and funny bit of business. Charlie, looking his shabbiest and acting his most elegant, strolls down a slum alleyway, only to be deluged by streams of garbage thrown out of windows. He then discovers a crying baby lying next to some garbage cans, and immediately looks up—perhaps this bit of "human garbage" was also thrown from a window. Suddenly comedy and drama become one, merging to make a terrible point about the value of life in the slums. It is a grim joke indeed.

As Chaplin's success grew and he had more time to spend on his films, elaborately planned object transformations like the roll dance replace the seemingly spontaneous ones that fill the Mutual films. As *The Kid* continues, Charlie turns his tiny garret apartment into a nursery. The infant lies in a makeshift hammock and nurses from a coffee pot fitted with a nipple on the spout; the coffee pot hangs from a string for easy access, like a crib mobile. Meanwhile, Charlie is busily cutting a hole in a cane chair and placing a cuspidor beneath it for a potty. Five years later the Kid (now played by Jackie Coogan) reciprocates, preparing Charlie's breakfast as he lounges in bed, smoking a cigarette and reading the *Police Gazette*. Summoned to table by the industrious lad, Charlie stretches, and his foot pokes through a hole in the bedspread. Moving to the foot of the bed, he puts his head through the hole and rises, effortlessly transforming the spread into a serape-like dressing gown. This scene is said to have taken Chaplin two weeks of shooting to perfect, a luxury he could hardly afford in the film-a-month schedule of the Essanay and early Mutual comedies. The slight loss in spontaneity that results from such carefully prepared props and calculated effects is more than compensated for by beautifully conceived and flawlessly executed gags.

This is certainly true of the last major object transformation in a Chaplin film, the large globe that turns out to be a balloon in *The Great Dictator*. The scene serves as a visual counterpoint to Chaplin's vocal lampoon of Hitler's maniacal ranting earlier in the film. There he presented him as a preening, gibberish-spouting buffoon. Here he reduces his monstrous craving for power and domination to an infantile desire to play with a toy balloon. The resulting dance sequence is mesmerizing, featuring all the fluid grace, comic ingenuity, and oily charm Chaplin can muster. The use of an overtly symbolic prop such as this globe-balloon is highly unusual for Chaplin, but certainly no more so than his decision to play Hitler in the first place, and the sequence remains a remarkable tour de force of purely visual political satire.[7]

2. Setting/Setting

When Charlie uses one object as if it's another, he's implicitly pretending that he's in a different place as well. It's a side effect, as it were, of the primary transformation. When he dissects that alarm clock the pawnshop itself becomes, by extension, a doctor's office, a dentist's office, a jeweler's counter, a department store, and so on. We don't have to think about how the setting changes when we watch him take apart the clock, but at times the object transformation forces our attention to the reimagined setting.

The Tramp costume itself allows Chaplin to enact his most characteristic setting transformations. An ill-fitting assemblage of formal clothing, it is richly suggestive of strong contrasts—rich versus poor, elegant versus bedraggled, child versus adult—which Chaplin exploits so effectively as his "gentleman tramp" characterization evolves. The formal aspect of the costume is reinforced by Charlie's carefully trimmed mustache; fastidious, delicate movements; and courtly manners. But the shabbiness of the clothes and the inappropriate settings for such pretensions contradict the bid for elegance. Thus, Charlie cleans his fingernails (*The Tramp*) or prepares a meal (*The Vagabond*) as if he is in a well-appointed mansion, while he is in fact outdoors, in the rural countryside. Similarly, in the rude cabins of *The Gold Rush* Charlie creates mock gourmet meals for Thanksgiving and New Year's feasts.

Often Charlie reveals aspects of his "true" character by acting as though he is in a different setting. In *The Adventurer* he's an escaped convict who's been taken in by a rich family after bravely rescuing both the wife and the daughter from drowning. He wakes up in the morning wearing striped pajamas, and for a panic-stricken moment thinks he's back in prison garb. His alarm deepens as he touches the bars of the brass headboard behind him—prison bars? Later he mistakes the popping of a champagne cork for a gunshot. Charlie can't escape his past, for almost every sense—sight, touch, and hearing—conspires to remind him of it. The dislocation gags continue throughout the film.

Thanksgiving Dinner in *The Gold Rush*. The nail becomes a wishbone.

Escaped convict Charlie sees the church choir as a jury. *The Pilgrim.*

In *The Pilgrim* Charlie is once again an escaped convict. While wearing stolen minister's clothing and buying a railway ticket to get out of town, he instinctively grasps the ticket window bars as if he's back in his jail cell. Even after he realizes his error, his hands unconsciously stray back to the bars.

The fish-out-of-water theme climaxes later in the film when Charlie, still trapped in his minister's identity, has to conduct a Sunday service. He sees the number "12" superimposed above the grim-looking church elders seated to his right, begins to light a cigarette (until he sees the shocked look on their faces), leans casually against the lectern, and, drinking a glass of water, reflexively lifts his foot to find the bar rail. After his sermon he takes elaborate curtain calls, so pleased with himself that he doesn't notice that no one is applauding except one small boy. Charlie's actions transform the church into settings more familiar to the convict—a saloon, a courtroom, and a vaudeville theatre. We become aware of the change of setting through Charlie's amusing and unintentionally revealing behavior.

Both Buster Keaton and Harold Lloyd became adept at transforming settings as well. In *Cops* Keaton *seems* to be saying goodbye to his girl from behind prison bars. But in the next, wider shot we see that the bars are actually the gates of her mansion, and that she is telling him to make good if he wants to win her. It's a nicely ironic beginning to a film about Buster's inability to make good at anything, aside from arousing the animosity of the entire police force; by the end of the film he *is* in jail. In *Safety Last*, made a year after *Cops*, Lloyd *appears* to be in the death house, behind bars, with an apparent scaffold and noose in view. A prison official stands by, a parson offers consolation. His girl sobs on the other side of the bars. But as Harold heads toward the noose the next shot reveals a much more innocuous scene. The group is actually in a railroad station, the bars merely the gate to the platform; the official is a conductor, the noose a mail carrier, and the parson only one of a group of friendly townspeople there to wish Harold off. The transformation from the death house to the platform both underscores the sinking feeling of watching a loved one depart and foreshadows the story to come, in which the perils of making it in the big city will be exemplified by Harold's involuntary, death-defying climb of a skyscraper.

The key difference in Chaplin's use of the device is that his setting transformations don't involve audience-fooling camera shots, but are a product of his character's movement and habits. His gags are gags of the actor; theirs of the director-writer. The onscreen Buster and Harold are only passive participants in the comedy of their scenes, while Charlie drives the comedy in his.

For example, after playing the violin for Edna outside the gypsy wagon in *The Vagabond*, Charlie takes a series of elaborate curtain calls, exactly as if he's in a huge concert hall. He dashes "offstage" around the side of the wagon, then modestly returns as the ovation—Edna's enthusiastic applause—continues.[8] In *Pay Day* a drunken Charlie, mistaking a food stall for a streetcar, strap hangs from a salami. He assumes his own swaying is the motion of the moving streetcar, and casually reads a newspaper. When the owner throws him out Charlie merely hands him a coin, simultaneously paying for his "fare" and the salami, which he holds onto as he's pushed from the stall. The identity of the setting as both a streetcar and a food stall has been scrupulously maintained, and Chaplin caps the sequence by transforming the salami a second time, striking a match to light it as though it's an enormous cigar.

The transformations described above reflect Charlie's misperception of reality, but he usually knows perfectly well what's going on, and uses setting transformations to bamboozle other characters. For example, in the dressing room of *The Cure*, Charlie has accidentally caused a fight between two men by throwing his shoes over his dressing-room curtains (exactly how he causes the fight is discussed later in the chapter). The two men face off in front of the curtain, but just as they're about to come to blows Charlie's *pants* come sailing over. They whip apart the curtains to reveal him frozen in a swashbuckling pose, his cane held like a sword. He breaks from his pose to close the curtains.

The dumbfounded duo pulls them open again, and this time Charlie strikes a coy *September Morn* position, modestly covering his bathing-suit-clad form. The third

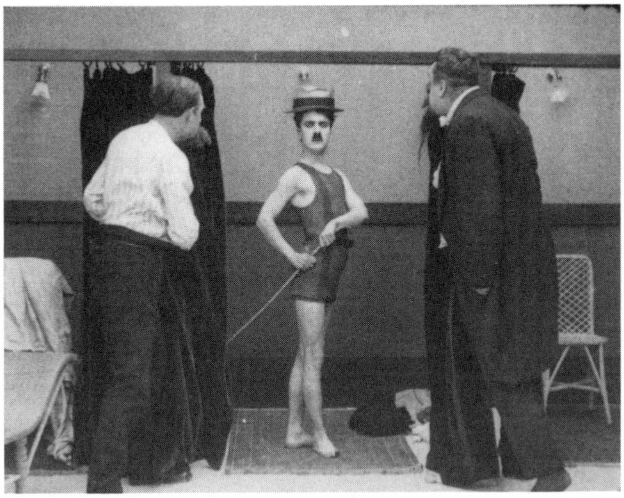

Artistic statue posing. *The Cure.*

time he becomes a ballerina: He jumps up and twiddles his feet, then blows kisses and bows in a mincing way to the presumably cheering throng. Then he abruptly ends the performance by striding past his flabbergasted audience. The dressing room has become a music hall display of *tableaux vivants*, the "living statue" scenes popular in the first two decades of the century. Often these scenes were an excuse to show some female flesh on stage in an "artistic" manner, and Charlie obliges with his scanty attire and portrayal of *September Morn*, the famous nude painting that adorned many living rooms of the era.

Even more playful is Charlie's break from the film's action during a melodramatic moment in *The Cure* to take a decorative little bow to the camera, transforming filmic reality into a stage performance for the benefit of the film audience. He does this twice in *The Pawnshop*, once after a tightrope routine performed on a piece of rope on the floor (no one else is present during the scene; it's performed strictly for our benefit), and a second time at the film's finale, after he has saved the day by conking villain Eric Campbell over the head with a rolling pin. These bows to the camera take to the extreme the many glances and smiles at the camera so central to Chaplin's presentational acting style, and they don't occur in his work after the Mutual series.

Tightrope act on the floor. *The Pawnshop.*

Chaplin called the Mutual period the happiest time of his career, and it shows in the films. To this day their buoyancy, exuberance and express-train speed sweep viewers up, daring audiences not to be drawn into the action despite Chaplin's occasional outrageous flaunting of dramatic conventions. Their fierce and joyous energy is not found again in films until the Marx Brothers' manic masterworks of the early thirties.

Although setting transformations usually emanate from Charlie's actions, sometimes other characters in the films initiate the change. After getting drunk on Charlie's liquor, which has been thrown into the mineral water well, the glum spa residents in *The Cure* turn the place into an orgiastic dance hall. One man sits "playing" a lamp as if it is a clarinet, while others dance or pursue women. In *Modern Times* Charlie's a waiter trying to carve a duck for a customer; he inadvertently tosses it to a group of drunken college men, who immediately start playing football with it. Charlie intercepts and scores a "touchdown" by diving onto his unfortunate customer. Less subtle is the film's "expressionistic" opening shot, in which a flock of sheep dissolves to people emerging from a subway (the film's original title was *The Masses*).

Chaplin's most elaborate setting transformation is turning a slum street into heaven for the dream sequence of *The Kid*. Although a straightforward set redressing is done, making this more of a camera trick than is usual in Chaplin's work, the dissolve of the set around the sleeping Charlie, nestled in a doorway, is nicely executed. The dissolve back to reality is more interesting because of the way it merges the dream world with reality. In the dream, angel-Charlie has been shot down midflight. The angel-cop shaking the dead angel-Charlie dissolves into a real cop shaking the sleeping Charlie. The action matches perfectly, and Charlie comes to consciousness in his slum doorway, still flapping his "wings."[9]

3. Body/Object

The violence so prevalent in Chaplin's films is considerably softened by a third type of object transformation, the treatment of human bodies as if they are inanimate objects. As we've already noted, he treats his own body this way. His selective, geometrically precise, and highly controlled movements lead to comic freezes to elude

Lifting himself onto a curb. *The Pawnshop.*

pursuers, and to Charlie becoming "thinglike"—a tree in *Shoulder Arms*, a fun-house mechanical figure in *The Circus*, and so on.

But the gag also takes on more subtle dimensions. In both *The Pawnshop* and *The Circus* Charlie literally pulls himself upward by the seat of his pants, violating the laws of gravity and physics, and separating himself into "lifter" and "liftee." By treating himself as an object, Chaplin conveys the idea that he feels little or no pain getting knocked about the way he does, so his many mishaps become funny rather than painful to watch. When he falls backward into a tub in *The Vagabond* or off a park bench in *A Woman*, his legs jackknife straight up as if he's a hinged toy. Bodies, after all, can feel pain, but toys cannot.

Other characters fare no better in the films. Kicking people in the rear end is one way to puncture their dignity, but Chaplin found he could accomplish the same thing by treating them as objects. Thus, fallen bodies are trod over as if they're carpets, rear ends are gently moved aside and then put back as Charlie passes, or dusted like pieces of furniture. In *The Bank* he solicitously takes a man's pulse, looks at him in a concerned way, and asks him to stick out his tongue, only to moisten a stamp on it.

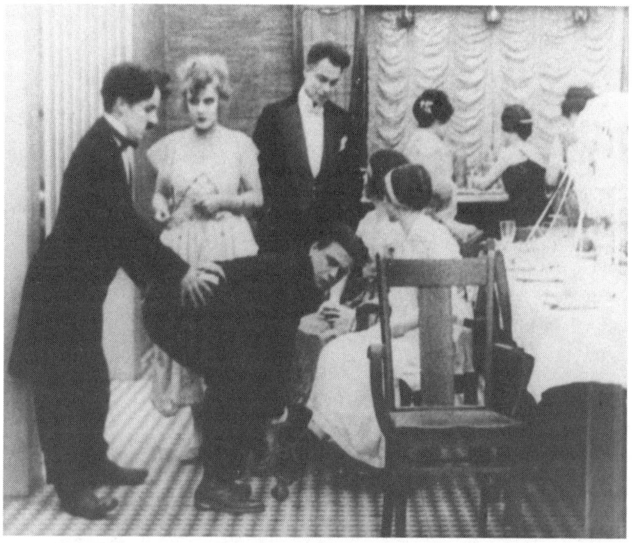

Charlie politely moves the man's rear end aside so Edna can pass, and then puts it back in place. *The Rink.*

While no one is ever seriously injured, sometimes their pain is played for laughs. In *The Cure*, a virtual ballet of careening bodies, Eric Campbell's bandaged foot becomes the painful focal point of the film, stepped and sat upon, caught in revolving doors, and kicked. Yet Eric is so obnoxious—he's a hothead who makes unwelcome advances toward Edna—that we feel only delight at the many assaults to his swollen extremity perpetrated by the resourceful Charlie. The viewer is also prevented from identifying with Eric's suffering by the very exaggeration of the hugely bandaged foot, along with the frequency of Charlie's attacks upon it. Eric also loses sympathy because gout was at the time considered a disease of the wealthy, resulting from overindulgence in rich foods and alcohol.

Chaplin's last extended routine using the body as an object is the wonderful musical routine with Buster Keaton in *Limelight*, during which Charlie's leg mysteriously shortens as if drawn up by a string, forcing him into a hilarious lopsided walk. We will examine this scene in detail in chapter 14. For now, suffice it to say that the illusion of the leg shortening, as though Charlie is some kind of telescoping toy, is perfectly achieved.

Another subtle variation on the body-as-thing idea is when Charlie compulsively repeats movements, which makes him seem machinelike. He often forms instant habits; for example, running back and forth behind a bed to elude Eric Campbell in *Easy Street*, he becomes so quickly habituated to his pattern that he fails to notice that Eric has reversed direction and nearly runs headlong into the arms of the brute. Dusting the back room in *The Pawnshop*, he immediately goes on automatic pilot, absently raising a cloud of dust, then dusting his fellow worker and finally an electric fan, which shreds the duster into a blizzard of swirling feathers.

Sometimes Charlie uses other people's tendency to mechanically repeat motions to his advantage. After Charlie has apparently been beaten by his coworker in *The Pawnshop*, Edna consoles him by patting his face; when her hand drops, Charlie simply puts it back to resume its patting. In *The Rink* he sits next to a woman who is absently kicking her crossed foot; bending to pick up his cane, Charlie gets a light kick in the rear, which he chooses to interpret as a flirtatious gesture, even though the woman hasn't even noticed him. He gets her attention by holding his hat in the path of action and pretending that she's kicked it onto his head, applauding her "feat." He continues the flirtation by leaning backward against the wall to tip his hat, wagging his eyebrows suggestively at her. She is not remotely amused, but we are, and Charlie knows it, for he looks at the camera repeatedly during this playful sequence. He's really flirting with *us*.

Habits persist even in sleep. In the flophouse of *The Kid*, a sleeping pickpocket probes Charlie's pockets. With an indulgent smile Charlie lets him proceed, knowing there's no money to be found. But the wandering fingers come up with a quarter in Charlie's vest pocket. Startled and delighted, Charlie plucks the coin away, then stuffs the hand deep into his pants pocket—who knows what buried treasure might be uncovered by the those expert fingers?

Objectifying people occasionally leads Chaplin into the cruel humor so prevalent in his early films. In *The Floorwalker* Chaplin coaxes comedy from the involuntary repetitive movements of a palsied old man shopping for toys. Charlie helpfully places a stringed instrument under his shaking fingers so the fellow can hear the sound. While it may seem shocking to a contemporary audience to see Chaplin making light of physical infirmity in this way, from Charlie's point of view, he's simply being a courteous employee.

Repetitive movement gives Charlie a decided advantage in the fight scene of *City Lights*. His rhythmic repetitions so hypnotize his opponent and the referee that they begin fighting each other, in a scene described in detail in chapter 9.

The culminating body-as-mechanical-object scene in Chaplin's work is the brilliant factory sequence that

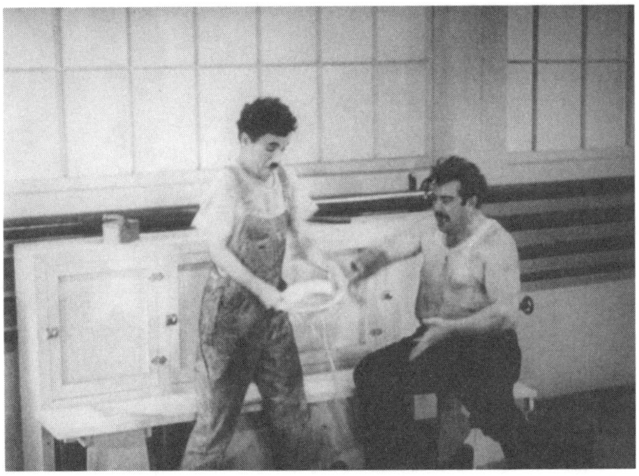

Charlie reflexively twists the soup bowl while handing it to his friend. *Modern Times*.

opens *Modern Times*. A slave to the assembly line, Charlie's job is tightening the nuts on passing metal plates with a pair of wrenches. He has to deal not only with the stultifying repetition, but with the belt's ever-increasing speed, as management pushes the workers to their limit. So programmed does Charlie become by his repetitive movement that he can't stop, even during breaks. At lunch, when he tries to pass his fellow worker a bowl of steaming soup, his arms reflexively twitch and spray the hot soup everywhere.

The factory sequence contains two elaborate high points, in both of which Charlie literally becomes part of the machinery. In the first, Charlie is strapped to a prototype feeding machine, designed to allow employees to eat while they continue working, thus eliminating the lunch hour. Predictably, the machine goes berserk, tormenting Charlie by throwing soup into his face, pushing large metal nuts into his mouth, and spinning a corncob

Charlie gets some use out of affliction. *The Floorwalker*.

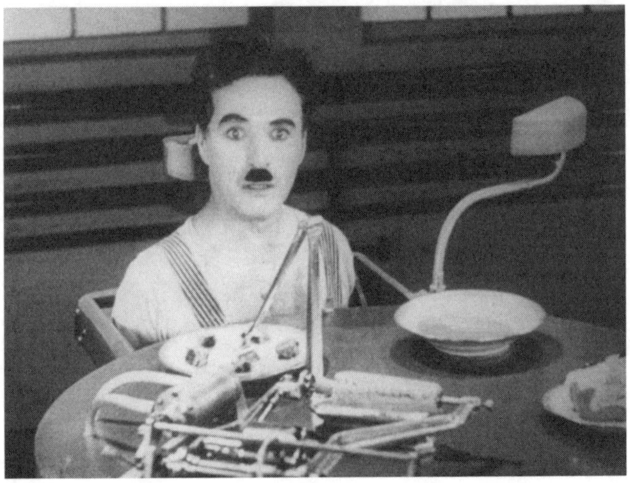

In the feeding machine. *Modern Times*.

Into the bowels of the factory. *Modern Times.*

against his teeth so fast that the spraying kernels look like teeth flying out of his mouth.[10]

In the equally celebrated second scene Charlie, trying to keep up with a speedup on the assembly line, follows a nut plate into the bowels of the machine and is literally "eaten" by the contraption. Accompanied by music box music, he weaves a serpentine path through the giant cogwheels, only to be "regurgitated" when the machine is reversed.[11] He emerges from the gaping maw to plunge into a "nervous breakdown" dance, tightening everything in sight with his wrenches, squirting oil on the faces of his coworkers, and generally wreaking havoc on the well-ordered routine of the factory.

In the factory scene Chaplin's long preoccupation with the comic possibilities of mechanical movement come to a logical and triumphant conclusion, as he satirizes one of the most pressing social issues of the industrial age, the psychological toll exacted by the mindless repetition of factory life.

4. Animated Objects

The complement to treating bodies as objects is treating objects as though they are alive. We've already seen how Charlie animates the innards of an alarm clock in *The Pawnshop* and reacts to stuffed animals and a willful bed in *One A.M.*

Another object that seems to have a life of its own is Charlie's cane, which often becomes an extension of his arm. In *Getting Acquainted* (1914) Charlie raises his hand to his head, which causes the cane to hook and lift Mabel Normand's skirt—whereupon he sternly reprimands it. A source of much comic business in his early films, it grabs people around the neck, trips them at the ankle, corkscrews them in the belly, and draws pretty girls on park benches toward him. In *A Night Out* (1915) a drunken Charlie tenderly puts it to bed.

Within a few years Chaplin had pretty much used up the comic possibilities of his cane, and since those films remained in more or less constant circulation, competing with releases of his later films, he had to find other objects to achieve the same effects. His golf club in *The Idle Class* "accidentally" snags the clubs out of a passing golfer's bag; the arms of his tree costume in *Shoulder Arms* end in convenient knobs and pointed sticks, for wartime mayhem; he conks people with the knobs and sticks them in the butt with the points.

Occasionally Charlie mistakes an object for a person. In the comic and poignant finale of *The Bank*, janitor Charlie has bravely foiled a bank robbery and won the fair Edna. But it's all been another dream; he wakes to discover that he's kissing not Edna but his mop, and tenderly caressing its "hair."

Charlie fares no better in his encounter with a boxing dummy in the Keystone film *Mabel's Married Life*. This remarkable scene is one of Chaplin's earliest and most elaborate explorations of the comic possibilities of a single prop, and merits a close look.

In the film Charlie is too cowardly to defend Mabel when a lustful Mack Swain tries to force his attentions on her in the park. Instead, Charlie cravenly accuses her of encouraging him, and orders her home. En route, she sees the dummy outside a store and purchases it, thinking that perhaps it will inspire Charlie to shape up. Meanwhile, Charlie is consoling himself with drink at the bar, only to be further terrorized by various patrons, including the unrepentant Swain.

When a drunken Charlie returns home and sees the dummy, he at first thinks he's in the wrong apartment. Then, because the figure is wearing the same kind of cap and sweatshirt worn by the burly Swain, he concludes

An unsuspecting Charlie returns home. *Mabel's Married Life.*

Negotiating with the enemy. *Mabel's Married Life.*

Love triangle. *Mabel's Married Life.*

that the lecherous bully has followed Mabel home. Filled with outrage and fueled by alcoholic courage, he takes off his coat to do battle, but accidentally brushes against the dummy, causing it to sway toward him on its rounded base. This movement terrifies Charlie, and he hastily pulls his coat back on, coughing nervously. He tries to make light of the situation and strike up a conversation, but naturally, the dummy remains mum.

He turns the thing around to face him, and, because it sways again, Charlie concludes that it, too, has had one too many. Now he's on more familiar ground, and he points to it, chuckles, and mimes a drinking motion to show his unwanted guest that he knows what's what. Emboldened by their new intimacy, he orders the intruder to leave. The dummy is unresponsive. Charlie gives him a little push, and the dummy rebounds and pushes back. The fight builds. Mabel watches with amusement from the bedroom, until the dummy bats Charlie into the bedroom onto her. He once again accuses her of encouraging Swain's advances, choking her and pulling her into the living room. Now it becomes a three-way argument. Unlike his later heroines, Mabel fully participates in the roughhouse, taking as many blows and falls as Charlie.

By this time, alarmed neighbors are beginning to gather in the hallway outside. Finally, Mabel is able to get it through Charlie's befuddled brain that he's been fighting a dummy. He laughs and the couple reconciles. But the dummy has the last word, flooring them both as the film ends.

The scene is fascinating to watch because of the way Chaplin develops his relationship with the dummy, exploring every possible way of animating it, and cleverly escalating the conflict by gradual stages. He manipulates the object so skillfully that we see it exactly as he does, as an adversary who is by turns stubborn, drunk, vindictive, and strong. It's a stunning example of sophisticated comic choreography, particularly when Mabel enters the fray. Made only six months into his film career and running nearly four minutes, it's an early showcase of Chaplin's ability to spin seemingly endless variations from a single comic idea and a simple prop. His sustained, bravura performance is comparable to the best of his later work.

5. Person/Animal

In *Behind the Screen* Charlie filches bites from the huge, meaty bone being gnawed by coworker Albert Austin. When Austin catches him in the act, Charlie barks at him like a mad dog, then holds his "paws" up and begs. While this is more imitation than transformation, it serves to remind us that many of Charlie's "natural" movements are doglike as well; he wipes his feet by shuffling in place, and shakes his head, his leg, or his whole

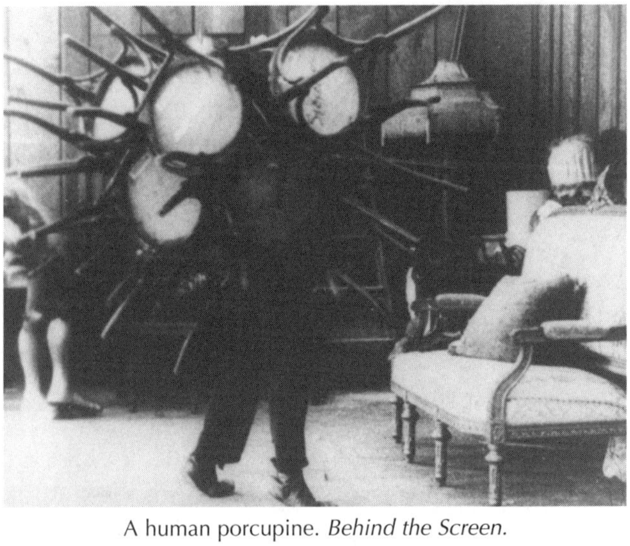

A human porcupine. *Behind the Screen.*

Charlie turning chicken. *The Gold Rush.*

An unusual sleeping position. *The Gold Rush.*

body like a dog shaking off water. Chaplin's identification with dogs reaches its pinnacle in his symbiotic relationship with Scraps, the pooch he rescues in *A Dog's Life*.

Nor are Chaplin's forays into the animal kingdom limited to dogs. In *Behind the Screen* he effortlessly swings eleven bentwood chairs onto his back, in a startling image that makes him look like a human porcupine.

But Chaplin's most elaborate animal transformation is a literal one, complete with costume. In *The Gold Rush* Charlie's starving cabinmate (Mack Swain again) "sees" him as a chicken, in a series of nicely matched dissolves. Chaplin is hilarious as a giant chicken, but the brilliance of the scene is the way he continues to act like one when he returns to human form. He flaps his arms like wings, and we suddenly realize that Charlie has *always* moved something like a chicken. Unwittingly, he taunts the ravenous Swain beyond endurance: "Chicken or no chicken, his friend looks appetizing." Charlie hurriedly buries the rifle, finishing the job by kicking snow backward, exactly like a chicken scrabbling at the dirt. Moments later he has to hastily retrieve it when Mack comes after him with an axe, and his first instinct is to dig for it with his feet. The scene wonderfully showcases Chaplin's protean ability to take on the physical characteristics of anything he pleases.[12]

6. Body Part/Body Part

After Swain tries to feast on chicken à la Charlie, the intended prey understandably goes to bed armed and wary. Yet the next morning we find him apparently snoozing away, his feet sticking out from under the blanket and shifting around comfortably. Suddenly his head pops up from between them. It's a hilarious image of impossible body contortion. In a moment we see that Charlie has merely reversed position, sleeping with his hands in his shoes to keep a watchful eye on his hallucinating companion. It's a bizarre but eminently sensible strategy.

While Chaplin usually doesn't employ the kind of eye-fooling setting transformations favored by Keaton and Lloyd, he delights in fooling the audience by confusing body parts, just the way he fools us here by sticking his hands into his shoes. Usually he uses two actors for this type of gag. In *The Kid* Jackie Coogan is hiding under a flophouse bed to elude the suspicious proprietor. When the man stoops down to peer underneath the side of the bed, Jackie immediately scoots out the end; Charlie lifts and lowers his legs like a drawbridge as Jackie springs under the covers. In a flash Jackie's head "becomes" Charlie knees under the blanket. When the proprietor straightens up he immediately notices Charlie's strangely enlarged knees. Charlie rubs them to demonstrate how sore they are, but it's no soap. Jackie is revealed, and Charlie has to pay with the found quarter.[13]

By this time in the film we've seen several amusing domestic and work routines perfected by Charlie and the Kid, so we believe in the improbable smoothness of this one. The transformation happens with mechanical precision, partly due to the way Chaplin raises and lowers his legs without bending his knees, like a hinged box lid opening and snapping shut.

Chaplin spins his richest variations on the gag of confusing body parts in the First National series of films, made between 1918 and 1923. He seldom uses it before that time, and when he does, it's not designed to fool the eye. For example, in *A Night in the Show* a drunken Charlie takes Edna's husband's hand, thinking it's hers. It's a decent gag, but the drunk fools only himself, not us. How much more interesting when Charlie's arms become

Charlie substitutes his arms for Albert Austin's. *A Dog's Life.*

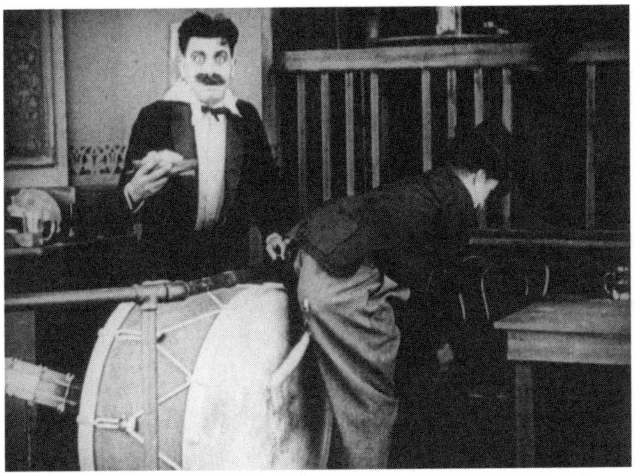

A dog in Charlie's pants beats the drum. *A Dog's Life.*

those of the unconscious Albert Austin in *A Dog's Life*; when a thief's arm becomes Charlie's in *The Idle Class*; and when Charlie mistakes Sydney's foot for his own in *Shoulder Arms*. In an inventive variant, Charlie stuffs his dog down his pants to sneak it into a café in *A Dog's Life*; this makes for a startling and vaguely obscene image, as its white tail wags madly out of a hole in the seat of the pants. It also neatly encapsulates the symbiotic relationship between dog and man in this film.

One of the best examples of the gag occurs in *The Kid*. As Charlie flirts with a laughing woman, her husband's hand comes through the window to choke him. From Charlie's point of view it's her hand choking him, and his panic mounts as the apparently homicidal woman laughs hysterically.

Chaplin's last major body-part-confusion scene is an elaborate one that opens *City Lights*. A new city monument ("Peace and Prosperity") is unveiled, revealing Charlie asleep on the lap of the middle figure of three. By the end of this ingenious routine Charlie has "violated" all three statues: He impales his pants on the sword of one and sits squarely upon its nose; places his foot upon the outstretched hand of another to tie his shoe; and, innocently tipping his hat to someone in the crowd below, manages to give a giant nose-thumb to the crowd by pressing his nose against the third's outsized, open hand.

Charlie can't understand why he has no feeling in Syd's foot. *Shoulder Arms.*

7. Action/Action

One of the subtlest variations occurs when Chaplin transforms one kind of action into another. After Charlie turns that thick branch into a fishing pole in *The Vagabond*, he takes the object transformation one step further. He winds an imaginary reel and smiles ingratiatingly back at the gypsy. Suddenly, he apparently hooks something. The gypsy obligingly peers over his shoulder, allowing Charlie to conk him soundly on the head as he

Charlie flirting in The *Kid.*

Charlie inadvertently thumbs his nose at the crowd below. *City Lights.*

. . . the boss appears. *The Pawnshop.*

pulls up his "fish." The stick has gone from branch, to weapon, to fishing pole, and back to weapon.

In *The Cure* Charlie watches Henry Bergman "massage" a victim by brutally stretching him out—Bergman presses against the poor man's chin with his bare foot while yanking on both legs. Charlie taps the table three times, hoists Bergman's arm in the classic victory pose, and shakes his hand. Then it's Charlie's turn, and the wrestling match begins in earnest. Charlie first tries to evade Bergman by sliding from end to end on the slippery tabletop, then gets up on all fours in the classic wrestler's start position. He flips off the table to face the massive Bergman, crouched for action with his arms outstretched. He does his best to get a grip on the advancing behemoth, but only his slippery agility saves him.

In *The Pawnshop* Chaplin transforms four fights with fellow employee John Rand into other activities. Fighting in the back room when boss Henry Bergman enters, they both immediately become worker bees: With absolutely no break in the rhythm, Charlie is suddenly energetically washing the floor as Rand scribbles busily at his desk; falling into one of his repetitive motion trances, Charlie also washes a violin. Outside, he traps Rand between the rungs of a ladder and "shadow boxes" with the helpless man until a policeman appears on the scene; then Charlie's fancy footwork easily transitions into a graceful dance, and he glides back into the pawnshop. Back in the back room, Charlie is getting the better of Rand, leaping on him and pummeling him mercilessly. Charlie hears Edna approaching and immediately drops to the floor, cowering at the feet of the dazed and bewildered Rand. This subterfuge earns Charlie Edna's ministrations. The final fight takes place in the kitchen, where Charlie and Rand go at each other with the dough. When boss Bergman again comes in upon them, they both, again without a break in the rhythm of their movement, begin "helping" Edna with her kitchen duties; Rand peels spuds as Charlie passes dough through the clothes wringer and rapidly trims it as a piecrust.

Fighting until . . .

Charlie cowers to win Edna's sympathy. *The Pawnshop.*

Occasionally the gag doesn't work as well. Masquerading as a German officer in *Shoulder Arms*, doughboy Charlie is surprised to see his CO brought in as a prisoner. Their hugging reunion turns into slapping when the Kaiser's chauffer glances back at them. The routine is, for Chaplin, a bit forced, but works better than does a similar, earlier version in *The Floorwalker* with Eric Campbell.

Camouflage is often Charlie's purpose in transforming one action to another, as the examples above show. In *The Adventurer* he drops ice cream down his pants. To disguise his action of shaking it out of his pant leg, he stands up, leans toward Edna, and chucks her on the chin. In the same film, escaped convict Charlie mistakes the sound of a champagne cork for a gunshot. Reflexively, he raises his hands, only to smooth his hair when he realizes his mistake. He gives a back kick to the baffled butler for scaring him.

One of Chaplin's best action transformation sequences occurs in *The Gold Rush*. Villainous Black Larson and Big Jim (Swain) are struggling for possession of a rifle in the small cabin, equally matched as they flail about. Despite Charlie's frantic attempts to avoid it, the rifle somehow always points directly at him. The earnestness with which the men fight combines with Charlie's desperation to get out of the line of fire to make this sequence utterly convincing. It's almost as though we're watching two films at once: a drama in which two men struggle over a gun, and a comedy in which a man innocently becomes a moving target. Charlie has to scamper over every square inch of the cabin to avoid being shot in this riotous and exciting sequence.

An interesting sidelight to this routine is that a year earlier, Buster Keaton had performed a very similar solo bit in *The Navigator*. Buster's just lit the fuse of a small cannon, and as he walks away his foot becomes entangled with a rope attached to it. Whichever way he moves, the tiny cannon follows. Several years later he reworked the gag with a large cannon in *The General*.

Whichever way the men turn, the rifle points at Charlie. *The Gold Rush.*

Perhaps the most ingenious of all Chaplin's action transformations occurs in *The Idle Class*. Rich, alcoholic husband Charlie gets a note from his wife: "I have found a new place to live until you stop drinking." He picks up her photo from the table and gazes at it longingly. Turning his back to the camera, his hands drop, his head sinks, and his back and shoulders begin to heave. He appears to be crying uncontrollably—until he turns briskly toward the camera to reveal that he has actually been shaking a cocktail, which he nonchalantly pours and drinks. Essentially, this is a superior reworking of the opening gag from *The Immigrant*, in which Charlie bends over a shipboard rail, his whole body heaving as though seasick, only to turn to reveal the fish he has just caught.

8. Relationship/Relationship

In the world of Chaplin's films, one kind of relationship can change instantly to another. These transformations involve inner issues of emotion and character, rather than outer issues of physical appearance. They don't always involve visual puns, but they do share with the other transformations the confusion of appearance and reality. Just as Chaplin's other transformation gags are at the heart of his comedy, so relationship transformations are at the heart of his character. Chaplin's conception of Charlie and his world centers on mutability of character.

Relationship transformations often result from body part confusions. Thus, in *The Idle Class* Chaplin sets up a scene in which Charlie will be mistaken for a thief. Charlie sits down next to a well-dressed man on a park bench and innocently begins to read a newspaper. Crouching behind the bench is a pickpocket, whose hand emerges from the side of Charlie's open newspaper in such a way that it appears to be Charlie's. As the hand reaches into the man's jacket, Charlie looks down at it wonderingly; he's fooled by the perfect illusion as well. The intended victim feels the hand and whirls around to grab Charlie; in the fray the pickpocket scurries away, unseen by either of them. In the eyes of the intended victim, Charlie is a thief, just as in Charlie's eyes the laughing woman in *The Kid* turned into a violent maniac. It's all a matter of point of view.

A scene in *A Dog's Life* develops the idea further. Two thieves have stolen Charlie's money (ironically, it's actually "their" money—they stole it from a rich drunk earlier in the film, and Charlie found it after they buried it). As they sit drinking in a café, Charlie, behind a curtain, knocks the walrus-mustached Albert Austin out cold. Quickly sliding his arms under Austin's and convincingly substituting them for those of the unconscious thief, he uses hand gestures to continue Austin's conversation with his partner in crime, eventually knocking the second thief out with a beer bottle and making off with the wallet (this sequence is examined in greater detail in chapter 7).

So far, it's been a straightforward body part substitution. But then Austin wakes up and rubs his painful noggin. He picks up the broken beer bottle and looks at his companion curiously, just as the other man wakes up to find Austin staring at him with the telltale bottle in hand. Each of them now believes, credibly, that he's been smashed over the head with a beer bottle by the other. The partners in crime become instant enemies.

During their ensuing fight, they come upon Charlie at the foot of the bar. He's been nabbed by the bartender as he tried to sneak out. The bartender has seized the stolen wallet, assuming it couldn't be Charlie's. As Charlie reaches for it, the bartender jerks it away, allowing one of the thieves to grab it. The other thief reaches for it, but because they no longer trust each other, the first one jerks it back, allowing the bartender to grab it again, which gives the resourceful Tramp *his* chance to grab the money and run. The scene happens with breathtaking speed, the wallet traveling from right to left and back again like the baton in a relay race. Yet because we understand the perceptions and misperceptions of each of the four characters, the rapid-fire action is entirely plausible. The comedy of confused identity is perfectly clear, perfectly credible, and perfectly hilarious. This is physical comedy at its peak, performed with brio, psychological sophistication, and impeccable choreography.

The struggle over the wallet. *A Dog's Life.*

When Charlie becomes Austin's puppet master he purposely fosters confusion, making Austin act like someone he's not. Often, however, relationships in Chaplin's films become confused by accident. For example, in the *tableaux vivants* scene described earlier from *The Cure*, Charlie's simple act of throwing his shoes over a dressing room curtain inadvertently causes two strangers to become mortal enemies.

Here's how Chaplin triangulates the relationships to bring this about. The men sit back to back on cots at opposite sides of the room, taking their shoes off. Charlie is changing behind a small curtained-off area in the center. His first shoe strikes Eric Campbell, who wrongly assumes it was thrown by the other man, a scrawny fellow. Short-tempered Eric simply throws it back at him. The man reacts but doesn't retaliate. But then Charlie's second shoe comes sailing over and hits the poor little sap, who of course now believes that Eric has thrown *both* his shoes at him. This is too much! He throws the second shoe back at Eric. Each man now thinks, quite reasonably, that the other has thrown *two* shoes at him, making their anger perfectly understandable. They each grab one of Charlie's shoes, ready to do battle. But they never come to blows, because the next moment Charlie's *pants* come sailing over the curtain. They whip the curtain open to reveal Charlie in the first of his artistic statue poses, so confounding the men that they simply gawk at him as he goes through his act and strolls away.

In *The Idle Class* such identity confusions are at the heart of the film, unifying its various sequences. Nothing in this film is what it seems. Charlie's being taken for a thief is only the beginning. In a more extended sequence on the links, golfer John Rand becomes the unfortunate victim. Rand tees off and his ball rolls between Charlie's legs; Charlie assumes it's his and promptly drives it down the course. As Rand rushes up and begins upbraiding Charlie, Mack Swain tees off, and his ball lands near them. Charlie points it out as Rand's, and after Rand slams it down the fairway they stroll along affably, suddenly the best of friends. In a conciliatory gesture Rand offers Charlie a cigarette from his case. Charlie graciously accepts, handing one of the cigarettes to Rand and nonchalantly pocketing the case. Whereupon the fuming Swain catches up to them, knocks Rand down, and begins pummeling him. Charlie just walks on more quickly.

The sequence is capped a few minutes later. Charlie beans Swain with one ball, then shatters his liquor bottle with a second. The loss of his illicit liquor (prohibition was in force) reduces Swain to tears. When Charlie steps on Swain's straw hat, it's the last straw for Swain. His pain and frustration boil over into rage just as the unfortunate Rand, his eye blackened from their previous encounter, saunters by. Swain once again assumes Rand is at fault, and once again he pulverizes the innocent man. Both sequences of Swain brutalizing Rand are made funnier because we don't actually see Rand being hit; rather, we see Swain from the back, hammering away astride his prone victim.

Charlie, of course, doesn't fit in among the idle rich, yet he can dream. Early in the film he gazes longingly at Edna as she rides past him on horseback. He daydreams of making a heroic rescue when her horse gets out of control, and then, in a few quick dissolves, of marrying her and having a family. Later, when he sees a woman lying on the ground next to a horse, he assumes it's Edna. But when he rushes over and lifts her to a sitting position she turns out to be a homely woman. Charlie quickly lowers her back to the ground with a look of distaste. (An earlier version of this cruel but funny gag occurs in *The Adventurer*, when Charlie chooses to rescue Edna from drowning before he rescues her mother.)

All the identity confusions in *The Idle Class* climax, appropriately enough, at a masquerade ball. Here, Charlie does fit in, since everyone takes his normal clothes for a tramp costume. Inevitably, he is confused for his drunken millionaire counterpart, who is unrecognizably trapped in a suit of armor with its visor stuck shut. After a poignant "reconciliation" scene between Edna, who turns out to be the drunk's wife, and the adoring Tramp, whom she mistakes for her husband, Mack Swain enters. It develops that he's not just a frustrated golfer, but Edna's father as well. When he introduces Charlie as Edna's husband to another guest. Charlie protests, "Oh, no—we're not married," making Swain puff apoplectically. He's already had a bad day on the golf course, and now his dissolute son-in-law insults his daughter!

The merry confusion of identities is underscored by the fact that Chaplin plays dual roles. He does that in only a few films, most notably *The Great Dictator*. But even when he plays only one role, Charlie's identity is highly flexible. Not only does he have the ability to alter the relationship of others with his behavior, he can alter his own character as well, in an instant.

Although Chaplin's "Charlie" persona is commonly referred to as "the Tramp" or "the Little Tramp," and his clothes mark him as such, he's usually gainfully employed, at least for some of the time, in his films. In a few instances he's even married with a family. What gives his portrayals consistency is that, whether playing rich man or poor, and regardless of his circumstances, he's always a fish out of water. As a vagrant he assumes the airs of a gentleman. As an employee he makes mischief like a child at play or confounds his employers with his incompetence. It all boils down to the comic principle of contrast, setting Charlie against the world so that comic sparks fly. Chaplin put it simply:

> My means of contriving comedy plot was simple. It was the process of getting people in and out of trouble.[14]

The great physical skill we've been celebrating in this book manifests in Charlie's uncanny ability to perform many tasks with extraordinary skill. He becomes a super violinist, cop, roller skater, bricklayer, soldier, father, singing waiter, and so on. Complementing his facility of action is his fluid ability to morph into any role called for in a given situation; he can masquerade as anyone, albeit usually with comically disastrous results. Many of his early films exploit this by casting Charlie in imposter roles: He impersonates royalty, rich men, women, and so on. In his later films he becomes animals, fun-house figures, Adolf Hitler—there seems to be no limit to his ability to become whomever and whatever he wants.

Charlie relies on this mutability for basic survival in a harsh world that threatens and excludes him. In *Police*, for example, he has broken into Edna's house to rob it. The police capture him, but by the time they arrive he has won her over by protecting her and her ailing mother from his thuggish partner. Edna kindly saves him from arrest by introducing him as her husband, whereupon Charlie convincingly takes on the role, flexing his knees, pulling out a cigar, every inch the man of the house. The police turn deferential and Charlie shows them out. It is role-play as camouflage. In *The Adventurer* he has been collared by the police after a long chase. Reverting to the part of the gentleman he's been playing in the house, he introduces his captor to Edna, the lady of the house, and she to him—and back and forth, until the cop finally lets go of him to shake Edna's hand, whereupon Charlie is off again.

His virtuosity at role-playing allows Chaplin to get away with a strain of sexual humor that, in less skilled hands, would be unfunny or offensive. Facing his double in *The Floorwalker* as though looking in a mirror, he suddenly plants a kiss on the man's cheek. Watching Eric, the king tough of *Easy Street*, roll up his sleeve for a knockout punch, Charlie pecks him on the fist. In *The Adventurer* he's got Eric trapped in pocket doors and gives him a big smooch on the nose before taking his leave. The jokes get bolder. In both *The Cure* and *A Dog's Life*, Charlie

Charlie tries to charm Mack Swain. Note that his face is directed more at the camera than at Swain. *The Gold Rush.*

Charlie sneaks a glance at the nude. *City Lights.*

misinterprets the actions of other men as flirtations, and he responds by coyly flirting back. Yet in the context of Charlie's world, where people's identities and even the functions of objects are ever changing and slippery, these gags don't come off as the sort of homosexual-baiting humor then common in popular entertainment. A few moments after he kisses his alter ego in *The Floorwalker*, the men decide to change clothes; Charlie modestly goes behind a chair to change his pants.

In all these instances Charlie is simply reacting to the immediate situation, shifting roles, playing with people's heads, being whatever he needs to be, whether it's a woman, a child, or a hero—the more outrageous, the better. As Edna would tell him before he shot a scene, "Go on. Be cute."[15]

The film in which Chaplin weaves his most elaborate fabric of role switches is *City Lights*. Charlie's millionaire friend knows him only when the millionaire is roaring drunk, a blind girl thinks he is a millionaire, the police think he's a thief, and he's gay. The four story threads are closely interwoven, deepening and enriching each other. Cumulatively, they bring the character of the Tramp, with all his contradictions, into sharp focus.

How they interweave is made clear if we follow the thread of sexual humor. *City Lights* contains more homosexual joking than any other Chaplin film, yet *we* never for one moment think that Charlie is gay. A critical scene at the beginning ensures that. While sneaking glances at a large nude statue in a window, Charlie pretends to study a small statue of a horseman. As Charlie backs away from the window like an art connoisseur studying a masterwork, a sidewalk elevator descends, then rises just as he steps onto it. Chaplin, by this time a veteran of two shotgun marriages and the resultant scandal-riddled, headline divorces, knew better than most that sex has its perils; the floor can literally drop out from under you. Discovering his danger, Charlie sternly reprimands the worker coming up on the elevator—until the man emerges fully, revealing that he stands about a foot and a half taller than Charlie, who meekly tips his hat and skulks away. Nothing is what it seems in this little scene. Art lovers are really looking for a little voyeuristic pleasure, sidewalks vanish without warning, and people can grow to monstrous proportions.

It's a very amusing set piece, beautifully choreographed and played. But the thematic importance of the scene is how it effortlessly establishes Charlie's heterosexuality through his fascination with the female nude statue. For the rest of the film that sexuality will be questioned by other characters in the film. In scene after scene with the millionaire, and later with the boxer, Charlie pats, rubs, kisses, and flirts. But as the thread weaves its way into his relationship with the blind girl, it becomes clear that in this film Charlie's sexual "unmanliness" is translated to unworthiness. He struggles mightily, and successfully, to provide basic necessities for the blind girl. But he does so at the cost of great personal sacrifices, which include going to prison. Yet despite his noble actions, is he worthy to be loved by her? After all, he's done it under false pretenses, masquerading as a millionaire. He's known all the while that his masquerade must end, and he will stand revealed—as he does at the end—stripped of disguises. Without sexuality and without money, is he worthy of love? What, after all, does it mean to be a man?

One gag from *City Lights* serves to show how sophisticated Chaplin had become in his depiction of the deceptive difference between the appearance of people and their

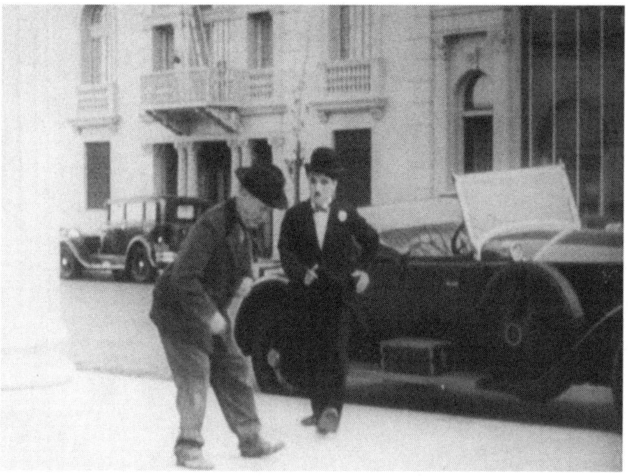

The bum gets a lesson in economics. *City Lights.*

reality. Despite the fact that the mercurial millionaire has given Charlie a Rolls-Royce and evening dress, when he wakes up cold sober the next morning he has no idea who Charlie is, and has him thrown unceremoniously out onto the street. A man strolls by smoking a cigar, and the aroma is irresistible. Charlie, true to form, hops into his Rolls and follows the smoker down the street. When the man discards the butt, Charlie stops the car and goes for it, pushing away a tramp who gets there first. Charlie snatches the cigar from the sidewalk and rides away, leaving the baffled, outraged bum to stare at this astonishing demonstration of the rich robbing the poor. Since we know the truth underlying the appearance, we appreciate each man's point of view, and marvel at the brilliance and resonance of the gag. The effect is similar to the abandoned baby gag in *The Kid.* The typical audience response is to laugh, and then laugh again as it sinks in.

It's actually a gag Chaplin reworked from *The Gold Rush.* As newly rich prospectors Charlie and Mack Swain sail home "on the good ship success," fur-coated Charlie reflexively picks up a cigar butt from the deck. Mack scolds him and offers a cigar from a fancy case. It's a good example of how Chaplin recycled and improved material; the dumbfounded bum in *City Lights* makes the gag much sharper. Startling and poignant to Depression-era audiences, it remains just as relevant today.

New millionaire Charlie forgets that he no longer has to pick up cigar butts from the ground. *The Gold Rush.*

Audiences found Chaplin's character and his stories more satisfying than those of most of his comic contemporaries because of the visual sophistication and emotional depth of his transformation gags. By and large he avoided impossible film gags; such gags, like magician's tricks, leave the audience dazzled, impressed, and awed, but ultimately unsatisfied, because they understand that there is a secret technique—a cheat—employed. Chaplin discovered, as did Keaton and Lloyd after him, that executing his gags with physical skill presented without any obvious film trickery was more satisfying, because audiences got the pleasure of the magical surprises without the cheat. The magic remains, but its mechanics become transparent.

This is one of the qualities that makes Chaplin's films engaging to watch even after repeated viewings. Knowing beforehand what's going to happen allows the audience to savor Chaplin's great skill at setting up and executing his gags. Indeed, in his best films—notably *The Gold Rush*—the setups contain such good gags themselves that they dovetail with the "payoff" gag sequences. Chaplin often achieves such a merging of conception, choreography, and characterization that repeated viewings are virtually necessary to appreciate the many levels on which his films operate. A first viewing draws us into the story and delights us with the magical surprises of his comedy. With later viewings we can savor the beauty of Chaplin's movement and the elegance of his choreographic style of directing, while *still* becoming involved with the story and laughing helplessly at the rich, apparently inexhaustible humor in the gag sequences. Details and nuances continually reveal themselves, rewarding each new screening.

Transformation gags aren't the only way Chaplin acts like a magician in his films. At times he becomes a trickster without the aid of such gags. He often fools the other characters with deft, magical ploys. Thus, as his pockets are being emptied by a thief in *Police,* he simultaneously picks the thief's pocket. As his shrewish wife takes the money hidden in his hatband in *Pay Day,* he retrieves

A Chaplin gag setup: In another moment the flypaper Syd is peeling from the child's legs will be pushed into his face. Chaplin's position enables him to do the actual pushing while making it appear as though the kid is doing it. *The Pilgrim.*

some from her purse and slips it back into the hatband. He manages to cadge a few pieces of fruit even as the butler throws him out of the mansion in *City Lights*.

In addition to his characteristic gestures, Chaplin has a repertoire of tricky moves he executes with all the flash and polish of magician's flourishes. Just as a magician will cut a deck of cards with one hand, or roll a coin around his fingers, Charlie is fond of "popping" his hat off his head in the act of apparently trying to put it on, or rolling it down his arm to hand it to someone, pulling it back just as his victim reaches for it.

He's also adept at creating new subterfuges, using the liquid smoothness of his movement to befuddle people, such as when he manages to swipe John Rand's cigarette case in *The Idle Class*. In *The Pawnshop* he flips Rand's

Another gag setup from *The Pilgrim*. The kid has covered a cake with Syd's bowler, then distracts Charlie so he doesn't notice as he pours the icing over it.

Chaplin as trickster: He twists his ear, "causing" smoke to come out of his mouth. *Modern Times.*

coin, which somehow ends up *in* his hand rather than on the back of it; the second time he does it he manages to swipe the coin as well. In *Modern Times* he's been arrested for not being able to pay for his lavish meal at a restaurant; he manages to con a few puffs of an after-dinner cigar under the nose of the cop who collars him. When the cop whips the cigar from his mouth, Charlie nonchalantly grasps a puff of smoke with his hand, taps it onto the top of his hat, twists his ear and—*voilà*—another puff of smoke magically emerges from his mouth. Similarly, in *The Great Dictator* he pours water into his ear and simultaneously squirts it from his mouth.

Like the transformations, these dexterous maneuvers delight us by their sheer audacity. We believe he would fool or bamboozle the other characters with such clever gambits, and are swept up by the beauty of their design and execution. Such streetwise ruses and playful flourishes are central to Charlie's character, non sequiturs that express both the indomitable spirit of the Tramp and the great élan with which he goes through life. The transformations, trickster moves, and idiosyncratic gestures are more than a grace note appended to the saga of the Tramp, they fuse with the comic and dramatic content of the films. They aren't just something Charlie *does*; they *are* Charlie, defining his character and his relationships with other characters. They are inseparable from him, in the same way that his heavy, masklike makeup somehow seems naturalistic rather than artificial on his face.

It may seem odd that the transformation gags that Chaplin performs with such panache, along with his frequent displays of super-competence, are complemented rather than contradicted by his frequent periods of blundering incompetence. The most obvious reason for this is that Chaplin plays the clumsy fool with such evident, consummate skill, and his comic mishaps are choreographed as carefully as any ballet. To take a fall in real life is painful and sometimes tragic; to fall repeatedly and without harm on film, as Chaplin does in almost every film he made, is to make light of life's inevitable misfortunes.[16] To turn incompetence, conflict, and pain into a kind of dance, both graceful and comic, is to offer a refreshing respite from life's sorrows; indeed, such respite is one of the main reasons we turn to the arts.

But there is a less obvious reason why Chaplin's comedy of incompetence complements his comedy of skill. His laughably inept attempts to work—in factories, farms, banks, pawnshops, restaurants, department stores, film studios, and so on—imply a question: If he's so good at so many things, why can't he hold a simple job? The answer, of course, is that Charlie, who has seemingly infinite capacity to endure physical abuse, has absolutely no tolerance for the suffering most of us are willing to endure for the sake of making a living. His incompetence calls into question the value of the work itself. When Charlie isn't good at something, it's usually because that thing is boring, oppressive, or meaningless. There are simply too many possibilities out there for fun and adventure to get stuck in one job, one role, one place. We share his distaste for the dull routines of life, his horror of being held captive by the expectations of others. We rejoice in his free-spirited rebellion against whatever and whoever constrains him, and eagerly join him on his journey down the open road.

But there's a flip side to Charlie's freedom, and it's what gives the films their darker side, their underlying dramatic power, and their universality. Charlie's inability to conform and fit in means that his path leads inevitably toward poverty and loneliness. For that reason he must wrestle, again and again, with satisfying the most basic needs of survival. In film after film he struggles to acquire what most of us take for granted—food and shelter. At the same time, he wants more than mere physical survival. He's a romantic, longing for beauty and love. Even when he does achieve these things, it's only temporary, for in the end he remains an outsider in a hostile world. Because this strange outsider does cope—imperfectly, but with incredible panache—he earns our admiration, affection, and gratitude.

He copes from moment to moment by improvising inventive strategies. He is street-smart, a consummate imposter. His "coping mechanisms" are ingenious, bold, graceful, and comic responses to an inhumane society, and chief among them is his magical ability to transform reality.

The cumulative effect of all the transformations and related gags that permeate Chaplin's films is of an unstable, fluid world, and at its center a character adept at assuming many roles and possessing a seemingly endless array of skills. The vision crystallizes in the Mutual films, which contain the densest concentration of transformation gags. This is a world of objects and characters in constant flux around the dancing figure of Charlie. While the character mellows and saddens with age, his core characteristic remains his magical ability to transform the world according to his imaginative vision.

Chaplin often repeats his gags, but almost always in ways that improve upon the original versions. Frequently he puts them into a new context that changes their meaning or sharpens their impact, as he does with the cigar gag that migrates from *The Gold Rush* to *City Lights*. He is just as careful about not overexposing his special skills; for example, he roller-skates in only two films, made years apart, and ditto for playing the violin. No doubt he felt intense pressure to create new material, since even his earliest films remained in constant circulation. This, along with the aesthetic conundrum of dealing with sound after 1930, partially accounts for his diminishing output as the years passed.

But another clue may be found in the transformation gags themselves. When we trace how they evolved through his career, a distinct pattern emerges. Object and action transformations proliferate during the Mutual period, and body part transformations during the First National films. More elaborate transformation gag sequences, sometimes involving large props, provide most of the highlights of the features through *Modern Times*. *The Great Dictator* has a number of notable transformation gags, but they no longer dominate the film, and there are even fewer in the films that followed, as if Chaplin found them to be incompatible with verbal comedy. While their absence fuels theories about Chaplin's artistic decline, their gradual disappearance in his films suggests that he simply outgrew them.

But up until that time Chaplin is the consummate magician of comedy, manipulating reality to his own great delight, and ours.

Notes

1. Charles Chaplin, *My Life in Pictures* (New York: Grosset & Dunlap, 1975), 28.

2. Charlie introduces it by saying (in a subtitle), "I'll dance the Oceana Roll." Audiences of the time would have recognized the name as a punning reference to a popular ragtime tune published in 1912. The "roll" of the song was the rolling sea, rather than bread rolls. In his sound film reissue of the film in 1942 Chaplin omitted the song reference.

3. Theodore Huff was the first commentator to offer an extended commentary on these gags, in his pioneering *Charlie Chaplin* (New York: Henry Schuman, 1951). Huff's book was for many years the standard biographical and critical work, and it is still valuable and highly readable. Fine discussions of the subject may also be found in Gerald Mast's *The Comic Mind* (Indianapolis, IN: Bobbs-Merrill, 1973), Walter Kerr's *The Silent Clowns* (New York: Knopf, 1975), and Raoul Sobel and David Francis's *Chaplin: Genesis of a Clown* (New York: Quartet Books, 1977).

4. *Photoplay*, October 1915, cited in Gerald D. McDonald, Michael Conway, and Mark Ricci, eds., *The Films of Charlie Chaplin* (New York: Bonanza Books, 1965), 106.

5. Like much of his comic business this is very much like a classic *lazzi* of the commedia dell'arte, mendicant troupes of performers who toured Italy and Europe from the fourteenth through eighteenth centuries. For example, the servant Arlechino would, with great relish, pull apart and eat a fly. The exaggerated comic characters and boisterous physical comedy of commedia greatly influenced later forms of comedy, including circus clowning, British pantomime, and the British music hall tradition, all of which nurtured Chaplin's talents. His work has often been compared to commedia by his more academic critics, though it's unlikely that he actually knew much about the tradition. He simply absorbed and channeled it.

Another connection between commedia and Chaplin is that the commedia players used a paddle with a hinged flap to create a cracking sound when they would whack somebody on the behind. It was the original slapstick, a word that became synonymous with physical comedy. The term came to haunt Chaplin, for it connoted the crudest, most lowbrow form of physical comedy. While this pretty well described his work during his formative years, he later professed dislike for both slapstick comedy and his own early films. Nevertheless, his later films retain plenty of crudity, vulgarity, and lowbrow comedy, which are a key to their continuing appeal.

6. David Robinson reports that the audience at the Berlin premiere went so wild after the roll dance that the projectionist had to rewind the film and show it again. Apparently this happened in other theatres as well. Robinson, *Chaplin, His Life and Art* (London: Penguin, 2001), 381.

7. Not everyone agrees. Woody Allen professes to dislike the scene—"I don't find it funny or a brilliant metaphor," he says in Richard Schickel's 2003 documentary *Charlie: The Life and Art of Charles Chaplin*. But for most people it remains one of the highlights of Chaplin's career.

It is now known that Hitler saw the film, twice, but not what he thought of it.

8. Interestingly, Chaplin performs the same sequence self-aggrandizing bows in *Caught in a Cabaret*, an early Keystone, but the gag is ineffective in the context provided in the earlier film—Chaplin the actor was way ahead of Chaplin the scenarist.

9. Three years later Buster Keaton used the dissolve-transformation idea with incredible ingenuity in *Sherlock, Jr.* Movie projectionist Buster walks right into the movie screen, but then has trouble merging with filmic reality. As the setting suddenly changes around him, Buster's body remains in place; he's trapped inside the film, at the mercy of a capricious editor. In the days before computer graphics and complex matte photography, the scene had to be accomplished by measuring Buster's position in the frame, traveling to a new location, and resuming the filming, precisely matching Buster's position and action. Slight changes in the lighting on Buster are the only thing that mars the nearly perfect illusion that Buster is being "cut" into eight different settings. It is a masterful and thought-provoking sequence that still thrills film lovers.

10. Chaplin actually worked the feeding machine himself so that he could control the speed and rhythm of its assaults upon him.

11. Via reverse-action filming.

12. Chaplin originally had someone else don the chicken costume. Technically, that would have made the shot easier to achieve, since in those days such dissolves had to be done in the camera by rewinding and reshooting the film. With a second actor the effect could have been done without the time required for a costume change, and the risk that the camera might move or the lighting might change. Luckily, he was dissatisfied with the filmed result, so he got into the costume himself for the scene and did his wonderful chicken mime.

In *The Idle Class* he plays a double role, and in the last scene both "Charlies" appear together. To accomplish this Chaplin had an actor double for him; but even wearing a suit of armor and perfectly made up, it's apparent that it's not Chaplin. He was hard to imitate!

13. The hide-and-seek scene is an example of Chaplin's storytelling running at peak efficiency, for it is only the centerpiece of a well-developed sequence about finding the money to pay for overnight lodging. Here's how it plays out: Charlie is broke, and that's why he has to sneak Jackie into the doss house; he finds a coin to pay for his own admission only by scouring his own pockets. Thanks to the sleeping pickpocket he has the means to pay for Jackie after the proprietor uncovers the lad. The simple idea of finding shelter for a night thus becomes a hilarious comic sequence rich in psychologically revealing behavior.

14. Charles Chaplin, My *Autobiography* (New York: Simon & Schuster, 1964), 211.

15. Reported in Robinson, *Chaplin, His Life and Art*, 218.

16. In 1915 a rumor circulated that Chaplin had killed himself doing a stunt, as indicated in several letters to *Photoplay* magazine in July 1915.

CHAPTER SIX

Cast of Characters

"We look . . . for some little incident, some vignette that fixes the other characters. The audience must never be in any doubt about them. We have to fix them on sight. Nobody cares about *their* troubles. They stay the same. You know them every time they appear . . . *He's* the one we develop."[1]

When Chaplin walked through the gates of the Keystone Film Company late in 1913, he encountered a vibrant stock company of buffoons, goons, dudes, and damsels, in all shapes and sizes. Many of the players had well-established comic trademarks, such as Chester Conklin's huge, drooping mustache and equally drooping clothes, and the bizarre triangle of hair that bisected Mack Swain's forehead. They also had distinctive behavioral trademarks, such as Fatty Arbuckle's cherubic grin and incongruous displays of acrobatic agility. A lot of them, including some of the women, were skilled comic acrobats. It was an intimidating company for any young comedian to join, but Chaplin soon found his place among the ricocheting bodies of the Keystone universe, and before long he set those bodies in orbit around his own emerging character.

Sennett told Chaplin, soon after hiring him,

> We have no scenario—we get an idea, then follow the natural sequence of events until it leads up to a chase, which is the essence of our comedy.[2]

The chase finale offered Sennett a neat solution to the problem of cranking out a dozen or so visual comedies a month. Characters and conflict could be established in a perfunctory manner, resulting in the fight or chase climax. Given such a recipe, it is understandable that people's behavior in the films is stereotypical and clichéd rather than naturalistic. Keystone players portray types rather than fully developed characters. Their reactions to the events in these furious, fast-moving films is larger than life and visually unambiguous, befitting the simple plots.

But lest we be tempted to dismiss these early comedies for their crudity, it must be kept in mind that the clichéd plots and characters were part of the joke; audiences of the time would have seen them as parodies of familiar stage potboilers, occurring in accelerated time. The silence of the medium necessitated that the actors find ways of translating extreme emotions into clear gestural expression and unambiguous action, sometimes resulting in over-the-top performances. The emotions had to be instantaneous and reflexive; a single performance might include rapidly alternating displays of jealousy, rage, cruelty, cowardice, and bravado. It was all part of the fun.

Because the silliness, simplicity of plot, cardboard characters, and emphasis on slapstick action in Sennett's films was similar to the stage world of the Karno sketches, Chaplin found this new comic world highly congenial, and from the bumper crop of zanies he gathered the seeds to populate his own films. In the process he turned them into supporting characters who are still viable dramatically today, unlike their Sennett counterparts, who have, for the most part, ended up in popular entertainment's dustbin.

Like any evolutionary process, the transformation took time and involved a good deal of trial and error. Fleshing out characters from a world of violent slapstick has perils. For example, if a character seems to be "really" hurt by the action, either physically or emotionally, the distance necessary for knockabout comedy vanishes.

There is tremendous violence in the Laurel and Hardy films, but it's exaggerated in such a way that we never take it seriously—we never believe they're really hurt, just as we never believe Eric's really hurt when Charlie keeps stepping on his gouty foot in *The Cure*. These are bodies presented as comic targets. But it's different when Chaplin is shot by a gun and injured in *The Tramp*. While the viewer may admire Chaplin's dramatic acting skill, the gossamer fabric of film reality is ripped by the abrupt shift in tone from comic to serious.

Chaplin, of course, eventually became adept at introducing serious content into his films, and he suffers physical injury—without damaging his film—in such later works as *The Adventurer* and *The Kid*. Mixing comedy and drama became one of his signal achievements, but it was a delicate balancing act, made even trickier by his tendency to mix Sennett-style caricatures with more naturalistic characterizations throughout his film career. When he manages it successfully, the stereotypes become more than mere conventions; they become archetypes, primal embodiments of certain human personality types.

Sennett's cast of characters—the heavies, heroines, buddies, and heroes Chaplin found on the lot—provided the starting point. In learning to work with them he discovered who he was onscreen.

Heavies

While heavies were the standard-issue villains of silent films, at Keystone the term was more inclusive, since it involved not only the hissable villain beloved of melodramas, but almost every other male character as well. Almost all of them had undesirable traits, comic foibles that set the plots moving. They tended to be a cheerfully larcenous group, cheating, stealing, and exploding into violence at the drop of the hat, usually over a woman. Chaplin would refine this simplistic notion of motivation, adding richness of characterization and surprising moral complexity to his films.

Sennett hired Chaplin because some of his leading male comedians, in the heady glow of newfound film fame, were departing for the greener pastures of other film companies. Fred Mace had done so in 1913, and Sennett feared he was about to lose Ford Sterling as well, which he did, less than two months after the untried Chaplin arrived on the lot.

Sterling gave essentially the same overheated performance whether playing a flirtatious rogue, a married man, or the chief of the Keystone Kops. It's clear that Chaplin observed him closely, for in his first Keystone film, *Making a Living*, he co-opted both Sterling's characteristic frock coat and his unsavory, aggressive character. He used the outfit twice more, in *Cruel, Cruel Love* and *Mabel at the Wheel*, adding a Sterling-type goatee in the latter film. These are among Chaplin's least engaging performances. But Sterling evidently made a strong impression, for even after Chaplin settled on the Tramp outfit for his character, he occasionally substituted the top hat favored by Sterling for his derby. He later paid him the tribute of using a Sterling look-alike when he created his own version of the bumbling Kops in *Easy Street*.

Most critics dismiss Sterling as a bad example that Chaplin had to overcome, but he may have exerted a more positive influence than he's generally given credit for. He walked with his feet splayed, which may have inspired Chaplin to develop his famous walk; certainly, no extant review of Chaplin's stage work mentions a distinctive funny walk. The wealthy drunk Chaplin played on stage was also closer in appearance, if not in behavior, to Sterling's frock-coated dandy than to the Tramp.

But Chaplin quickly absorbed and outgrew Sterling's physical repertoire. For example, although he hops in place like Sterling to indicate surprise or anger in several early films, he almost immediately substitutes a much more interesting movement: his distinctive way of skidding into a scene on one foot and skip-hopping to change direction.[3] Even when aping Sterling's movements, Chaplin executes them with a delicacy and precision that is beyond Sterling's capabilities. Not that Sterling was awkward or oafish; he was a decent physical comedian, and took his pratfalls with ease. But compared to Chaplin, both his movement and his character are unappealing and one-dimensional.

Chaplin mirrors Ford Sterling in *Between Showers*. In the background are Chester Conklin and Emma Clifton.

Sterling throttles Chaplin in *Tango Tangles*.

The contrast between them is apparent in their two co-starring films. *Between Showers* showcases the essential characteristics of Keystone comic heavies of this period: amorality, quick tempers that lead to violent altercations, and an abiding interest in picking up pretty women. The paper-thin plot revolves around Sterling's rivalry with Chaplin over the possession of a stolen umbrella, and their unsuccessful attempts to woo a couple of women. While the men share similar eccentricities of movement and pretty much mirror each other's behavior, scholar Harry Geduld neatly summarizes the critical difference in their performances: "Sterling's mean-spirited, irascible attitude contrasts at every turn with Charlie's good-humored, mischievous playfulness."[4]

In *Tango Tangles* he and Chaplin duke it out over another woman, this time in a dance hall. This fascinating film is like watching a rehearsal, since both men act in character but wear street clothes. It's intriguing to see their movements and facial expressions unadorned by their characteristic getups. Sterling plays his usual hotheaded self, and Chaplin reverts to his drunk act as he dances with Sterling's girl. Particularly notable is Chaplin's mock-heroic posturing during the inevitable fight scene, anticipating his performances in *The Champion* and *The Cure*. As he cocks his pelvis back and to the side expressively, his flexibility and fluidity are impressive.

But despite his superior physicality and the attitudinal grace notes Chaplin brings to bear, as a Keystone comedian he fits right into the amoral comic-heavy mold. In fact, he's even cruder and crueler than the rest of them, flicking cigarette ashes into a woman's open hand, sticking knives into posteriors, pushing people into lakes, and enthusiastically smashing his adversaries in the face with bricks. But from his Karno training and his long experience playing in front of live audiences, Chaplin knew exactly how to get away with such brutality, adding a casualness to his cruelty that undercuts it, and modulating the ferocity of his assaults with choreographic panache. He also takes as much abuse as he dishes out, and his many falls are a study in how to collapse comically.

The Chaplin-Sterling Keystones are good examples of Sennett's guiding rule of getting quickly to the larger actions of fights and chases, without dwelling on the niceties of character motivation; hence the extraordinary fuss made over that stolen umbrella in *Between Showers*, and the speed with which the men come to blows in *Tango Tangles*. Chaplin recognized and fought against this rudimentary storytelling approach. Fresh from his years of performing the audience-tested Karno repertoire, he knew in his bones how a solid story with believable antagonists drove comedy. But he had never written a whole story by himself. Chaplin's brother Syd had created several original sketches for Karno, but Charlie had never presumed to do that. However, Sennett's very offhandedness about the process of creating comedy made Chaplin feel confident in his ideas and abilities, and before long he announced to Sennett that he could do a park comedy as well as anyone.

And so he could. But his first self-directed Keystone films were hardly revolutionary. More than he would later admit, Chaplin found the Keystone recipe congenial, with its reliance on simple plots and elasticity about character motivation. But while his Tramp would always embody some of the ethically flexible characteristics of the Sennett heavy, Chaplin became skillful at justifying Charlie's more questionable behavior by grounding it in dramatic necessity. For example, he *must* steal or deceive to get food or shelter, and he *has* to fight to protect himself from larger and more powerful adversaries. The actions that seem gratuitous in his early films become admirable in later ones.

Chaplin also found that he could make his character more appealing by transferring many of the crasser elements of the Keystone heavies—in particular, jealousy, lechery, bullying, and cowardice—to other characters in his films. Often the heavies in his later work—the orphan officials and doctor in *The Kid*, or the circus ringmaster in *The Circus*—are just as cardboard as their Keystone forebears. If anything, they are even more limited by being better focused; the doctor is simply callous, the orphan official simply pompous, and so on. But by exporting some of the less appealing traits to other characters, Chaplin enables Charlie to become admirable by contrast.

But all that came later. Chaplin began his filmic journey as a total rogue, outdoing Sterling and the others in sheer destructive power. Chaplin's first full-fledged starring vehicle, *A Film Johnnie*, made between *Between Showers* and *Tango Tangles*, is far superior to the other two. A fairly elaborate production, its settings include a movie theatre, the Keystone studio itself, and a burning house that the onscreen filmmakers rush to film for a scene. It's intriguing to see a near documentary of early moviemaking, but the real interest of the film is Chaplin's performance. Although he's the titular hero, Chaplin plays the role in full heavy mode. He's a lascivious, belligerent pest who slaps and kicks an old doorman for no apparent reason. Even so, there's a certain anarchic joy in watching him sabotage the enjoyment of the onscreen moviegoers and the work of the onscreen filmmakers.

The film, which Chaplin neither wrote nor directed, features a Charlie so dumb that he confuses scenes being filmed with reality, so he rushes in to "save" the heroine on the movie set. But Chaplin obviously came up with most of the inventive gags, such as picking his teeth with the barrel of a pistol, then firing it to light his cigarette. It's also clear that he came up with much of the comic choreography, including some neat tangles with stagehands who are moving set pieces and props around. No one else at Keystone was staging action like this. After Charlie shoots up the set and everyone ducks for cover, there's a funny bit of peek-a-boo action as he struts around in triumph and whirls around to catch them looking at him; he would do exactly the same bit as a cop in *Easy Street* a few years later.

Chaplin's performance is all the more striking because the other players, except when they're being filmed within the film, are completely naturalistic—Sterling, Sennett, Arbuckle, and others all play themselves, not their customary screen characters. Even when tussling with Charlie, they react naturalistically. Charlie, despite his outlandish costume, is presented as part of the real world of the filmmakers. This makes his behavior seem even more bizarre and obnoxious, yet he remains engaging because of his quirky movement and inventive gags.

While audiences liked this irresponsible troublemaker, Chaplin understood that they would tire of him if he limited himself to playing an agile, disruptive rogue. But he faced a dilemma: Playing against Sterling-type heavies forced him to compete against other eccentrics who behaved much like he did, yet setting himself off by playing the heavy in a world of ordinary people, as he does in *A Film Johnnie*, made his slapstick violence too gratuitous. So during the course of his year at Keystone, he gradually made himself more sympathetic by channeling his aggressive behavior into better-motivated storylines with more believable adversaries. *His Trysting Place* and *The New Janitor*, two late Keystones that he both wrote and directed, are good indicators of his progress.

At first glance, *His Trysting Place* seems like a typical Keystone romp. But it actually has a surprisingly intricate, well-worked-out storyline, an interlocking domestic tangle of mistaken perceptions. Simply by switching coats at a café, both Charlie and Mack Swain get into big trouble with their wives. Charlie's coat contains a baby bottle he's bought for his infant son, and Mack's has a love letter he's been asked to mail by a lady in his hotel lobby. Both wives, of course, assume the worse when they discover the goods.

The film is comprised of three amusing dustups that illustrate Chaplin's growth as both a scenario writer and creator of physical comedy. It opens on a familiar scene of domestic discord, as wife Mabel complains to Charlie about her worn-out shoes and their poor living conditions, emphatically driving her points home by throwing horseshoes at him and painfully closing the door on his legs and fingers. But the slapstick violence doesn't obscure the fact that the argument itself is believable, and played quite realistically. By making Mabel the aggressor, Charlie earns sympathy as the henpecked husband. Although he is irritated with her and snaps back verbally, he earns further kudos by not retaliating physically or bearing a grudge; when they make up, he affectionately makes funny faces at their son to stop the boy's crying, and smooches Mabel with such spontaneous affection that it seems to catch her off guard. He cheerfully departs on his errand to buy the baby bottle.

Before returning home, though, he stops in the café for a bite to eat. As though to make up for his equanimity on the home front, he begins the scene by behaving like his scrappy character from *A Film Johnnie*. There are

Charlie is offended by Mack's table manners. *His Trysting Place.*

no seats, so Charlie torments an old man sitting at the counter into giving up his. He samples the oldster's food, wipes his fingers on the man's long beard, then pretends to find a bug in the beard. The indignant oldster leaves in a huff, and Charlie promptly takes his seat, next to Swain. Charlie's abuse of the old man is cruel, selfish, and quite funny.

But the ensuing contretemps with Swain is better because it's less gratuitous, motivated by a carefully escalating series of irritating actions on each man's part that occur in one long, uninterrupted take. As Swain noisily slurps his soup, Charlie mocks him by "accompanying" his slurping on an imaginary violin. Then he accidentally shakes pepper into Swain's face, causing the big man to sneeze. Swain pretty much ignores Charlie because he's preoccupied with his soup. He burps and sprays some of it onto Charlie. When he reaches across Charlie's face to get some mustard, Charlie irritably bites his arm, causing Swain to drop some of the mustard into Charlie's soup. Swain then scratches his head with his soup spoon, giving Charlie a sympathetic itch. After Charlie carelessly throws his meat bone into Swain's soup, Swain slaps him. Now the battle begins in earnest. Charlie flicks a spoonful of soup into Swain's face, and then, after some more slapping, his whole bowl.

We cut to a longer shot as everyone in the café gets drawn into the fray. When Swain exits in a hurry, he understandably grabs the wrong coat. The well-developed scene has actually been a setup for the mix-ups to come between the men and their wives.

The resulting spousal battles climax in the park, where Mabel knocks Charlie repeatedly into a trash can, and Chaplin takes the falls with his customary geometrical precision. She swings away as he pops in and out and pleads with her to stop. Before long Mack winds up in the trash can as well. Finally, the coats are restored to their proper owners and all is well—until Charlie innocently brings Mack's wife the love letter, which now does double-duty as an agent of discord. Mack's outraged spouse whacks away at him with her umbrella, while Charlie and Mabel enjoy the spectacle from a nearby park bench. He presents the new baby bottle to Mabel, and the film ends with the little family enjoying another loving domestic interlude.

Mack presents Charlie with a prime target. *His Trysting Place.*

The inevitable violence that punctuates all Keystone films is executed here in Chaplin's now characteristically bravura style. In addition to the well-choreographed action sequences and clever storyline, the film is set apart from the usual Keystone product by its well-defined and clearly motivated characters. The café sequence is particularly well worked out. Before Charlie enters, Chaplin sets up the comedy of manners to come by introducing another character who's exiting as Mack enters. This filthy fellow, who looks like he just emerged from the sewer, is an even bigger slob than Mack. He picks his teeth, spits, and carelessly tosses his used napkin behind him onto the counter in front of Mack and the oldster, who gawk at him in disgust. Now the stage is set for Charlie's boorish behavior toward the hapless old man, and Mack's boorish behavior toward a suddenly fastidious Charlie. By the time it's over we're with Charlie all the way, for he's striking a blow against all the slurpers, snifflers, loudmouths, and other jerks that we've all suffered in public.

But however deftly worked out and appealingly played, the stakes are low in the story, its typical bedroom-farce misunderstandings quickly resolved after the requisite comic battles. There is considerably more at stake in

Charlie and Mabel enjoy the show as Mack's wife goes at him. *His Trysting Place.*

An unusually subdued Charlie as *The New Janitor.*

The New Janitor, arguably Chaplin's best Keystone, and certainly his most touching.

Chaplin plays the title role with his customary polished ineptitude, but the story is anything but typical for either Chaplin or Keystone. In a poignant little scene in which he is both dignified and endearing, Charlie gets fired for his incompetence. But before his departure he answers one last summons and ends up bravely foiling a would-be embezzler. There's no amorality about this heavy; he's a genuine crook, stealing the company payroll to pay off his gambling debts, and he's ready to use his gun against anyone who crosses him.

For the sake of the story Chaplin mutes Charlie's usually feisty character, making him seem worn down by his menial duties as cleanup man. He's meek and compliant toward his boss, and doesn't retaliate against a nasty elevator operator who forces him to climb many flights of stairs rather than using the elevator. This makes his sudden turnaround, when he foils the crook with some bold and comically graceful maneuvers, quite exhilarating.

What is also notable is that for the first time Chaplin brings an ironic social dimension into his work. While several of the characters in earlier films make fun of Charlie's comical clothing, nothing is made of his inferior social status. But in this film, Charlie's lowly social status is central to the plot. When the boss returns to the office to find Charlie holding a gun on the crooked office manager, he automatically assumes the bedraggled former janitor must be the thief. The secretary saves the day by revealing the truth just as a cop is about to haul Charlie off.

The almost instant popularity of his films enabled Chaplin to assert a measure of artistic independence at Keystone, but he was relegated once again to the role of an actor—and a supporting one at that—for the company's most ambitious project to date. Mack Sennett brought in the celebrated Broadway comedienne Marie Dressler to star in *Tillie's Punctured Romance*, the first-ever feature-length comedy. It was based on one of Dressler's well-known stage vehicles and directed by Sennett himself. While it doesn't hold up well today, it proved to be a huge success for all involved at the time, and confirmed Chaplin's growing reputation with the public. He and Mabel play the heavies—more conventional heavies this time—a larcenous couple who try to swindle the ignorant, elephantine farm girl Tillie out of her inherited fortune. Though he retains his large shoes, cane, and characteristic walk, Chaplin doesn't wear his Tramp costume. Instead, he dons the sort of city slicker clothes he used in some of his first films, behaves like his early amoral screen self, and wears a conventional split "villain" mustache rather than his trademark toothbrush. Chaplin realized that his character was the key to his popularity, so he took care to distance him from this sleazy opportunist.

Chafing for more freedom and more money, Chaplin finished out his contract and left Keystone. No one else would ever direct him again.

At Essanay Chaplin got more of the independence and salary he craved. Brought in as an established star with an astronomical salary that was nearly ten times what he earned at Keystone, he was able to work without rival directors and stars breathing down his neck, particularly the intimidating Sennett, who basically invented modern screen comedy. During his year with Essanay, Chaplin made variations of many of the films he had done at Keystone, freely recycling plots and characters to meet the ever-increasing demand for new films.

Admirably, he also continued to develop artistically. The moral dimension of the Tramp character that he introduced in *The New Janitor*, with its attendant thread of social awareness, filters into his Essanay films. Crime, and particularly theft, became a more important plot element.

In *The Tramp*, often cited as a watershed work, Chaplin for the first time explicitly defines his character as a wandering tramp, while at the same time making it clear how he is different from the other, more common tramps depicted in the picture. They are little more than lowlife criminals, and he has to fight them to protect Edna, which lands him a job on her family farm. There he performs his tasks with characteristic incompetence, but later he's shot in the leg thwarting a robbery attempt by the tramps.

Recuperating in relative luxury, his hopes for a romance with Edna are dashed when he sees her embracing her sweetheart. He leaves a pathetic farewell note and departs, concluding the film with a bittersweet ending that would become emblematic of the Tramp character: Shuffling off slowly down the dirt road, barely able to drag himself along, he suddenly perks up and strides jauntily off, his knees pumping and his spirit restored, eager for the next adventure.

Everything later audiences came to love about Chaplin is contained in this film: his gallant knight in bum's clothing; his graceful, acrobatic fight sequences; and his equally graceful comic inability to do the most simple, conventional tasks. In addition, the intrusion of real-world violence in the form of a gunshot that actually injures him, and his painful romantic disillusion, were virtually unprecedented in comic films up to this time. Chaplin was well aware of what he was doing, and agonized to interviewers over whether he could get away with stretching the boundaries of comedy in this way.[5]

While some critics rightfully pointed out that the jarring notes struck by the naturalistic and serious elements are not well supported in this particular film, no one questioned the superb ending. Through his eloquent mime, Chaplin makes the simple act of walking down the road into a celebration of the indomitable human spirit. Described in words, the scene sounds clichéd, but seeing it—even out of context, as most modern viewers are likely to do—it remains compelling. With this ending Chaplin moved into cinematic immortality. He would do variations on it in *The Pilgrim*, *The Circus*, *Modern Times*, and *Monsieur Verdoux*.

A few months later Chaplin resurrected his unlikely *New Janitor* hero for *The Bank*, borrowing the foiling-the-robbery theme from the earlier film and skillfully combining it with the unrequited love theme from *The Tramp*. This time Charlie is no sad sack, but his typical self, a feisty, unrepentant bungler, wreaking messy havoc with mop and bucket. And although Edna's love interest in *The Bank* proves to be a cowardly cad during the robbery, Charlie *still* doesn't win her, because both the robbery and Charlie's heroics take place in a dream. Charlie is bereft, but for Chaplin it's a triumph, a significant advance in storytelling in which the comic and serious elements perfectly balance each other, just as they had in the shorter Keystone film.

Police, which ends the Essanay series, once again contrasts Charlie's values with those of the criminals he meets at the lower end of the social ladder. It begins with a sequence that was probably shocking to some members of the 1915 audience: A crooked street preacher picks Charlie's pocket while lecturing him about going straight. Chaplin's social commentary was growing more pointed. A remarkable scene of people entering a flophouse features a comic but unsparing gallery of the victims of poverty, a far more realistic gathering than in any Keystone film. They include the suspicious Jewish proprietor; an alcoholic Italian; a filthy man wearing an eye patch; a pudgy, flamboyant homosexual; a "dude" in ragged clothing and a battered top hat; and a deathly pale, hollow-cheeked consumptive, who coughs weakly and looks ready to keel over. The proprietor sympathetically allows the ailing man in for free, but bars Charlie, whose tiny reserve of cash has been filched by the street preacher. Charlie tries to con his way in by coughing, but even sucking his cheeks into a "fish face" doesn't work. Because there's nothing mean-spirited about Charlie's imitation, we can't take offense at this early example of sick humor; in fact, it's startling and quite funny. The gag would not have worked nearly as well if Charlie were playing his earlier aggressive self, but in this film he is himself a downtrodden victim of poverty.

Denizens of the slum seek shelter for the night in *Police*.

The consumptive. *Police*.

Thrown out of the flophouse, Charlie runs into his old cellmate, a tough-looking, scowling thug who offers him work—burglarizing a home. But Charlie proves to be more a bungler than a burglar, and has no idea how to choose objects of value. He makes such a racket by overturning things that they are soon discovered by the lady of the house, played once again by the stately and lovely Edna. She cooks a meal for the would-be crooks and begs them not to disturb her ailing mother upstairs. Charlie is so struck by her beauty and touched by her kindness that he has a change of heart. As he had in *The Tramp*, he sacrifices his own short-term gain by turning against his larcenous cohort to protect her.[6]

While in New York to sign his Mutual contract in February 1916, Chaplin came upon an old Karno comrade, Eric Campbell, starring in a Broadway operetta. Chaplin immediately signed him for his new series, and it was one of the best professional decisions of his life. Eric proved to be a superb comic heavy. At 6 feet, 4 inches tall and nearly three hundred pounds, he towered over Charlie; more importantly, he was more powerful and threatening than any previous adversary. Chaplin featured him in eleven of the twelve Mutuals, and his contribution to their success can hardly be overstated.

Before Karno discovered him, Campbell had played in many straight melodramas in his native Scotland, as he demonstrates in the films by the ease with which he assumes the classic attitudes and postures of the genre. A large, barrel-chested man, he had a penchant for standing balletically on his toes with one foot extended. His outrageous makeup, almost always featuring huge, sharply pointed Mephistophelean eyebrows, enhances his performances, as does his ludicrously tapering bottom half, the opposite of Charlie's physique. In addition, his strong, sweeping gestures perfectly counterpoint Chaplin's light, quicksilver movements. His performances are gems of comic exaggeration. They're more funny than frightening, but contain just enough menace that we believe the bully of *Easy Street* and the waiter in *The Immigrant* might really pose a threat to Charlie. With this giant as a foil, Chaplin was able to bring a new kind of excitement to his chase and fight scenes, climaxing in their epic battles in *Easy Street*.

Working with Campbell inspired Chaplin in other ways as well. For the first time he fully justifies his insult humor by making his adversary one up on him: Eric is invariably richer, of a higher social class, Charlie's employer, or simply a brutal Goliath to Charlie's David. Chaplin stacks the deck further by combining Eric's physical or social superiority with bad behavior: He's a thug, a thief, a bully, short-tempered, mean, a masher—

Eric Campbell confronts Charlie in *The Rink*.

in short, he's all the Keystone comic heavies wrapped into one package, bursting at the seams with hostility toward Charlie, his natural enemy. Against Eric's boiling antagonism and outraged dignity, Chaplin is able to spin exhilarating triumphs, and the resulting explosion of insult humor is at the heart of the two funniest Mutuals, *The Cure* and *The Adventurer*. With Campbell, Chaplin arrived at the apotheosis of his Keystone rogue character. While he would go on to wreak havoc in circuses, factories, and restaurants, it was never again such carefree and joyous havoc.

Chaplin signed Campbell for his First National series that began in 1918, but his great adversary died in an automobile accident after filming *The Adventurer*. How Chaplin's films might have been different had Campbell lived, we'll never know. Certainly, the big man had a greater dramatic range than he demonstrated in his brief film career in the Mutuals. We see glimpses in several films, notably *Behind the Screen*, in which Eric plays the sleepy, gluttonous boss of uncomplaining workhorse Charlie. The only time Eric perks up, before the inevitable fight that climaxes the film, is when he sees Charlie kissing Edna, improbably disguised as a male stagehand. Eric's mincing, mocking dance shows his agility and versatility, and hints that he would have gone far beyond his angry bully roles, just as Chaplin went beyond what he had done in the Mutuals.

With the First National series of films, the stories become more complex, the sets more realistic, and the heavies more naturalistic. The thieves in *A Dog's Life*, *The Pilgrim*, and *The Kid* seem more like hardened professional criminals than Sennett stereotypes. By contrast, when Eric plays a thief in *The Pawnshop*, he melodramatically strokes

Eric enjoying his lunch in *Behind the Screen.*

his handlebar mustache and practically drools over the loot he intends to pilfer. He's powerful, but over the top enough that he poses no serious threat. Even Eric's slum tough in *Easy Street* is a caricature of real power, a parody of the classic melodramatic black-hearted villain, as exemplified in the scene in which Eric prevents Charlie from leaving his apartment by effortlessly swallowing the large key. One can almost hear the audience hissing. Against such an adversary night sticks have no effect; to subdue him, Charlie has to gas him or drop an iron stove from a second-floor window onto his head. Even handcuffs can't restrain him—Eric rips them apart like paper.

Chaplin's continuing growth as a storyteller led him to tone down the exaggeration. Some of the thugs in the First National films still sport funny mustaches, but, with the sole exception of Charles Riesner's bully in *The Kid*—his upper half padded to resemble Eric's—they no longer play comic superhumans.

The first film in the new series sets the tone. Stealing is more than a plot device in *A Dog's Life*; it becomes the film's central motif. The film begins with Charlie as a thief, stealing his breakfast from a hot dog vendor. Charlie's theft is justified because he's homeless and hungry, woken from his slumber in a vacant lot by the wafting smell of hot dogs on the other side of the fence. He filches one easily, but before he can finish it, a cop appears. The scene is a lively little comic ballet of desperation, a merry chase in which the cop laboriously circles the fence while Charlie simply rolls back and forth under it, managing in the process to untie the cop's shoelace and stick a pin into his rear end. Later Charlie steals pastries from a lunch wagon. He and the proprietor, played by his brother Sydney, turn it into a game: Charlie stuffs pastry after pastry into his mouth, while Sydney whirls around again and again, determined to catch him in the act.

By themselves, these two scenes would put Charlie in a role similar to that of his old Keystone rogue, except for several elements: the gritty slum environment, Charlie's evident need to stave off starvation, and, most importantly, the fact that in between the scenes is a third scene in which Charlie, again in a rhythmically intricate sequence, tries and fails to get a job from the local employment office—tougher men "steal" his place in line, until he's the only one left without a job. Charlie, in other words, steals because he is unable to find work, not because he is of the criminal class, and not because he is looking for something for nothing. There is no flaw in his character. On the contrary, he even rescues a starving dog from a pack of more aggressive hounds. Charlie has no means, but he has a heart. He's hungry, homeless, and abandoned by the callous world, but he has some surprising inner resources that enable him to make his way.

As he had in earlier films, Chaplin contrasts Charlie's resourcefulness and generosity with the hard-heartedness of the heavies of the film. After pulling a drunken millionaire into an alley, the two thieves emerge to find cops in pursuit. Except for the sudden jerk of the millionaire into the alley, nothing about the theft is comic. Nor are any of the characters individualized. They don't have to be—the choreography of the scene clearly defines who they are. The crooks see the millionaire offscreen, then duck into the alley as he rounds the corner and comes into view, toddling unsteadily down the sidewalk toward the camera. They yank him into the alley, but the actual mugging is left to the imagination. An instant later, the thieves emerge with the wallet and are immediately chased off, in opposite directions, by two cops. After they vanish, the millionaire staggers out of the alley, rubbing his head.

As well as being an ingeniously designed pattern of movement, the scene leaves no time for comic posturing; the thieves *are* the action of mugging and fleeing. It is filmed, as usual, in a single long shot, interrupted only by a cutaway showing Albert Austin eluding his cop by ducking into the empty lot, then cutting back to the first shot to show the millionaire emerging from the alley. One directorial detail shows Chaplin's ever-increasing mastery of visual storytelling: A wooden sign sticks out from the alley at about head height, and it knocks the millionaire's top hat off as he disappears into the alley. The hat drops to the slum sidewalk, a forlorn reminder that this inebriated swell has staggered into the wrong neighborhood. When he emerges, dazed but apparently none the worse for wear, he staggers back up the sidewalk the way he came, leaving the hat behind.

Later, in the Green Lantern Café, one of the thieves wants to dance with the new singer, Edna. He pulls her to him roughly. There is none of the comic exaggeration Eric Campbell brought to such scenes, wiggling his eyebrows or making kissing motions with his fingers to his lips. This man seems to have more than flirtation on his mind. When the shy and naive Edna resists, she is promptly fired by her boss. While the exchange is ostensibly about dancing with customers and encouraging them to drink, it's the first hint in a Chaplin film, however muted, that a stock movie character like a saloon singer might in real life be a prostitute; Chaplin had found Charlie's natural milieu in the slum streets, but he refused to romanticize it. Instead, he offered the viewer a glimpse into the harsh reality of poverty.

When Charlie created the misunderstanding between two men in the dressing room of *The Cure*, it was gratuitous. When he does the same thing with the two thieves in the arm-substitution scene of *A Dog's Life* it is not only a satisfying reversal, but reveals the darkness at the heart of these thieves. As we saw in the last chapter, they quickly go from being "thick as thieves" to mortal enemies. And this time they are holding not shoes or fake Sennett bricks, but a broken bottle. When Charlie dives headlong into the lunch wagon, they fire away at him with guns. Chaplin makes the scene comic by transforming the wagon into a shooting gallery—Charlie and Sydney's heads pop up like mechanical targets—but that doesn't alter the evident danger as the bullets shatter the cups hanging behind them. Charlie sticks a plate in the line of fire so that the bullets punch two eyeholes into it and, with characteristic absurdity, holds it in front of his face as a shield. The scene climaxes when the thieves charge the wagon and quite viciously choke Charlie on the countertop. When the police show up to arrest them, Charlie escapes with a graceful backward somersault as they're hauled away. As a little coda to the violent sequence, a dazed and bedraggled Sydney emerges from behind the counter, plucking shattered crockery from his collar.

It is only one short step from these thieves to Chaplin's ultimate heavy: Black Larson in *The Gold Rush*. As indicated by his name, Black Larson is villainy and treachery personified. We watch him cold-bloodedly murder two policemen and leave Charlie and Mack Swain to starve in a snowbound cabin.

Black Larson is no caricature. A powerful-looking man with a full, natural-looking beard and mustache, he goes about his business efficiently. Even the thieves of *A Dog's Life* retained some comic exaggeration in their movements and in Austin's droopy mustache. But Black Larson is played perfectly straight, not even scowling as he guns down the cops. He is also the first major character to die in a Chaplin film.[7] The only time his cold, expressionless demeanor changes is after Big Jim has wrested a rifle from him. He crouches, feral and panting, glaring at Jim with icy rage. Since his role in the film is that of a malevolent force of nature, utterly ruthless and beyond human redemption, it is fitting that an act of nature eliminates him—"The North. A law unto itself." Larson is caught on a collapsing cliff and plunges to his death. This end gets around the problem of tone that would arise if a less naturalistic character like Big Jim killed him. Certainly Charlie couldn't do it.

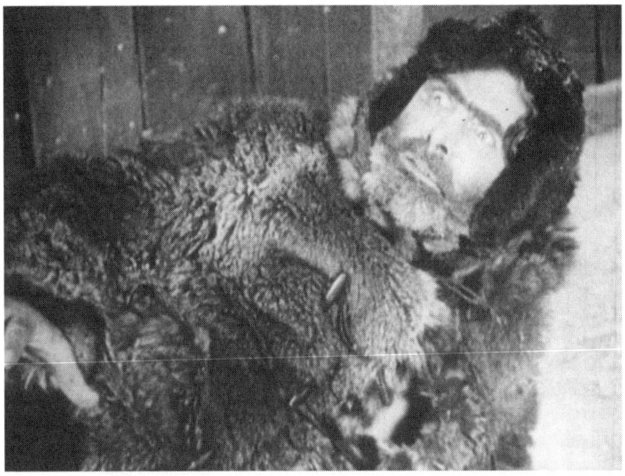

Tom Murray as Black Larson. *The Gold Rush.*

Larson is an archetypal killer, but the progression from type to archetype in Chaplin's films is neither linear nor absolute. Throughout his career, types and caricatures drawn from Keystone models, his stage experience, and his memories of Victorian theatre continue to populate the films. Following *The Gold Rush* Chaplin made *The Circus*, in which his adversary is the owner-ringmaster of the circus. The ringmaster controls more than the action in the ring; he's a puppeteer who controls all the other characters, and whose pitiless actions drive the plot. At the film's opening he throws the pretty equestrian—his stepdaughter—to the ground because she fails to execute a trick properly. He's not only a mean boss, he's a lousy parent. He's also a melodramatic cliché, down to his handlebar mustache and whip. But although cruel, he's neither evil, like Black Larson, nor comic, like Mack Swain and Eric Campbell. It's not a bad performance, simply a bit one-dimensional for a major character in a feature film.

Though they are cut from the same cloth as the ringmaster, the performances of the orphan officials and the doctor in *The Kid* work much better. First, such characters seem to emanate from the Dickensian slum setting

Chuck Riesner, Edna, and Charlie in *The Kid.*

Riesner as a pickpocket. *The Pilgrim.*

of *The Kid*, with its palpable poverty and scruffy, marginal inhabitants. Second, their callousness is effectively played against a gripping and urgent reality: As they bicker with Charlie, the pale-faced Kid lies listlessly in bed behind them. Chaplin's brilliant comic reactions to the men underscore their pomposity without undercutting the real power they wield over him and Jackie. The stakes—Jackie's health and Charlie's tenuous guardianship of the boy—are high. By contrast, the scenes with the ringmaster lack emotional depth.

On the other hand, the *comic* heavies in Chaplin's films, derived directly from their Keystone counterparts, are refreshingly well drawn. Mack Swain, with whom Chaplin had worked so effectively at Keystone, is very funny as both the apoplectic golfer in *The Idle Class* and Charlie's impatient boss in *Pay Day*, before giving his final and most brilliant performance for Chaplin as Big Jim, Charlie's gruff but lovable cabinmate in *The Gold Rush.*

Two of the best comic heavies in the First National series are played by Chuck Riesner, who also worked as Chaplin's assistant director during this period.[8] In *The Kid* Riesner plays a bully, brother to a boy the Kid has bested in a fight. He's the ultimate brute, a simian creature with cauliflower ears and ridiculously padded shoulders. Riesner is doing an obvious variant on Eric's *Easy Street* character, right down to bending a lamppost and experiencing a religious conversion. But Riesner, a former boxer himself, puts his own stamp on the portrayal with his expression of punch-drunk idiocy.

In *The Pilgrim* the versatile Riesner plays a completely different kind of character, all slippery cunning and guile as yet another of Charlie's ex-cellmates. He sniffs opportunity when he sees Charlie, dressed up as a bogus minister, strolling down the street in the company of Edna's family. Charlie shoos him away, but Riesner determines to loot the rubes, with or without Charlie's cooperation. A gregarious backslapper, he effortlessly talks his way into the home. However, Charlie outwits the nimble thief at every turn in a scene of delightfully conceived one-upmanship: Riesner deftly lifts Mack Swain's wallet, and Charlie just as deftly lifts it from Riesner and returns it. When Riesner retrieves it Charlie performs a mock magic trick, flourishing a handkerchief at both men and producing the wallet he has "mysteriously" transferred into Riesner's pocket. The smooth editing of the complex scene reinforces the elegant movement pattern of the actors, so that the viewer can fully appreciate the desperate game being played out with the stolen wallet under the noses of the unwitting family.

Money motivates the scene, just as it motivates so many scenes in Chaplin's films. His strong feelings on the subject influenced how he developed the roles of his heavies, and led him to infuse his films with their distinct vein of social commentary.

Keystone films only occasionally use the world of the rich as a background for rude physical comedy, *Tillie's Punctured Romance* being the notable exception. For the most part they are little concerned with exploring the niceties of economic and class distinctions. But class consciousness, the yawning gulf between haves and have-nots, is an important feature of Chaplin's work almost from the outset. He was acutely aware of the rigid class system that limited his prospects in his native country, and perhaps that's why he delighted in portraying bogus noblemen or members of the upper crust in stories that revolve around the discovery of his imposture. At Keystone he does it in *Making a Living, Caught in a Cabaret*, and *Her Friend the Bandit*; at Essanay in *A Jitney Elopement*; and at Mutual in *The Count, The Rink*, and *The Adventurer*. Along the way he also plays genuine men of means in *Cruel, Cruel Love*, *The Rounders*, *A Night in the Show*, *One A.M.*, and *The Idle Class*.

In his Keystone period, Chaplin's sketchbook stage, he experiments freely with mixing and matching both costume pieces and character traits; the only real constants are his mustache and the big shoes. As the Tramp evolves into the penniless vagabond who stars in Chaplin's feature films, an interesting pattern emerges. Whenever Chaplin departs from his standard characterization to play more "solid" members of society, he becomes seriously flawed. When he's rich, he's invariably a drunk (*One A.M.*, *The Cure*, *The Idle Class*). When he's a lower-middle-class citizen, such as the henpecked construction worker in *Pay Day*, his preoccupations are drinking and philandering. In Chaplin's world, having money releases one from the struggle for survival, but it also seems to lead to dissipation—or worse.

When he joins the middle class, he becomes *Monsieur Verdoux*, whose "business" is marrying and murdering wealthy women. Verdoux, of course, is a sinister variation on the many fake French counts he plays, who unsuccessfully try to woo heiresses. For Chaplin, to have real power means to abuse it, as he shows us when he becomes the maniacal dictator in *The Great Dictator*. Chaplin's dictator is a preening idiot, the apotheosis of Sterling and all the hotheaded clowns Chaplin found at Keystone—except that this idiot has ended up as the malevolent, war-mongering leader of an all-too-willing nation of followers.

In his last starring performance Chaplin finally plays a genuine aristocrat, the deposed and powerless head of state, Shahdov, in *A King in New York*. This regal personage is, for once, a moral and well-intentioned man, despite his former wealth and position. But he's also completely ineffective at achieving his goals. No one is interested in his Utopian plan for disarmament and world peace, and he can't even save a similarly idealistic young boy from the horror of betraying his parents during the Communist witch-hunt of the McCarthy era. On the contrary, he is trivialized, duped by advertising executives into using his celebrity to help advertise products. For his final role Chaplin, who entered films playing a sharper in *Making a Living*, ends up as a flack for modern sharpers.

Clearly Chaplin had strong negative feelings toward the rich and powerful, no doubt stemming from his years of childhood privation. While his films are often compared to the novels of Charles Dickens, they are devoid of the kind, wealthy benefactors who brighten Dickens's gloomy world. In his autobiography he rebukes anyone who would romanticize either poverty, including the picturesque poverty of his films, or the world of privilege:

> I found poverty neither attractive nor edifying. It taught me nothing but a distortion of values, an overrating of the virtues and graces of the rich and the so-called better classes. . . . Wealth and celebrity, on the contrary, taught me to view the world in proper perspective, to discover that men of eminence, when I came close to them, were as deficient in their way as the rest of us.[9]

Wealth, at least, bought freedom, and Chaplin valued that above all else. It is clear from his employment history how he rankled under any form of authority. He'd had about all the bossing he could take under the authoritarian Karno, and as a filmmaker he proved intractable about artistic compromise, demanding complete artistic control almost from the outset. His increasing popularity eventually gave him the clout to achieve it, though he burned through four different employers in as many years. It is worth noting that in his last film for Essanay Chaplin played a prisoner getting out of jail, and in his

Free at last. *Police*.

And again. *The Pilgrim*.

last films for Mutual and First National he played a prisoner escaping to freedom.

Chaplin's uneasy relationships with his bosses is reflected in Charlie's invariably poor relationships with his. Some of those bosses are stock characters, their only flaw that they present an obstacle to Charlie's fun. For example, Charlie runs rings around Henry Bergman, the proprietor of *The Pawnshop*. Poor Bergman is only trying to run his modest business, but his simple demands prove hugely oppressive to the irrepressible Charlie, who would rather fight, flirt, and generally cut up.

While the natural antipathy between bosses and workers has been a perennial theme of movies from the beginning, Chaplin complicates the equation with telling twists and ironies. In *The New Janitor*, as we saw, Charlie's bumbling incompetence gets him fired, but he shows his mettle by foiling a theft. While his admirable qualities are lost on his boss, the integrity of Charlie's blue-collar menial is pointedly juxtaposed with the white-collar criminality of the supposedly respectable store manager.

Two other early films contain effective touches of the same cynical view of bosses. An uncomplaining Charlie becomes a literal workhorse in *Work*, pulling a cart through city streets and up an impossibly steep grade. His boss sits back in the cart smoking, occasionally goading Charlie helpfully along by whipping him enthusiastically with Charlie's bamboo cane. In this film Charlie's incompetence provides poetic redress, as he wreaks havoc on the boss and the household with paper, paste, brush, and ladders. Chaplin retools the idea, with Eric as the boss, in *Behind the Screen*. This time Charlie is his super-competent self, doing all the work as Eric snoozes. Somehow Eric repeatedly gets the credit while Charlie is unjustly blamed for being lazy. Again, a violent finale balances the scale.

The telling culmination of Charlie's uneasy relationship with his employers occurs in *Modern Times*. The boss of the factory sits at his desk in his huge office, trying to distract himself with a jigsaw puzzle and the funny papers. His job has been almost automated out of existence, and he has little actual work to do. He doesn't even have to walk onto the factory floor—he communicates with his employees through closed-circuit television. Years before George Orwell introduced Big Brother in his dystopian novel *1984*, this omniscient manager even spies on Charlie taking a smoke break in the bathroom.

Charlie has two direct encounters with the man. In the first, the boss chooses Charlie as the guinea pig to demonstrate the new feeding machine, with predictably disastrous results. Later, after Charlie reduces the factory routine to shambles, he sprays oil into the boss's face, a final coup de grâce before being carted off to the lunatic asylum. But unlike Charlie's previous unreasonable, uncomprehending, lazy, or incompetent bosses, this man is as much a victim as Charlie. He's an ordinary bureaucrat going through the motions, just doing his job.

Still later in the film, when Charlie encounters thieves during his rounds as night watchman in a department store, they turn out to be unemployed factory workers, like Charlie the victims of strikes and the Depression. "We ain't burglars—we're hungry," says Charlie's old pal. As Chaplin had earlier learned to ground Charlie's larcenous behavior in necessity, so now he justifies—or at least, sympathizes with—the antisocial behavior of his traditional adversaries; it has been forced upon them by their circumstances. Looked at in this way, even the callous doctor and orphan officials in *The Kid* aren't evil villains, but rather simply the unfeeling representatives of an inhumane society. Even bosses and thieves become sympathetic when seen in the proper context, their actions emblematic of social problems rather than personal character flaws. The result, ironically, is that the Tramp of the feature films becomes a true outsider, since he is comfortable neither with individuals nor with the society that spawns them. Society itself has become the heavy.

Because of their omnipresence in his films, the police represent a special class of heavies for Chaplin. Tracing the way they developed throughout his career reveals the emerging moral dimension in his work, and the extraordinary distance he traveled as a filmmaker.

While Charlie is intimidated by the police at Keystone, he is able to outmaneuver them pretty easily. Except for the shambling Conklin, the police in his films are played fairly naturalistically. They try, usually without much success, to maintain order when the park shenanigans grow too rowdy, and they're always handy when a chase is required.

By the end of his Essanay year, police are the subjects of more pointed satire. When a panicked Edna calls the police as burglars loot her house in *Police*, they are taking their tea—and their time. They proceed to her house at a leisurely pace, enjoying the ride in the backseat of their car, yawning and puffing away at their cigars. Chaplin continues the mockery in *Easy Street*. Here the cops are totally ineffective against slum violence, so cowardly that a small child is able to terrify them by pointing his finger and saying, "Bang." It's up to Charlie to join the force and clean up the neighborhood.

Usually he's on the other side of the law, of course, leading lines of cops on merry chases in the other Mutuals, notably *The Adventurer*. But with the First National films the cops change, becoming less humorous and more threatening. No longer human oddities with comic makeup and fumbling behavior, they develop into formidable presences, more than ever objects of fear and avoidance for Charlie. In *The Gold Rush* the cops are played with complete naturalism, staying warm in their tent until Black Larson discovers and murders them. Types cannot be killed, but characters can.

In *Modern Times* cops are omnipresent, part of the background milieu of the Depression, and they clearly represent the interests of the haves over the dispossessed have-nots. They arrest Charlie several times, prevent angry strikers from entering the factory, and break up a peaceful demonstration by riding through the crowd on horseback. Jail becomes a haven for Charlie in this film, an irony clear to anyone who had followed his cinematic journey. The ironies multiply, as Charlie becomes the hero of the jail by foiling a jailbreak attempt, his superhuman strength and courage the result of an accidental snort of cocaine. Charlie gets the royal treatment after that, including a private cell, the morning paper, and friendly guards to chat with. But when offered a pardon, Charlie doesn't want to leave; as the film makes clear, the real prison is the harsh, Depression-battered outside world.

In *The Great Dictator* the cops take on the specific and ominous roles of Nazi storm troopers. These goons march in lockstep and whitewash the word "Jew" on store windows. When Paulette Goddard stands up to them and calls them cowards, they pelt her with tomatoes, ruining her clean laundry and bringing her to tears; she mutters, "Pigs!" But in this case the tonal mix doesn't quite work, because the slovenly looks, exaggerated sarcasm, and slapstick behavior of the Nazis undercuts their power, and doesn't properly set up Paulette's strong reaction. It works much better in their subsequent scenes with Charlie, because he *can* fight back, and they simply become bumbling, ineffectual cops; the scenes, in fact, become characteristic Keystone Kops melees.

Years later Mel Brooks would effectively lampoon Nazis in *The Producers*, both onscreen and in a wildly successful Broadway show. But Brooks, of course, is an equal opportunity offender, gleefully poking fun at every taboo subject under the sun. There's not a serious soul in sight—nor was there an impending Nazi threat looming over the audience.

Chaplin, facing the threat head-on, had made a career of combining comic and serious elements. One wants the trooper scenes to work better because of Chaplin's sensationally successful lampoon of Hitler elsewhere in the film. *The Great Dictator* drew mixed reviews at the time and continues to be an artistically controversial work, although its historical importance is incontestable. But it was very well received by its intended audience, becoming the biggest hit of Chaplin's career.

Tom Murray as the good policeman. *The Pilgrim.*

Other attempts to deal with the subject in a seriocomic way drew similarly mixed reactions, including Ernst Lubitsch's *To Be or Not to Be* (1942) with Jack Benny, which, while a modest box office success, was savaged by critics. The topic was too loaded; even half a century later Roberto Benigni's *Life Is Beautiful* (1997), though it won an Oscar as best foreign film, had its detractors.

Chaplin made it clear what a law officer *ought* to be in an earlier film, *The Pilgrim*. Even as this sheriff arrests Charlie at the end of the film, he realizes that, despite being an escaped convict and bogus minister, Charlie is, in fact, a genuinely good human being. After all, he has recovered and returned Edna's stolen money, risking his own life and freedom in the process. So, taking the law into his own hands, the sheriff boots Charlie over the border into Mexico. This extraordinary act makes this lawman unique in Chaplin's films. By recognizing Charlie's higher morality and bending the law to free him, he proves himself to be Chaplin's one cop hero.[10] In the world of Chaplin's films the rest of the force is a motley crew of bunglers and cowards—or worse, the insensitive enforcers of an unjust social order.

Heroines

Despite the presence of many beautiful women, the Keystone film world was anything but romantic. The reigning comic beauty was Mabel Normand. Like the once-potent comedy of the Keystone films, much of Mabel's humor has dimmed with the passage of time, so her indisputable position as the outstanding comedienne of silent films may seem puzzling to modern viewers. Comedy producer Hal Roach said,

> Whatever she did the audience would roar with laughter and to this day I don't know why. She was sort of a pixie, I guess, but you knew that if a guy kicked her, she'd kick him back.[11]

She certainly was a pixie, a cover girl for celebrated artists like Charles Dana Gibson before she found movie fame. And on screen, she is an appealing and vibrant presence: her huge, dreamy eyes gazing directly at the camera with all the insinuating boldness of Chaplin's; her cupid's bow mouth held in a knowing pout. For audiences of the time, the comedy likely stemmed from the startling contrast between her demure good looks and her uninhibited physicality. Mabel matched the antic male comics around her stunt for stunt, punch for punch, and fall for fall. Assertive and given to such "masculine" behavior as driving race cars, motorcycles, and planes, Mabel is a clear embodiment of the "New Woman" heralded by Ibsen and Shaw. But the story has been Americanized and given a Horatio Alger twist; like Mary Pickford, she often plays penniless, plucky young women who must make their own way in the world.

Today Mabel is remembered primarily for the scandals that rocked her career, and for being Chaplin's first female costar. He could hardly have had a better one to help him launch his career. Mabel was so popular that her first name was often used in the titles of her pictures, including four that she made with Chaplin. As we've noted, their relationship in the films is one of equals. Once their initial offscreen tussle over artistic control was worked out, they worked wonderfully well as a team. While Charlie often abuses and takes advantage of Mabel, she repays him in kind, such as when she tricks him with the boxing dummy in *Mabel's Married Life*. And when required, she could charmingly play a standard ingénue to set off his antics.

Mabel, like Lucille Ball after her, is that great rarity, a pretty clown. Usually female clowns are funny-looking, like the formidable Marie Dressler. At Keystone, Louise Fazenda often played a caricatured hick country lass, and goofy-looking Polly Moran was, for a time, the reigning queen of broad slapstick, specializing in uninhibited, man-hungry tomboys. At Mutual, Chaplin found an equally eccentric "female" in portly Henry Bergman, who looked properly grotesque in drag. Bergman is terrific as a flirtatious wife in *The Rink*, complete with pratfalls, and, of course, he's the woman who rolls around the rocking deck so memorably in *The Immigrant*.

Character actresses such as Phyllis Allen and Alice Davenport—plain, stout, and a bit older—often played the sweethearts or wives of secondary lead characters like Mack Swain, and frequently figure in the farcical mix-ups between couples in the park. They also play the crucial roles of battle-axe wives, there to lower the boom on their errant husbands. Allen plays Chaplin's disapproving wife in several Keystones, and reunited with him for his last short comedy, *Pay Day*. Her baleful gaze and hostile demeanor understandably drives poor Charlie to seek boozy companionship in a local saloon.

It is the last time Chaplin plays a henpecked husband until the battle-axe reemerges in a blaze of glory in the form of Martha Raye in *Monsieur Verdoux*. Raye is the apogee of the battle-axe as the crass, indestructible Annabella, who looks into the water while fishing with Verdoux and declares, "I see one. Ooh, it's a monster—no, it's me!" A monster, yes, but the one truly comic performance by a woman in the Chaplin canon. Her non sequiturs, braying laugh, and gullibility make a wonderful contrast to fussbudget Verdoux, and their scenes together are the highlights of the film.

The clowns and character actresses at Keystone are outnumbered by the more innocuous ornamental heroines, and it was this role that became most important in Chaplin's later work. Minta Durfee, Cecile Arnold, and other more or less interchangeable lovelies are the objects and victims of Charlie's affections in the Keystones, doing little more than standing demurely around to be flirted with, on occasion rejecting his affections, but as often as not tolerating them. Chaplin found in such women a vein of romantic and comic inspiration for his character that he would pursue in the coming years. A poster for Chaplin's eighth Keystone film, *Cruel, Cruel Love*, shows Charlie gazing worshipfully up at Durfee; the poster prophetically describes him as "Sentimental Charlie."

Chaplin played female roles himself, twice at Keystone and once at Essanay. In *A Busy Day*, a short Keystone quickie improvised at a military parade, he plays an unattractive and violent termagant. His portrayal is straight out of the pantomime dame tradition of English pantomime, but with more acrobatic humor. Chaplin tries to wring laughter from such unfeminine behavior as wiping his nose with his dress, taking spills, and fighting, especially when he catches husband Mack Swain with another woman. The reissue title, *The Militant Suffragette*, tells us what appeal such an abrasive character must have held for a contemporary audience, like a later generation's crude jokes about bra-burning feminists.

The Masquerader, a fascinating backstage film, is another matter. Charlie arrives at the studio in street

Edna Purviance in *The Immigrant.*

clothes and puts on his Tramp outfit and makeup, skirmishing the while with fellow actor Fatty Arbuckle. He dons female clothing after he's fired for being an incompetent movie actor, returning to the studio to very effectively "vamp" the director. In this film, as in *A Woman*, made a year later at Essanay, Chaplin becomes a genuinely seductive female, surprisingly attractive, establishing many of the demure postures and gestures that his later leading ladies employed under his direction. The comedy is much richer in the two later films, because we get the triple treat of marveling at how well Chaplin portrays a sexy woman, enjoying the spectacle of how "she" holds the drooling males at bay, and relishing the inevitable revelation scene.

Soon after leaving Keystone for Essanay, Chaplin discovered Edna Purviance. Then nineteen years old, Edna became the leading lady in almost every film Chaplin made from 1915 through 1923.[12] Although she plays many different characters in these thirty-six films—naive country girls, chambermaids, rich women—there is a consistency about her movements and her relationship to Charlie that makes all her portrayals variations on the same theme, just as Chaplin played variations on his character. A beautiful blonde woman, Edna was definitely an ornamental heroine. But Chaplin was at first doubtful of her acting ability:

> I doubted whether she could act or had any humor, she looked so serious. Nevertheless, with these reservations, we engaged her. She would at least be decorative in my comedies.[13]

Edna, who had no prior acting experience, would become far more than decorative. With her gravity, measured movements, fair coloring, and comfortable, slightly fleshy body, she provided a background that anchored Chaplin's performances both physically and emotionally. She brought great dignity to her roles, as well as a concentration on Chaplin that helped the audience focus on his more subtle movements.

The combination of Eric Campbell as antagonist and Edna as heroine helps to give the Mutual films their peculiar iconographic quality, for Edna's role came to represent an idealized vision of womanhood—beautiful, placid, receptive. Though cultural values a century on have changed our standards of female beauty and demeanor—many would prefer Mabel's feisty character—Edna's portrayals remain appealing not only because of her timeless beauty, but because her relationship with Charlie is brimming with quiet humor and genuine affection. Outtakes of the Mutual films only confirm the great rapport between them. They also attest to the effort that went into making Edna's performances seem so natural and relaxed.

Although Charlie often flirts outrageously with Edna, he never kicks her in the pants as he did Mabel. The slapstick action invariably happens around her, not with her. Which is not to say she is a passive participant in the films. A huge amount of screen time is devoted to scenes of their meeting and getting acquainted, a virtual catalogue of flirtation and budding romance that unfolds over their nine-year working relationship. Although Charlie and Edna are never seen in anything like a passionate embrace, Chaplin's ease in touching her gives their scenes a warm and sensuous ambiance. In some films—notably *The Bank*, *The Vagabond*, and *The Idle Class*—Edna is out of his league, and the romance just a poignant fantasy on his part. But usually she is charmed by him and quite responsive to his advances.

There are two notable anomalies in the Charlie-Edna saga: *Sunnyside*, in which they are sweethearts at the outset, and *A Day's Pleasure*, in which they are a married couple with children. These films, both made in 1919, mark a decided, if mercifully short, creative slump in Chaplin's career. Chaplin later attributed it to his personal unhappiness during the period. Late in 1917 he and Edna ended their offscreen romance, and soon after he embarked on a disastrous shotgun marriage with seventeen year-old actress Mildred Harris. While he was shooting *A Day's Pleasure*, Mildred gave birth to a physically impaired son, who lived only three days.

It's tempting to see in the failure of these two films a reflection of Chaplin's romantic and personal woes, and particularly the ending of his relationship with Edna, the longest and most loving relationship in his life up to that time. Charlie's sweet, hayseed romance with Edna in *Sunnyside* is threatened by a suave city slicker who charms her, just as three years earlier an artist had charmed her in *The Vagabond*. But this time the threat is a red herring; this slicker charms Edna only in Charlie's paranoid dream; she's actually steadfast and true. The self-pitying dream follows on the heels of another dream sequence, this one a self-indulgent idyll in which Charlie is thrown by a bull, knocked unconscious, and then dances, à la Nijinsky, with wood nymphs. While the often-reproduced stills from this scene are appealing, the scene is dramatically inert, as is the whole film, whose plot and gags seems listlessly recycled from earlier, better work, including a surprisingly mean-spirited sequence with Edna's dim-witted brother that might have come out of an early Keystone—except that it's not even remotely funny. Chaplin reprises his passive hero from *The New Janitor*, but without either that film's satisfying turnaround or a bittersweet ending as in *The Bank*. Emotionally, the film is a cipher.

Nor is there any tension, romantic or comic, in the throwaway film that follows, *A Day's Pleasure*. One subtle, if trivial, marker of Chaplin's disengagement is that it's the only film in which he has "hat hair." This time Chaplin and Edna are a married couple with two children, but there's no real interaction between them other than a perfunctory dance on the pitching deck of an excursion boat. These boat scenes pale in comparison to the shipboard scenes of *The Immigrant*. But the earlier film resonates with the excitement and optimism of young love, and features a poignant ending in which the two penniless immigrants get married on a rainy day. Late in life Chaplin said that *The Immigrant* "touched me more than any other film I made."[14] There is nothing touching about Chaplin's two 1919 films, which are, in fact, boring to watch. It's like seeing a good Chaplin impersonator; he's got the moves, but not the animating spirit.

But Chaplin immediately pulled himself out of his slump, embarking on his most ambitious film to date, *The Kid*. Chaplin began working on the film a scant ten days after his child died, interrupting production of *A Day's Pleasure*. As biographer David Robinson points out, it would be presumptuous for any commentator to connect the dots between Chaplin's personal tragedy and his screen incarnation as a perfect parent in *The Kid*—although the connection is so blatant that it's impossible to ignore. However, it is just as reasonable to surmise that it was a great relief for Chaplin to make a film about the love between a father and son, rather than reprise the never-ending romance with Edna yet again. In *Sunnyside* he even introduces the obligatory courtship sequence with the title, "And now, the 'romance.'" He might as well have said, "Time to move on." He does move on. In *The Kid* romance is only a bitter echo, in the form of Edna's shame as the unwed mother of the Kid.

The long cinematic relationship between Charlie and Edna ended gracefully a few years later, in their elegiac farewell scene in *The Pilgrim*. Chaplin realized that Edna was no longer the svelte ingénue his comedies now required. He tried to launch her career as a dramatic actress in *A Woman of Paris* (1923), his only venture into straight drama. She portrays a country girl gone wrong who becomes the mistress of a Parisian playboy. The role effectively ended her career, although, given her stardom, it seems likely that she could have gotten other roles if she had wanted them. Instead she simply retired from the screen, shunning the public spotlight and living out her days with all the quiet dignity she brought to her onscreen incarnation.

It is touchingly clear from his autobiography that Chaplin loved Edna as much as the evidence of the films suggests. He kept her on his studio payroll until her death in 1958. Toward the close of his autobiography he prints two of her last letters to him, admitting that through all the years he never wrote to her. He says simply,

> Shortly after I received this letter she died. And so the world grows young. And youth takes over. And we who have lived a little longer become a little more estranged as we journey on our way.[15]

Aside from his personal feelings for Edna even after their offscreen romance ended, in keeping her on his payroll, Chaplin was undoubtedly acknowledging her crucial importance in the films he made during the seminal years of his artistic development.

Several of Chaplin's heroines after Edna's departure are cast in the same pliant mold: Merna Kennedy, in a

Virginia Cherrill in *City Lights*.

Georgia Hale in *The Gold Rush.*

Paulette Goddard in *Modern Times.*

sweet, if bland, performance in *The Circus*; and Virginia Cherrill, in a sensitive performance as the blind heroine of *City Lights*. But both Georgia Hale in *The Gold Rush* and Paulette Goddard in *Modern Times* and *The Great Dictator* are made of sterner stuff. Small, dark, willful beauties, they are closer to the feisty Mabel in appearance and spirit.

While Chaplin had never played against a sophisticated heroine himself, Edna's final screen incarnation, as the mistress of a worldly and cynical playboy, may have emboldened him to create the role of the world-weary dance hall girl in *The Gold Rush*. Hale's performance, more than that of any other Chaplin heroine, seems bound to period. With her slouchy posture, insouciant air, and disdainful manner she is every inch a 1920s heroine. Nevertheless, she gives a very effective portrayal as the spangle-dressed saloon girl, although her precise duties, along with those of her hard-bitten girlfriends, are left to the imagination. Whether flashing with anger as she quarrels with her loutish suitor, Jack, or pretending an innocence she doesn't possess to toy with the smitten Charlie, she represents, in this epic film, the harshness of the brutal landscape, from which spring murderers like Black Larson. In this boomtown love is a commodity, a corollary to the pursuit of gold. It is only by fortuitous twists of fate that Charlie is able to find either. Interestingly, in the presence of the steely Georgia, Charlie takes on the qualities of the ingénue: He is sweet, demure, and utterly at her capricious mercy.

Goddard is unique among Chaplin's heroines in that she's more a buddy than a girlfriend. Rather than being a vision of beauty inspiring Charlie's worship and motivating his actions, she frequently initiates the action herself, dragging him along in her wake. In *Modern Times* she meets Charlie by literally bowling him over in her attempt to escape capture for stealing a loaf of bread. Soon after, she instigates their escape from a police van, finds jobs for both of them, and locates a shanty for them to set up house in. Her dynamism in the film is enhanced by the sped-up action and Chaplin's movement design for her, exemplified by her key gesture of balletically jumping in the air and twittering her feet when excited. Though more constrained by her role as an orphaned Jewish laundress in *The Great Dictator*, she retains her high-octane energy as a fast-talking dervish who's all too willing to take on the storm troopers.

The leading ladies of *Monsieur Verdoux*, Chaplin's most antiromantic film, are the comic but sexy Martha Raye and an assortment of decidedly less sexy variations on the battle-axe type, including the haggard and embittered Lydia, an older version of the harpy Chaplin plays in *A Busy Day*. She is rightfully suspicious of Verdoux's intentions, unlike the stately dowager Mme. Grosnay, who is vain and all too willing to fall for Verdoux's flattery.

There is also an ingénue, as in all Chaplin's films, but this time she appears only in a subplot, and her scenes with Chaplin play out with a sardonic twist. Verdoux picks up the Girl, played by Marilyn Nash, on the street one rainy night, figuring that she's a prostitute and thus a suitably "disposable" subject on which to test his new poison. She explains how she came to her present state: Trying to provide for an invalid husband, she foolishly pawned a rented typewriter. By the time she was released from prison, her husband had died. This tale softens Verdoux's heart, since he, too, practices his immoral trade to support an invalid spouse. So instead of poisoning her he feeds her, gives her some money, and sends her on her way. It is fascinating to watch Chaplin deal openly with a theme he only alludes to in earlier films like *A Dog's Life* and *The Gold Rush*, how prostitution is a form of sexual degradation that poverty imposes on women. Nash later reappears as the mistress of a wealthy munitions manufacturer. She has achieved a measure of success at her chosen profession, and the film makes it clear that her "client" operates on an even lower moral plane. As in *The Gold Rush*, love is merely another commodity.

Unselfish love reasserts itself in *Limelight*, in which Chaplin returns to a theme he dealt with twenty years earlier in *City Lights*, helping the heroine overcome a physical handicap. In this case, Claire Bloom plays a suicidal ballerina who suffers from hysterical paralysis. Chaplin plays Calvero, a washed-up, alcoholic music hall comedian. He has to muster his inner resources to nurse her back to health and artistic success.

Limelight, in a sense, continues where *City Lights* left off. The earlier film ended with the moment that the blind girl, her sight restored, sees her millionaire benefactor for the first time as he really is, a ragged derelict. It leaves the audience exquisitely poised on a dilemma: What can possibly happen next? *Limelight* addresses that uncomfortable question by doing something unprecedented in a Chaplin film: allowing the hero and heroine to switch roles. As the ballerina achieves success, Calvero's comeback attempts fail, and he goes into a decline. She then becomes *his* enthusiastic booster. Although she wants nothing more than to marry and care for him, he is convinced that her love is just gratitude. Besides, there's a daunting difference in their ages. He nobly rejects her and disappears from her life, leaving her brokenhearted.

Years later he resurfaces, and she helps him to organize a triumphant comeback performance. That finishes him, in a blaze of artistic glory, and releases her to fulfill her destiny. As in so many Chaplin films, there is no storybook happy ending. But this time there is also no bittersweet walk into an uncertain future. There is only sorrow, remembered laughter, and the consolation of art, passed from one generation to the next like a bright torch.

Love makes an encore in the voluptuous form of Sophia Loren in Chaplin's swan song, *A Countess from Hong Kong*. Chaplin, who appears only in a cameo, directed the international star in a performance that virtually reincarnates the vivacious Mabel Normand. Indeed, Loren's many attempts to avoid detection while wearing a pair of men's pajamas summon up *Mabel's Married Life*. Alas, the film features many of the old hijinks, but conjures little of the old inspiration. Thematically, at least, it's right on target, capping Chaplin's long preoccupation with the dance hall girl/prostitute theme, and placing Loren in the role of a Charlie-like stowaway on a ship bound for America—the immigrant, yet again. But despite Loren's game and energetic performance, the film is more a tribute to Chaplin's appreciation of female beauty than his ability to create a world illuminated by that beauty.

Buddies

A role that hardly exists in the amoral world of Keystone is the buddy or sidekick. At Keystone this role translates into *rival*. There is no friendship as such in the Keystones, since friends become enemies at the first appearance of a pretty woman to fight over. Everything is a pretext for the ubiquitous fights and chases.

Chaplin carries this rival role into his first two Essanay films, *His New Job* and *A Night Out*. Ben Turpin as Charlie's "friend" takes an enormous amount of physical abuse—much more than Chaplin gave Fatty Arbuckle in the similar Keystone drunken-spree film, *The Rounders*. While some of the routines in the two Turpin films are ingenious, so gratuitous is the cruelty that one is left with the impression that Chaplin genuinely disliked Turpin. He also chose not to include Turpin as a member of the stock company he was assembling.

As implied above, often buddies turn to heavies, as when Charlie must turn against his former cellmates in *Police* and *The Pilgrim*. In fact, friendship is a rarity for the solitary Tramp, and when it happens, its tenuous at best, as in Charlie's relationship with Mack Swain in *The Gold Rush*—friendship that evaporates when starvation sets in and Swain tries to eat Charlie. Such inconstancy becomes a driving force in Charlie's relationship with the millionaire of *City Lights*, who recognizes him as his bosom buddy only when roaring drunk.

This attitude about the inconstancy of friendship was echoed in Chaplin's life. On film the Tramp is more often rejected than rejecting—a reflection of the shy Chaplin who entered films at age twenty-four. But with professional success Chaplin found friendship pressed upon him from all sides. While he earned the fierce loyalty of his stock company and technical staff, many of whom stayed with him for years, by all accounts he did not enjoy the same success in his personal life. He had a disconcerting habit of capriciously breaking or "forgetting" appointments without notice, and his sudden enthusiasm, for people as well as projects, would unpredictably wane. "I like friends as I like music, when I am in the mood," he says in his autobiography. "To help a friend in need is easy, but to give him your time is not always opportune."[16]

Nevertheless, he goes on to dismiss as "nonsense" the many character sketches over the years that commented on his loner tendencies or his supposed incapacity for friendship. Alistair Cooke, who spent an intense summer helping him develop a film about Napoleon in 1933, had the opportunity to experience Chaplin's mercurial nature both personally and professionally. Chaplin abruptly canceled the film project, and the following summer literally left Cooke standing at the altar when he failed to show up as his best man. Chaplin later unapologetically feted the young couple. Recounting it in the 1970s, Cooke was philosophical and insightful:

> It was a trait I noticed later in other very poor boys who had grown very rich: a willful desire to flout the idea that there is any such thing as a duty or a social obligation.[17]

Friendship, in the sense of an affectionate relationship of equals, blossoms in only two films. In *The Kid* Jackie Coogan is not so much Charlie's adopted child as his younger self. For Chaplin, so plagued by film imitators during the teens,[18] it must have been immensely satisfying to train one of his own. And Jackie is such a brilliant little actor that he maintains his own personality even as he does some characteristic Chaplin gestures.

Another buddy. In *The Kid,* Chaplin created an icon of childhood that made Jackie Coogan into the first child star. Plaster statuette c. 1922.

Charlie's only adult buddy is Paulette Goddard in *Modern Times*. She alone shares his adventures and has some of her own, independent of his. She alone joins him in that final walk down the road.

Heroes

In action films the plot usually centers around a protagonist who has close to superhuman courage, strength, wit, attractiveness, and often all of the above. Although the outlines change, the basic characteristics remain the same, from John Gilbert to Clark Gable to Robert Redford to Tom Cruise.

At Keystone, conventional heroes are objects of ridicule, parodied by the likes of the cross-eyed, idiotic-looking Ben Turpin. But as the major comedians moved into feature productions, they had to become credible heroes to sustain the increased length of their films. Douglas Fairbanks provided the model, making a series of popular, light comedies in the teens that often featured the familiar plot of the meek worm turning and triumphing in a thrilling action finale. In the 1920s he turned to swashbucklers, becoming the screen's first major action hero.

The great silent comedies are, of course, also action films. Harold Lloyd followed Fairbanks's lead in playing a handsome, regular-guy type who finds himself in extraordinary situations. Both his square-jawed good looks and the thrill finales of his films made him a believable action hero; his goofy smile and round glasses stamp him as comic, but not so much that he can't play touching romantic scenes with standard ingénue lovelies.

The plots of Buster Keaton's comedies are similar to Lloyd's, but his hero is a stoical eccentric, far more passive than the go-getters played by Lloyd and Fairbanks. His leading ladies don't simply spur Buster to action; they become part of the action, usually greatly complicating the hero's task of rescuing them. His courtship scenes similarly parody the dramatic convention of the dashing hero winning the beautiful damsel; while Charlie courts his women (in his films of the teens) with insolent abandon, Buster, equally attracted, approaches them with the excruciating self-consciousness of an adolescent, resulting in scenes of hilarious discomfort.

For Chaplin, playing the comic hero became problematical as his character evolved, particularly with respect to justifying the romances in the films. Sexually aggressive in the rough-and-tumble Keystones, as his social milieu came into focus romance became more unlikely. The outsider status, vulnerability, and heart-tugging emotion he experimented with in *The New Janitor* blossomed in the Essanays and Mutuals. Increasingly, Charlie had to struggle to attain the most basic elements of survival. Chaplin still played the cheery incompetent for comedy, but his ineptitude became limned with the ever-present threat of unemployment, imprisonment, starvation, and indigence. Life on the margins of society became the subject of some of his most celebrated short films, including *The Tramp*, *The Vagabond*, *Easy Street*, *The Immigrant*, *A Dog's Life*, and almost all his features. Ultimately, it defined the Tramp character in the public mind.

Doug is an action hero. Harold is a conventional young man whose determination to make good and win his girl somehow leads him into danger. Buster deadpans his way through similar adventures, conveying that the whole struggle is some kind of cosmic joke not to be taken seriously; he triumphs anyway. They all do, again and again, with flying colors—heroes with happy endings.

Charlie's stories don't always have happy endings, nor are they reassuring Horatio Alger parables of success. Charlie shares with the other heroes of the time his athleticism and ingenuity, adding to it his distinctive grace of movement and charming, courtly mannerisms. He also embodies several distinctly Christian virtues: meekness, poverty, and self-sacrifice. His circumstances, his values, and his valiant behavior make him stand out in the harsh world around him. He doesn't always win the heroine's heart, but he always wins ours. In so doing Charlie becomes a genuine, if unconventional, hero.

Interestingly, Chaplin also introduces a number of conventional leading-men types into his films, but they almost always appear in unsympathetic roles. In *The Bank*, as we've seen, Edna is in love with the cashier;

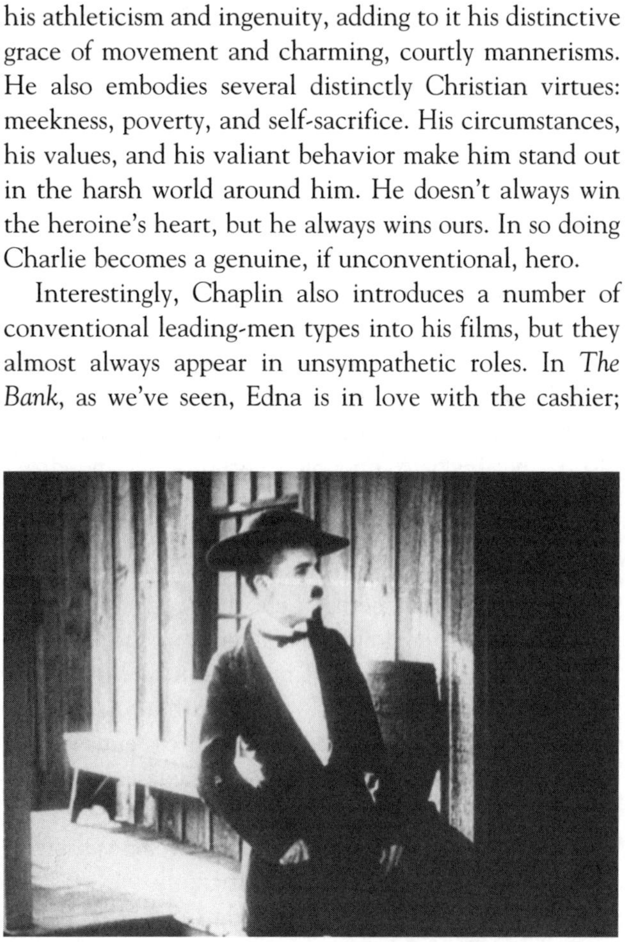

Charlie becomes a Western hero by transforming his minister's costume into that of a young Buffalo Bill. *The Pilgrim.*

Chaplin ensures that he gets none of our sympathy by casting a rather homely man in the role and having him behave like a coward, even if only in Charlie's wish-fulfillment dream. In later films along the same lines, Chaplin stacks the deck a bit more subtly. The artist in *The Vagabond* and the tightrope walker in *The Circus* are conventionally handsome men, to all appearances decent sorts. Certainly they aren't cads, criminals, or cowards. But their very blandness contrasts with Charlie's fascinating intensity, his adoration of the woman in question, his deserving character, and his noble, self-sacrificing actions.

Even when not part of a love triangle with Charlie, conventional hero types don't fare well in Chaplin films. Another handsome artist, played by Carl Miller, gets Edna pregnant in *The Kid* and then abandons her. In his modest garret studio he gazes longingly at a snapshot of her, then accidentally drops it into his fireplace. He plucks it from the flames, but, realizing it has burned beyond recovery, tosses it back. He uses a small stick from the fireplace to light his pipe as the photo burns. It's a subtle and visual way to show that he's not the standard unfeeling cad of melodrama. He still cares for her, but their relationship, like the photo, has gone up in smoke. Chaplin doesn't even bother to explain why; take your choice from the standard options. It's life.

As that scene might have been the downbeat conclusion to Edna's romance with the artist she meets in *The Vagabond*, so *A Woman of Paris* provides an alternative ending to the saga of the fallen woman Edna plays in *The Kid*, even to the point of casting Miller as an artist again. This time he's not even slightly caddish; Edna has left Miller—a simple, small-town artist—because she mistakenly believes he has spurned her on the night of their intended elopement. She goes to Paris, where suave playboy Adolphe Menjou takes her as his mistress. The foreword to the film states that people "sin only in blindness," that only the ignorant condemn and judge—thus setting the tone for a film in which Chaplin attempts to turn the conventional clichéd portrayal of heroes and villains on their head. He succeeds—the motivations of all the characters are complex, subtle, and clearly expressed directorially by Chaplin and the fine cast. Miller is a good guy, but rather boring and weak; he ends up committing suicide. Menjou, on the other hand, the putative villain of the piece, though not wholly sympathetic, is amusing and appealing.

In writing and directing *A Woman of Paris* Chaplin was making a bid to separate himself as a filmmaker from his great creation. Part of this must surely have been burnout; it had taken him five years to complete the eight films required to fulfill his First National contract, and they vary greatly in length and quality. As we've seen, he rankled under the yoke of employment. Even when he attained full independence as a founding member of United Artists, he dismayed his famous partners Fairbanks, Pickford, and D. W. Griffith by making this serious drama as his first release. It flopped decisively at the box office.

Chaplin got the message, and buckled down to the task of making feature-length Tramp films. He made two brilliant silent features, *The Gold Rush* and *The Circus*, and two bold silent-sound hybrids, *City Lights* and *Modern Times*, before finally capitulating to sound films in his political spoof, *The Great Dictator*. The film is the swan song for the Tramp. Chaplin puts aspects of him into both the Jewish barber and maniacal title character, a Jekyll-and-Hyde split that serves his urgent need to speak out about the current world crisis.

Having played the hero and villain as separate characters, for his next film Chaplin puts them together in the dapper form of *Monsieur Verdoux*. For the first time in his career he abandons the square mustache and big shoes to play a normal-looking character with gray hair and conventional good looks. He looks a bit like Clifton Webb, then about to embark on his successful series of films as the urbane and fussy Mr. Belvedere. But *Verdoux* is no light comedy, for the title character earns his living by marrying wealthy widows and murdering them for their money. It's all to support his crippled wife and young son during the Depression years, and he feels totally justified because of the way world war has made a mockery of any rational moral code. Chaplin clearly takes savage delight in this role, exorcising his contempt for a world that allows monstrous atrocities on a global scale and monstrous profits for war profiteers, while at the same time deluding itself with patriotic and religious pieties. Once again, the qualities of the heavy are embodied by the culture itself.

Chaplin's last starring performances allow him to tie up loose ends, as it were, by casting him in the roles of flawed heroes who embody many of the characteristics of his earlier incarnations, including the voluble fellow who holds forth in the final speeches of both *The Great Dictator* and *Monsieur Verdoux*. *Limelight*'s Calvero is part drunk, part philosopher, part selfless protector of a damsel in distress—as well as brilliant physical comedian. *A King in New York*'s Shahdov is royalty, with much to say but little ability to get the world to heed his words. He also fails in his attempt to protect a kindred spirit, a defenseless young boy. Long before, Charlie, despite his limited means, had been able to help a boy survive the harsh world. But times have changed, and now even a king must admit defeat. Even physical comedy, the great engine of Chaplin's art, is down to a low idle.

In the silent era all characters were defined by movement. Chaplin's mastery of movement led him to demand full artistic control of his films, not only from producers but from other actors as well. This is confirmed by the many eyewitness accounts of Chaplin at work, most of which stress his directorial method of acting out all the roles himself. Robert Parrish, who played the pea-shooting newsboy in *City Lights*, described it well:

> He said he found it best to show people rather than tell them. . . . He became a kind of dervish, playing all the parts, using all the props. . . . Finally, he had it all worked out and reluctantly gave us back our parts. I felt that he would much rather have played all of them himself.[19]

In fact, it is possible to trace the development of virtually every role in any later Chaplin film back to a Chaplin performance during the Keystone period. This makes his films, if not solo performances, about as close as they can be to them. Every actor's performance is molded directly by Chaplin, through repetition and imitation. This is a controversial method of directing, and some actors, notably Marlon Brando, bridled at the indignity of being told what to do down to the minutest detail. But the results speak for themselves, except in Brando's case—he gave the most wooden performance of his career in *A Countess from Hong Kong*. Nor was he the only one to complain; Virginia Cherrill said that she learned essentially nothing about acting from her years of shooting *City Lights*.[20] Most others, however, such as Adolphe Menjou, Jack Oakie, and Martha Raye, spoke in glowing terms of the experience for the rest of their lives.

On a first viewing it is difficult to fully appreciate the function of other actors in Chaplin films, since their performances so effectively focus our attention on his. But within a single film there is a startling variety in depth of characterization, from two-dimensional Keystone stereotypes to rounded, realistic characters. *The Kid* is a prime example. The ladies of the slum are hard-boiled characters who seem not to be acting at all; the same is true of most of the bums in the flophouse. But Edna, her artist lover, the orphan officials, and the doctor seem to have stepped off the stage of a Victorian melodrama. The bully is a caricature exaggerated beyond Sennett's imagination.

In *A Dog's Life* Chaplin creates a Daumier-like gallery of human caricatures.

Charlie is his usual highly stylized self, and the Kid is a mirror image of him. Yet everyone fits smoothly into the fabric of the film.

Chaplin's great skill at characterization lies in his ability to balance this wildly varied cast of characters into a filmic universe that comfortably accommodates them all. Although there is a general movement toward realistic characterization in the films of the late teens through the 1930s, the enormous variety remains. For example, Chester Conklin's performance as the factory mechanic in *Modern Times* could have come right out of a Keystone film, where Conklin was a leading comic two decades earlier.

Nor can the persistence of caricature and stereotype be seen as a flaw or a stubborn anachronism on Chaplin's part. They are organic necessities to make the Tramp a believable protagonist, serving to ground his broader acrobatic comedy and strongly physical style of acting.

With sound, the film world became necessarily less stylized, complicating Chaplin's balancing act. He falters in parts of *The Great Dictator* and *Monsieur Verdoux*. But, up to that time, the miracle is that the act is so smooth the effort doesn't show. The disparate elements orbit in beautiful configurations, set into motion by this master juggler of human images.

Notes

1. Chaplin, cited in Alistair Cooke, *Six Men* (New York: Knopf, 1977), 33.

2. Charles Chaplin, *My Autobiography* (New York: Simon & Schuster), 141.

3. Both the walk and the skid-turn were reportedly developed, or at least used onstage, by Karno comedian Fred Kitchen. No extant review or personal recollection mentions Chaplin doing these movements on stage, although it's likely that he did, since Karno comedians were expected to learn every role in the repertoire. Even if he didn't perform them onstage, his uncanny gift for mimicry would have imprinted them in his memory.

4. Harry Geduld, *Chapliniana*, vol. 1: *The Keystone Films* (Bloomington and Indianapolis: Indiana University Press, 1987), 35.

5. See Charles A. McGuirk, "Chaplinitis," *Motion Picture Magazine*, August 1915, 89.

6. Charlie is shot in this film, as he was in *The Tramp*, but this time it's played strictly for laughs. Charlie hops up and down at the piano in a cartoony way as his partner shoots him repeatedly in the rear end. Since it's a Keystone-style shooting, Charlie suffers no apparent ill effects.

7. There is a perfunctory gunfight featuring some Mexican banditos at the end of Chaplin's other "western," *The Pilgrim*, made two years earlier, but the killings are more a joke of the genre rather than true dramatic action. The same is true of Chaplin's *Burlesque on Carmen*, made in 1915, in which he kills a fellow soldier in a duel, suffers melodramatic remorse, and later kills Edna and himself in a murder suicide—after which the duo promptly come back to life, and Charlie demonstrates his fake knife.

8. Riesner was an important member of Chaplin's creative team from 1918 to 1925, contributing several key performances, assistant directing, and, perhaps most critically, working as a gagman. Indeed, there is some evidence that he helped Chaplin develop the longer, more elaborate comic routines that fill the First Nationals, including the bravura body part confusion gags. Chaplin expert Hooman Mehran notes that during Riesner's absence in 1919 Chaplin went into a creative slump, making his two weakest films of the period, *A Day's Pleasure* and *Sunnyside* ("Chaplin's Directing and Writing Collaborators," paper delivered at the London International Chaplin Conference [October 2005]). While Riesner's contribution remains speculative, it is undeniable that Chaplin made a sudden and significant artistic advance with his First National films; Theodore Huff and others have called *A Dog's Life* Chaplin's first masterpiece, and his next film, *Shoulder Arms*, cemented his reputation as not only the world's most popular actor, but its most important filmmaker as well.

9. Chaplin, *My Autobiography*, 271. Interestingly, though Chaplin had been a millionaire for the better part of his life by the time he wrote those words, he still included himself among the "us" who *don't* have wealth and celebrity.

10. Ironically, the actor, Tom Murray, also played Black Larson.

11. Roach, cited in Betty Harper Fussell, *Mabel: Hollywood's First I-Don't-Care Girl* (New York: Limelight Editions, 1992), 57.

12. The exceptions are *His New Job*, Chaplin's first Essanay, and *One A.M.*

13. Chaplin, *My Autobiography*, 170

14. Chaplin, *My Life in Pictures* (New York: Grosset & Dunlap, 1975), 150.

15. Chaplin, *My Autobiography*, 497.

16. Chaplin, *My Autobiography*, 269.

17. Cooke, *Six Men*, 37.

18. He began his Mutual series by implicitly mocking them. *The Floorwalker* opens with a character who looks very much like Charlie, sporting his toothbrush mustache and some characteristic gestures. It's the actual floorwalker, or floor manager, of the department store, with whom Charlie will soon switch places. After the switch, when the floorwalker exits wearing Charlie's clothes, he does a rather clumsy version of Chaplin's walk as well. By First National the joke had evidently worn thin, for Chaplin was signing the opening credits of his films, taking imitators to court, and putting ads in film magazines warning his fans to beware of imitation Chaplin films.

19. Robert Parrish, *Growing Up in Hollywood* (New York: Harcourt, Brace, Jovanovich, 1976), 42–43.

20. Virginia Cherrill, author interview, 1978.

CHAPTER SEVEN

Shall We Dance?

"Your comedy is *balletique*, you are a dancer."—Vaslav Nijinsky to Chaplin, 1916[1]

From the beginning of his screen career, Chaplin linked himself closely to dance through his posture. With his splayed feet, tilted-back pelvis, and regal bearing he presented a virtual parody of a classical ballet dancer.

The crisp precision of his movements was also dancelike. Apparently this was automatic with Chaplin both onscreen and off, as noted by many observers, including Alistair Cooke:

> One of the permanent pleasures of being with him was to watch the grace and deftness with which he performed all physical movements, from pouring syrup to swerving like a matador just out of the line of an oncoming truck.[2]

Arabesque on a ladder. *The Floorwalker.*

But the dance aspect of Chaplin's films goes beyond his posture and the paradoxical gracefulness of his personal movement. It goes beyond the many dance-floor scenes that enliven the films. It even goes beyond his highly choreographed fight scenes.[3] One of his signal achievements was to translate to the screen movement qualities usually seen only on the stage. Like good dance, Chaplin's films have the effect of sweeping viewers along, leaving them exhilarated and awestruck by the expressive power of movement, and more aware of their own physical selves. This is dance in its broadest sense, as movement that draws attention to itself, bringing pleasure and insight to viewers because of its formal qualities. The movement in Chaplin's films is so carefully composed that it might fairly be said that his films are not so much directed as choreographed.

Until the Mutual series of films in 1916–17, scenes with the unmistakably choreographed look that characterizes his later work appear only intermittently. But with the first Mutual, *The Floorwalker*, a dramatic change occurs. Masquerading as the store floorwalker, Charlie measures a lady's foot for shoes. The touch of her foot so excites him that, after climbing a wheeled ladder to get her a pair, he pushes off the wall with his foot and gracefully sails back to her, one leg balletically outstretched in an arabesque. His walk and posture had suggested ballet from the beginning, but this is the first time Chaplin uses a specific quotation from the ballet repertoire for a comic effect.

Later, Charlie discovers a satchel full of money and literally dives into it in his exhilaration. A moment later embezzler Eric Campbell enters, finds Charlie with the goods, and knocks him down—whereupon Charlie springs up and dances a little solo for the dumbfounded crook, complete with twirls, entrechats,[4] and mock toe

Diving into a satchel. *The Floorwalker.*

Dancing his joy. *The Floorwalker.*

dancing. He ends the dance with a graceful spread-eagle bow, whereupon Campbell promptly knocks him down again.

Such moments percolate through the Mutual series, reflecting Chaplin's exhilaration during what he later called the happiest period of his career. Confident of his popularity, demonstrated tangibly each week by his fabulous $10,000 paycheck, he went from success to success, well supported by his handpicked stock company of players and technicians. With the anchoring onscreen triumvirate of Charlie, Edna, and Eric, Chaplin could play out his wildest ideas with abandon, including the transparently autobiographical moment above, in which Charlie plays an imposter who discovers a satchel stuffed with money.

He dove into the Mutual series as he dove into that satchel, with a new boldness that enabled him to take an artistic as well as a physical leap. It wasn't just his happiest period, it was also his most creative. The twelve Mutual films build upon what had come before and go further, establishing the prototypes for all his work to come. Nor is their value simply transitional. By themselves, they constitute a unique artistic achievement, unarguably the best film comedies that had been produced to that time. For many people, they remain Chaplin's best work—funnier, simpler, and unburdened by the serious content of his later films.

Audiences flocked to the Chaplin Mutuals, and Charlie's glances at the camera grew bolder than ever, deepening the rapport between him and his vast public. He fills the series with teasing in-jokes, using a look-alike in the opening scenes of *The Floorwalker*, beginning *The Vagabond* with a shot of his feet shuffling along under saloon doors, starting *The Immigrant* bent double over the ship's rail, mooning his audience with that famous posterior.

But it was his deepening understanding of how to use the elements of dance that was the key to his artistic leap. During this time he discovered how to press the dance impulse into the very fabric of his films, not just with non sequitur bursts of mock ballet dancing, but by creating comic ideas based on the natural laws of movement. He learned, for example, how he could play with the idea of gravity itself to suit his comic purposes.

A classical ballet dancer plays with the audience's perception of gravity by creating the illusion of being able to float. As the chapter on Chaplin's mime pointed out, he became adept at manipulating the audience's sense of his weight or the weight of props he handled. He creates a comical illusion of weightlessness when he hoists himself by the back of the pants onto the curb in *The Pawnshop*, and later makes a doughnut look like it's made of lead. In *Easy Street* he adds apparent weight to a fake iron stove he's about to drop on Eric. Chaplin's simple but subtle displacement of his own weight to achieve these effects shows how he gently bends, rather than breaks, the law of gravity. While Mack Sennett might have shown the doughnut crashing through the floor, Chaplin makes his point with skillful movement, which is why the gag remains both funny and pleasing to watch.

Sometimes Chaplin conjures comedy from the actual weight of objects, as he does in a charming sequence from *The Pilgrim*. Charlie is helping Edna to prepare a cake. She picks up a breadboard with a rolling pin on top of it, absently tilting the board so that the pin rolls off, and Charlie must catch it before it hits the floor. He rolls it onto a high shelf, and when he turns around it rolls off and hits him on the head. He returns it to the shelf and it happens again; finally, he places a milk bottle on the shelf to hold the rolling pin in place. Moments later Edna reaches for the milk, and Charlie must lunge to prevent the rolling pin from hitting *her*. He holds the pin in place with his hand until she moves away, then absentmindedly turns away, allowing the pin to hit him yet again.

Naturally, the subject of the routine is not the rolling pin, but the budding romance between Charlie and Edna; what happens with the rolling pin visually expresses their distracted state. The delightful sequence is built from the simplest of props and actions, and a slightly tilted shelf that allows gravity to do its work. Chaplin's movement in the scene, rolling the pin to the back of the shelf and turning around just as it rolls off, is exquisitely timed, and the pattern of his movement is elegantly worked out. One cannot imagine another comedian doing the routine in this way, with variation after variation. Despite its apparent simplicity, the sequence would look too ornate for the more prosaic movement styles of Keaton or Lloyd.

One of Chaplin's most ingenious gravity jokes is the startling *anti*gravity image he creates in *The Great Dictator*, when his open-cockpit plane flips upside down. The film image flips as well, so that we see Charlie right side up and share his perception of a world gone topsy-turvy, in which his pocket watch seems to float in front of his face and water from a canteen flows upward.

Chaplin builds many such inventive routines around the invisible but omnipresent force of gravity. For all of Charlie's lightness on his feet, his films are filled with reminders of gravity's power, which he ignores at his peril.

Gravity, of course, is also the unheralded force that gives many sporting events their meaning: How high can the athlete jump? How far can the ball be thrown? The laws of inertia and momentum become part of the equation as well: A moving object will keep moving unless stopped by another object or force—like the opposing team. Sporting events celebrate the human body's ability to overcome inertia and channel momentum.

Ballet dancers, equally interested in pushing physical limits, seek to create the theatrical illusion that gravity, inertia, and momentum don't really apply to them. Their powerful musculature is dedicated to belying the effort leading up to the leap and the shock of the landing. The flow of energy in the movement is unnaturally even, so they appear to defy not only the law of gravity, but the laws of inertia and momentum as well.

Chaplin sometimes uses physical skill and illusion to deny the effect of momentum, as when he breaks into his quick-freezes. But more often he exaggerates it. A kick, a revolving door, or a fall is an excuse for a display of visual and acrobatic pyrotechnics. In *The Cure* he is spun by a revolving door into the lobby, up the stairs, and through the health spa, coming to rest only when he plunges into the pool. He maintains his improbable momentum with balletic smoothness as he rockets from room to room, revolving in place from time to time as he careens through the spa. The spinning door seems to cause Charlie's movement, a false causation made plausible by speeding up the film. Speedup also enhances Charlie's impressive mastery of momentum when he runs, his head bent backward as if reacting to the forward thrust of his movement, or when he performs athletic feats like skating rings around the other skaters in *The Rink*.

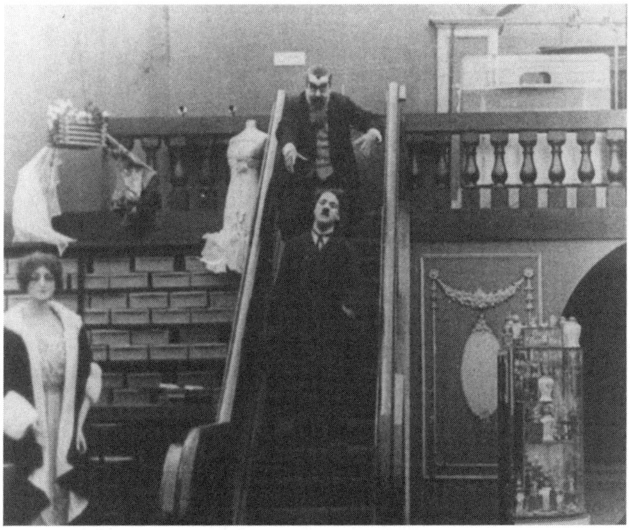

The escalator chase. *The Floorwalker.*

Occasionally Chaplin plays with opposing forces that cancel one another out, creating moments of comically strained equilibrium. We've seen how he does that in his titanic struggle to mount the stairs in *One A.M.* By the time of the Mutuals, Chaplin had fallen down so many flights of stairs that for *The Floorwalker* he came up with an ingenious variant: a *moving* stairway. Charlie, of course, laboriously works his way down the up escalator; pausing to rest at the bottom, he is carried back up again. The climax of the film is a quintessential chase image as Eric chases Charlie down the escalator, both of them running in place in a tableau-in-motion of the pursuer and the pursued. In another memorable sequence, from *The Gold Rush*, it's a strong wind that Charlie struggles against, once again straining to get ahead, and once again remaining in place. The escalator returns in *Modern Times*, and this time Charlie's on skates, a good example of how Chaplin inventively recycles his gags by combining them.

Chaplin's most delicate expressions of equilibrium are his various balancing acts, and perhaps the most splendid one takes place atop an A-frame ladder in *The Pawnshop*. Rocking back and forth as he tries to clean the store sign, he finally goes too far and the ladder topples backward. The viewer's anxiety in watching this sequence—the ladder is at least ten feet tall—is matched by that of a policeman, who sways back and forth and draws in his breath in time to Charlie's precarious movement. As always in such scenes, the payoff occurs in a sustained long shot. When the ladder finally falls, Charlie hits the road in a graceful back somersault, hopping up immediately to check his watch. His solicitous concern for his timepiece also reassures us that he is himself still ticking.

Both Lloyd and Keaton came to specialize in this sort of thrill comedy, surpassing Chaplin by their greater willingness to risk life and limb in some truly hair-raising sequences. Chaplin, however, does a most effective thrill sequence on the tightrope in *The Circus*, and in *Modern Times* he reprises his graceful roller-skating from *The Rink* with an added thrill element: showing off for Paulette Goddard, he dons a blindfold and skates along in graceful arcs, forward and backward, oblivious of the danger as he glides perilously close to the edge of an unfinished floor (discussed in detail in chapter 10). But such stunt comedy played less of a role in his films than in those of his great silent colleagues, especially as he grew more adept at making his films dance.

For Chaplin, no dance element was more important than rhythm. He had two aids on the set: the loud clicking of the silent camera, imposing a steady beat and telling him how much the film was being undercranked, and the occasional presence of musicians who played to help establish the mood. Virginia Cherrill, costar of *City Lights*, said that musicians, often a trio, were in constant attendance during the two-year period of filming, playing "whatever Charlie felt like that day."[5]

As noted in chapter 5, Chaplin often extracts humor from the Tramp's tendency to mechanically repeat actions. Thus, Charlie begins dusting in *The Pawnshop*, maintaining a steady rhythm as he dusts his hat, his cane, a coworker's desk (causing the man to sneeze violently as a cloud of dust rises), and an electric fan (creating a snowstorm of feathers as the duster is shredded). Later, transforming a fight into furious floor washing when the boss appears, he grabs a violin and starts scrubbing it in the soapy water, until the boss yanks him to his feet and orders him to leave. In these sequences, as in many others like them, it is Charlie's blind adherence to a regular rhythm that makes his actions funny and persuasive. Such gags also reveal things about Charlie's character:

On the assembly line. *Modern Times*.

The dusting expresses his boredom, the floor washing his quicksilver ability to cover his tracks—or try to—by instantly substituting one action for another.

The ultimate expression of Chaplin's use of rhythmically repetitive movement for comedy is the lengthy three-part factory sequence that opens *Modern Times*. In the first part Charlie struggles to tighten nuts as they speed past him on the assembly line, while various distractions make it difficult to keep up the pace. The stultifying repetition so programs his nervous system that even after a man relieves him to take a break he continues to jerk involuntarily; finally, he manages to "squeeze" the movement out of himself with a mighty compression and release. When the lunch break is called the same problem causes him to spill steaming soup all over a coworker.

During lunch Charlie is chosen to test a new feeding machine, a contraption designed to help management eliminate the lunch hour by feeding employees while they work. Predictably, the attempt to rhythmically regulate the act of eating has disastrous results. A soup bowl lifts and tilts so that Charlie can sip the steaming soup, but malfunctions and throws the soup into his face; a food-pusher shoves morsels into his mouth, including several large metal nuts that have accidentally been placed on the rotating plate; a corncob revolves slowly against his mouth and moves slowly from side to side so he can chew, but soon spins out of control. After each violation to Charlie's person, a mouth wiper gracefully arcs to wipe his lips, an ironic rhythmic counterpoint to the abuse—until it, too, goes haywire and bats away at him.

In the third sequence the pace of the assembly line accelerates until Charlie is driven mad. Chaplin had met the legendary dancer Vaslav Nijinsky late in 1916 and

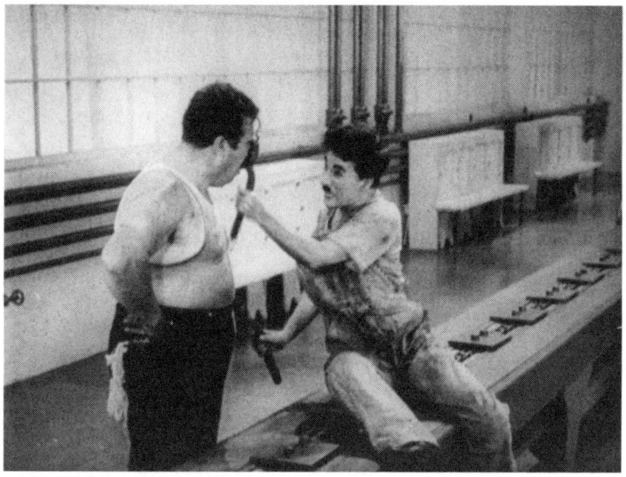

Tightening everything in sight. *Modern Times.*

Charlie going balletically crazy in *Modern Times.*

marveled at his performance in *The Afternoon of a Faun*. Soon after that poor Nijinsky went permanently mad. Chaplin was haunted by both events, and now combines them in the brilliant climax to the factory scene. Unlike his pallid tribute to the dancer in *Sunnyside*, in this scene there is a strong dramatic purpose for the parody.

After obsessively following a nut plate into the bowels of the machine and being "regurgitated" back out, Charlie emerges in a batty state. He is all mock-ballet elegance as he gracefully twirls to tighten several nuts, along with the noses and nipples of a couple of workers. When he sees a comely secretary he flips his wrenches above his ears like horns and wags his eyebrows lasciviously; what excites him is not the woman, but the buttons on her dress. He tears through the factory twisting every nut-like object in sight. He's also foxy, for he understands that none of the workers dare break their own factory-imposed rhythm, and he keeps restarting the assembly line so they have to return to work rather than chasing him. Chaplin's chase scenes were always dancelike, but never was there one so filled with leaps, pirouettes, and arabesques. Charlie wreaks choreographed chaos, utterly disrupting the inhuman mechanical rhythms of the factory and replacing them, for a few precious minutes, with his own eccentric ones.

Charlie flipping out. *Modern Times.*

That Chaplin was fully aware of the importance of repetitive rhythm and the power of habit in his work is demonstrated by a short story he published a couple of years after *Modern Times* came out. Entitled "Rhythm: A Story of Men in Macabre Movement," it deals with an officer who must give the order for a firing squad to shoot a friend of his. He blanks out and shouts incoherently, which his men interpret as the "present arms" order. Then habit takes over, with disastrous results.

> The rhythm of their action set his brain in rhythm, and again he shouted. Now the men took aim.
>
> But in the pause that followed, there came into the prison yard hurrying footsteps, the nature of which the officer knew meant a reprieve. Instantly, his mind cleared. "Stop!" he screamed frantically at the firing squad.
>
> Six men stood poised with rifles. Six men were caught in rhythm. Six men when they heard the scream to stop—fired.[6]

Chaplin's most rhythmically sophisticated film is much less well known than *Modern Times*. In his autobiography Chaplin states that it was with *A Dog's Life* in 1918 that he began "to think of comedy in a structural sense, and to become conscious of its architectural form. Each sequence implied the next sequence, all of them relating to the whole."[7] Indeed, *A Dog's Life* has a nicely worked-out little plot, but what makes it outstanding is the remarkable rhythmic structure of the nine major comic sequences that make up the film, and the way they complement each other.

In the first, Charlie is sitting coyly on the ground in a vacant lot. He's just replaced the stolen hot dog that was to be his breakfast, because a cop caught him in the act. The cop stands on the other side of a wooden fence, glowering down at him, and gestures with his head for Charlie to come over to his side. Charlie responds by flirtatiously gesturing with his head for the cop to join *him*. The back-and-forth exchange is a teasing prelude to the chase that follows. The cop runs through a door in the fence, but Charlie simply rolls to the other side through a gap, then back as the cop runs around again. Charlie then reaches under the fence to untie one of the cop's shoes; when the cop pauses to tie it, Charlie unties the other. When the cop reties that one Charlie, for good measure, sticks him with one of those straight pins that always seem to be conveniently attached to his vest. In perfectly matched shots the camera cuts from one side of the fence to the other as the chase accelerates. Finally, the cop tries to squeeze under the fence, giving the agile Charlie the chance to run around and boot him soundly in the butt a few times. They round the fence a couple more times, and Charlie, feeling safe and a bit cocky with the fence between them, offers the cop a mocking bow—only to find his outstretched hand touching the badge of a second cop. Rolling under the fence and dashing through the gate a last time, he eludes both cops. He runs to the next street, hop-skidding into a brick wall to break his momentum. He starts running again, but quickly slows his pace to a casual walk, hands in his pockets, to fool yet another of the omnipresent cops.

As he had at the beginning of the Mutual series, Chaplin makes a significant artistic leap with his initial First National offering, and once again, it's connected

Mocking the cop. *A Dog's Life.*

to his dancelike movement. Charlie's standard flight from the cops is presented with such choreographic ingenuity and compelling rhythmic variety that watching the scene is like watching music made visual. One can practically hear the opening crescendo as the sequence begins, the tempo quickening as the chase accelerates, the percussion accents as Charlie kicks and jabs the cop, and finally the explosive release as he makes his escape in a run, followed by the quick diminuendo when he hits the wall, slows to a walk, and strolls away. It's a comic chase scene, and it's also a dance. There's no longer any difference. Without quoting a single ballet movement or pulling himself from the regular action to create an incongruous *moment* of dance, Chaplin has married comedy with choreography. In addition, Charlie's ease and clear enjoyment as he taunts and mocks his way through the sequence make him something more than a vagrant eluding a cop; he's a performer exulting in his skill.

That exultant quality was present in many of the Mutuals as well, especially when Chaplin bows to the audience in films like *The Pawnshop* and *The Cure*. But those bows mocked the reality of his own film. In *A Dog's Life* Chaplin is after bigger game. He mocks other characters, but no longer his film. Charlie is more deeply embedded in this film, a more realistic figure, more grounded in his slum environment. We see where he sleeps, at least for one night. We see that, like all of us, he's hungry when he wakes up, and has to find food. We see that even a petty crime like stealing a hot dog is difficult to pull off, because cops are everywhere in these grimy streets.

Charlie's hunt for the means of survival leads him into the second sequence, another rhythmically rich scene that follows on the heels of the first. The scene addresses a basic question about Charlie: Why is this artful dodger indigent, even though he's so resourceful that he can dance rings around the cops?

Charlie strolls past an employment office. A sign on the blackboard proclaiming "Men Wanted for Brewery," for some reason, attracts a crowd who had been indifferent to one asking for "Strong men for Sewer work." Charlie gets into the office first and sits expectantly on a bench. But when the window opens, just as he reaches it one of the other men slips in ahead of him. He returns to his seat. It happens again. As he's going back to his seat a second window opens and he heads for it, but someone gets there first too. Charlie's pace accelerates steadily as he tries to reach one of the windows, but somehow, someone's always there just ahead of him. He overshoots and slams into a wall, enabling yet another man to slip past. By the time it's over ten men have gotten jobs, and Charlie is running full tilt from window to window.

Running from window to window in the employment office. *A Dog's Life.*

Sibling rivalry. Charlie filches pastries from his brother, Sydney. *A Dog's Life.*

Each of the windows slams shut as he reaches it, decisive percussive bangs that conclude the sequence. One of the clerks emerges and Charlie skids into him. He asks for a handout. The clerk looks at him as though to say, "Why don't you get a job?" Of course, we've just seen why. Charlie is a vagrant because he *can't* find work in his world.

The bravura window sequence is shot in one continuous take, and it's thoroughly convincing. None of the men seems to rush to get ahead of Charlie, they're just *there*. Only Charlie rushes, faster and faster as it goes along. The sequence, for all its speed and apparent spontaneity, is choreographed with such painstaking precision that it unfolds with almost stately inevitability.

Hunger has driven the first two sequences, and it drives the next one as well. Once again, the scene deepens our understanding of Charlie, showing him to be a compassionate being. He pauses in his own search for sustenance to help another hungry creature, Scraps, the "thoroughbred mongrel." Scraps is a small white dog who is being overpowered by larger and more aggressive dogs fighting over a scrap of food, exactly as Charlie had been overpowered by the scruffy crowd in the employment office. While Chaplin can't impose the same careful rhythm to a dogfight that he imposes on the film's other carefully rehearsed sequences, he comes pretty close with the use of editing, cutting away from the main action for amusing rhythmic accents such as dogs peering out from around corners before joining the fray. Charlie lifts Scraps from the leaping, mangy pack, and with her in tow he charges off, chased by the hungry curs. The chase allows Chaplin a bit more control over the action, and he varies it with such details as a determined dog that attaches itself to the seat of his pants and hangs on as he whirls to dislodge it; finally it trots off in triumph with its morsel of cloth. Actors rhythmically reinforce the action as well; a group of ladies sitting on their stoops (including the ubiquitous Henry Bergman) topple backward like dominos as Charlie and the pack charge past.

The dog becomes Charlie's alter ego in the film, and from this point on their fates will be intertwined, as each helps the other to survive. As Walter Kerr points out, this "small narrative motor" helps to drive the film.[8]

But it is the rhythmic comedy that makes it memorable. Scraps becomes part of the fourth sequence, another of the catch-me-if-you-can scenes of which Chaplin was so fond. Leaning against the counter of a lunch wagon, Charlie feeds the dog with a couple of sausage links he filches from a frying pan, then systematically devours a plateful of pastries. Tension mounts throughout the routine as Charlie stuffs pastry after pastry into his mouth—eleven in all—and freezes each time proprietor Syd Chaplin whirls around to catch him. Syd is perfectly aware that the pastries are rapidly vanishing from the plate, and he knows that Charlie's taking them, but it doesn't matter; he's determined to catch him in the act. Charlie's starvation—his clothes were never baggier on his body—is played out as a delightful comic game, and the teamwork between the brothers in their first onscreen peformance together is a wonder to behold.

Once again Chaplin finds intriguing ways to vary the action. As the pastries grow fewer, Syd starts whirling around unexpectedly, and Charlie has to cover his approaches with a series of little feints. Finally, he pretends to catch a fly and swat it on the counter, a decisive percussive beat. As Syd stares down at the counter Charlie turns around and wolfs down another pastry. The sequence ends with another visual beat: The cop who caught Charlie

Edna as the soulful singer in *A Dog's Life.*

Henry Bergman as a crying patron of The Green Lantern. *A Dog's Life.*

stealing a hot dog turns up, spies him reaching for the last pastry, and tries to collar him. Instead, he gets the crack on the head intended for Charlie by the salami-wielding Syd, who's finally had enough of the game. Charlie has more than earned his hard-won breakfast.

Although this sequence is constructed in several shots, the eccentric stop-start rhythm of filching-eating-whirling-freezing is reinforced by the fluid editing. The cutaways, showing Scraps licking her chops, Syd glaring at her suspiciously, and the cop peering in through a small opening in the back of the lunch wagon, lend variety, and also allow Chaplin to empty his mouth between takes—although he does somehow manage to cram six of the things into his mouth in a single take.

The fifth sequence stems not only from a musical rhythm, but from the power of the music itself. Now that he and Scraps have eaten, Charlie goes to the Green Lantern Café, hoping for a drink and a bit of entertainment. After an exuberant hoochie-koochie dancer gyrates frantically on the stage, Edna is introduced with a title, "A new singer sings an old song." Edna's song is so sad, and so evidently heartfelt—she must dab away tears herself—that it makes everyone in the café burst out crying. This is a rare instance of Chaplin letting other characters get laughs. The sentiment inspires the bartender to return filched money to the cash register. A fat woman (Bergman again, of course) douses Charlie with tears and seltzer water. Patrons fall on each other weeping. Even the musicians have trouble playing; the one-eyed violinist weeps copiously and the bald-headed pianist must blow his nose. All of them are caught up in the heaving, uncontrollable rhythm of crying, and it's apparently a very therapeutic group catharsis.

The hard-boiled crowd's overreaction to Edna's sentimental song is very funny, and since we laugh at them crying, it is a master stroke for Chaplin to climax the sequence with a gag that confuses tears and laughter. The band's drummer, played by the reliable Chuck Riesner, is racked with sobs like everybody else, until the sight of the bawling Charlie, sitting next to him, makes him start laughing. This cracks Charlie up, too, which inexplicably infuriates Riesner, who turns away and *pretends* to be crying, although he's clearly still laughing. The rhythmic similarity between the spasmodic movements of laughing and crying makes the sequence both bizarre and hilarious, a reversal of emotion similar to the strangling/laughing woman scene Chaplin would do a couple of years later in *The Kid.* Eventually, Riesner and Charlie both start sobbing in earnest again, but once more Riesner spoils Charlie's enjoyment of his cry, blasting him with several foul-smelling expulsions of air and spittle. Finally, with a demure bow, Edna exits, the frantic dancer returns, and the spell is broken.

Charlie is doused by Bergman's tears, which he thinks are raindrops. *A Dog's Life.*

In the sixth sequence Charlie dances with Edna. Unfortunately, her talents lie more in singing; she bounces up and down so vigorously that her shoulder knocks Charlie's chin up and down like a punching bag, making it difficult for him to keep his hat on. She maintains her bouncing beat, but Charlie can't; he steps in gum and gets into an altercation with the fat lady and her diminutive dancing partner. For once, the humor comes from the mismatched rhythm between Charlie and Edna. After they sit down, Charlie, unable to buy her a drink, is unceremoniously thrown out.

In a series of quick transitional scenes two crooks steal a rich man's wallet and bury it in Charlie's vacant lot; Charlie discovers the wallet when Scraps digs it up; Edna is fired for refusing to dance with one of the crooks; Charlie returns to the Green Lantern; the crooks quickly recapture the wallet from him; and he's given the bum's rush and thrown out again.

In the seventh major rhythmic sequence Charlie must overpower the crooks to regain the wallet. To do that he slips into a curtained booth behind the men and knocks out the one played by Albert Austin. After substituting his arms for Austin's, Charlie engages the other crook in a lively conversation, using only his hand movements rather than speech. He justifies his silence with gestures cautioning the other thug to keep quiet, lest they be overheard. Charlie then demands his share of the stolen loot. When the partners toast their success, he manages to drain Austin's beer mug, wiping Austin's mouth with a handkerchief as he finishes. Throughout the sequence he keeps manhandling Austin to keep him unconscious, choking him viciously in the guise of tightening his tie, and punching him surreptitiously on the jaw when he begins to wake up. Finally, beckoning the other thug closer, Charlie crowns him with a beer bottle, then emerges from behind the curtain to grab the wallet, leaving the two thieves slumped unconscious on the table. The comedy of the sequence derives from the way Charlie's rhythmically fluttering hands bring the inert, open-eyed Austin so convincingly to life, while at the same time dealing with such obstacles as returning Austin's handkerchief to his pocket and making sure he remains unconscious.

In the eighth sequence, following on the heels of this one, the two crooks, Charlie, and the bartender battle for possession of the wallet. It might have been timed to the beats of a metronome, so regular is the rhythm as the wallet is pulled from right to left and back again; after four even beats Charlie grabs it on the fifth and bursts toward the camera and out of sight. Once again, prosaic movements are transmuted into striking and effortless-looking comic choreography.

The lunch wagon becomes a shooting gallery. *A Dog's Life.*

The strong staccato rhythm of that brief exchange leads like a drum roll to the ninth and final sequence, in which Charlie and Sydney pop up alternately like ducks in a shooting gallery as the crooks fire at the lunch wagon. The gunshots punctuate the scene, until the last one shatters the plate Charlie holds up to shield himself. As the crooks rush the wagon and begin choking Charlie, Scraps saves the day by retrieving the wallet from him.

These nine sequences give *A Dog's Life* a quality unique in the Chaplin canon. A different rhythm dominates each scene and provides its structural underpinning, just as the bass line in a musical piece underscores the more obvious melody line. Even the transitions between scenes make inventive use of visual rhythms. For example, when Charlie is bounced from the Green Lantern the first time, he angrily grabs a brick and winds up to throw it into the café before noticing that one of the omnipresent cops has come up beside him; without breaking his rhythm he tosses the brick offscreen instead, as if tossing a stick for Scraps—a familiar act of camouflage. Then, as Charlie and Scraps briskly exit the screen on the lower right, the scene cuts to show the two thugs entering quickly from the lower left; their action seems to pick up Charlie's momentum.

The rhythm that percolates through *A Dog's Life* also imposes a playful quality to what we're actually witnessing in this film, a surprisingly grim and uncompromising depiction of the desperate fight for survival in the slums. It was a giant step in storytelling for Chaplin as he sought to infuse more serious content into his films. The ebullience of the comic sequences justifies the improbable storybook happy ending, in which Charlie and Edna buy a farm with the money in the wallet. In the last shot they look lovingly down into a bassinet, and the camera pans down to reveal—Scraps and her litter.

In most other Chaplin films the rhythm and unity of the best sequences are superior to those of the film as a whole. *City Lights* may have the best plot, and it certainly packs the biggest emotional wallop, but its comic routines are inconsistent in quality; the dramatic subplot of *The Circus* is a bit shaky; *The Kid* has some dated expositional sequences; and so on through the films. These are hardly fatal flaws in incontestable comic masterpieces, but no such qualifications need be made of *A Dog's Life*. For once, form and content merge completely. One would be hard pressed to pick a comic high point, so consistently brilliant are the comic routines. Yet the great variety in the sequences ensures that there is no monotony.

In *A Dog's Life* Chaplin achieves an effortless blending of comic and serious content, bound inextricably together by the rhythmic relationship of its nine primary sequences, resulting in a "structural" film that is unified by much more than a good plot. It is not only Chaplin's first masterpiece, but arguably the most perfect film of his career. Only *The Gold Rush* approaches its rock-solid consistency, narrative drive, and comic inventiveness.

While Chaplin shares with classical ballet a preoccupation with gravity, momentum, and rhythm, he naturally uses these dynamic movement qualities in a very different way than dance choreographers. It is his use of a fourth dynamic element—space—that links his films most with classical dance. In ballet the major principle of spatial design is the circle. The body is visualized as a series of interlocking circles, and the various ballet positions approximate the geometric perfection and precision of a series of interlocking circles and arcs.

Sometimes Chaplin quotes from the ballet repertoire of steps and positions, such as when he pushes down the large lever in *Modern Times*, his leg extended in an arabesque, or leaps into entrechats in *The Floorwalker* and *The Cure*. These moments invariably occur in inappropriate places, which, of course, is what makes them funny. They are totally out of place in such mundane settings as factories, department stores, and health spas.

But even when he's not quoting ballet moves, Chaplin's world seethes with the fertile juxtaposition of the plain and the fancy. His most pedestrian movements—lighting matches on the seat of his pants, his walk, his entire repertoire of eccentric kicks and falls—have stylistic embellishments that make them fascinating to watch and link them formally to classical dance. Like a ballet choreographer, Chaplin is in love with circular patterns. A mock magic trick from *The Pawnshop* serves as a good illustration of how he takes a mundane action,

An entrechat on the factory floor. *Modern Times.*

Arabesque on a switch. *Behind the Screen.*

in this case flipping a coin, and turns it into a surprisingly intricate bit.

Charlie and fellow employee John Rand argue over which one of them should go out of the shop to retrieve a bucket of water from under the nose of an angry policeman. They decide to toss a coin. Charlie borrows the coin from Rand and flips it into the air with his right hand, catching it in the same hand. At this point Charlie *should* complete the movement by slapping the coin down onto the back of his left hand. Indeed, his right hand circles as though to slap the coin down, but as the hand descends his *left* hand suddenly plucks an imaginary coin from the air and slaps down onto the back of the right. Charlie lifts up his left hand and feigns surprise at the disappearance of the coin, before "finding" it in his right.

If this is somewhat confusing to read, let it be said that it's also quite befuddling to watch. We can more or less see how he's faking Rand out, but the movement is so slick that it fakes us out as well. Charlie repeats the flip a minute or so later, so that we can enjoy it again—and see how he does the trick, if we missed it the first time. The spatial pattern, balletic in its use of interlocking circles, contributes to this mesmerizing bit of movement magic. Charlie makes a hypnotic series of circles and arcs with his hands, both of which describe loop-the-loop patterns perpendicular to each other. We *see* that he's already caught the coin, but the confusing double motion of his hands that follows gets us every time.

Like the moment when Chaplin manages to refill his glass of wine by bumping it into someone else's in *The Adventurer*, the coin trick is one of the innumerable "magical" stylizations of pedestrian actions that fill Chaplin's films. While such sequences might seem to be non sequiturs, meaningless displays of skill, magician's flourishes, they almost always serve a specific dramatic purpose; in this case, Charlie uses the confusing coin flip to cadge the coin from Rand, even though it takes him two flips to do it.

Critic William Paul does a good job of describing the paradoxically ornate yet efficient movement that characterizes so much of Chaplin's work:

> There is always such an abundance of detail in a Chaplin performance that his acting might well be described as rococo. Yet Chaplin's every gesture, every facial expression is so economical that he always seems to make a necessity of unnecessary movement, transforming his whole body into the expression of one emotion . . . every emotion he feels finds an external expression in his body.[9]

Those "unnecessary" movements, like the coin flip, are necessary to the films because they convey vital information in a visually engaging way. Chaplin's increasing choreographic mastery led him to develop many such sequences, which are, in fact, much more sophisticated than his occasional ballet parodies. In *The Kid*, for example, Charlie wants to get rid of an orphan official—the driver of a truck carting the Kid away—without leaving the Kid behind. The official is already running away from Charlie because of the way Charlie managed to jump into the moving truck and rescue the Kid from another official. Whenever the terrified official pauses to look back, Charlie simply runs in place in a burst of explosive movement, as though he's charging toward the guy. It's not exactly logical that the guy would be fooled by Charlie's "threatening" movement, but it works in the context; it's funny, interesting to watch, and makes sense dramatically.

The formal beauty of Chaplin's movement is even more obvious when he departs from pedestrian actions for more presentational scenes. In *The Great Dictator*, for example, the dictator is addressing the assembled throng, extolling the beauty of "der Aryan maiden." He supplements his suggestive gibberish—describing her face as a "delicatessen"—with descriptive gestures, assuming her coy expression and saucily tilted head, while he circles his face caressingly a couple of times with his hand. His hand movement flows into a sinuous depiction of her long, curly hair, "flaxen mit der stress" before blending smoothly into a double-handed depiction of the swell of her enormous bosom, "und der *Holsteins*." As he completes the arc his palms turn up, and Chaplin softens the risqué image somewhat by raising his shoulders slightly, turning his movement into a shrug, as though to say, "Can you believe it?" This subtlety allows him to pull off a double double-entendre of visual and verbal naughtiness. He doesn't linger over it, smoothly transitioning into the familiar "strong man" pose as the maiden flexes her powerful bicep ("mit der muss"); she needs big muscles to cradle all the "kinder Katzenjammer" she must raise. Chaplin's tender cradling gesture, followed by his staccato indication of the heights of the brood—nine in all—completes his elegant visualization of this burly, fertile beauty, a dead-on parody of the Nazi feminine ideal. It's an enchanting bit of mime, as florid and fluid as any dance movement—and funny, to boot.

The circles, arcs, and revolutions in Chaplin's personal movements are extended in the way he and the other characters move across the screen space. Visualizing the actors' movements as seen from above makes it apparent that they often move in gracefully interlocking arcs. The cumulative effect of such choreography is to lend the two-dimensional movie screen a unique sense of depth, since space in Chaplin's films is defined by the human movement within the frame rather than by camera movement. While it left him open to the complaint that his films were too stagy, this approach allowed him to develop his eloquent conceptions of comedy based on gravity, momentum, rhythm, and space. Like the best stage dance and film musicals, his work celebrates the movement of the human body in space.

Few films succeed in doing this, so it is interesting to compare Chaplin's work in this respect with that of another master, Fred Astaire. Like Chaplin, Astaire became adept at filming his work so that his stage dancing skills translated to the film medium. His use of sustained long shots—often entire dances are filmed in a single shot or two—forces us to be aware of Astaire's great facility and the brilliance of the choreography, which always serves to advance the story of the films. His dances, of course, are the essence of his art. Because they are so well integrated into the stories, and presented with such apparent simplicity, they help to ground Astaire's highly stylized acting.

A critical difference in their films is that Astaire's choreographic conceptions are rooted in the real time and space of a Broadway stage. Of course, no Broadway stage would be large enough to accommodate the huge hotel rooms and other settings he dances through so gracefully, nor could any dancer—not even Astaire himself—be precise enough to pull off some of his effects night after night. That was something borne out of the opportunity of shooting take after take, week after week, until he achieved the desired effect. Nevertheless, the intimacy of his performance style derives precisely from the *illusion* that we are watching him do a live performance, as though we have a privileged front-row seat in the theatre.

Chaplin's performances, while equally intimate, do not conjure up the world of the theatre. The silence of Chaplin's pre-1940 films and the sped-up action puts us into a very different filmic reality. Aside from their focus on movement to tell their stories, the work of these two artists could hardly be more different. One uses song and dance and breezy dialogue; the other, silence and sophisticated mime. One presses the limits of movement at normal speed; the other, what can be achieved using sped-up action. One offers a stylized and sympathetic reflection of the world of wealth and privilege; the other, of the world of poverty.

Within their respective filmic worlds, however, they both shared a taste for occasionally pushing the envelope by doing something that could be achieved only through the union of movement skill, choreography, and film technology. Astaire does it when he dances on the walls and ceiling in *Royal Wedding*, and Chaplin when he catches bricks in *Pay Day*.

In his last two-reeler Charlie is a construction worker preparing to stack some bricks onto a scaffold. Workers below throw the bricks up to him, which he improbably "catches" with the aid of reverse action. The routine is complex and elaborate; in a total of five reverse-action shots, Charlie catches seventy bricks. What makes it noteworthy are Chaplin's entertaining variations on the act of brick catching, and the deceptive way the reverse shots are combined with the forward-motion shots to throw us off the track. Indeed, until some of the more impossible-looking catches are made toward the end, one isn't quite sure that the action *is* reversed. Many viewers will chalk it up to yet another demonstration of Chaplin's incredible physical skill.

The routine begins with a long master shot showing Charlie on a scaffold and two other workers, Sydney Chaplin and Henry Bergman, on the ground below. Wiping his hands with his handkerchief in the time-honored manner of a circus performer about to do a difficult feat, Charlie drops the handkerchief down to Syd, who catches it and tosses it back up (the handkerchief has a weight in it to facilitate its movement). This opening gambit is a nice touch, since it establishes in the viewer's mind the paradigm that Charlie will be catching objects thrown upward from below. Charlie's bravura manner tells us that this is going to be something to behold.

And so it is. With a balletic twirl, Charlie turns his back, bends over, and wriggles his backside. We can practically hear the drum roll. A cut to a tighter shot below shows Syd reaching into his brick pile and rapidly tossing bricks straight up and out of frame. In the next shot Charlie, intent on his work, plucks the bricks out of the air and begins stacking them. He reaches behind him to either side and through his legs. The reverse action is effectively disguised by the way Chaplin releases the bricks; in reality, he picks up a brick from the stack, reaches back, pauses a moment, and drops it straight down. The slightest hint of a tossing motion on his part would destroy the illusion. It is only gradually that we realize that Charlie is catching most of the bricks without even looking at them.

Almost immediately Chaplin begins a series of surprise variations, catching bricks in the crooks of his knees, on top of his feet, on the back of his heel, on his butt, and between his legs at the crotch; he even catches one on top of another. Boss Mack Swain comes along and puts Henry to work as well, so now they are thrown up and caught at a dizzying pace. The editing cuts smoothly back and forth between workers tossing bricks below and Charlie retrieving them above. The payoff shot shows Charlie catching six bricks in a row—one in each hand,

Making a fancy catch. *Pay Day*.

one under each arm, one under his chin, and the last one between his legs. The foreman blows his whistle and Charlie, in an unreversed shot, drops the brick that's between his legs onto the foreman's head, ending the act with another of those decisive bangs.

It is doubtful that there exists another example in all of cinema of such successful, extended use of reverse action; Jean Cocteau used it briefly in several of his surrealistic films, notably *Beauty and the Beast*, but to achieve a dreamlike mood rather than a comic effect. With the exception of a few brief moments in later films,[10] Chaplin himself never again returned to it. But then, the brick throwing scene would be hard to top, even by Chaplin.

Isolating scenes makes it easy to see how Chaplin uses the various elements of dance—or, more accurately, the laws of Newtonian physics along with some of the aesthetic principles of dance movement—to conjure comedy from the mundane actions of everyday life. Of course, viewers don't have to recognize the sophisticated underpinnings of his physical comedy to appreciate it, which makes his achievement all the more impressive. Chaplin's highly stylized movement comes to seem so natural that we stop noticing it *is* stylized. Instead, like a good movie soundtrack, it becomes unobtrusive. Yet dance—in this larger sense—is central to the meaning of Chaplin's films, helping him to define his character and strongly affecting what subject matter he is drawn to. It intertwines with the films' content.

Chaplin's original source for consciously choreographed action was the Sennett chase (or "rally," as Sennett called it). Those weaving lines of men and autos supplied Chaplin with a basic story element that he would refine in his own work. While Keaton developed the chase by finding unusual adversaries (locomotives, boulders, cows), and unusual locations (ocean liners, antebellum Southern mansions, raging rivers), Chaplin focused on increasingly complex formal designs. What in Sennett's films remains chaotic and one-dimensional becomes, in Chaplin's, something to appreciate on several levels—for the story line, the gags, and the brilliant choreography. For Chaplin, the chase became a dance—a functional dance of pursuit.

As his career developed many of Chaplin's other "functional" movements edged toward dance as well. In *The Pawnshop* Charlie turns a fighting movement into a little dance to fool a cop. All of his action transformations are dancelike, and they almost always serve as camouflage, as when he conceals a passionate advance toward the elderly dowager Madame Grosnay in *Monsieur Verdoux* by pretending to chase a bee. It's the same with his rhythmic breaks from frenzied action into sudden freezes.

Violence camouflaged. A moment before the woman entered, Charlie had kicked Chuck Riesner across the room. *The Pilgrim.*

Posture tells the story. Charlie and his drunken millionaire buddy Harry Myers give each other a little support, while butler Allan Garcia stands impassively by. *City Lights.*

Nowhere is Chaplin more dancelike than when he portrays altered states of consciousness—madness in *Modern Times*, grogginess when he's hit on the head, most notably in *The Great Dictator*, and, most frequently, drunkenness. In *City Lights* Charlie rises, drunk, from a chair, circles around a piano bench to the keyboard, flexes his fingers to play, but instead completes his circle by rounding the bench and staggering backward into his chair. The momentum is too much to resist. He tries again, but this time walks straight into the bench, hitting the piano keyboard with his forehead. The circle, the straight line, the right angle. Chaplin was in love with geometry, and he knew that when people move in perfect lines and curves, especially when drunk, they tend to look ridiculous.

The drunken or absentminded state provided Chaplin with some of his best opportunities for both large- and small-scale choreography. Two of the finest examples occur back-to-back in *The Idle Class*. The chronically drunk husband (Chaplin in full dress as a millionaire) stands in front of his dresser and notices, by comparing wife Edna's arrival time from a telegram with his clock, that he's already late to pick her up at the train. Still, he wants to make sure he looks his best. Picking up his comb and brush, he notices in the mirror that he is wearing his top hat, so he puts down the comb and brush and takes his hat off; unfortunately, he puts it down on top of the brush, because he's been distracted by a bottle of cologne on the dresser. He sprays his forehead with the scent and picks up his comb, but now he can't find the brush. He locates the brush under the hat, but absently puts his hat back on his head so he can pick it up. When he goes to brush his hair, the hat's back on his head.

Every action Charlie does seems perfectly reasonable, but makes the simple task of brushing his hair impossible. In this film Chaplin doesn't stagger to show that he's drunk, as he had always done previously. It's *what* he's doing, not *how* he's doing it, that gives him away. Chaplin turns Charlie's distractibility into a highly choreographed sequence of self-defeating actions.

The confusion continues. Turning away from the dresser, he pats his breast pockets and notices that he has forgotten his handkerchief. He turns back, takes a handkerchief from a drawer, sprays it with the cologne, and, as he studies himself one last time in the mirror, absently folds the handkerchief, replaces it in the drawer, pats his breast pockets again, and strides off.

That's when we see that he's forgotten to put on his pants, and is about to go out in public wearing oversized boxer shorts.

Chaplin now brilliantly extends the man's self-deception to his totally unwitting deception of an entire hotel lobby full of people. Charlie walks in through a curtained entrance at the upper left of the screen. An elderly lady with a lorgnette, sitting on a bench along the left wall, turns to look at him at the same moment that a pipe-smoking workman, carrying a curtain rod with hanging drapes, enters from the right and conveniently shields Charlie's lower half from view.

Millionaire Charlie enters the hotel lobby and the workman covers him with the drape. *The Idle Class*.

Charlie politely doffs his hat to the dowager. Two other ladies enter from a doorway on the upper left, followed by a bored bellman, who leans against the door opening. One of the ladies continues diagonally out of frame to the lower right, but the other stops in the center, facing the camera; she has forgotten something. The workman turns around counter-clockwise, looking for a place to hang his curtains, which have now swung *behind* Charlie, exposing him to view.

Charlie takes a few brisk steps to the right as the woman checks through her purse. He turns his back and

The workman revolves, exposing Charlie.

He revolves again and covers him up.

walks a step or two toward a phone booth as the workman revolves again, completing his circle and covering Charlie once more, just as the woman with the purse turns and walks a few steps towards them.

The woman turns away again and exits to the lower left, as the workman exits to the upper left, and Charlie turns and enters the phone booth. As he closes the door, the woman with the lorgnette looks toward him again.

The scene lasts a mere fifteen seconds, yet so much happens in it that it seems longer. Each of the six characters seems relaxed and behaves in a natural and plausible way, yet their movements mesh together like the gears in a complex piece of machinery. Every time one of the ladies looks toward Charlie, the workman covers him with a drape. Every time they look away, he is uncovered. Repeated viewing reveals the elegance of the pattern, a gem of comic choreography.

The workman and the lady leave as Charlie enters the phone booth.

The courtly elegance of the tramp. He offers Edna his cane to help her skate, as he might offer her his arm on the street. *The Rink.*

In this scene, as in the brick-catching scene, the viewer can't help being aware of Chaplin the writer-director at work behind the scenes. This is atypical, because usually the choreography in the films seems to emanate from the personality of the Tramp himself. His dancelike movement stresses his gentlemanly aspect, the suave and elegant demeanor he maintains even as he's flicking his cigarette ashes into a lady's hand, a top hat, or someone's open mouth.

Chaplin uses both form and rhythm to convey Charlie's courtly behavior. In *The Cure* Charlie efficiently dispatches two drunks who are harassing Edna, then, without any break in his rhythm, he doffs his hat and bows to her. Escorting her from the scene, he considerately hooks his cane on the arm of one of the

Charlie watches the Apache dancers with mounting alarm in *City Lights.* The woman at left is Jean Harlow, who appeared as an extra in this scene, though she didn't make it into the final cut.

Charlie's pants have fallen down, and he holds them up with a rope, unaware of the dog attached to the other end. The dog is about to lunge for a cat. *The Gold Rush.*

drunks, rolling him over to make a path for Edna, and just as considerately rolls him back when she has passed. Charlie's silken smooth movement as he twirls through the sequence makes his rescue of Edna seem as casual and effortless as if he had merely opened a door for her.

As we would expect, Charlie is an excellent, if eccentric, social dancer. However, in the innumerable delightful scenes in which he dances in cafés, saloons, nightclubs, and society parties, things invariably go awry. In most cases, after beginning in a promising way, he encounters obstacles such as slippery floors, wads of gum sticking to his shoe, dogs tied around his waist, or partners who are unwilling, too bouncy, or too fat.

Social dancing gives Chaplin the chance to display some of the dance steps he learned on the music hall stage. The charming and poignant dance of the rolls in *The Gold Rush* and the distinctive sliding back step he uses in *Shanghaied*, *The Count*, *Modern Times*, and *Limelight* are a few examples of how he transformed stage dancing effectively into film.

Unlike the mimic qualities in Chaplin's work, which were there from the start, dance elements enter the films gradually and become more pervasive as his career evolves. Dance bursts out spectacularly in *The Floorwalker* when Charlie dances in sheer high spirits, setting the tone for the whole joyous Mutual series. Three of them—*The Count*, *The Cure*, and *The Adventurer*—contain scenes of social dancing, but more important is Chaplin's subtle use of dance elements to create new gags and enhance old ones. He livens up his chase and fight scenes with choreography that turns Charlie into a dervish of comedy, a troublemaker who somehow gets everyone dancing to his tune. Only a few dramatic moments, in *The Vagabond* and *The Immigrant*, are allowed to interrupt the comic momentum.

Charlie doesn't dance as often for sheer joy after that, but both drama and dance elements become more tightly woven into the films' fabric. The immediate result was his first masterwork, *A Dog's Life*, a film that pointed the way toward the great work to come.

In the virtuoso comic rhythms of *A Dog's Life*, Chaplin achieved a unique fusion of dance with the plot. Thereafter, there are choreographic high points in each film: brick catching in *Pay Day*, the dream sequence in *The Kid*, the David-and-Goliath sermon in *The Pilgrim*, the roll dance in *The Gold Rush*, the mirror maze in *The Circus*, the boxing match in *City Lights*, the factory and waiter dances in *Modern Times*, the balloon dance from *The Great Dictator*, and the music hall routine with Buster Keaton in *Limelight*. These are the sequences that burn into the memory as the comic or poetic highlights of the films. They are unique achievements—no one else has so successfully fused dance, drama, and comedy into single works of art.

Even Chaplin occasionally falters. In *Modern Times* waiter Charlie tries to carry a duck dinner across a crowded dance floor, accidentally impaling the duck on a chandelier as he passes under it. But his movement as he positions the duck onto the chandelier's prong seems too deliberate. In *The Idle Class* some of the scenes with the Tramp are perfunctory compared to the well-developed scenes with the millionaire.

What is amazing, though, is how often Chaplin hits the mark, successfully blending the various elements of dance with the content of the films. The choreographic high points remain just that, high points, not mountain peaks isolated from the rest of the film. The silent films, particularly, are spectacularly integrated in this respect. The seams don't show.

Comedian Dick Van Dyke often publicly stated his preference for Stan Laurel over Chaplin:

> Chaplin is great, a genius—but with Chaplin I can always see the technique showing. Lord knows it's great technique, and I admire it very much—but with Stan the technique never shows. Never. And that to me is proof that he is a better craftsman than Chaplin—an infinitely better craftsman.[11]

Leaving aside the issue of whether invisible technique is the mark of a better craftsman, there is a kind of truth in Van Dyke's statement. Only at rare moments are we aware of Stan Laurel's great physical skill. In *Liberty*, one of his silent films, he gets a crab down his pants and jumps and freezes in odd and funny positions as the crab bites him. Later in the same film he does an incredible legs-trembling routine on high girders. In *Sons of the Desert*, the team's best sound film, he takes about five minutes to go through a doorway; it's addled comic choreography as sophisticated as any of Chaplin's drunk scenes. More often than not, however, Stan's notable movements are silly or impossible, as when he wiggles his ears or "lights" his thumb. Smooth and graceful movements simply don't fit the slow-thinking, awkward, childish Stan character.

The Tramp is a far more complex creature. Childlike in many ways, he is never childish. While Chaplin muted the Tramp's raffish sexuality after 1918, he replaced it with serious romantic and dramatic content that would be alien to the world of Laurel and Hardy. Stan's lovable simplicity elicits simpler responses from viewers than Chaplin's multifaceted character.

And who, after all, is this character? We've seen that he embodies many contradictions: He is both tender and cruel, naive and knowing, romantic and cynical, courtly and streetwise. The list goes on. Within the familiar silhouette of the Tramp his creator explores the boundaries of his own artistic vision. A case can be made that Charlie is not really a coherent character at all, but a hollow device that serves a different purpose with each appearance. Chaplin conjures a golem from a mask of a face, an expressive costume, and complex, stylized movements. The character seems to have depth, to suffer, to have a soul—but he is in the end a glittering shell that expresses his creator, whose ideas, ultimately, could not be contained in the familiar outline. While the character had an extraordinary quarter-century run, Chaplin felt more and more constrained by the limits that seemed necessary to maintain his vast audience. Ultimately he lost that audience, but not before taking them into realms that no other film artist ever reached. A look at two of Chaplin's last dance scenes, both from *The Great Dictator*, makes his achievement clear.

Chaplin's famous dance with the globe is often called balletic, but, except for an initial leap, Chaplin's movements aren't really balletic at all. Instead, they have all the pretentiousness and deadly solemnity of bad modern dance. Chaplin moves dramatically toward the globe, gazing at it with adoration, a crazed Aristotle contemplating the bust of Homer. He picks it up, unsurprised to find that it's a balloon—it is, after all, his world, as he tells us: "Emperor of the world. My world." He laughs maniacally and spins it on his fingertip, a prime mover setting the world spinning on its axis. He taps it gently over his head to the other hand, and back again. But he is a capricious deity; he borrows the Tramp's back kick to send it high into the air. When the camera pans back down, he has assumed a coy female position, his ankles crossed, his hands clasped demurely in front of him: an exotic dancer, Sally Rand in clothing. He bats it back into the air with his head, then becomes a circus strongman, striking a series of "artistic" Atlas-like poses with the balloon. He rocks back and forth on his toes as though preparing to do an astonishing feat—and back kicks it again. He lies down on his desk like a sated Bacchus, bored with overindulgence, and bats it with the bottom of his foot, his backside, then spins it again on his fingertip. Back on the floor, he releases the balloon and it floats up on its own; he floats up after it, alighting weightlessly on the desk as the world descends into

Emperor of the world. *The Great Dictator.*

The prime mover. *The Great Dictator.*

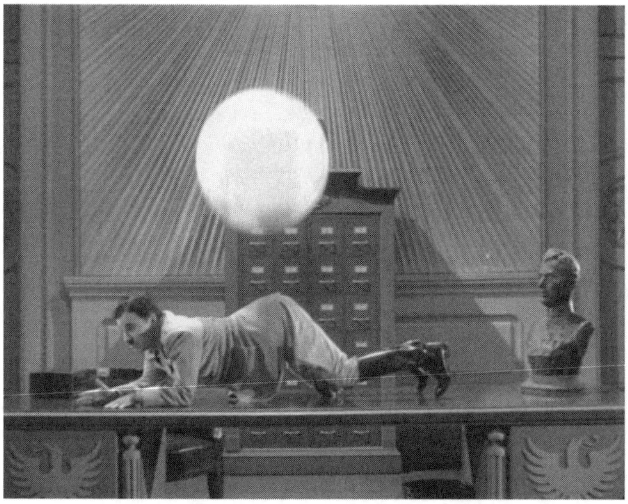

The butt of the joke. *The Great Dictator.*

his hands: The dictator has himself become a heavenly body, floating in the void of his own ego.

There are, of necessity, many cuts in the sequence to allow Chaplin to accomplish all this, including the shot in which he seems to float, another skillful use of reverse action. But the editing is seamless and fluid, reinforcing the stately rhythm set by the movement of the balloon hypnotically ascending and descending, as the syrupy Wagner music on the soundtrack provides perfect, ponderous accompaniment. The dictator is totally mesmerized by his dream of omnipotence—until he hugs the balloon with a little too much enthusiasm, and it breaks. He turns his back and collapses onto his desk, sobbing uncontrollably, a child who's just broken his favorite toy. If ridicule could have prevented a war, this scene would have done it.

The sequence that follows is a lark by comparison. We cut to the barbershop and hear a cheery radio announcer saying, "Make your work a pleasure. Move with the rhythm of music." And that's exactly what the barber does as he shaves his customer (Chester Conklin, sans his "walrus" mustache, making a final appearance with Chaplin). Everything Charlie does—lathering Conklin's face, stropping the razor, shaving, toweling, combing—is choreographed into a precise and functional dance, set to the lively and familiar strains of Brahms's Hungarian Dance Number 5. The scene derives its comedy from the barber's adherence to the rhythm and dynamic changes in the music at the expense of his customer's comfort. As usual, there are many delightful choreographic grace notes, such as the way Charlie's elbows and knees jut out to the beat as he strops his razor. He uses the last three notes of music to whip off the sheet, clamp Conklin's hat on his head, and extend his hand for payment.

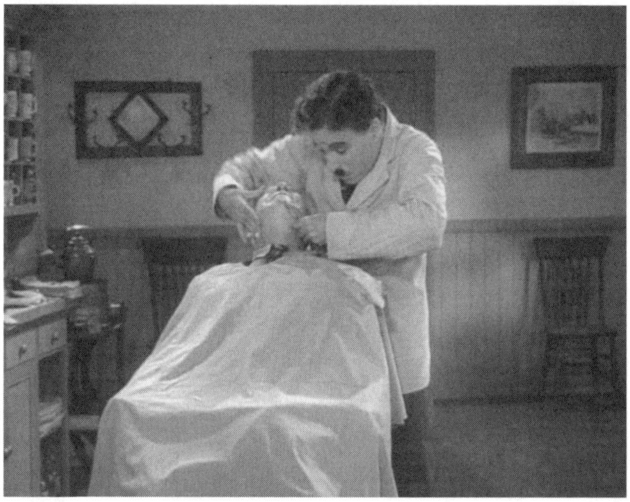

A close shave. *The Great Dictator.*

For the first time, one of Chaplin's rhythmic routines is motivated by music that we can hear. We also hear the underlying rationale, previously unspoken, behind so many scenes of Charlie at work—"Make your work a pleasure." The scene is shot is one uninterrupted take, increasing our appreciation of both the choreography and the performance. The unpretentious actions, elevated by Chaplin's art into a delightful comic dance, tell us all we need to know about the barber's all-too-human character, in stark contrast to the dictator's grandiose, mad, and infantile will to power.

At the end of Federico Fellini's *8½*, all the characters join hands around a circus ring and gravely dance in a symbolic acknowledgment that life is like a circus.

For Chaplin dance is not merely symbolic. It is at the heart of his filmic world, and it takes many different forms. It goes far beyond the playful joy and exuberance of the Mutuals, and even the elaborate, addled factory ballet in *Modern Times*. For to view life in all its aspects as dance is more than childish play—it is divine play. To integrate that vision into film is great art.

Notes

1. Charles Chaplin, *My Autobiography* (New York: Simon & Schuster, 1964), 192.

2. Alistair Cooke, *Six Men* (New York: Knopf, 1977), 26.

3. Fight scenes in all movies and stage productions have to be carefully choreographed so that the actors can avoid injury. The term *fight choreographer*, though not coined at the time, now denotes an important specialist in film and theatre production.

4. A movement in which the dancer jumps in the air and "twitters" his feet by rapidly crossing them back and forth.

5. Virginia Cherrill, interview with the author, 1978. However, according to David Robinson, who studied the

studio records, the frugal Chaplin rarely employed musicians. Robinson recounts that he did employ the Hollywood String Quartet, and then the cheaper Abe Lyman Orchestra, for the shooting of the New Year's Eve scene in the cabin in *The Gold Rush*. This makes sense, given his dance with the rolls. Robinson, *Chaplin, His Life and Art* (London: Penguin, 2001), 374–75.

6. Charles Chaplin, "Rhythm. A Story of Men in Macabre Movement," originally published in *Script* 18, no. 445 (January 15, 1938), reprinted in Peter Cotes and Thelma Niklaus, *The Little Fellow* (New York: Citadel Press, 1965), 167–68.

7. Chaplin, *My Autobiography*, 209.

8. Walter Kerr, *The Silent Clowns* (New York: Knopf, 1975), 168. Kerr provides one of the best and most extended discussions of this film in his book, on pages 163–68.

9. William Paul, "The Gold Rush," *Film Comment* 8, no. 3 (September–October, 1972), 17.

10. He does it for one shot during the balloon dance in *The Great Dictator*, and again for a shot in *Limelight*, discussed in chapter 14.

11. Van Dyke, cited in Al Kilgore and John McCabe *Laurel and Hardy* (New York: Ballantine Books, 1976), 11.

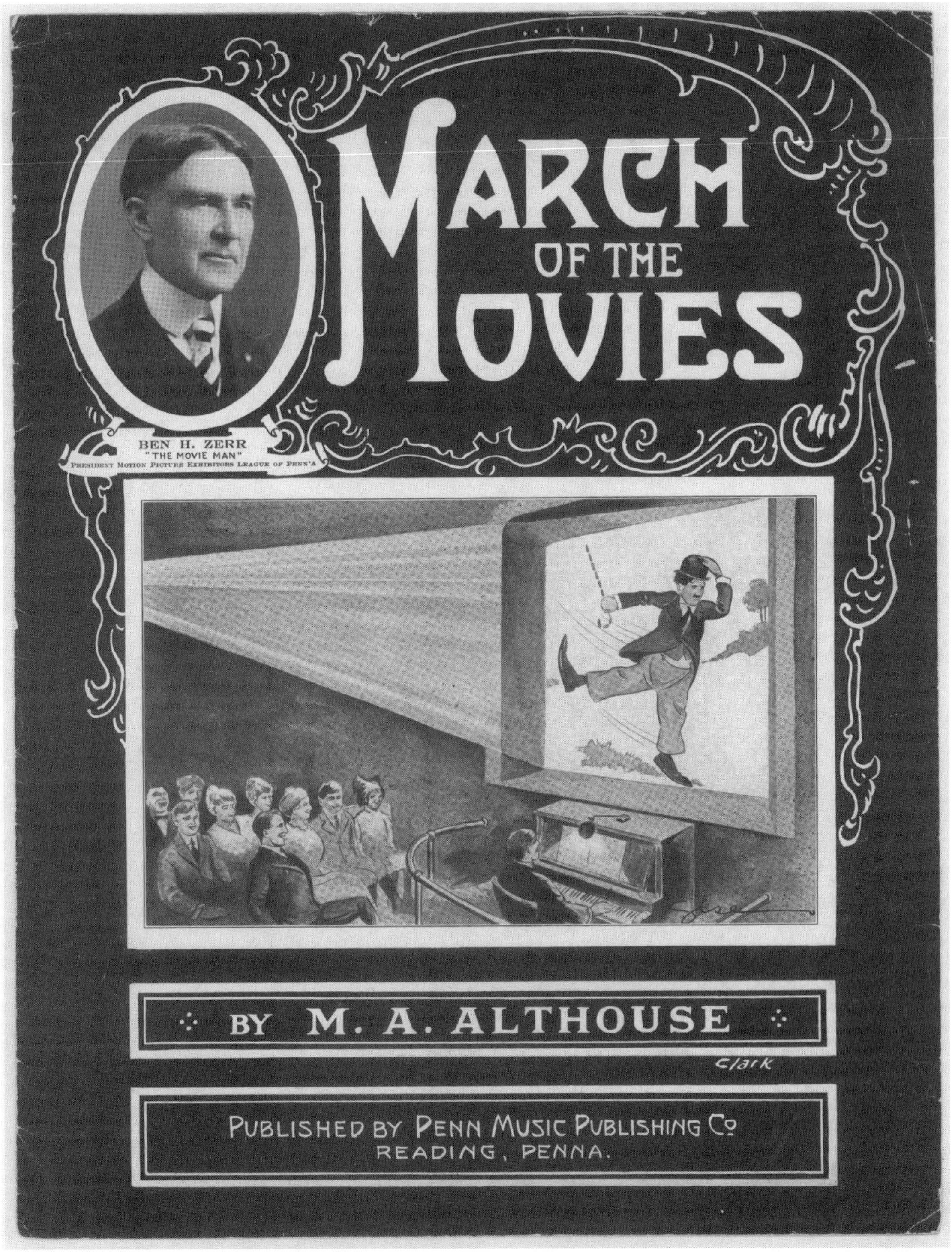

PART THREE

March of the Movies, 1915. This instrumental piece was published by the Motion Picture Exhibitors League of Pennsylvania, using Chaplin's image to promote movies themselves. During this period movie theaters were casting off their lowly and rather disreputable origins and positioning themselves as places of wholesome family entertainment. The well-dressed audience includes both women and children, and even the pianist is laughing at Charlie's antics.

CHAPTER EIGHT

Facing Sound

The Sounds of Silents

Although Chaplin's silent films are an eloquent argument for the notion that actions speak louder than words, words play an important role in his films, and in silent films generally, in the form of subtitles.[1] Subtitles grew more elaborate throughout the silent era, particularly in those films that derived from literature or aspired to literary-type significance. In retrospect, this tendency is seen as a wrong direction. Cinema has always been more visual than verbal, and too many dialogue or expositional subtitles in a silent film signals a failure of the visual imagination. The better filmmakers recognized this, though few pushed it to the point of F. W. Murnau, whose 1924 film *The Last Laugh* contains only one. Most simply prided themselves on their sparing use of subtitles, and Chaplin was no exception.

One way Chaplin minimized the use of subtitles was to find reasons for his characters not to talk. In *The Immigrant*, for example, the language barrier causes comic clashes as immigrant Charlie struggles to order a meal from surly waiter Eric Campbell. Charlie mimes playing a flute to order a plate of beans, "the musical fruit" of the popular naughty rhyme[2] (it's a quick moment that is often lost on modern viewers). Even in his sound films Chaplin often found reasons for characters to have to communicate through action. Forty years after *The Immigrant*, the king in *A King in New York* is having difficulties ordering a meal in a nightclub over the raucous sound of a loud jazz combo. Like his 1917 counterpart, this later-day immigrant is forced to resort to pantomime. Chaplin thus makes stylized silent action sequences seem natural by grounding them in necessity.

In plays and sound movies, dialogue conveys essential information, and the emotional meaning behind the words, the subtext, is conveyed primarily through vocal inflection. In silent films, both information and emotional content must be conveyed through actions. The way people relate to each other physically, as well as the way they handle objects, takes on heightened importance. That's the function of that pesky rolling pin in *The Pilgrim* as Charlie and Edna are shyly getting to know each other. There's only one subtitle, as Charlie asks, "May I help you?" Though the couple exchange a few more words during the scene, there's no need to translate them, because we can plainly see what they're talking about from the context. The scene unfolds visually. Similarly, fights and chases, ubiquitous in silent films, are a more visual way to express dramatic conflict than verbal exchanges.

Dialogue, of course, isn't the only kind of sound missing from the films. An intriguing aspect of silent films is that they're not really silent. An image of someone screaming, for instance, has such strong associations that viewers automatically "fill in" the sound in their heads. This makes possible a whole class of unique sound gags that work *only* in a silent film world. When Charlie "plays" the wooden spoon for Edna and sings to her in *The Pawnshop*, we can easily imagine the Hawaiian kitchen serenade; in a sound film the sequence wouldn't be as amusing, because we'd hear Charlie singing, but not the imaginary ukulele music. Similarly, when butler Albert Austin pops a champagne cork in *The Adventurer*, escaped convict Charlie automatically throws his hands up, assuming the cops have arrived with guns blazing. It works well visually because the audience can see the cork popping and Charlie reacting at the same instant. Hearing the sound of the cork would hardly improve the gag, since a cork popping sounds little like the deafening report of a gun.

Yet reissues of silent films in the sound era often supplied them with just such synchronized sound effects; in the first sound reissues of the Mutual films, we hear the cork popping and the ukulele playing.[3] While such after-the-fact sounds may make the films more accessible to young children, synchronized sound effects fit oddly in a silent film world, stressing the absence of naturalistic sound elsewhere in the film. This is an aesthetic dilemma in the contemporary scoring of silent films. For example, in Harold Lloyd's *Why Worry* there is a scene in which Harold simulates cannon fire with a combination of cigar smoke, lobbed coconuts, and bass drum beats. This unlikely subterfuge is credible in silence, or with stylized instrumental music as an accompaniment. But in a 1970s reissue we hear authentic-sounding cannon and explosion sounds, which stretches plausibility. A more recent score corrected the misjudgment.

Chaplin's own reissue soundtracks for his 1918–1928 films, which he composed from the early 1940s through the 1970s, offer an object lesson in the proper way to score a silent film. Sound effects are used sparingly, and the music seldom "Mickey Mouses" the action in the way now associated with early sound-era animated cartoons. Instead, it establishes mood and reinforces the action with jaunty, up-tempo dance tunes, marches, and melodic waltzes.

In the silent era subtitles were as important as music in accompanying the silent action. In addition to providing essential information, they offered comedy filmmakers the chance to add verbal humor to their stories. One of the first things a modern audience will notice about the subtitles in Chaplin's 1914–1917 films is his fondness for silly names.[4] A carryover from the British music hall tradition generally, and from the Karno sketches and Sennett films specifically, such names continue a venerable theatrical tradition that peaked with eighteenth-century Restoration playwrights like Richard Brinsley Sheridan, who delighted in such character-revealing names as Lady Sneerwell, Lydia Languish, and Snake. Chaplin's character names tended to be more bluntly descriptive than clever—Edna as a society woman is Miss Moneybags, Henry Bergman in drag is Mrs. Stout, Chaplin is Weakchin the caveman, who battles Mack Swain's King Low-Brow. He gets a bit more inventive with punning names like Count de Broko, Count Chloride de Lime, Count de Beans, and Sir Cecil Seltzer, C.O.D. In his parody of *Carmen*, Don Jose becomes Darn Hosiery. Silly names disappear from the films after 1918, only to return with a vengeance in *The Great Dictator*.

Often the subtitles in Chaplin's films serve to humorously label scenes or characters. In *The Immigrant*, after a lot of comedy derived from the movement of the wildly pitching deck, the audience is treated to "More rolling" in the form of a craps game. The construction workers in *Pay Day* are "Hard Shirking Men"; Charlie's termagant wife, pacing back and forth outside the construction yard on payday, is "His wife—and First National Bank." If these jokes seem rather tame, it must be said that they seldom get laughs in the viewing. Mildly amusing, they primarily serve an expositional function.

Chaplin occasionally scores with a funny line in his dialogue subtitles. Capturing thirteen German soldiers by himself in *Shoulder Arms*, he casually describes his success by explaining, "I surrounded them." After Albert Austin leaves the pawnshop with his dissected alarm clock, he is approached by a bum who asks him, "What time is it?" The innocent question brings a laugh, and Austin tops it when he angrily pushes the hapless derelict to the ground. In *A Dog's Life* Charlie uses Scraps the dog as a pillow but is soon scratching his head, noting, "There are strangers in our midst." But as he moved into feature film production Chaplin largely abandoned jokey titles, not wanting words to compete with his visual comedy.

Not that verbal comedy in subtitles is incompatible with visual comedy. Both Keaton and Lloyd made extensive use of comical subtitles. While the original subtitles for Lloyd's films are somewhat dated, Keaton's remain surprisingly fresh.

It is ironic that Keaton, taciturn in real life, used subtitles with far greater wit and sophistication than the more voluble Chaplin and Lloyd. He set the droll standard in his first independent film, the 1920 short *One Week*. Sitting on the end of a plank extending from the second floor of his partially completed house, he is about to finish sawing it in two when he is called to supper by his wife. "I'll be right down," he accurately replies. In *Cops*, through an intricate series of misunderstandings, Buster believes he has shrewdly bought a wagonload of furniture to resell. In fact, the actual owners think he is a moving man. He accepts their generous if puzzling help loading the wagon and goes on his way. While the family anxiously awaits him at their new home, Buster naps on the seat as his horse pulls the cart along at a snail's pace. Looking at his watch, the father exclaims, "Maybe he was arrested for speeding." The next title introduces the police parade: "Once a year the citizens of every city know where they can find a policeman." Buster accidentally throws an anarchist's bomb into the parade; rides over a fire hydrant, drenching the assembled dignitaries; and overturns the cart. During the ensuing melee the police chief accosts the mayor with "Get some cops to protect our policemen." Meanwhile the father, innocent of the fact that all his worldly possessions have been destroyed, points excitedly toward his wife and says, "Do you suppose anything could've happened to our furniture?" This running verbal commentary not only stems naturally from the action, it complements it, adding greatly to the film's visual humor. Keaton maintained the same high level of verbal wit throughout his silent career.

Chaplin hardly needed verbal wit to ensure the success of his silent films, but with the coming of sound he faced a much greater problem. Both subtitles and silent film were rendered obsolete by the new technology.

Facing the Revolution

From the mid-1920s on, Chaplin was defensive about the subject of sound movies. Visiting William Randolph Hearst's palatial home, San Simeon, he stalked furiously out of the room when Hearst dared to suggest that sound films might be a natural and acceptable successor to silents. Chaplin was well aware of the reasons for his anger:

> [I]f I did make a talking picture, no matter how good I was I could never surpass the artistry of my pantomime. I had thought of possible voices for the tramp—whether he should speak in monosyllables or just mumble. But it was no use. If I talked I would become like any other comedian. These were the melancholy problems that confronted me.[5]

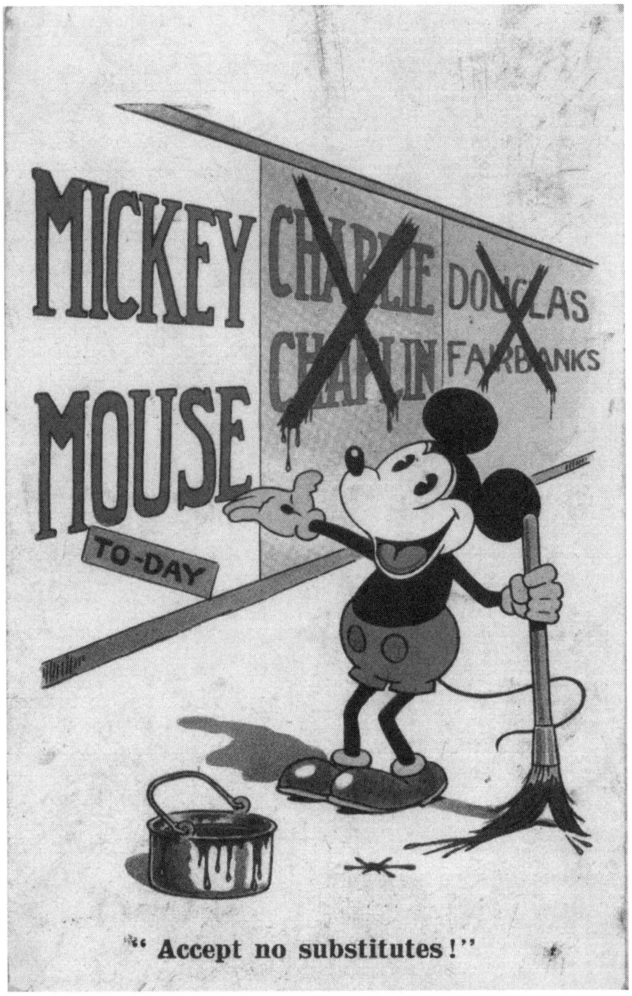

Sign of the times: A postcard from 1932. © Disney Enterprises, Inc.

Chaplin was justifiably appalled by the poor quality of many early sound films. Sound technicians ruled the day, and actors, now frequently stage imports with no screen experience, were forced to restrict their movements to a limited area, and speak their lines with excruciating deliberateness and overarticulation to be picked up by the crude early microphones. The once-fluid silent camera had to be encased in an immobile, soundproof booth, so that its loud whirring didn't spoil the take. In addition, the fledgling technology sometimes produced unintentionally humorous sound effects.[6]

Films had finally become what one of their original names suggested they were—photoplays—except that the early sound films were far more static and stilted than any stage play. Yet at first the audience overlooked the problems, flocking to the new sensation of pictures that talked as they had thirty years earlier flocked to crude nickelodeon theaters to see the novelty of pictures that moved. Although for a time the country went musical mad, the subject matter hardly mattered, since it was the illusion that was the attraction. And soon the technology improved, and a new breed of performer emerged for the new medium.

For sound films were not merely silent films with sound added. They were an entirely new medium. The soundtrack eliminated many of the basic characteristics of silent film storytelling—the use of variable speeds, the need to tell the story visually with the use of a few subtitles, the presence of live musicians to provide the sound accompaniment. The screen itself seemed to open up, edging closer to reality with the sound of voices, breathing, dialogue, and ambient sound. Music, before this largely a local affair put together by the music director of each theater, was for the first time under the absolute control of the filmmakers. No longer did music have to accompany every moment of the film the way an orchestra accompanies a ballet. Now it could be used more selectively, sometimes disappearing entirely, at other times fading to a low volume to underscore dialogue. In early sound films it was thought odd to have "disembodied" music that wasn't associated with an onscreen orchestra playing,[7] but that soon changed as new rules quickly evolved for the new medium.

For Chaplin it was as though the rug he had labored so long to weave was suddenly yanked out from under him. Unlike the rugs he had slipped on so gracefully in *One A.M.*, this time the threat was all too real. He recognized it as both a personal crisis and a crisis for an entire art form,[8] and he wasn't shy about expressing his feelings in interviews. In an article he wrote for the *New York Times* two weeks before the premiere of *City Lights*, he defended his position not only as the master of silent comedy, but as its sole remaining exponent. Despite the fact that silent films had been completely replaced by the three-year-old phenomenon, Chaplin blithely stated:

> Because the silent or nondialogue picture has been temporarily pushed aside in the hysteria attending the introduction of speech by no means indicates that it is extinct or that the motion picture screen has seen the last of it. *City Lights* is evidence of this. . . . I am confident that the future will see a return of interest in nontalking productions because there is a constant demand for a medium that is universal in its utility. . . . I consider the talking picture a valuable addition to the dramatic art regardless of its limitations, but I regard it only as an addition, not as a substitute. . . . Silent comedy is more satisfactory entertainment for the masses than talking comedy. . . . Pantomime . . . is the prime qualification of a successful screen player.[9]

In fact, Chaplin had halted production midway through *City Lights* to consider the advisability of making a film that would seem anachronistic to its intended audience. Harold Lloyd virtually remade his completed silent film *Welcome Danger* in 1929, eagerly embracing the new medium, a move that Chaplin, who rarely talked about his colleagues publicly, condemned in a magazine interview the same year.[10]

Buster Keaton, no longer his own boss at MGM, made two excellent silent films in 1928 and 1929 but, weary from creative battles on the job, a personal battle with alcoholism, and a dissolving marriage, capitulated to MGM's "guidance" of his career into swift oblivion in a series of uninspired sound films. Of course, there are moments when some of the old brilliance returns; in *The Hollywood Revue of 1929*, he plays Neptune's daughter in an eccentric dance sequence that recalls the breezy parodic style of his two-reelers. But Keaton's days as a major filmmaker were over, as were those of Douglas Fairbanks, Mary Pickford, Gloria Swanson, and most of the other major stars of silent cinema. Lloyd made some excellent sound features, but public interest in his films waned as the decade wore on. Of the silent clowns, only Laurel and Hardy seemed to make the transition to sound without major aesthetic fuss, and they went on to become even more popular than they had been in the silent era.

But waiting in the wings were a new breed of comedian. Many of them were of Chaplin's comic generation, but had styles of comedy too dependent on the spoken word to succeed in silent films. The Marx Brothers virtually exploded onto the screen and into the hearts of a public shocked and disheartened by the Depression. W. C. Fields, a stage star from the early 1900s on, was a modest hit as a silent film comedian, but a major one in sound. The cynical, antiromantic content and tongue-in-cheek style of these films perfectly matched the national mood, and by the mid-1930s Fields was being labeled "the funniest man in the world."

And what of the King of Comedy? Now the statement had to be qualified: The King of Silent Comedy. A king whose kingdom had completely vanished, despite his vigorous protests. Privately, Chaplin expressed both his fear of being outdated and his contempt for the newcomers:

> Modern humor frightens me a little. The Marx brothers are frightening. . . . They say, 'All right, you're insane, we'll appeal to your insanity.' They make insanity the convention. . . . Knocking everything down. Annihilating everything. There's no conduct in their humor. They haven't any attitude. It's up-to-date, of course—a part of the chaos. I think it's transitional.[11]

It wasn't transitional, of course. The kingdom had irreversibly altered, leaving its king to adapt as best he could. On one occasion he met with Fields and outraged the comedian by never once referring to his screen work. He did manage to tell Groucho Marx how much he admired his great verbal facility, but basically he felt confounded and threatened by the new developments.

Working against the prevailing trend and the heartfelt advice of his film colleagues, Chaplin elected to continue making *City Lights* as a silent film.[12] But the anomaly of releasing a silent film in 1931 hit home forcibly when he found that United Artists, his own company, was reluctant to risk money promoting *City Lights*. He took over the New York premiere himself, renting an out-of-the-way theatre and personally supervising the ad campaign. The film, of course, proved to be a huge popular and critical success, one of Chaplin's greatest triumphs. It was an auspicious beginning for a sound career marked by bold artistic choices.

Notes

1. *Subtitle* is the original term for any text cards after the main title and credits. The term *intertitle* is preferred by modern film scholars to differentiate silent movie subtitles from foreign film subtitles, which appear superimposed over the image. This book adheres to the original usage.

2. "Beans, beans, the musical fruit/The more you eat, the more you toot."

3. The Van Beuren Corporation acquired the rights to the Mutuals in 1932 and added jazzy soundtracks to the films. For many years these were the only sound versions of the Mutuals available to the public. While some people find the soundtracks annoying, they are very lively, and possess a certain early jazz charm, like much of the cartoon music from the period. The most recent DVD release of the films boasts new scores by Carl Davis, a well-known composer who has done many excellent silent film scores.

4. Scholars have agonized over the authenticity of the subtitles of Chaplin's early films, since they were repeatedly "modernized" with new ones. In the 1920s particularly, many of Chaplin's Keystones were gagged up with lengthy and unfunny editorial commentary and dreadful puns (Chaplin's brother Sydney was one of the offenders). In later years Chaplin himself altered both scenes and subtitles in reissues of his post-1918 films. For example, in *Shoulder Arms* he eliminated a "three on a match" gag; the old superstition held that it was bad luck to be the third person to light a cigarette off the same match.

5. Charles Chaplin, *My Autobiography* (New York: Simon & Schuster, 1964), 387. The great French comedian Jacques Tati speaks in monosyllables in his brilliant series of Mr. Hulot films from the 1950s through the 1970s.

6. An excellent and highly entertaining account of the transition to sound films can be found in Scott Eyman's *The Speed of Sound* (New York: Simon & Schuster, 1997).

7. For that reason many of the early film musicals were about stage musicals, including *Gold Diggers of Broadway*, the top-grossing film of 1929. That's also the reason the seminal early film *Dracula* (1931) is virtually without music. Philip Glass was commissioned by Universal to compose a soundtrack in 1999.

8. He wasn't the only one to recognize the crisis, of course. Late in 1931 Mary Pickford told an interviewer, "Isn't all art development a process of simplification . . . a search for a universal idea, a universal medium? It would have been more logical if silent pictures had grown out of the talkie instead of the other way round" (Anne O'Hare McCormick, "Searching for the Mind of Hollywood/An Inquiry into the Influences Molding the Vast Flow of Motion Pictures," *New York Times Magazine*, December 13, 1931, 21). Pickford's comment, provocative at the time, now sounds rather plaintive, particularly to the many silent film aficionados who agree with it.

9. Charlie Chaplin, "Pantomime and Comedy," *New York Times*, January 25, 1931, sec. 8, p. 6.

10. Gladys Hall, "Charlie Chaplin Attacks the Talkies" *Motion Picture*, May 1929, 29.

11. Chaplin, cited in Max Eastman, *Enjoyment of Laughter* (London: Hamish Hamilton, 1937), 108.

12. It did provide Chaplin with the opportunity to develop and demonstrate his talent as a composer of film music.

CHAPTER NINE

Swan Song with Music: *City Lights*

In his articles and interviews attacking talkies, Chaplin had thrown down the gauntlet, declaring silent film to be a viable art form and offering up *City Lights* as the proof. The embattled tone is evident in the film's opening credits. Addressing an audience that hadn't seen a silent film, or a new Chaplin film, in nearly three years—an audience moreover "hysterical" over what he considered the passing fad of talking pictures—he succinctly subtitles his picture "A Comedy Romance in Pantomime." Three years earlier no one would have described a film as pantomime, because they were *all* pantomime. But now Chaplin stood defiantly alone, the last holdout.

After the main credits, Chaplin repeats the title with a theatrical flourish. We see a bustling night scene of the central city street where much of the film's action will take place; sitting unobtrusively in the background is the civic monument that will be used in the opening scene. Letters pop up across the screen, each one formed from white dots, like the glowing electric bulbs on a flashing movie marquee, spelling out the words CITY LIGHTS. It's a pleasant conceit, subtly reminding the audience that this, too, is a movie, despite the fact that it's a *silent* movie, and at the same time reinforcing the title, the best one Chaplin ever came up with.

Originally conceived as a silent film, *City Lights* can be viewed silently without losing most of its meaning and humor. However, Chaplin couldn't resist beginning it by taking another gibe at talking pictures, this time in the form of a sound gag. A crowd is gathered for the unveiling of the civic monument, and various pompous dignitaries speak, accompanied on the soundtrack by kazoo-like squawks synchronized to their lip movements (Chaplin made the sounds by speaking through a saxophone mouthpiece). By presenting their utterances as unintelligible gibberish, Chaplin pokes fun at filmed speech as superfluous. While the reference to garbled movie soundtracks would have been more meaningful to a 1931 audience, the gag still works, since any audience is going to get the point about empty ceremonial babble. And when Charlie is revealed asleep in the lap of the statue, and then disrupts the ceremony with his characteristic antics, no further demonstration is necessary that words *are* superfluous in a film—at least, in a Charlie Chaplin film.

Three later scenes make use of naturalistic, synchronized sound effects. At a party Charlie swallows a whistle, which tweets each time he hiccups, interrupting the performance of a pretentious classical singer (whose singing we *don't* hear on the soundtrack). During the prizefight scene we hear the bell ring several times. And a scene of Charlie escaping the police includes the sounds of gunshots and sirens. But most of the film takes place in the charmed silent world of Chaplin pantomime, accompanied for the first time by Chaplin's own music.

The Gold Rush and *City Lights* are the two films most often singled out as Chaplin's best, and they complement each other in so many ways that it is illuminating to consider them in relation to each other. In *The Gold Rush* Chaplin achieved unity, in part, by the fusion of comedy and drama in the individual scenes, a series of set pieces of remarkable quality and consistency. The cabin scenes, such as the struggle for the rifle, the eating of the shoe, Mack Swain imagining Charlie to be a chicken, and the cliff-hanging finale, are all comic, but it's comedy on the brink of the abyss, as Charlie wages life and death struggles against cold, hunger, and his cannibalistic cabinmate. As these scenes deal with Charlie's physical survival and his tenuous relationship with Swain,

Charlie, a bit more dapper than usual, in *City Lights*.

the romantic scenes with Georgia focus on his equally urgent need for love, and they unfold through a series of equally outstanding comic sequences. The romantic plot climaxes when Charlie is stood up by the dance hall girls on New Year's Eve and does his dance of the dinner rolls. This tour de force, at once comic, graceful, and poignant, mirrors the shoe-eating sequence that provides the centerpiece of the film's survival story.[1]

City Lights also features parallel plots about tenuous friendship and romance, this time with the twist that both stories hinge on identity confusion. In the friendship story Charlie saves a drunken and depressed millionaire from committing suicide by drowning, becoming the millionaire's bosom buddy—but only when the man is roaring drunk. Sober, the swell has no idea who Charlie is. In the romance, the blind flower seller believes Charlie is himself a millionaire. It is this relationship that drives the action of the film, for Charlie must earn money to supplement her slender income and keep up his masquerade.

In *The Gold Rush* the romance and friendship plots each play out separately. Georgia doesn't even appear until the film is a third over, and then we remain with her and the smitten Charlie until he returns to the frozen hills to make his fortune, secure in the mistaken belief that he has wooed and won her. He only rediscovers her by chance, on the voyage home, a plot device that allows Chaplin to bring the two halves of the film neatly together.

In *City Lights* Chaplin intricately interweaves the blind girl and millionaire scenes. The girl and the millionaire never meet, but their stories are closely linked by the dual themes of money and blindness. Money, meaningless to the millionaire, is in desperately short supply for Charlie and the girl. The millionaire's metaphorical blindness—he has to be blind drunk to "see" Charlie—permits their friendship, unthinkable in the harsh daylight of sobriety. This inconstant friendship helps Charlie to perpetrate the deception that he's the girl's wealthy benefactor, a deception, in turn, that wouldn't be possible without the girl's literal blindness.

Chaplin set himself an ambitious problem in unifying these very different stories, for there is a great tonal difference in the comedy. The scenes with the millionaire are raucous, taking place in nightclubs and at orgiastic drunken parties. While the millionaire remains suicidal throughout the film, the stakes aren't as high as in *The Gold Rush*, since it's only the capricious drunk who's at risk, not Charlie himself. The comedy is therefore lighter, a return to the cheery, pratfall-filled drunken comedy of Chaplin's early days. On the other hand, the girl's affliction limits the kind of comedy—invariably at his own expense—that Chaplin can use.[2] Obviously, a handicapped heroine lends a perilous gravity to a comedy film, and the slightest misjudgment could tilt it toward mawkishness or bad taste. As it turns out, the scenes between Chaplin and the blind girl, quiet and full of delicate humor, are among the marvels of the Chaplin canon.[3]

The contrast in tones is reflected in the changes in Chaplin's facial makeup. In scenes with the millionaire, particularly in the nightclub, it is highly exaggerated—more so than in any other Chaplin film. His eyebrows are large half-moons on his chalky-white face, giving him a clownish look. But the makeup is more subtle and naturalistic in the scenes with the blind girl.

Another notable change in the makeup is that Charlie's mustache is smaller than usual, exposing more of his upper lip and making his face look more "naked," and therefore more vulnerable. This is appropriate, given the film's focus on Charlie's vulnerabilities. In addition to reducing the size of his trademark mustache, Chaplin lets some of the gray in his hair show through. While Chaplin had never tried to hide from the public his prematurely graying hair, which had gone white by 1928,

Chaplin with Harry Myers as the eccentric millionaire. Note Chaplin's exaggerated facial makeup.

this is the first time he let it any of it show through in a film. It's tempting to think that he wanted us to glimpse Chaplin, the artist, through Charlie, his masklike comic creation.

Chaplin's musical soundtrack is of inestimable help in unifying the disparate elements of his film. Though he never learned to read music, Chaplin had always been an enthusiastic musician and composer. During his stage career he traveled with a violin and cello, taking occasional lessons from the music directors of the theatres on his tours, and practicing for hours in his rented rooms. In 1916 he self-published several songs—"I think we sold three copies," he wryly reports in his autobiography.[4] However, anything associated with Chaplin was commercially viable, and one of them, "The Peace Patrol," was recorded on a single-sided, six-inch disk. In 1925 two more of his songs were recorded, this time with Chaplin conducting Abe Lyman's popular orchestra. These songs were published by established music publishers, and the covers linked them to the release of *The Gold Rush*, though neither song has any connection with the film.[5]

However, Chaplin didn't avail himself of the most logical outlet for his compositional skill, the scores that were sent to theaters playing his films.[6] Very few silent films commissioned full original scores, and it may be that the pressure of producing his films left Chaplin with neither the time nor the inclination to do so. However, with movie pit orchestras as obsolete as silent film itself, he prolonged *City Lights*' release date for several months to compose and record his own score.

During the transitional period between the silent and sound eras, a number of silent feature films, beginning with John Barrymore's *Don Juan* in 1926, were released with recorded musical soundtracks and some sound effects. Comparing Chaplin's score with the soundtrack for Keaton's *Spite Marriage*, released in 1929, reveals the sophistication of Chaplin's maiden effort as a film composer.

The film was Keaton's last silent, and his first to have a recorded soundtrack. Its score, while pleasant and serviceable, occasionally uses cartoony sound effects such as slide whistles to accent the falls and action sequences. While such sounds were fresh and perfectly acceptable to the original audience, by today's standards they cheapen rather than highlight the comedy.[7] The score also incorporates synchronized human sounds, including applause and crowd laughter, which has the unintended effect of highlighting the absence of other naturalistic sounds, especially dialogue.[8]

The score for *Spite Marriage*, as was customary during the silent era, incorporates a number of popular songs, whose unheard lyrics would have been familiar to contemporary audiences. Thus songs like "This Is My Lucky Day," "I'm More Than Satisfied," and "That's Just My Way of Forgetting You" explicitly comment on the scenes they accompany. However, the music, as a whole, is undistinguished, and does little to enhance the film.

The score for *City Lights* also incorporates and paraphrases a number of popular tunes, notably "La Violetera" as the blind girl's principal theme.[9] However, there the resemblance ends, for Chaplin's score is tuneful, inventive, and almost wholly original. Chaplin uses the Wagnerian leitmotif method of identifying each character with one or more specific musical themes. The score is filled with lilting waltzes; tangos; rumbas; delicate love themes; jazzy, blaring "city" music to set off some of the drunken slapstick sequences; and several witty parodies of operatic and classical music at appropriate moments. For the most part it avoids comical effects—Chaplin didn't want the music to compete with the visual comedy.[10] Sound effects are used, but very sparingly, so that we never get the strange dislocation between the sound and silent film worlds that occurs in *Spite Marriage* and other early scored silent films.[11] The score does more than accompany the film. It enhances its comedy and deepens its emotional power, helping Chaplin to tie his film together as it builds inexorably toward its powerful conclusion.[12]

That buildup begins when the millionaire goes to the Continent for an extended vacation, leaving Charlie to fend for himself. When the girl falls ill, he gets a job as a street cleaner to help provide for her. But he loses his job just when she's threatened with eviction. Desperate for money to save her, he enters a prizefight. But despite his valiant effort in the ring, he's knocked out.

Later that night, aching and discouraged, he comes upon the drunken millionaire, who gives him not only money to pay the girl's back rent, but enough for the operation that will restore her eyesight. This encounter ties together the two plots of the film, but there are further complications. Before Charlie can leave with the money, the millionaire is knocked out in an attempted robbery. Charlie thwarts the thieves and summons the police, but when the millionaire comes to he has no memory either of Charlie or of having given him the money. Charlie grabs the cash and runs, thereby becoming a fugitive. He bids the girl a final, furtive goodbye, giving her the money for the rent, and for the operation that will forever alter their relationship.

The fight scene is particularly important in setting up this dramatic turn of fortune, because the film flags somewhat during several of the earlier comic scenes, particularly the party sequence at the millionaire's house in which Charlie swallows the whistle. But in the boxing scene, working opposite Keystone veteran Hank Mann, Chaplin comes triumphantly into his own again; it is one of the longest, funniest, and most elaborately choreographed scenes he ever devised.

Chaplin had done boxing scenes twice before, once at Keystone in *The Knockout* and again at Essanay in *The Champion*. Even a casual comparison demonstrates Chaplin's growth as a creator of physical comedy in the fifteen years that separates these films from *City Lights*. The new scene leaves the viewer breathless with laughter. In addition to featuring better gags and much more sophisticated choreography, it's also perfectly set off by Chaplin's subtle but lively background music, which underscores the visual rhythms of the action without ever "Mickey Mousing" it. There are no effects or musical accents when the men punch and fall; instead, the metronome-like repetition and precision of the routine are reflected in the music, which consists of a piccolo playing a simple and sprightly motif over a rapid rhythmic tattoo, or ostinato, played by the strings.

The match itself is preceded by a very funny dressing-room scene that runs about seven minutes. The boxer who had agreed to go easy with Charlie and split the take has to scram because the police are after him. He is replaced by the stolid Mann, who's tough enough to effortlessly knock out the winner of a previous bout. Charlie's panic mounts as Mann refuses to make the same deal. It will be winner take all. Charlie mincingly tries to ingratiate himself, but Mann interprets his coy overtures as homosexual advances, and pointedly ducks behind a dressing curtain to change to his boxing trunks. After much additional byplay the match begins. Running a full six minutes, it's a virtual catalogue of boxing gags.[13]

When the bell rings Charlie immediately maneuvers the referee between himself and Mann, shadowing the referee's movements so that Mann can't get to him. Establishing a pattern of movement they will repeat throughout the scene, the men hop from side to side;

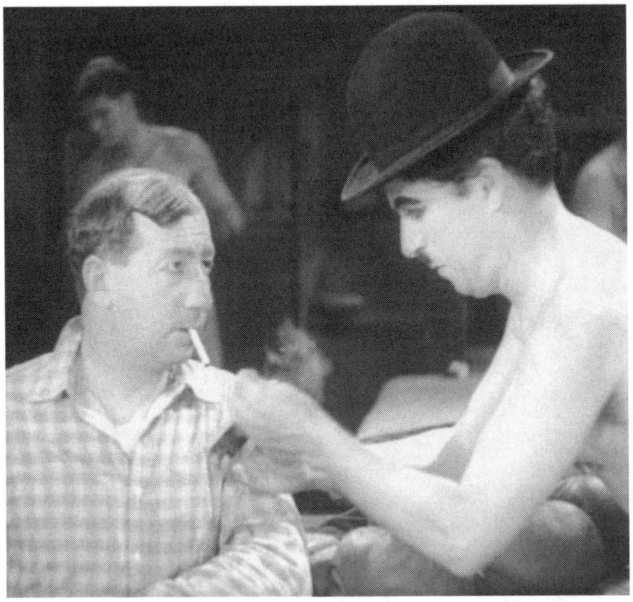

Hank Mann evidently isn't used to having his cigarette lit by a man.

Charlie maneuvers the referee between himself and Mann; Charlie and the referee hop one way, Mann the other.

the referee and Mann face each other and hop in opposite directions, while Charlie, keeping safely behind the referee, hops along with him. It's as though all three have been instantly programmed by the hypnotic pattern. They circle around the ring and repeat it on the other side, then return to their original positions and begin it again. But this time Mann breaks the rhythm by stopping. The moment the referee hops out of the way, Charlie uses the opportunity to punch Mann, whereupon they resume the original pattern of circle, hop-hop-hop, circle back, hop-hop-stop-PUNCH. But this time Mann gets a swing in at Charlie, who ducks and grabs him in a bear-hug. The referee breaks up the clinch, and again the men move into the same pattern of hops, circles, punch-duck-clinch.

A variation is introduced when Mann swings so hard that he spins around; Charlie grabs him in a clinch from behind and Mann tries to buck him off. Charlie stays on, even though his legs fly into the air, and he butts Mann in the rear end with his knee. The referee breaks this up and then moves aside, giving Charlie another opportunity to punch Mann.

The original pattern begins again, but then the participants execute an intricate circling movement during which they change positions while staying in rhythm. Now Charlie and Mann face each other, ineffectually hopping from side to side, while the referee hops along beside them and looks on. Charlie, ever the master of the situation, gets in another punch, shaking his hand from the pain. He runs in a circle around the now thoroughly befuddled Mann and punches him again. Mann begins

Charlie tries to push Mann down.

to sink to the floor, but then rises, and Charlie helpfully pushes down on his shoulders. But again Mann rises, as if powered by an internal spring.

Steadying Mann, Charlie backs off and takes a flying leap (via an unseen wire), butting Mann in the stomach with his head and knocking him down. When the resilient Mann gets up, Charlie butts him again. The referee then moves to block Charlie and gets butted down himself.

After a couple more futile swings by Mann, and more futile attempts by Charlie to push him down to the canvas, Mann finally connects with his first punch of the fight, causing Charlie to stagger around the ring in a semicircle, one leg lifting decorously as he totters precariously on the other. Though bewildered, he somehow

A clinch.

Charlie steadies the dazed Mann prior to butting him with a flying leap.

A flying leap. Note the wire.

A role reversal: Charlie becomes the referee.

manages to duck Mann's next few punches, then falls into clinches with Mann, the corner pole, and his own second, who has come into the ring to retrieve him after the bell rings, signaling the end of round one.

During the break the dazed Charlie imagines that his tough-guy second turns into Virginia. She strokes his brow and comforts him, and he grabs her hand and begins kissing it—but the image dissolves back, leaving him kissing the hand of the indignant pug, who threatens to clobber him. Once again, Charlie's innocent actions are misinterpreted as homosexual overtures, this time in the very proving ground of masculinity, the fight ring. When

Virginia appears to the dazed Charlie.

Virginia appears to Charlie, soft violin music replaces the lively fight theme, which returns as he shakes off his reverie. The bell signals the next round.

The second round starts like the first, and once again the trance-inducing rhythm causes the men to shift positions. This time Mann and the referee face each other while Charlie hops along behind Mann. The referee recovers and points at Charlie, who winds up and punches Mann when he turns around. Charlie ducks Mann's return punch and clinches with the referee. Pushing him away, the referee receives the punch intended for Charlie. Mann catches the staggering official, and Charlie seizes his opportunity to separate *their* clinch. Fooled by this latest role confusion, the referee swings at Mann, who ducks and grabs him in another clinch. Once again Charlie separates them, and once again the referee recovers and points at Charlie, who begins running in a circle around him, chased by Mann.

The enterprising Charlie runs over to the bell rope, pulls it, and heads back to his corner. But the referee immediately pulls it again and they all return to the original hopping pattern. Suddenly Mann clips Charlie with a hard right, and Charlie staggers in another semicircle; Mann clips him with a left, and Charlie staggers the opposite way. But when Mann hits Charlie with yet another right Charlie suddenly becomes a furious fighting machine, revolving his gloves around each other, punching Mann, circling around him, and ducking Mann's now futile punches, until both men deck each other with simultaneous haymakers.

The referee gives the count over Charlie, but Charlie rises just before he counts ten, so the ref turns to Mann, who also manages to get up just before the count is completed. But now Charlie collapses to the canvas again, and the referee whirls to count *him* out, but again Charlie rises. Then once again *Mann* drops. The hapless referee whirls from man to man, trying to count *someone* out. Both men finally stagger to their feet at the same time. Mann swings, Charlie ducks and grabs him in a clinch, and they stagger against the ropes, where the bell rope wraps around Charlie's neck.

Now every time Mann knocks Charlie down, the bell rings, and every time he trots back to his corner, he unknowingly rings the bell again. The referee removes the rope from Charlie's neck, and a final punch from Mann leaves Charlie out for the count.

The elegant comic choreography and perfect rhythms of the sequence are, of course, impossible to fully convey in print. Like the boxers and referee, the viewer is literally swept up in the hypnotic, irresistible flow of the action. It is instantly hilarious, and maintains its comic momentum with seemingly endless inventive variations. The mechanical quality of the movement, established at the outset with the hop-hop-hop pattern, is reinforced by the way Mann keeps springing up like a toy, Charlie turns into a furious punching machine, and each man collapses just as the other man gets up. The circles, and circles within circles, give the whole thing the appearance of a dance. Yet, though it is obviously tightly choreographed, the sequence unfolds so naturally that everyone's actions are totally believable. Charlie is the driving force. We've seen his rising fear in the dressing room, and the comedy of the fight scene comes right out of his instinctive self-protective behavior as he seeks to survive in the ring.

Out for the count.

The scene is so engaging as a comic set piece that it's easy to lose sight of the fact that it's more than just a funny sequence. For one thing, it subtly but insistently recapitulates the two main themes of the film—identity confusion and money: the boxers and referee keep switching roles throughout the sequence, and Charlie's desperate need for money is what got him into this predicament in the first place. The scene also deepens our esteem for Charlie. While he acts terrified throughout much of it, the fact that he's fighting for Virginia's rent money makes his actions gallant and courageous, and the nasty battering he takes makes us admire him all the more. Finally, the boxing match, like the roll dance in *The Gold Rush*, fills us with awe for Charlie's—and Chaplin's—grace and ingenuity.

After getting the money from the millionaire, Charlie gives it to the blind girl, an act of sacrifice and love that will have doubly grave consequences for him. First, taking it has made him, however unjustly, a criminal in the eyes of the law. Second, his gift will inevitably destroy the illusion he has so painstakingly built up of being a millionaire. Charlie's sadness as he bids her farewell tells us that he's perfectly aware of what is to come.

Sure enough, Charlie is almost immediately captured and jailed. Months pass, and we again meet the girl. Her sight now restored, she is bright eyed and well dressed. Evidently the money included enough surplus for her to open a flower shop, which seems to be thriving as she eagerly awaits the return of her benefactor.

Charlie pursued romance, risked danger, and suffered great hardships in *The Gold Rush* as well. That film ended happily, as newly minted millionaire Charlie reunited with his beloved dance hall girl on the voyage home from the gold fields. Posed by a news photographer in a close embrace, they slowly draw together for a kiss. The photographer declares, "Oh, you've spoilt the picture." The subtitle is one of Chaplin's slyest direct addresses to the film audience, since it's an ironic dismissal of those viewers cynical enough to quarrel with the film's improbable fairy-tale ending. Charlie simply waves the photographer off and continues his kiss as the scene fades. Chaplin knew that, having lived through Charlie's emotional and physical trials in the film, his audience would feel that he has more than earned his reward.

If anything, the audience watching *City Lights* wants even more to see Charlie rewarded. He has, after all, behaved with the utmost nobility throughout the film, and his trials are endured not for his own survival, but for the survival and comfort of the impoverished blind girl. In

After prison—his spirits dampened.

Charlie is thrilled to see the change in Virginia; she finds the adoration of the bedraggled vagrant hilarious.

addition, for a world devastated by the hardships of the Great Depression, Charlie's familiar state of poverty has acquired a new poignancy.[14]

But the plot of *City Lights* leads inexorably to vision, which will shatter illusion. In the conclusion of *The Gold Rush*, a man who looks like a bum to his love is in reality a millionaire, whereas in *City Lights* he is, except for his inner nobility and spirit, truly a bum.

Even that spirit seems dampened when Charlie is released from prison. Seen in a long shot as he rounds the old street corner where the girl had sold flowers, his silhouette is a study in downtrodden defeat. The clothes, this once, are not the clownish motley of the genteel Tramp, but the genuine, tattered rags of a real tramp. In *The Gold Rush* Chaplin had toyed playfully with his iconic costume, eating his shoe and turning rolls into big dancing feet. Now the clothes tell a harrowing tale. We are left to imagine what happened to him in prison that left the clothes in such a sorry state. His hat is battered and broken. He is tie-less, vest-less, shirtless. His collar is turned up, his coat buttoned tightly to protect him from the chill autumn air.

Chaplin's mime is here seen at its most powerful. He stands stooped over, his head bowed. His walk is slow and halting as he passes the flower shop. He picks up a flower from the gutter, then turns and sees the girl through the shop window—and breaks into a wide grin. It isn't the happy or mischievous grin we've come to expect from the ebullient Tramp, but the weary smile of someone at the end of his tether, full of despair and exhaustion. Nevertheless, he lights up when he sees what he has wrought, sees her *seeing* for the first time. The petals drop from his flower as he gazes at her in wonder.

The girl laughs, saying, "I've made a conquest!" Her unwittingly cruel comment prepares the audience for the utter seriousness of the final moments, as she comes out of the shop to give Charlie a fresh flower and a coin. He shuffles away, not wanting to break the illusion he had so carefully nurtured. But he cannot resist her as she beckons. In another heartrending bit of mime he grins, this time the guileless grin of a child being offered a treat, as he shyly reaches for the flower. He knows what

Charlie reluctantly takes her flower.

Virginia recognizes Charlie.

The final expression.

will happen, but he can't help himself. He is utterly entranced as Virginia draws him toward her, pressing the coin into his hand.

Suddenly, her face changes as recognition dawns. A close-up of their hands, her touch becoming a caress, makes clear that she is seeing once again the way she saw before—through touch, through feeling.

She runs her hand up his arm, along the familiar lapel. Haunting close-ups of their faces alternate with the film's final, eloquent dialogue titles. Virginia says simply, "You?" Charlie nods shyly, then, pointing to his own eyes, says, "You can see now," confirming—as if further confirmation were necessary—his identity. She responds in a final, heartbreaking title, "Yes, I can see now." She grasps his hand to her and dissolves into tears as the full impact settles in. In the last shot of the film Charlie, holding the rose, shyly biting on his forefinger, breaks into a radiant, tremulous smile as he stands revealed before his love. He gives a little laugh as the scene fades.

Touch confirms his identity.

We simply don't see this ending coming. In his feature films, Chaplin had always wrestled with the problem of getting a pretty girl interested in his indigent Tramp character. It was a movie convention that there be a romance, and he had always provided it. But, except for the wish-fulfillment ending of *The Gold Rush*, Charlie usually doesn't get the girl. It makes more sense for him to walk off into the distance, as he does in *The Pilgrim*, *The Circus*, and other films, saddened but eternally optimistic.

In *City Lights* Chaplin doesn't walk off, but confronts the problem head-on. The blind girl enters a relationship with Charlie because he's fooled her into thinking he's someone else, someone normal, someone solvent—more than solvent, wealthy. When she finds out who he really is, we're poised, like Virginia, on a precipice. She can't very well send Charlie on his way, but he isn't the person she was expecting, either. So we fade out on Charlie's beautiful, terrified expression.

Everything in the film has led us to this moment, and suddenly it all makes sense in a new way. As Charlie was literally unveiled before the public at the beginning of the film, so at the end he is unveiled on a deeper level. The running gag about his sexuality repeatedly calls his manliness—his worthiness—into question, as does his inability to earn money. Now Virginia finally sees Charlie in all his shabby imperfection. We've laughed at the manifestations of that imperfection throughout the film, just as the newsboys who torment him in front of the flower shop laugh. And now it's her turn to laugh, amused at his incongruous dignity as he wipes his nose with a rag, folds it carefully, and puts it into his coat pocket as though it's an elegant handkerchief. She laughs even harder when he turns and sees her through her shop window, his face beaming with naked adoration.

Even this moment of revelation is foreshadowed earlier in the film, when Charlie looks through another shop window to steal glances at the statue of the beautiful nude woman. Virginia is that idealized woman made flesh: Pygmalion to Charlie's Galatea, she has been miraculously delivered from her life of poverty and darkness through his devoted efforts. This time there's nothing furtive about his look. He gazes at her directly, with pride and awe at his accomplishment.

When Virginia realizes who he is her laughter curdles, just as ours has already curdled. The darker implication of the elaborate charade Charlie has put on for her benefit settles in: *He* doesn't consider himself worthy either, not even of the attention of a blind street peddler. And now that she can see him, he's not at all surprised by her reaction. Despite his dignified airs he knows that, in the world's eyes, he's an object of ridicule and contempt.

But we know better. We've seen that he's also compassionate, loving, and even heroic. And now the girl made whole by his sacrifices finally sees him as we do, for what he is. It is a painful moment as they gaze at one another, their emotions a complex swirl. On her part there is shock, sadness, disappointment, and gratitude; on his, shyness and delight.

But where is love in this stew of emotion, the romance promised in the opening subtitle? Charlie's love for Virginia has been evident from the start, but his loving care, provided at such cost, has actually widened the gulf between them. Her feelings are another matter. As soon as she touches his hand, ending his masquerade, she knows exactly how profound his sacrifice must have been—not, as she had been led to believe, the easy charity of a glamorous millionaire, but something truly extraordinary. Now that she sees him she understands that his generosity toward her is an act that can barely be fathomed, let alone repaid. The film ends at the moment of her discovery, leaving the question of her love tantalizingly unanswered.

Unanswered, at least, within the confines of the film. For there are two courtships being conducted in *City Lights*. Just as surely as Charlie has courted the blind girl, Chaplin has courted the film audience, not least with the return of his characteristic glances directly into the eye of the camera. But the interviews, the articles, and the film's opening jest about sound films have made it abundantly clear that he sees sound film as a threat to that relationship. So, just as he slyly addresses the film audience with the last subtitle in *The Gold Rush*, now, with the ending of *City Lights*, he addresses us again, this time with an urgent question about love.

In the world of the film, the question is, will the blind girl love Charlie now that she can see him? Or will she merely feel obligated, grateful for what he has done for her? Will she be blind to his virtues because she can't see past his bedraggled appearance? The very same question applies to Chaplin's vast film audience, which by 1931 had gone blind to the virtues of silent films, decisively rejecting them in favor of a newer, flashier attraction. Would they—could they—love even Chaplin in a silent film? Despite his bravado, he had good reason to fear the answer would be "no." So the overwhelming success of *City Lights*, the fourth top-grossing film of its year, must have come as sweet vindication. Indeed, many of the ecstatic reviews of the film, to this day, read like grateful love notes rather than dispassionate evaluations.[15]

The final half hour of *City Lights*, with its sublime blend of the funniest comedy and the most moving drama, is Chaplin at his best as performer, director, writer, and composer. The various musical themes associated with the Tramp and the girl are resolved decisively during the film's haunting final minutes. Facial close-ups, so rare in Chaplin's films, lend the final moments a startling intimacy and power. Even the titles contribute greatly to the final effect, which is as utterly disarming today as it was in 1931. *City Lights* is a unique achievement, transcending considerations of sound versus silent film. The final scenes are so skillfully set up and so beautifully acted that repeated viewings do not diminish their impact.

In 1949 James Agee, writing for *Life* magazine, called the final scene the highest moment in movies. More than half a century later, few would argue with that assessment. *City Lights* remains Chaplin's triumph of motion and emotion.

Notes

1. Julian Smith, in *Chaplin* (Boston: Twayne, 1984), points out the connection between the two famous scenes: "Whereas at Thanksgiving, his shoe became food, now dinner rolls become little shoes" (76). The deep affinity between the two scenes, both of which use Charlie's iconic oversize shoes as the subject for transformation gags, is an example of the remarkably

high level of dramatic, comic, and visual thinking operating in this accessible, unpretentious film. Seeing it, one appreciates anew why Chaplin's work was lauded as the pinnacle of cinematic art at the time, and why it remains vital.

2. It was a bold but not unprecedented move to make a comedy with a blind heroine. Harry Langdon, directed by Frank Capra, had pulled it off effectively in *The Strong Man* in 1926. In both films the blindness of the heroines leads them to misperceive their unsuitable suitors. Langdon, of course, is a childlike boob, and by the end we know that his blind sweetheart will have take care of *him*. For Charlie, a far more complex character, a resolution will not be so simple.

3. Interestingly, during the comic portions of these scenes Chaplin returns to his old trick of looking at the audience, and he does it more often and more directly than in any of his other features. Since the comedy of their scenes is based on Virginia being oblivious to Charlie's comic predicaments, he can be unusually bold in including us. It's a perfectly appropriate way to steal focus from the beautiful Virginia.

4. Charles Chaplin, *My Autobiography* (New York: Simon & Schuster, 1964), 226.

5. One of them, "With You, Dear, In Bombay," is incongruously illustrated with a still from *The Gold Rush* featuring Charlie shoveling snow.

6. According to David Robinson he did involve himself with the preparation of the musical cue sheets from 1923 on, but it's unclear how much. These sheets provided local music directors with suggested standard pieces to play for each scene. Theaters had extensive libraries of sheet music, from which the music director would assemble and adapt a score for the available players.

7. In the same fashion MGM's chosen name for Buster's character in this film and several others—Elmer—pigeonholed him as a slow-witted dunce character, rather than the elegant, if naive, character he actually played.

8. During the fascinating transitional period, 1926–1930, filmmakers experimented with many ways of incorporating sound into film. The celebrated breakthrough film, 1927's *The Jazz Singer*, is for the most part a silent film with the usual dialogue subtitles, along with music and some sound effects. What made it a sensation was the charismatic Al Jolson singing six of his characteristic songs, and uttering just a few lines of improvised-sounding dialogue. As Scott Eyman points out in *The Speed of Sound*, these scenes made the rest of the film—and silent film generally—seem lifeless by comparison.

9. This haunting melody, by the Spanish composer José Padilla, has been used in a number of films since, including *Scent of a Woman* (1992), and, perhaps most notably, in the underrated Gene Hackman–Barbra Streisand comedy *All Night Long* (1981).

10. There is one notable overlap in the soundtracks of the two films. *Spite Marriage* features a scene in which instruments mimic human speech as two characters talk. It's the same effect as the opening scene of *City Lights*, but without the later film's satirical intent. It is one of several minor but intriguing parallels between the films. Others include significant drunk scenes in and out of nightclubs, and a plot-advancing device in which a character in a dressing room has to make a quick exit because the cops are after him. In addition, veteran comic actor Hank Mann, the stage manager in *Spite Marriage*, plays the boxer in *City Lights*. Of course, the major silent comedians often reworked the same material; all three did boxing scenes: for example, Keaton in *Battling Butler* in 1926, and Lloyd in *The Milky Way* in 1936. None of the scenes is remotely alike. However, given the similarities it seems likely that Chaplin saw *Spite Marriage*, and that it lingered in his memory; he later reworked its main running gag for *The Great Dictator* (see chap. 11, n12).

11. In an interview with Rob Wagner during the making of *City Lights*, Chaplin described an earlier approach to the music of the film. The blind girl's theme (later "La Violetera") was to be on a record Charlie plays on a phonograph in the film. The title, shown to the audience on the disc itself, is "Wondrous Eyes, by Charles Chaplin." From that point on, throughout the film Charlie would hear it played by street musicians and in saloons. In the eventual film the music is not so naturalistically wedded to the image. Except for the sound effect moments mentioned above, it's done very much in the manner that a live orchestra would have accompanied a silent film. Even a scene in which Charlie plays a record on the blind girl's phonograph is not presented in such a way that we feel we're hearing the music on the record.

12. For an excellent analysis of the score, see Theodore Huff's "Chaplin as a Composer" in his seminal biography *Charlie Chaplin* (New York: Henry Schuman, 1951), 234–41.

13. Chaplin regularly attended the American Legion prizefights in Hollywood, and his knowledge of the sport obviously paid dividends when he came to create the boxing scene. Chaplin first met Virginia Cherrill at one of the fights. She had no acting experience, but she was a striking beauty, and, in her own words, looked "blind as a bat" without her thick glasses.

14. Chaplin, of course, had no way to know the Depression was coming when he began working on the film in 1928. It was a lucky accident for him that urban poverty, one of his ongoing themes and a main focus of *City Lights*, had become a global preoccupation by the time he completed his film. His anachronistic holdover from the silent era had become quite timely.

15. Of all Chaplin's films, this one has inspired the most rhapsodic commentary. See especially Alexander Woollcott's often-quoted contemporary review, "Charlie As Ever Was," reprinted in Woollcott's *While Rome Burns* (New York: Viking, 1934). Insightful discussions of the film can be found in Julian Smith's *Chaplin*, Gerald Mast's *The Comic Mind* (Indianapolis, IN: Bobbs-Merrill, 1973), Walter Kerr's *The Silent Clowns* (New York: Knopf, 1975), and Charles Maland's *Chaplin and American Culture* (Princeton, NJ: Princeton University Press, 1989).

CHAPTER TEN

The Machine Age: *Modern Times*

As he had done with *The Kid* ten years earlier, Chaplin went abroad to generate additional publicity for the European release of *City Lights*. The trip stretched to fifteen months, encompassing both Europe and Asia. Chaplin prolonged his trip, at least in part, to avoid coming home to an uncertain professional future. Despairing of following the success of *City Lights* with another silent film, he seriously considered retiring.

He probably could have continued making successful silent films with music, but he would have been alone. His great colleagues abandoned silent films, only to find themselves marginalized in the world of sound. Mary Pickford and Douglas Fairbanks retired from the screen by 1934, and Harold Lloyd's popularity and productivity declined to a quiet fadeout by the end of the decade. Buster Keaton had embarked on his depressing series of low budget sound shorts for Educational Pictures and Columbia, never to regain his former preeminence as a filmmaker.

Various of Chaplin's distinguished contemporaries argued that "only Charlie" could still get away with it. No less a commentator than Winston Churchill, in an article for *Collier's* magazine in 1935, publicly encouraged Chaplin to pursue this course. Churchill was aware of Chaplin's ambitions to do serious films, as well as his antipathy to sound, and he wrote:

> Pantomime is the true universal tongue. . . . [T]he future of Charlie Chaplin may lie mainly in the portrayal of serious roles in silent, or rather, non-talking films, and in the development of a universal cinema. . . . But let him come back—at least occasionally—to the vein of comedy that has been the world's delight for twenty years.[1]

But Chaplin dreaded leaving his vast audience behind by continuing in a style of film that had become old-fashioned.

Finally, he hit upon a compromise: another silent film with subtitles, but one in which sound effects and words were wedded in unusual ways to the image. He would give the people what they wanted—but, as always, on his own terms. And who could possibly consider a film called *Modern Times* old-fashioned? The subject of his film would be the pressing social problems of the day.

Chaplin reported that the idea for the film was stimulated by seeing the terrible effects of the Depression during his world tour, along with conversations about the mechanization of modern life in general, and the assembly line in particular, during the early 1930s. But in fact, he first had the idea for the feeding machine in 1916, and his friend Max Eastman recalled a scene Chaplin shot before 1920 in which crowds, moving like automatons, rush past a beggar seated on the sidewalk. Periodically one of the passersby turns to hand the beggar a nickel, which he rings up in a cash register. "That's modern life," Chaplin told Eastman, "everything mechanized and regimented—even charity!"[2] Since this tendency to visually translate the mechanical aspects of life was at the heart of Chaplin's comedy, the factory in *Modern Times* was a fitting final playground for the Tramp's silent film career. Significantly, choosing to make the film as a hybrid also allowed him to shoot at undercranked speeds, preserving the crispness of movement so essential to his art.

For all its up-to-the-minute satire of mechanization and the hardships of modern life, *Modern Times* is as much about Chaplin's artistic dilemma as it is about the times. As in *City Lights*, the insistent subtext of the film is Charlie's place—indeed, his very existence—in the world of sound films, and, by implication, Chaplin's place as a film artist. In fact, despite the later film's explicit depiction of the issues of the day—strikes, unemployment, police brutality, and so on—a case can be made that *City Lights*, with its stark contrast between the dissolute and empty life of the millionaire and the grinding poverty of the blind flower girl, more effectively evokes the mood of the Depression era. These characters epitomize the poles of society at the time, and we get to know them very well. In contrast, virtually all the characters in *Modern Times* are secondary, providing background for the Tramp's adventures. Even Paulette Goddard, the female lead, comes off more as Charlie's alter ego than a separate character. There is neither courtship nor conflict between them. The times in *Modern Times* serve mainly as a backdrop for the Tramp's characteristic misadventures.

Nevertheless, the opening credits forcefully assert the film's claim to topicality. A sleek, contemporary clock face fills the screen, its second hand sweeping around. The time approaches six o'clock, and the opening music adds to the sense of urgency, suggesting a factory whistle blowing and the percussive beginnings of machinery coming to life. The main title is superimposed in white lettering over the clock, in a 1930s typeface that looked contemporary then and now appears rather quaint, pleasantly evoking the "streamlined moderne" look of the era.

The credits end with a rousing subtitle: "'Modern Times.' A story of industry, of individual enterprise—humanity crusading in the pursuit of happiness." This is nothing like *City Lights*' opening subtitle, with its nostalgic promise of the comedy, romance, and pantomime of a Chaplin film. Instead, it seems like the beginning of a patriotic documentary. But the uplifting tone will prove ironic, since the film will demonstrate at every turn how "individual enterprise" is crushed and thwarted by industry and the forces behind it, making "the pursuit of happiness" an elusive goal.

The opening shot underscores the irony, as a rushing flock of sheep dissolves into factory workers emerging from a subway. So much for humanity's crusade. While this Eisenstein-style montage is a bit heavy handed, contained within it is another, quieter joke: A single black sheep in the center of the fold stands out because of its darker coat, just as Charlie always stands out because of his. It is the first of several subtle insertions in *Modern Times* not intended for all eyes.[3]

The president of the Electro Steel Company sits in his office, so idle and bored that he reads the funny papers and does jigsaw puzzles.[4] But Chaplin immediately un-

A black sheep in the fold.

dercuts the easy jibe that the man is living a life of ease, a parasite off the sweat of the sheeplike workers, by having the secretary bring him a pill. Even idle bosses have their problems; perhaps their very idleness stresses them out.

The president is underworked because technology has made it so easy for him to do his job. He doesn't even have to leave his office, because he can scan the factory via his large closed-circuit video screen. Television, of course, was the stuff of science fiction in 1936, and befitting the futuristic nature of the device he turns it on by activating a Jacob's ladder, that rising-spark device beloved of Dr. Frankenstein and other mad scientists of the era. Chaplin, more generous in his use of sound effects than in *City Lights*, accompanies the moving spark with a synchronized electronic sizzle. The president summons Mack, the strapping, shirtless controller of the generators and assembly lines. Mack, who looks like he just stepped out of a propaganda poster for industrial might, runs past a long row of enormous generators to the factory floor monitor. Over this monitor the president utters the first spoken words in Chaplin's cinema, "Section Five. Speed 'er up. Four-one." It is a most interesting juxtaposition of the worlds of sound and silent film, since Mack is clearly moving at quickened silent speed.[5]

As the scene cuts to "Section Five" and pans to reveal Charlie, a second voice is heard over a loudspeaker: "Attention foreman. Trouble on Bench Five. Check on the nut tightener. Nuts coming through loose on Bench Five. Attention foreman." Of course, Charlie is the nut tightener, and he is finding it difficult to keep up the relentless pace of the assembly line due to various distractions, including an itchy underarm and a huge bee hovering around his face.

The lengthy seventeen-and-a-half-minute factory sequence benefits greatly from Chaplin's excellent musical soundtrack. As in the boxing scene in *City Lights*, he uses music to establish a rapid and regular background rhythm to evoke the sounds of the massive machinery and set off the human action. The two men working behind Charlie tap the passing nut plates with their hammers and chisels after Charlie tightens them, and their taps are reflected in the music by rhythmic metallic clinking. For the most part musical themes, rather than comical stings and effects, are used to underscore the comedy.[6]

The president orders a speed up to "Four-seven." Charlie is saved by a passing relief man (identified as such over the loudspeaker). Charlie goes to the bathroom and lights a cigarette, but the president suddenly appears in a monstrous close-up on a huge TV monitor on the bathroom wall. "Hey! Quit stalling! Get back to work," he shouts. "Go on," he says, his eyes following Charlie, who hustles out at silent speed.

Yet another mechanical speech device is introduced as a formally dressed inventor in a swallow-tailed coat and his two lab-coated assistants meet with the president in his office. The inventor cranks up a phonograph, which plays the following prerecorded sales pitch as he and his assistants proudly display the machine:

> Good morning, my friends. This record comes to you through the Sales Talk Transcription Company, Incorporated. Your speaker, the Mechanical Salesman. May I take the pleasure of introducing Mr. J. Whillicombe Billows, the inventor of the Billows Feeding Machine, a practical device which automatically feeds your men while at work. Don't stop for lunch. Be ahead of your competitor. The Billows Feeding Machine will eliminate the lunch hour, increase your production, and decrease your overhead.
>
> Allow us to point out some of the features of this wonderful machine. Its beautiful aerodynamic streamlined body. Its smoothness of action, made silent by our electro-porous metal ball bearings. Let us acquaint you with our automaton soup plate—its compressed air blower—no breath necessary—no energy required to cool the soup. Notice the revolving plate with the automatic food pusher. Observe our counter-shaft double-knee-action corn feeder, with its synchro-mesh transmission, which enables you to shift from high to low gear by the mere tip of the tongue. Then there is the hydro-compressed sterilized mouth wiper. Its factors of control ensure against spots on the shirtfront.
>
> These are but a few of the delightful features of the Billows Feeding Machine. Let us demonstrate with one of your workers, for actions speak louder than words.
>
> Remember, if you wish to keep ahead of your competitor, you cannot afford to ignore the importance of the Billows Feeding Machine.

That the monstrosity is irrelevantly "aerodynamic" is only the least of its dubious wonders. In this scene Chaplin definitively fulfills his vision of "everything mechanized" by automating not only the eating process, but the sales call as well. The record player, the third mechanical speech device in the first ten minutes of the film, takes the factory's division of labor to an absurd extreme by separating the salesmen from their sales pitch. They are relegated to the role of mute gesticulators, turning the machine this way and that to point out its component parts.

The machine is a brilliant comic conception, and the effusive, jargon-filled description of its many features—Chaplin's first foray into audible verbal humor—is quite funny. But having a disembodied monologue acted out by silent performers pushes Chaplin's hybrid concept nearly to the breaking point.[7] The idea works very well during the opening factory scenes, in which we hear spoken words and at the same time see the actors moving at quickened speed. We're in a strange and magical new filmic world. But with the machine presentation things get a bit trickier.

To preserve the silent world even as we're hearing the record played in the room, Chaplin omits the ambient sounds that would put us unmistakably into a sound film reality. But at the same time he edges closer to that reality by shooting the scene at twenty-four frames per second, the first time we see actors moving at normal speed in a Chaplin film.[8] The slowed action, combined with the auditory isolation of the narration, has the effect of drawing our attention to the suddenly conspicuous silence of the actors and the room. This, in turn, makes their movements look all the more stilted and ritualistic, especially when they pause expectantly to wait for the next bit of narration to act out. Chaplin's decision not to accompany the narration with music only accentuates the arid quality of the scene. Of course, the arid quality is precisely Chaplin's point, satirizing the modern drive to mechanize everything in life. But a mechanized eating machine presented by mechanized salesmen may be too much mechanization for one scene. Chaplin, possibly sensing that actors playing second fiddle to a disembodied narrator and a machine might come off as a bit static, is at pains to move them about as fluidly as possible. He even allows the loopy inventor to ham it up a bit as he mimes his way through the product demo.

But despite the aesthetic and dramatic peculiarities of the scene, it is amusing, relatively short, and thematically important in reinforcing the role of sound in the film. It also fulfills its primary purpose, which is to set up the next scene, the inevitable test of the contraption on Charlie.

The silent and sound worlds mesh together perfectly once again as we proceed to the factory floor for the test. The soundtrack effectively underscores the disastrous demonstration with descriptive music and selective synchronized effects. After the soup is splashed into Charlie's face and the corn feeder goes out of control, the inventor declares, in the film's first dialogue subtitle, that "We'll start with the soup again." After the ensuing debacle, the president says, in another subtitle, "It's no good—it isn't practical."

The dialogue titles, which henceforth in the film are mixed in freely with the voices coming over mechanical devices, help to further isolate and define the role of spoken speech in the world of *Modern Times*. It is invariably mechanical and artificial, suitable for the orders of bosses to employees, or for glib sales pitches. "Normal" conversation—that is, face-to-face encounters—is shown in silent-film subtitles, as it had been throughout the silent era. With this brilliant act of transposition, Chaplin has managed to equate his own aesthetic problem with modern sound technology with the problem of the factory worker, who is victimized by the powerful forces of technological "progress." These forces dehumanize the worker by mechanizing his actions on the factory line, and attempt to mechanize and regiment everything about him, including his need for food, rest, and bathroom breaks—compelling him, in short, to conform. Thus, Chaplin's problem as an artist has been neatly joined to Charlie's problem as a character, which is an industrial-age variant of his customary role as the natural man beset by the constraints and injustices of the social order, the eternal outsider, the square peg in the round hole. Both Chaplin and Charlie are black sheep in the larger flock of conformists.

The feeding-machine sequence initiates a whole series of eating and being-eaten scenes in *Modern Times*, bringing to a climax one of the prominent themes of Chaplin's films. After "time marches on into the late afternoon" (the title alludes to the popular "March of Time" newsreel short subjects of the period), the president orders Mack to "give 'er the limit." Charlie can't keep up the pace and follows one of his nut plates into the bowels of the machine, "eaten" by it and then "vomited" back out when the belt is reversed. This celebrated sequence reinforces *Modern Times*' reflexive theme of Chaplin's confrontation with sound movies, because the machine, shown in a cutaway, resembles nothing so much as a giant film projector, with Charlie as the film threading through it. Since there's no other clue as to what the factory is producing, the nut plates he tightens may reasonably be assumed to be metaphorical representations of frames of film. The factory is a film factory.[9]

Charlie threading through the machinery like a strip of film.

Most audiences aren't going to see the scene metaphorically, of course, or tune in to Chaplin's problems at all. They'll only be concerned about Charlie's, which have now brought him to the breaking point. The nut tightener goes completely nuts, the unhealthy consequence of a too-intimate relationship with the demanding and voracious machine. His nervous breakdown takes the form of a destructive dance through the factory in which he tightens or squirts oil at everything in sight.[10] He manages, for a few exhilarating minutes, to disrupt the factory's relentless routine, and possibly damage some of its precious generators as well (fireballs flare as he plays with the switches). The burst of happy anarchy ends with Charlie giving the president a satisfying squirt in the face with his handy oilcan, before he's carted off to the loony bin.

Released from the mental hospital, Charlie is told, "Take it easy and avoid excitement." He is quickly mistaken for a Communist leader, however, and jailed. The scene, beautifully directed, is also remarkably prescient in light of the accusations that would dog Chaplin later.

Given Charlie's marginal existence, the specter of jail hovers over almost all his films. However, it is usually a place from which he had just been released, or from which he has just escaped; occasionally he is seen, via brief flashbacks, inside. But in *Modern Times*, for the first time, we join him inside. As he had faced the realistic complexities of the Tramp's romantic life in *City Lights*, for the second major section of *Modern Times* Chaplin looks unflinchingly at prison life, and in doing so he manages to insert several subtle and not-so-subtle references to its seamier aspects.

Ushered to his cell, Charlie sits down on the bunk next to his tough looking cellmate, who glares at him

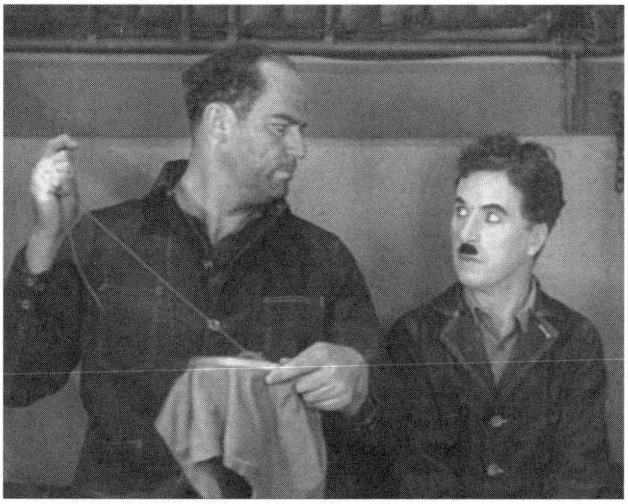

Charlie doesn't quite know how to take his cellmate.

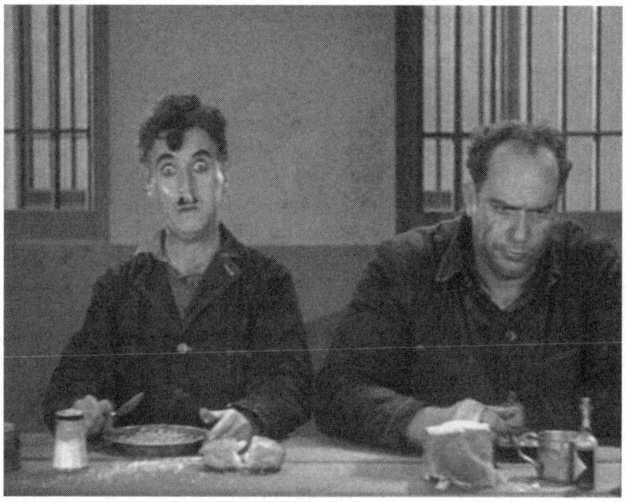

The "nose powder" energizes Charlie.

for a moment—then resumes his needlepoint. The incongruity of this bruiser doing needlepoint is funny, of course, as is the implication that such a creature might be gay. Charlie eyes him suspiciously, much as he had himself been eyed suspiciously all through *City Lights*. But in that film homosexuality was a running gag about Charlie's manhood, without the slightest suggestion that he might actually *be* gay. Here, it's something else, since this burly, unshaven fellow doesn't remotely resemble the "pansy" caricature beloved of audiences of the period. He even has bandaged knuckles on one hand, as though he's been in fight. Before we have time to dwell on it, however, Charlie, in a neatly worked out series of innocent actions, quickly brings the brute to a state of homicidal rage. First he inadvertently prevents the man from threading his needle; then he accidentally slams the upper bunk down on his head. The lug effortlessly hoists Charlie into the air and begins throttling him, but when the lunch bell rings he instantly forgets his rage, drops Charlie, and turns away. The Pavlovian response to the bell is an amusing and telling moment, demonstrating how prison is simply another kind of factory, one that controls behavior and regulates emotion. Aside from all the social commentary packed into in this brief, brilliant little sequence, it is pleasantly reminiscent of Charlie's encounters with Eric Campbell two decades earlier.

In the lunchroom Chaplin introduces another of the harsh realities of prison life. The authorities suspect that one of the convicts is smuggling drugs. The culprit, a rat-faced fellow sitting next to Charlie, is unmistakably and amusingly identified by a loud chord of music and a rapid iris to his pointy face. Before the cops apprehend him, he manages to pour his "nose powder" into the salt shaker. Charlie unknowingly sprinkles it liberally over his food, getting some on his finger in the process. When he wipes his finger across his nose he deposits a large dollop onto his mustache, and does several very funny wide-eyed comic takes as he inhales. His courage fueled by the cocaine, Charlie gets the upper hand of his cellmate in yet another nicely choreographed contretemps, asserting his right to the food in no uncertain terms by flicking a spoonful of stew into the man's eye.

As the group files out of the lunchroom, Chaplin includes another sly detail. In front of Charlie and his cellmate in line is a man who is ludicrously effeminate, walking with his hands bent upward at the wrist and swiveling his hips and shoulders. Because the viewer is riveted on Charlie revolving in his stoned state, this fellow invariably goes unnoticed in the several shots in which he appears. Chaplin was extremely bold to include, however covertly, such a blatantly homosexual character

Charlie, his cellmate, and the gay prisoner.

in his film. Acknowledgement of homosexual activity in prisons—or anywhere in life, for that matter—was virtually nonexistent in the mainstream media at this time.[11] The same thing goes for references to drug use, apart from alcohol. In this respect *Modern Times* was years ahead of its time.[12]

After Charlie thwarts a jailbreak attempt, in a scene reminiscent of his earlier feats of drug-induced heroism in *Easy Street*, he is granted a pardon. We discover this over the film's fourth medium of indirect verbal communication, the radio in the sheriff's office. A fast-talking announcer blurts out, "Local News. A pardon was granted the prisoner who so recently thwarted the attempted city jailbreak. Sheriff Couler will inform the prisoner of the good news sometime today." The sheriff picks up the phone and summons Charlie, his words conveyed in a subtitle.

Brought to the sheriff's office from his now-comfortable private cell, Charlie is left alone with the minister's frosty wife while the sheriff escorts the minister on his weekly rounds. Here the silence of the actors makes sense, for the haughty woman clearly has no intention of speaking with the lowly prisoner. Charlie's discomfort is established with a nice visual gag, in which he nervously sips from his teacup and accidentally takes the teaspoon into his mouth.

As they sit together in stony silence, sipping away at their tea, Chaplin introduces the first bodily sounds in his cinema. The tea gives both of them indigestion, which makes their stomachs gurgle alarmingly. Her little dog barks at each of them in turn when they gurgle. To distract attention from these embarrassing sounds, Charlie reaches back to turn on the radio, which blares, "If you are suffering from gastritis, don't forget to try—" before he snaps it off.

The routine concludes with a sound transformation gag. Taking out a pill for her indigestion, the minister's wife squirts seltzer into a glass. Charlie reacts to the sound with a startled leap, and looks very relieved and abashed when he sees it was just seltzer. Chaplin, as usual, gets away with vulgarity by alluding to it rather than showing it directly. The thought of this dignified woman—a minister's wife, no less—explosively emitting gas, or worse, is funny, and the scatological gag made it past the censors. They did, however, ask Chaplin to remove some of the stomach-gurgling that precedes it.[13]

But once again Chaplin's hybrid concept puts a strain on the proceedings. While pleasant enough, most of the scene unfolds in the same barren soundscape as the Mechanical Salesman scene, without music or ambient sound as "fill." The gurgling sounds are funny, but by isolating them Chaplin weakens the illusion that they emanate from the actors' bodies, making the effect less persuasive. On the other hand, the seltzer squirt, precisely synchronized, works fine.

Released from jail, Charlie gets a job in a shipyard, and Chaplin confronts another aspect of modern times in the form of the economical use of rear-screen projection. Charlie accidentally causes a ship under construction to slide into the water and sink. Chaplin had used rear-projection earlier in the film for the television sequences, but this is the first time a comic payoff shot depends on the special effect.[14] In the nicely executed combined shot, Chaplin, his back to the camera, watches the ship slide into the water; scaffolding bordering the screen neatly merges with filmed scaffolding to disguise the artifice, although film-wise audiences will spot it because of the slight differences in lighting and camera movement between the two shots. Chaplin, in any case, tops the shot with a funny cutaway to four dumbfounded workers gaping in disbelief.[15]

Charlie's failure in the shipyard makes him want to return to his comfortable jail cell. To do that, he nobly takes the blame for stealing a loaf of bread, which was actually stolen by a starving, orphaned gamine (Paulette Goddard). When that plan doesn't work, because a nasty woman fingers Paulette for the theft, he's more determined than ever to get arrested. He eats a sumptuous meal at a restaurant, then casually summons a passing cop to pay for it. That does the trick, and Charlie even manages to "purchase" a cigar in the same manner, managing a few refreshing puffs before being carted off. Meanwhile, Paulette has also been apprehended, and the two meet again in the police van.

Rear projection is used again to show their escape, and this time it's for technical rather than economic reasons.

In the next moment Charlie, the gamine, and the cop dive out the door to the right as . . .

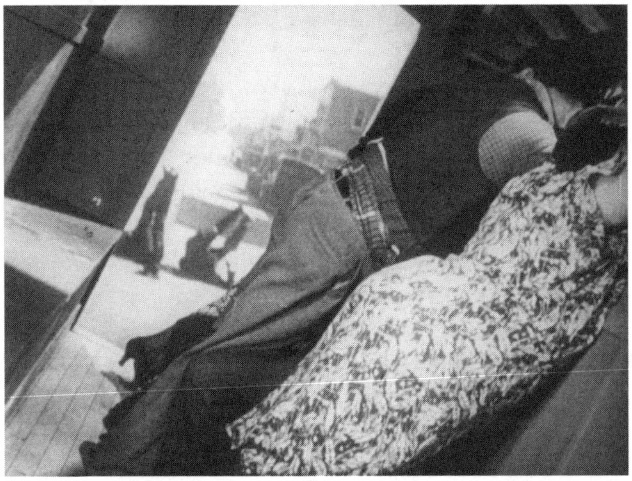

. . . the van tips and their images appear on the rear projection.

Eight passengers are seated along benches on either side of the van, and a cop stands on a running board outside the rear open doorway. The van rocks convincingly as the rear-projected road recedes in the distance through the door. Suddenly the gamine leaps up and struggles with the cop, and Charlie follows her. The van swerves to avoid an oncoming car (shown in a cutaway), and tilts wildly to the right. All three fall out of the van and out of sight, immediately reappearing in the rear-projected image as the van speeds away. It's an exquisitely timed shot, coordinating the tilting van, the passengers thrown against the right wall, and the rear-screen image. It all happens so smoothly and quickly that the artifice is undetectable. A cut to the trio lying stunned on the road completes the perfect illusion.

The gamine and Charlie steal away, pausing to rest on a curb in a suburban neighborhood. There, a happy housewife bids her husband an affectionate good-bye and skips back into her home. The exaggerated display of domestic bliss is made even sillier by being considerably undercranked. Charlie parodies her movements, tearing some pieces of grass and throwing them into the air in an orgy of simpering glee. This parody of a parody works because of Chaplin's skill and charm, and because the scene is underscored by the first introduction of Chaplin's beautiful romantic theme for the film, a tune that two decades later would become a worldwide song hit as "Smile."

Charlie mocks the happy couple, but seeing them inspires his delightful fantasy of himself and Paulette as suburbanites, which in turn inspires Charlie to find a home for them. "I'll do it! We'll get a home even if I have to work for it!" he declares boldly, before being hustled off the curb by another of the film's omnipresent cops. Once Charlie and Paulette join forces, their determination to find a home drives the action of the rest of the film. Unfortunately for Charlie, his next job, as a department store night watchman, ends as disastrously as his previous two. And unfortunately for Chaplin, with the department store scene the film begins to drag.

Part of the reason is that, despite the film's lovely musical theme, there really is no romance in *Modern Times*. Not that every film has to be a romance, but it usually was for Chaplin; romance had driven the plots of his previous three features. In *The Gold Rush* Charlie's unlikely courtship of the callous saloon girl complements his unlikely quest to find gold in the frozen wasteland. In *The Circus*, despite risking his life in the lion's cage and on the tightrope to woo his love, he ends up alone. In *City Lights* his attempts to provide for the blind girl while maintaining his masquerade of wealth lends poignancy and tension to their scenes together. In all three films the problematic romantic relationships are more than sufficient to engage the viewer.

But in *Modern Times* Charlie and Paulette instantly pair up, with no courtship or romantic tension. Charlie initiates the relationship by trying to take the blame for stealing the bread. Though he has an ulterior motive—wanting to return to jail—she doesn't know that, and his kindness both startles and touches her. Then he offers her his seat in the police van, comically inappropriate but nevertheless courtly behavior. Finally, he protectively follows her as she struggles with the cop. Paulette returns all this consideration by urging him to flee with her after they land on the road. He has to think about it; after all, what he really wanted was to return to the safety and relative comfort of jail. She persuades him with urgent gestures and the two run off, holding hands. From that point on, despite their hand-holding and Charlie's frequent affectionate looks toward her, they act more like siblings than lovers, and they often behave more like children than adults. The film's focus is not on their relationship, but on their joint effort to find a home for themselves. To achieve that goal, Charlie must become a breadwinner.

This is a perfectly reasonable story line, and a logical development from the first part of the film, for we've already seen how unsuited Charlie is for the working world; now the pressure is on for him to find and keep a job. Working is the only way the couple can achieve the American dream of home ownership, the "pursuit of happiness" promised in the opening credits. But for a variety of reasons their quest doesn't maintain the momentum of the film.

The lengthy nine-minute department store sequence begins as another pleasant domestic idyll. Charlie's job allows them act out their fantasy of a home life, as they turn the store into their personal playhouse. They eat, then visit the toy department, where Charlie shows off his skating prowess.

This brief but impressive sequence, in which Charlie skates precariously close to the edge of an unfinished floor while blindfolded, owes its impact to a number of clever illusions. First, Chaplin is able to see through his blindfold, a standard magician's gambit. Second, the camera greatly undercranks the action, shooting at fourteen and sixteen frames per second, allowing Chaplin to skate carefully while he appears to zip along with reckless abandon. Third, several reverse-action shots create the illusion that he's skating backward along the edge of the precipice, while he's actually skating forward. All these tricks enhance the palpable sense of danger in the scene, but the fourth and most impressive illusion ensures that Chaplin is in no danger at all, for there is no actual drop-off. The effect is achieved with an extremely deceptive "glass" shot, a painting of the floors below done on a sheet of glass placed in front of the camera. Thanks to this technique Chaplin was able to shoot the sequence over a four-day period without seriously risking life and limb. The painting aligns with the strip of wood that edges the apparent balcony floor; the small lip of the wood enables Charlie to stop securely as he skates backward towards the "edge" at the beginning and end of the routine. The illusion of the drop-off is made all the more convincing by the way the camera pans back and forth throughout the scene, and by a real plank of wood on a sawhorse that seems to extend over the drop off area. In actuality, we see the wood through a precise cutout in the painting. It took the studio team five days of testing and reworking to perfect the illusion, and their

The sign reiterates Charlie's apparent peril. The drop-off is an illusion painted on glass.

efforts paid off handsomely, for the artifice is virtually impossible to detect.[16]

The layered illusions, fused with Chaplin's graceful choreography, make this one of the most magical and memorable scenes of his career. It's not only funny and frightening to watch, it's also psychologically sophisticated. Charlie is in total control as long as he's unaware of his actual danger. He blithely glides along, one leg or another gracefully extended over the edge as he circles and twirls his way across the floor. Paulette can't call out to him, because she's afraid that if she does he might panic and take the plunge. Indeed, when he finally pulls off his blindfold and sees where he is, he *does* panic. His legs seem to skitter out from under him and his arms windmill in a frantic attempt to stop his forward momentum as he rolls toward the edge. Charlie's fear is expressed not only by his sudden inability to control the skates, but by his perverse attraction to the abyss. Paulette finally pulls him away and he walks off haltingly, holding onto her for dear life. The music underscores the irony that Charlie loses his ability to skate when he sees his actual danger by *not* changing to reflect his flailing movements. Instead, the lilting skating theme, interrupted by brief "awakening" music as he removes his blindfold, resumes as he struggles against his darker impulses.

In the bedroom department Charlie swaths Paulette in a fur coat and tucks her in for a nap while he skates along on his rounds. He immediately tangles with burglars, who turn out to be Charlie's old factory mates, now unemployed and hungry. Through no fault of his own, Charlie imbibes a huge quantity of rum and gets roaring drunk. The next morning he is discovered asleep on a fabric counter and promptly jailed once again.

Yet despite the many pleasures of this scene, notably Charlie's roller-skating, a slight sense of repetition begins to creep in. Charlie, who has already gone mad and gotten high, now gets drunk. He's already been carted off to the loony bin once and arrested twice, and now he's arrested a third time.

But if the film repeats, Charlie himself isn't so much going around in circles as spiraling steadily toward his goal. When he is released from prison ten days later, his dream of a life of suburban domesticity with Paulette turns into a pathetic, if comical, reality, one that would have been all too familiar to audiences of 1936. Paulette proudly shows him their new home, a broken-down little shanty in an empty field. The country at this time was dotted with whole communities of such makeshift dwellings, ironically dubbed "Hoovervilles" after the president deemed responsible for the Depression. Standing at the door of the decrepit shack, Charlie says, "It's paradise" and shuts the door, only to have a piece of hinged wood above the lintel conk him on the head (accompanied by the sound of wood blocks on the soundtrack).

Things keep falling apart during this third and last of Charlie and Paulette's domestic interludes, which ends with a jolt when Charlie reads over breakfast that the factories have reopened and are hiring men. Instantly galvanized, he bursts into action. "Now we'll get a real home," he declares to Paulette, gesturing melodramatically and popping his hat off his head in his excitement. Never was this hat-popping gag, which Chaplin did in many early films, used to better comic effect. He dashes out and, in a beautifully choreographed sequence, races across the field and plunges furiously through the packed crowd in front of the factory, calmly slipping through the gate in the nick of time before it's closed. This brief sequence is Chaplin at his best, and the film immediately perks up.

Alas, it loses its momentum again during the second factory scene. Charlie is hired as the assistant to mechanic Chester Conklin, whose job is to put the idle machinery in working order again following the strike or shutdown (we're not informed which). The first part of the scene, in which Charlie struggles to carry a large toolbox and then accidentally flattens Chester's heirloom watch in a large press, is not up to Chaplin's usual standard, while the rest basically reworks the eating gags of the first factory sequence. This time it's Chester who falls into one of the machines. Unlike Charlie, Chester is only partially regurgitated, his head poking out near the bottom of the machine, face up. When lunch hour is called Charlie, who in the earlier scene had been stuck in a machine and fed, now feeds the immobilized Chester, with similar messy results. It's very amusing, reminiscent of dozens of other fun-with-food scenes in Chaplin's films, but the reworking of earlier material contributes to the sense that the film is meandering rather than advancing.

In addition, as should be evident from the descriptions above, *Modern Times* contains many not-so-modern gags, and even whole sequences reminiscent of earlier films. A contemporary reviewer stated flatly that "all the old gags are brought out and dusted off for use. But they are such good old standbys that they still earn laughs."[17] Although critical reception of *Modern Times* was more mixed than for any previous Chaplin feature, Chaplin fared far better in this respect than Harold Lloyd, whose *Professor Beware* two years later was dismissed by *Time* magazine as "an overstocked museum of silent comedy technique."[18]

But it's not just because Chaplin recycles a few situations and gags that the film drags. He's at great pains to vary them from the originals, so his skating is now done blindfolded, on the edge of a drop-off, sharing with *The Rink* only Chaplin's incongruous grace and skill. His antics on the escalator shortly thereafter, unlike those in *The Floorwalker*, are done on the roller skates. The second factory scene concludes with one of his oldest film gags, smartly updated. The workers go on strike, and when Charlie leaves the factory the police are dispersing the angry strikers. One of the cops aggressively pushes Charlie away several times. Watching him warily, Charlie accidentally steps on a plank instead of stepping onto a curb, which catapults a brick onto another cop's head. It's a clever contemporary twist on his many brick-throwing battles of the past, not to mention his eternal battle with the cops. Like the hat-popping gag, brick throwing has been made new again, well motivated and beautifully executed.

Yet when he's arrested and packed off to jail for a *fourth* time, the repetition really starts to pall.

One of the harshest critics of the film was Sydney Chaplin, who sent his younger half-sibling a scorching eight-page, typed, single-spaced critique. Syd, who had been an important part of Chaplin's creative team in the teens and early 1920s, had retired and moved to Europe in the 1930s. He would rejoin his brother on *The Great Dictator*, possibly because of the way he felt Charlie had botched *Modern Times*. Writing six months after *Modern Times*' European premiere, Syd began his diatribe by ridiculing the "Nit wits" who worked with Charlie on the film, then went on to say:

> I think you made a mistake by trying to introduce too many factions [the brothers' word for major sequences]. . . . You started your picture off with a fast tempo then faded away. You gave them the best first instead of saving it until last. You had no *personal* heavy running throughout your picture, Your only heavy was inanimate machinery & conditions. . . . [Y]our dry good store & cafe were incidents in them selves & had no bearing on the story, except to show you trying to make an honest living.[19]

Syd then offered Charlie detailed critiques of the individual "factions," and suggestions for many gags his careless younger brother had missed. The department store scene, for example, would have been more exciting had it ended with him being chased on roller skates by the cops, who have mistaken him for one of the burglars, rather than simply using the skates to show off for Paulette. Syd went on to provide a detailed plot synopsis for how the factory could have provided a through-line unifying the film. In his view the factory should have manufactured something definite, such as cars, so that Charlie's mad dance would have resulted in a comical "freak car" being produced. In addition, the factory owner would be the film's continuing heavy; it would be him, not the minister, visiting the prison, so Charlie could interact with his haughty wife; he would also own the department store. Charlie and he could clash at every turn.

Chaplin could hardly have welcomed this Monday-morning quarterbacking, but he greatly respected his brother's opinions. And Syd tempered his scathing commentary—somewhat—by saying, "[Y]ou may not agree with me but you must admit that if I criticise, at least I try to offer some constructive ideas with my criticism."[20] That's very true; Syd's suggestions are both practical and shrewd, if a bit late. Several of them, remarkably, seem to anticipate the approach taken by French comedian-filmmaker Jacques Tati a decade and a half later, including his idea that Charlie remain a more or less silent character in his future talking films.

And Syd is right on the money in saying that the main problem of *Modern Times* is that Chaplin never tops his inventive opening factory sequence. The jailhouse scene comes very close; it moves quickly, with clear adversaries (first his cellmate, then the escaping prisoners) and bold comedy about homosexuality and drugs. Had Chaplin maintained that level of inventiveness and dramatic tension, the film probably wouldn't flag no matter how meandering its plot or repetitious its gags, and no matter how much we miss the usual romantic complications.

But there's something more subtle missing, and it's that Chaplin has failed to follow through on his initial premise, the inventive intermingling of the worlds of sound and silent film. After we leave the Big Brother world of the factory, with its voices, omnipresent two-way television monitors, and relentless, inhuman pace and regimentation, it's as though we're thrust backward in time, into the silent film world, with only a few sound effects here and there to remind us of the hybrid world Chaplin so brilliantly creates in his factory. Even when he returns to the factory, Chaplin fails to resurrect this world, instead offering a pallid variant on what had come before. In addition, the presence of Chester, a conspicuous relic of silent movies, forcibly reminds us that we're now in olden rather than modern times. Despite Chaplin's determination to keep the film current with continual references to the events of the day, it becomes a nostalgic evocation of bygone days, his filmmaking choices those of the unregenerate curmudgeon that Otis Ferguson, in his oft-quoted review of the film in the *New Republic*, accuses him of being.[21] Another way of saying this is that the film becomes too much about Charlie and not enough about Chaplin; it loses sight of its "shadow" plot of Chaplin confronting sound.

Things pick up considerably, however, during the lively café scene. Charlie tries in vain to serve a roast duck to a frustrated customer, but the huge crowd on the dance floor keeps jostling him away. Although a bit attenuated, the scene climaxes strongly when the elusive duck becomes a football for a drunken college reunion group. Charlie intercepts the flying duck and does a broken-field run to score a "touchdown," overturning his hapless customer's table and thrusting the duck into his bare hands.

As important as the sequence's tightened comic pace is the fact that Chaplin finally returns to his theme by allowing human sounds to reenter the film, in the form of whistles, cheers, applause, and a background buzz of conversation from the large café crowd. When the drunken college group takes the floor to sing their college fight song, there's no serious attempt to accurately lip synch their words, because we're not in a sound film—we're back in the hybrid world, where there are voices and sound effects, but everyone is still moving at silent speed. Sound is encroaching, though; this is the first time we've been permitted to hear voices and other sounds directly, without the intercession of a mechanical playback device. Even the music, mostly a series of lively dance tunes, is ostensibly played by a band that we see onscreen throughout the scene.

And now the two plots of the film—Charlie's problem with employment and Chaplin's problem with sound—merge definitively, for Charlie has reluctantly agreed to sing as part of his waiter job.[22]

Even without knowledge of Chaplin's previous career, or a concern about the aesthetic conundrums of sound versus silent film posed in *Modern Times*, an audience greets the knowledge that Chaplin is finally going to break silence with knowing laughter and anticipation, having sat through most of a feature-length film in which he has "spoken," as usual, in eloquent, silent pantomime. How will he finally confront his nemesis? As he had in *City Lights*, Chaplin brings the film to a sharp focus on the double dilemma faced by himself and his character. And as he had in *City Lights*, he rises to the occasion surprisingly and brilliantly.

"I hope you can sing," the café boss says (in a subtitle), after Charlie has demonstrated in no uncertain terms that he's not much of a waiter. Casting a doubtful glance at the camera, Charlie silently begins rehearsing his song in the dressing room, while outside a quartet of waiters files onto the darkened dance floor and begins singing. The waiters move at crisp silent speed, and the lip-synching is as shaky as it was during the earlier café scenes. Back in the dressing room Paulette joins Charlie, and as we watch them we hear the waiters in the next room launch into the old standard "In the Evening by the Moonlight."

Charlie is having trouble memorizing the lines of his song, so Paulette helpfully writes them on his shirt cuffs. This device allows Chaplin to prepare the viewer for what's about to happen by telling us all we need to know about the song:

> a pretty girl and a gay old man
> flirted on the boulevard
> he was a fat old thing
> but his diamond ring
> caught her eye

Charlie practices, periodically checking his cuffs for the lyrics as he sings and mimes his way through the song. As he rehearses, the rowdy crowd boos the quartet off and starts stamping impatiently for the next act. Following his introductory fanfare, Charlie, secure with the crib notes on his cuffs, marches onto a brightened dance floor to the lively strains of a popular tune of the day, "Titina."

English sheet music for "Titina," a French song about a Spanish beauty that Chaplin used for his multilingual gibberish song. 1925.

For the first time we see Chaplin moving to music, rather than hearing music as an accompaniment to his actions. The sprightly dance tune inspires him to throw his arms apart several times as he slides back and forth across the floor in bravura style. In the process, he accidentally flings his cuffs away. His step flows smoothly to a nifty sliding motion in which he "digs" his back foot into the floor as he drags his front foot backward, occasionally creating the amusing illusion that he's pulling himself backward by the seat of his pants.

But what's really notable is that we *hear* his feet scraping along the floor. For the first time, the synchronization is precise; what we hear fuses with what we see, enhancing the illusion of reality. For the first time ever in a Chaplin film, Charlie Chaplin moves at the speed of life. A door has opened, and we have finally entered the domain of sound cinema.[23]

Charlie moves front and center to sing, then realizes, to his dismay, that he has lost his cuffs. He resumes his drag-step around the floor to look for them. The band vamps. He can't see them anywhere. He gestures helplessly to Paulette, who's watching from the doorway of the dressing room. Moving at brisk silent tempo, she mouths "Sing!! Never mind the words." We see her words in a subtitle. The two worlds are now presented side by side, rather than overlapping.

The crowd is growing restive, and Charlie holds his hands out in front of him, motioning for them to calm down. The tempo of the band behind him slows down as well, in response to his movement. Taking Paulette literally, he begins to sing without words, in gibberish. His nonsense words are a fluid mishmash of Spanish, Italian,

Pulling himself by the seat of his pants to find the lost cuffs.

"A pretty girl."

The "gay old man" displays his ring and beckons the girl.

French, German, and English.[24] Simultaneously, he acts out the story in movement.

Chaplin faces the audience in the café and performs directly to the camera, engaging us, as he had so often done before, in an intimate one-on-one exchange. And once again he manages to slip some surprisingly bold material past the censors, and past most viewers.

In the first verse Chaplin shows us the "pretty girl" with descriptive arcs of his eloquent hands, first around her face and then her shapely figure, ending with one hand provocatively placed on her hip and the other stylishly holding a cigarette holder. Chaplin thus simultaneously describes the girl and becomes her. His movements are the same as those he practiced in the dressing room, but performed much more slowly, allowing us to appreciate his fluid grace and savor his mimetic skill. "Se bella" begins the verse, which ends, as every verse will, with a nonsense-syllable variant on "tra la la la la la la." The pretty girl holds her skirt up becomingly and turns around in a circle. The café audience laughs and applauds.

After completing his circle Chaplin becomes the "fat old thing," reinforcing his clear descriptive gestures with a number of recognizable, indirectly applicable words. He strokes his handlebar mustache, "la spinach," and draws his fingers along the long cigar, "la pusho," sticking out of his mouth. He joins his hands to encircle his ample belly, his "cigaretto potto-bello," then places "de rackie spaghaletto," his imaginary cane, against the floor and wiggles it from side to side as if gaining purchase. He twirls it jauntily as he circles around again, this time in the opposite direction.

Having established his two main characters with gibberish and mime, Chaplin continues the story for a while with mime alone. The band vamps as the fat man notices the girl. He checks her out with lascivious interest and tips his hat as she walks past. To attract her, he spits on and polishes his diamond ring, then looks down at the ring and flutters it invitingly. He wiggles his eyebrows and beckons her with a come-hither toss of his head. Evidently she is receptive, for he does a comical, predatory walk in profile toward her. When he reaches her he stops, pulls down his waistcoat, twirls his mustache, tips his hat again, and bows.

The fat man begins the third verse by singing to the girl. "Señora peela seela" (hinting that she is perhaps married), "voulez-vous la taxi meter?" He turns an imaginary steering wheel to reinforce the lyric, pauses to wait for her answer, then opens the door to the taxi and ushers her in with a graceful arm gesture, singing, "le jonta su la seata," then joins her in the taxi, closing the door behind him and instructing the driver, with a twirl of his hand, "to le tour le tour le wah."

Completing his circle he becomes the cabbie, driving along and occasionally squeezing his taxi horn (heard on the soundtrack but not precisely synced to his movements). Chaplin releases the steering wheel and holds his hands up in front of him as he did at the beginning of the song, signaling that he has become the narrator once again.

He begins the fourth verse by circling his face to show the girl, now sitting quietly in the back seat, her hands folded demurely over one another. Standing in the same place he becomes the fat man, stroking his mustache, eying her sideways, twiddling his thumbs, biding his time. The singsong turns to dialogue again as the man points to her, kisses his forefinger, then reaches over and pats her knee. She indignantly pushes his hand away and slaps it hard (we hear all these body sounds). It's a fascinating bit of mime, because he becomes both characters

Embracing.

The girl bids a demure goodbye.

at once, slapping "his" left hand with "her" right. She uses the refrain to scold him, singing, "se la putsh a tee la twa."

In the fifth verse the girl negotiates, touching her finger to her lips ("meena"), then pointing to her right forefinger and back to herself, demanding that he give her his ring. He hesitates, wipes away a tear, and somewhat reluctantly takes the ring off his finger and hands it over. He pulls her to him enthusiastically, then crosses his arms in a stylized embrace, turning his back and rocking rapidly back and forth on the outsides of his feet. While the rocking movement can be seen as a response to the lively music, a bit of eccentric dance—he does essentially the same movement with the dancing rolls in *The Gold Rush*—it makes his butt wiggle suggestively. If the movement is somewhat ambiguous, there is no ambiguity about what he does next. Reaching behind himself, he pulls down a window shade.

Chaplin turns around and walks rhythmically toward the audience for the sixth verse, his arms still folded, his expression neutral. He takes his time; possibly it is the next morning. He circles his face and becomes the girl. Clearly very pleased with herself, she strikes several coy poses, then chucks the fat man's cheeks, pulls him toward her by his mustache, gives him a big kiss, and waves good-bye as she goes on her way, singing a merry "tra la la la la la la," the first time we hear the refrain in its proper, simple form.

The café audience is vastly amused by Charlie's song, and so are we. The nonsense lyrics are perfectly understandable due to Charlie's sharp and amusing characterizations of the girl and her suitor, and his fluid dance-and-mime routine is utterly enchanting and hypnotic. So much so that it's easy to overlook the fact that Charlie is acting out a tidy little tale of prostitution. Although this is plain enough when the scene is described in words, Chaplin's singsong lyrics and intricate, fluid movements soften the impact, as does the fact that his characters are cartoony stereotypes—Betty Boop meets the Monopoly man. Even sophisticated viewers don't usually see the story for what it is, a racy account of a pickup, a financial transaction, and a one-night stand.[25] As he had done throughout he career, Chaplin gets away with risqué material that would be unacceptable in less skilled hands—and less eloquent bodies.

That the girl considers the ring payment for her favors was made even more explicit in the original release version of the film, which included a seventh verse in which she tries to pawn it. Demurely holding up her skirt and trotting along, she visits a pawnbroker, unambiguously identified as such in the lyric. She hands him the ring and asks him to tell her "how mucha?" Chaplin suddenly becomes a caricatured Jewish pawnbroker, screwing up his face and shrugging his shoulders expressively, look-

The pawnbroker.

ing very much like his childhood portrayal of Fagin in *Casey's Circus*.[26] He peers at the ring through his loupe and turns it skeptically from side to side, rejecting it with strong gestures as he declares it to be "punka wa le punka wa," the final "tra la la" variant. The girl throws her arms up in dismay, tears her hair, and runs off.[27]

The only real precedent for this routine in Chaplin's work is the David and Goliath sermon from *The Pilgrim*, in which Charlie as a minister assumes the roles of both David and Goliath. The waiter sequence is much more elaborate. A seemingly effortless blend of gibberish song, dance, and mime, it occupies a unique place in Chaplin's work, as well as virtually defining a type of mime performance in which a solo performer switches rapidly from role to role and uses illusionary props, a form of mime made popular by Marcel Marceau nearly twenty years later.[28]

As Marceau would find, however, effectively *filming* such stage mime routines is a daunting task. Chaplin, as we would expect, pulls it off magnificently. His performance of the three-minute song is presented almost entirely in long shot, strategically interrupted for two brief medium shots, perfectly matched on action, of the fat man flashing his ring and the girl later demanding it for her services, and one brief cutaway of Paulette laughing. And more importantly, the sequence is presented not as a self-contained set piece, but put into context—necessitated, one might say—by the plot of the film.

Like the ending of *City Lights*, the ending of *Modern Times* is perfectly logical, and like the ending of the earlier film, we don't see it coming. Chaplin hammers home his point, the point he's been making from the start of the film—indeed, from the start of his career: *Actions speak louder than words*. The nonsense song must have been particularly pleasing to non-English-speaking audiences, who, like everyone else, were waiting to hear Chaplin's voice.

But for the casual viewer it's easy to overlook another obvious fact: The man doing this routine no longer moves like the Tramp, nor does the content suit the innocent we've been watching bungle his way through the film. Instead, we are treated to the spectacle of Charles Chaplin, mime, the Tramp unmasked. The ending of *Modern Times* solves Chaplin's aesthetic dilemma by merging the Tramp with his creator.

But a question remains: Why does Chaplin sing this particular song, in this particular way, risking censorship and public censure by crossing the line into risqué material?[29] Is it simply another of his engaging non sequiturs, like twisting his ear and blowing cigar smoke from his mouth, which he does earlier in the film when he snatches a cigar from under the nose of a cop?

I think not. Charlie's routine is conjured, like all his best routines, to get himself out of a jam. The café audience has definitively rejected the quartet of waiters singing a hoary old favorite. There are drunks in this audience, and sailors with their girls. They're all out for a good time, and they want something sexy and sophisticated. Charlie gives them all that and more—an excursion to a sophisticated European cabaret. Singing the song in Euro-gibberish is a master touch, for American audiences expected Continental entertainment to be sexier than the home-grown product, and Chaplin delivers with a song about a girl who is "no better than she ought to be," in the euphemistic parlance of the music hall of Chaplin's youth. Intriguingly, as the singer of a comic, risqué ballad, Chaplin evokes not the Tramp but his own charming, doomed father, who topped the bill with just such risqué songs half a century earlier.

The scene also balances the film by allowing Charlie to turn, however briefly, into a sexual being. As we've noted before, following the Mutual series of films the Tramp had grown increasingly innocent, his courtships invariably chaste. Only occasionally, such as in the short scene with the policeman's wife in *The Kid*, or when he scrutinizes the nude statue in *City Lights*, does the Tramp evince mature sexuality. Overtly sexual behavior is usually relegated to such lustful secondary characters as the German officer in *Shoulder Arms* or Jack, "the ladies' man" in *The Gold Rush*.

In *Modern Times* Charlie is a comic satyr during his "mad" scene in the factory, lasciviously pursuing women, if only to twist their buttons. But the mad sexual impulse is suppressed from that time on, as Charlie and the gamine cavort like children through the rest of the film. But sex will out, just as words will out. After the film's long, teasing "foreplay," both words and sex finally burst free, in an explosion of nonsense that makes perfect sense, even if its implications are muted by the very virtuosity of the presentation. Everyone gets the idea that Chaplin is telling a sexy story. For those with the eyes to see, the tale that unfolds is a celebration of the power of sex, along with some of its disillusionments. Yet it's told nonjudgmentally, unadorned either by fashionable cynicism or the romantic halo that usually veils such stories in the movies.

After Chaplin's brilliant simultaneous display of mime, song, and dance, the viewer is once more completely engaged with the film. Charlie runs into the dressing room and suddenly the tempo quickens. His character changes as well, just as abruptly as he changed characters during the routine. He's the innocent again, uncertain of his accomplishment. Paulette gives him a reassuring hug. The café boss—the redoubtable Henry Bergman, making his last appearance in a Chaplin film—comes to summon Charlie out for a curtain call. Charlie reenters the dining room (at sound speed), takes a modest bow, and blows kisses to the crowd, which is standing and cheering. He returns to the dressing room, where Henry enthusiastically offers to keep him on. Henry speaks in a silent film subtitle, of course, for we've returned to the silent world, where the Tramp belongs.

Finally, Charlie has succeeded at a job, and Chaplin has both confronted and triumphed over sound. But the respite is temporary. The orphan officials are closing in on Paulette, so Charlie and his underage companion escape from the café and its brief promise of security.

The next morning finds the duo sitting by the side of a desolate road. Charlie is footsore after their night of travel, and Paulette is feeling discouraged. She breaks down and begins to cry. Charlie tries to cheer her up. "Buck up—never say die. We'll get along!" he tells her in the film's last subtitle. "You betcha. Let's go!" she mouths gamely, and they get up and start down the road, hand in hand. But her face is still grim. Charlie stops her, "draws" a broad grin across his face with his finger, and mouths the word "smile." She does, brightly and fiercely, ready again to take on the world.

In print, the little pep talk sounds like it might be cloying. In the film it becomes unexpectedly moving as the duo walks away from us down the long, empty road. We've seen Charlie walk down roads before at the end of his adventures, but this is different. This road is no rural dirt path, but a modern paved highway, with a traffic stripe painted down the middle and telephone poles running along the side. The sun is just coming up over the distant, mountainous horizon, silhouetting the two figures and bathing the scene in a warm, comforting glow. And most significantly, for the first time Charlie is not alone on his journey. It is heartening to know that his road will not be a lonely one.

But it is also deeply saddening for any viewer who knows that this would be the last walk down the road for the silent Tramp. As Chaplin's beautiful love theme swells on the soundtrack, we watch the familiar figure recede in the distance, a casualty of modern times.

Notes

1. Winston Churchill, "Everybody's Language," *Collier's* 96 (October 26, 1935); reprinted in Donald McCaffrey, ed., *Focus on Chaplin* (Englewood Cliffs, NJ: Prentice-Hall, 1971) 76–78.

2. Chaplin, cited by Max Eastman, *Great Companions* (New York: Farrar, Strauss and Cudahy, 1949), 225.

3. Chaplin was not generally given to in-jokes in his films, certainly not to the extent of Alfred Hitchcock, whose cameo appearances became a teasing challenge for knowing viewers. There are, however, subtleties to be found. For example, in *City Lights*, as boxer Hank Mann walks through the crowd toward the ring, he pokes a heckler. After the fight he returns by the same route and sees the heckler, who ducks out of sight. It's a nice, understated character bit. In *Modern Times*, as we'll see, the subtleties are much more subversive.

4. The actor, Allan Garcia, was a utility authority figure for Chaplin, appearing as the ringmaster in *The Circus*, the butler in *City Lights*, and several other films.

5. Shooting logs for the film reveal that Chaplin shot much of it at eighteen frames per second, or 25 percent faster than life, and some of the chase and other action scenes at sixteen frames per second. While Chaplin also shot some scenes at standard sound speed, the president, here and elsewhere, seems to move more quickly, and his words, dubbed in later, are almost, but not completely, lip-synced.

6. It is generally agreed that *Modern Times* is Chaplin's best score. It is certainly his most complex. Conductor Timothy Brock reconstructed the score from the original manuscript sheets, for the purposes of playing it as live accompaniment to the film. In the process he was able to reconstruct Chaplin's compositional process, which he recounts in a fascinating article on the subject. Brock reveals that the recording sessions lasted an incredible four weeks, because Chaplin would often listen to the music, then rework it in the presence of the orchestra. Brock also provides an in-depth analysis of the musical values of the score. His article may be found at www.timothybrock.com/articles_modern_times.htm (October 10, 2007).

7. In fact, Chaplin had contemplated making *Modern Times* as a standard sound film, and scripted many of the scenes with full dialogue. But after shooting sound tests and an initial scene he opted to make the film a hybrid.

8. Chaplin shot the scene at eighteen frames per second as well, but evidently the sped-up action didn't work with the narration. In the finished film the men stride into the office at a brisk eighteen frames per second; the inventor cranks the phonograph, then, following a cut to the president looking on curiously, the balance of the scene plays out at twenty-four frames per second.

9. There is no question that Chaplin intended for the machine to be taken metaphorically rather than literally, for tinkling music box music follows Charlie as he winds through the gears, compelling us to see it as a giant clockwork toy. Whether he consciously intended for that toy to be seen as a film projector remains speculative, but associating the machine with a music box makes it tempting to think so. A music box mechanically reproduces sounds, a film projector mechanically reproduces images, and *Modern Times* is a film self-consciously focused on the mechanical reproduction of sounds and images. If the interpretation is a stretch, it's not much of one.

10. We know that Charlie's gone nuts as much because of the music as by his crazy behavior. Twittering sounds accompany his "awakening" after he emerges from the machine, and the ensuing "mad" dance is accompanied by a series of lively variations on the factory theme music, each one carefully timed to match Charlie's actions. It's like watching a ballet, except that the music clearly follows his action, silent film style, rather than the other way around.

11. "Pansy" characters such as those played by Franklin Pangborn in the 1930s and Clifton Webb in the 1940s and 1950s were a staple of entertainment, but most viewers would have seen them as harmless comic fops, bookworms, or mama's boys rather than homosexuals. Gays were off the public radar in popular entertainment until the late 1960s.

12. The gay character originally figured more prominently. In the cut of the film Chaplin submitted to the Production Code office, Hollywood's self-censorship arm, the man actually enters a cell where Charlie is sitting alone. Alarmed, Charlie immediately demands to be moved, only to end up in the cell with the brutish man doing needlepoint. This makes the needlepoint gag even funnier and more pointed, of course: In prison, you can't get away from gay people, or apparently straight people acting gay. However, Joseph Breen, head of the Code office, demanded that Chaplin remove the earlier sequence, although he allowed the gay character to remain in the rest of the scene. Why he didn't require Chaplin to excise the man altogether remains speculative. I can think of three possibilities. First, he may not have wanted to force Chaplin to do expensive retakes. Second, he may have thought no one would notice. Third, he may not have noticed himself. Breen also required Chaplin to remove the word "dope" in a subtitle in the scene, evidently finding "nose powder" more acceptable.

13. There were two sound transformation gags in *City Lights*. In the first Charlie mistakes the sound of a loud piano chord for a gunshot; in the second he swallows a whistle, and each time he hiccups he emits a wheezing sound, first summoning a cab, then a pack of dogs.

14. It must have been galling to Chaplin to have his filmmaking criticized as old-fashioned, given the sophisticated use of special effects photography in *Modern Times*. He also uses a number of "glass" shots, matte shots, and "hanging miniatures" in the film. By strategically placing a sheet of glass, part of which is painted with a realistic image, in front of the camera, glass shots could create the illusion of massive sets, skylines, and such. Matte shots use the same principle, but are more controllable because they rely on paintings that are later double-exposed onto the original negative, which has been shot with the area to be double-exposed carefully "matted" out. A matte shot creates a nonexistent factory in *Modern Times*' opening montage; actual workers walk over an actual bridge, while above them a huge (painted) factory looms. The illusion is made even more persuasive by smoke that billows from one of the painted smokestacks, which was shot as a separate element and added to the master negative. Before and after production shots of this scene can be found in John Bengtson's impressive *Silent Traces: Discovering Early Hollywood Through the Films of Charlie Chaplin* (Santa Monica, CA: Santa Monica Press, 2006), 265. Hanging miniatures, small three-dimensional models that serve essentially the same function as glass shots, are used to complete several interior shots of the factory as well. In *City Lights* Chaplin used both glass shots and a hanging miniature to create his city skyline. See *Silent Traces*, 253–54, for revealing production shots.

15. Both a full-scale section of the boat and a miniature were used for the sequence. In the shot immediately preceding the sinking, Charlie knocks the wedge holding the boat in place away, and it begins its stately slide into the water. The miniature was used for the rear-projection sinking shot. It would have had to be a pretty large scale miniature to sink properly and look convincing; sinking a boat of any size presents quite a technical problem, as Keaton discovered when shooting the full-size boat in *The Boat* (1921). After several failed attempts his special-effects man ended up dragging it under with steel cables connected to a winch, driven by an engine. See Rudi Blesh, *Keaton* (New York: MacMillan, 1966), 195. Keaton and Lloyd, in their heyday, wouldn't have countenanced rear projection for a comic payoff shot, as both prided themselves on painstaking authenticity in such scenes. But the times were imposing new economic constraints on filmmakers, and Chaplin's films were always expensive due to their protracted shooting schedules.

16. It's so well done, in fact, that it caused a lively debate among an impressive circle of Chaplin experts during the writing of this book. Despite being unequivocally labeled as a glass shot in Jeffrey Vance's *Chaplin: Genius of the Cinema* (New York: Abrams, 2003), confirmed by studio records provided by Kate Guyonvarch of Association Chaplin, several expert observers held that the term "glass shot" *might* have been used generically to include what they saw as a trompe l'oeil painting on the floor next to where Chaplin is skating. The camera movement and wooden plank support that view, while the lack of shadows on the drop-off area suggest a glass shot. Weighing in on the debate were David Totheroh, grandson of Chaplin's cameraman Rollie; Chaplin scholar Bruce Lawton and his grandfather, cameraman Karl Malkames; classical guitarist and Chaplin aficionado Alice Artzt; author/editor Hooman Mehran; and Glenn Mitchell, author of *The Chaplin Encyclopedia* (London: B.T. Batsford, 1997). The matter was finally settled by Craig Barron, coauthor of the definitive book on glass painting, *The Invisible Art: The Legends of Movie Matte Painting* (San Francisco: Chronicle Books, 2002), whose sharp eye caught one of Chaplin's skate wheels disappearing behind the painting in a couple of frames. Welcome to the world of special effects before matte photography, blue screen, and computer animation.

17. Cited in Gerald D. McDonald, Michael Conway, and Mark Ricci, eds., *The Films of Charlie Chaplin* (New York: Bonanza Books, 1965), 203.

18. "Also Showing," *Time*, July 18, 1938, 21.

19. This remarkable letter was reprinted in full in *Modern Times-Tempi moderni*, ed. Christian Delage and Cecilia Cenciarelli (Chaplin Project No. 2, Cineteca di Bologna, Le Mani, Bologna, Italy, 2004), 336–50.

20. Delage et al., *Modern Times-Tempi moderni*, 342.

21. Otis Ferguson, "Hallelujah, Bum Again," *New Republic*, February 19, 1936.

22. Charlie's job interview is wittily played out in musical terms. As he had done in the opening scene of *City Lights*, Chaplin lets instruments comically represent human voices. The rotund café boss quizzes Charlie in a low bassoon growl. Paulette "speaks" on Charlie's behalf in a rapid, high-pitched twittering made with strings and flute. It's a variation on the birdlike musical motif that accompanies her throughout the film, perfect for a character whose key movement is twittering her feet excitedly. When the insecure Charlie speaks for himself, his voice is a reedy oboe.

23. The musical performance was recorded while the scene was being filmed, rather than being prerecorded in a sound studio or dubbed in afterward. This accounts for the perfect synchronization of sound and image. A fifty-piece orchestra accompanied Chaplin offscreen. See Vance, *Charlie Chaplin: Genius of the Cinema*, 219.

24. Chaplin, like Sid Caesar after him, had the gift of being able to speak in foreign-language gibberish that sounded very convincing. He would astonish Douglas Fairbanks by "conversing" fluently with his Japanese servants, for example.

25. Most people I have asked about the routine, including some longtime Chaplin buffs, see it simply as a charming but essentially meaningless demonstration of Chaplin's mime skills. Several told me they saw the ring exchange as an offer of marriage. Hardly!

26. Chaplin reprints a photo of himself in the role in *My Autobiography* (New York: Simon & Schuster, 1964), 91.

27. It's unclear why Chaplin cut this stanza prior to re-releasing the film in 1954. Perhaps the war had changed his attitudes about doing a Jewish caricature, or perhaps he wanted to soften the commercial aspect of the transaction. Eliminating it makes for a bit of a jump cut as Charlie runs back into the dressing room. The original version can be found in the Image Entertainment release of the film on DVD.

28. The film, and this scene in particular, also inspired the classic 1945 French film *Les Enfants du Paradis* (*Children of Paradise*). The great French actor and mime Jean-Louis Barrault, playing the great nineteenth-century mime Baptiste Deburau, begins the film by reenacting a robbery he has just witnessed. Barrault's brilliant mime of a pretty woman, a fat man, and a crafty pickpocket owe much to Chaplin's mime characterizations in the waiter dance.

29. The Production Code Administration was established in 1934 to preclude the rising calls for governmental censorship of movies. Prior to that time many films had racy content that included prostitutes, for example the comedy *If I Had a Million* and the drama *Rain*, both from 1932. After 1934 such topics were still allowed, but had to be dramatically justified and done in "good taste"—that is, the questionable behavior had to be condemned within the film. The Code office asked Chaplin to alter several scenes in *Modern Times*, but not the song. As he had done since the beginning of his career, Chaplin was able to push the envelope of good taste through the brilliance of his mime.

CHAPTER ELEVEN

Split Personality: *The Great Dictator*

On September 9, 1939, barely a week after Adolf Hitler began World War II by invading Poland, Charlie Chaplin began shooting *The Great Dictator*. All of Chaplin's films had been eagerly anticipated, but none more so than this cinematic showdown between the funniest man in the world and the most terrifying.

In retrospect it seems inevitable that Chaplin play Hitler. During the 1930s political cartoonists, pundits, and comedians had a field day with their bizarre resemblance. A British music hall song from 1939 comically contrasts the two, suggesting Hitler would be a flop as a filmmaker, but that if Chaplin waged war—

> With him in charge the battles would be fun,
> And the chief of his Gestapo
> Wouldn't be Karl Marx, but Harpo,
> And he'd soon have Shirley Temple on the run.
> —*Who Is This Man? (Who Looks Like Charlie Chaplin)*

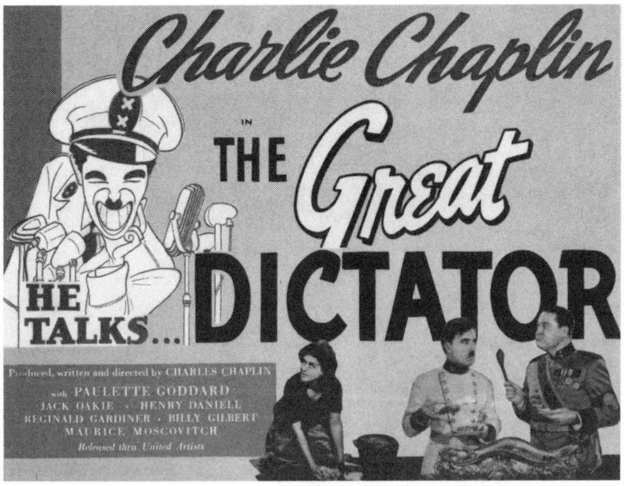

Al Hirschfeld's distinctive artwork helped to promote *The Great Dictator,* here trumpeting the fact that "HE TALKS!" To the movie-going public of the time, this was almost as startling as the fact that Chaplin was playing Hitler. The phrase echoes the famous GARBO TALKS slogan used a decade earlier to advertise Greta Garbo's first talkie, *Anna Christie*. But in Chaplin's case the words and images combine to announce not only that he talks, but that he has something important to say. Illustration © Al Hirschfeld. Reproduced by arrangement with Hirschfeld's exclusive representative, the Margo Feiden Galleries Ltd., New York, www.alhirschfeld.com.

The Nazis, in their turn, attacked Chaplin. A friend sent him a repellent propaganda paperback published in Germany, entitled *Jews Are Looking at You*. It featured full-page photos of prominent Jewish figures, retouched to make them look grotesque. Chaplin was included, with a caption that read, "This little Jewish tumbler, as disgusting as he is boring."

Chaplin wasn't Jewish, but he was perfectly willing to turn his Tramp character into a Jew on screen if that's what it would take to strike back at the Nazis' virulent anti-Semitism. And if Hitler had stolen Chaplin's mustache, Chaplin would reclaim it with a savage caricature of Hitler as a preening, gibberish-spouting buffoon.

But however satisfying it might be for Chaplin personally, making *The Great Dictator* represented an enormous risk on several fronts. First, in the volatile political climate, a comedy about Hitler could well become a box office disaster—or even unreleasable. Second, lampooning Hitler put Chaplin at risk personally; he received death threats and crank letters throughout the preparation of the film. But the most significant risk was artistic, for this was to be Chaplin's first full-fledged talking picture. Would the public accept him as a speaking comedian? For that matter, would they permit any comedian—even Chaplin—to speak out about Hitler?

As with all his feature films, Chaplin agonized for years over the conception of the film. Max Eastman recalls coming upon his distraught friend in a hotel room in New York, years before he made *The Great Dictator*. Chaplin had just been offered $877,000 to do twenty-five fifteen-minute radio broadcasts.

> "I can't do it, you know," he said. And then, with increased mournfulness: "I need the money too! The government just relieved me of a million dollars."
>
> "Why can't you do it?" I said. "You can make a speech!"
>
> "It isn't that," he said. "You know how I love speech-making. I can't come that close to my public. I have to remain a little remote and mysterious. They have to romanticize me. I would lose more than that at the box office if I made myself real and familiar over the radio."[1]

To keep this distance, Chaplin had created the unique treatment of sound in *City Lights* and *Modern Times*. In *The Great Dictator*, his first true talkie, he was able to find another compromise, one that allowed him to give his Tramp a reprieve by capitalizing on Hitler's resemblance to the beloved figure. He would enter the world of dialogue comedy on his own terms, making full use of his talismanic character, his gift for gibberish, and his mimetic abilities.

> As Hitler I could harangue the crowds in jargon and talk all I wanted to. And as the tramp I could remain more or less silent. A Hitler story was an opportunity for burlesque and pantomime.[2]

This was a bold decision on many levels. Like *Shoulder Arms* it was an attempt to find humor in the madness of war before the passage of time provided a safe vantage point. But unlike *Shoulder Arms*, which was released just three weeks before the armistice, *The Great Dictator* was begun more than two years before Pearl Harbor, during a period when popular sentiment in America was overwhelmingly isolationist.

The earlier film, which both Chaplin and his distributor released with some trepidation, proved to be Chaplin's greatest success up to that time, setting a standard by which his films were judged for years to come. Once he had hit upon the idea for *The Great Dictator*, it must have been an irresistible temptation to try to repeat his early triumph, and to do for World War II what he had done for World War I—even more, for this film could conceivably alter the tide of the war. And whatever criticism he might receive, no one could complain that *this* film wasn't about modern times.

War comedy, 1918. Charlie as a doughboy in *Shoulder Arms*.

But to make a true sound film, two things would have to change: his character and his comedy.

> Some people suggested that the tramp might talk. This was unthinkable, for the first word he ever uttered would transform him into another person. Besides, the matrix out of which he was born was as mute as the rags he wore.[3]

He does become another person, albeit a close relative of the silent Tramp. Even though Chaplin keeps the Tramp "more or less silent," as his brother Syd had suggested he do henceforth in his critique of *Modern Times*, by giving him even minimal dialogue, a nationality (German), a job (barber), and a religion (Jewish), he removes the non-specific Everyman quality of his great vagabond. More critically, by placing him in a sound film world he slows him down, since dialogue had to be shot and projected at twenty-four frames a second, the speed of life. No longer the comic dervish of the silents, the Tramp becomes uncharacteristically passive, as the essential comic energy and driving force in the film shifts to the dictator.

The presence of dialogue meant Chaplin had to change the nature of his comedy as well. After so many years of creating visual puns, Chaplin now peppers his film with verbal ones. No one could miss the litany of insulting names—Goebbels becomes Garbitsch, Göring becomes Herring, and Benito Mussolini becomes Benzino Napaloni, a pungent combination of a petroleum derivative, the emperor Napoleon, and baloney. This "fragrant" disrespect extends to country and city names as well. Napaloni is the dictator of Bacteria, whose capital is Aroma; Germany becomes Tomania, a name that neatly fuses the nauseating digestive condition with the idea of mania. Tomania's mania is its enthusiasm for its crazed leader, Adenoid Hynkel, a blustering tyrant whose noxious ideas are spewed out in pun-filled pseudo-German that often sends him into coughing fits, as though he's choking on the bile of his poisonous thoughts.

The Great Dictator begins with two subtitles that establish the light tone and silly humor that will permeate much of the film:

NOTE
ANY RESEMBLANCE BETWEEN
HYNKEL THE DICTATOR AND
THE JEWISH BARBER IS PURELY
CO-INCIDENTAL

This is a story of the period between
two World Wars—an interim in
which Insanity cut loose, Liberty
took a nose dive, and Humanity
was kicked around somewhat.

The story begins at the end of World War I. As the camera tracks across the landscape soldiers scurry through trenches like ants, and bombs explode everywhere. An urgent-sounding voiceover narration tells us that in the waning days of the war, the Tomanian nation set its hopes on a new weapon, a giant gun called Big Bertha. The cannon's absurdly long barrel is aimed at the Cathedral of Notre Dame in Paris. Charlie, one finger in his ear, yanks the pull cord with a characteristic double twisting motion, falling to the ground from the mighty reverberation of the gun. But the shell only manages to destroy a nearby outhouse.

An officer tells him to get back to his station for another try. Charlie mutters, "Yes, sir," the first unambiguous words Chaplin speaks on the screen. This time the monstrous weapon emits a series of constipated sounds and the shell plops lazily out, falling onto the ground with a hollow metallic thud. The shell is in effect defecated by the gun, a funny and vulgar image that calls into further question the military competence of the Tomanians. Charlie shrugs at the soldiers gaping at the scene behind him, and they shrug back in unison. Charlie, low man on the gun crew, is naturally the one ordered to check the fuse on the unexploded shell.

Up to this point we've watched the action at sound speed, which makes some moments, notably Charlie's fall and the simultaneous shrug of the men, look a bit sluggish. But things perk up in the next shot, which is undercranked. As Charlie carefully approaches the smoking shell it suddenly begins revolving, matching his speed and direction as he runs back and forth in frantic circles to elude it, its point always perversely aiming right at him. It's much like that menacing rifle in *The Gold Rush*, except in that film there was a more logical reason for the wild movement of the gun—two men were struggling over it. Here's it's the apparent malevolence of the thing itself. When it begins spewing sparks Charlie and the others dash away, diving to the ground just as it explodes.

Charlie tries to control the antiaircraft gun.

Enemy aircraft appear, and Charlie is ordered (at sound speed) to man an antiaircraft gun. We revert to silent speed again as he does his familiar skip-turn and mounts the gun's attached chair. He's unable to control the weapon, however, and it flails around wildly, sending the other soldiers scurrying. Finally the chair upends, dumping him unceremoniously onto the ground.

Chaplin thus establishes the film's strategy of doing some of his physical comedy at sound speed, and undercranking other passages as of old. *Modern Times* was shot almost entirely at an unapologetically brisk silent pace; *The Great Dictator* will have plenty of silent speed action, but Chaplin is at pains to disguise the speedup with post-synched dialogue, ambient sound, and smooth editing. This film will not pit the virtues of silent film against sound—he fought that battle in his previous two films. This time, Chaplin's got bigger game in mind. In *The Great Dictator* the physical comedy is much more subtly integrated with the sound comedy, becoming just another weapon in the comic arsenal he's aiming at Hitler.

The sneaky speedup continues when Charlie, trying to throw a hand grenade, accidentally drops it down his sleeve. As he begins frantically digging through his clothing, another soldier comes up to him and says, "Say, this is no time to scratch." The scene could easily have come out of *Shoulder Arms*, except for two things: the

A hand grenade down the sleeve.

fact that Charlie's on the German side this time, and the inconsequential bit of dialogue, meant to cover the speedup. The fifty-year-old Chaplin performs with all his old zest, managing several comic takes as he scrambles to retrieve the grenade. When he finally fishes it out of his pants, we hear the sound of his clothes swishing as he tosses it away, and then the explosion a moment later. A relieved Charlie collapses into the soldier's arms. In another nicely post-synched bit of dialogue the soldier says, "Here, pull yourself together. Take this." He hands Charlie a rifle and sends him scampering into the fray. It's stealth silent comedy, slipped into the sound era.

After some more *Shoulder Arms*–like business in the drill formation, Charlie marches off with the others and almost immediately gets lost in a haze of gunfire smoke. We return to sound speed as he calls out, "Capitaine! Woo, woo." As the smoke clears he discovers himself marching among American soldiers. "Oh, there you are," he says cheerfully. They look at each other with dawning horror. Politely, he exclaims, "Oh, excuse me," drops his rifle, and runs for dear life.

Chaplin's cultured, rather prissy voice matches the Tramp's courtly manners, but it's somehow jarring to hear it coming from him. Without the dazzling mix of gibberish, song, mime, and dance at the climax of *Modern Times* we hear Chaplin's voice unadorned. As he well knew, no voice could have matched the inner voice in people's imagination as they watched his silent performances. Nevertheless, the voice and the comic tone are distinctive and pleasant. Charlie's courteous, self-effacing manner, along with his British accent, make him sound like a more diffident Stan Laurel.

For all Chaplin's subtle intermingling of silent and sound comedy, the four sequences of the film thus far have been like a less effective sound update of *Shoulder Arms*. Much of the broad physical humor recalls comedy films of the early 1930s, such as *Million Dollar Legs*,[4] which used sped-up action and lots of pratfalls, along with sound comedy shorts by the likes of the Three Stooges. But mainstream comedy—and mainstream physical comedy—had become more sophisticated. Pratfalls and other physical gags were selectively and effectively integrated into sound films by directors such as Howard Hawks, Frank Capra, and Leo McCarey, all of whom had learned their craft in the silent era.

Chaplin, of course, had reigned as the supreme comedy creator during the silent era, and he reasserts his mastery in the next sequence, integrating physical and verbal comedy so skillfully that the distinction is virtually obliterated. Charlie helps Schultz, a wounded aviator played by the dashing Reginald Gardiner, into his plane. Schultz has vital dispatches for the unfortunately named General Schmelawful. Too weak to fly the plane himself, Schultz asks Charlie if he can do it. "I can *try*," Charlie replies brightly as he climbs into the cockpit.

As they lift off Charlie helps Schultz with the controls, but to his alarm the aviator begins to grow faint. Under Charlie's control the plane flips upside down, which revives Schultz: "I feel better now," he says. "The blood's returning to my head. How's the gas?" "Terrible," replies Charlie, "it kept me awake all night." "No, no, no, the gasoline in the tank," says Schultz.

As they continue to chatter away, unaware that their plane is flying upside down, we cut to a shot in which the plane is right side up, so that we're seeing things from their point of view. This enables us to appreciate Charlie's reaction to the bizarre behavior of his pocket watch, which dangles in front of his face as it seemingly

Charlie's watch defies the law of gravity.

Model plane, puppet Charlie, which cuts smoothly into . . .

floats upward on its chain. The water from his canteen similarly flows upward. Understandably, Charlie's seat belt feels uncomfortably tight, and when he loosens it he suddenly flips out of the plane, hanging onto the control stick for dear life. The image flips as well. When Schultz demands that he let go Charlie replies with a terse "Impossible." It doesn't matter, for at that moment the plane runs out of gas, plummets downward, and crashes. It's a terrific sequence from start to finish, expertly blending miniatures, rear projection, rapid-fire verbal banter, and Chaplin's ingenious antigravity gag of a topsy-turvy world.

All of this is a prologue that serves to establish Charlie genteel character and his postwar fate—after the plane crash he lives in a hospital for years, a victim of amnesia. It also sets up Chaplin's clever way of incorporating physical comedy into the sound-film world.

. . . full-scale plane, real Charlie.

That mix doesn't always work as well as it does in the flying sequence, and unfortunately, the musical soundtrack doesn't help to bridge the gap the way it did in *Modern Times*. For the first time, Chaplin doesn't take a composer credit, for much of the music was delegated to musical director Meredith Willson, later to earn fame as the author and composer of *The Music Man*. The music is very good, and includes several haunting themes, but there's far less of it. Chaplin lets many scenes, including most of the twelve-minute prologue, play out with dialogue and sound effects alone. The film would probably have benefited from a bit more underscoring, but, racing against time to release it, Chaplin allowed only a three-week period for the composition and recording process. He took almost five months, by contrast, for *Modern Times*. Intermittent music, of course, was the rule of the day for sound films, and Chaplin was exploring the use of ambient sound and dialogue in comedy.

The dialogue alone provides sufficient musicality when we first meet the dictator. Newspaper headlines, accompanied by the newsreel-type narrator, have shown the passage of time and the dictator's rise to power. Now Hynkel stands on a platform in front of the assembled multitude, his loyal core of officers in grandstand seats behind him. He speaks in a fluent-sounding Germanic gibberish that's the direct descendant of the song from *Modern Times*, but this time almost everything he says is perfectly intelligible, because he throws in so many familiar words. "Wiener schnitzel, lager beer und sauerkraut," he shouts, going into a coughing fit after spluttering a purse-lipped stream of gutturals. To cool himself down he takes a drink of water, then pours some down his pants. Suddenly the Tramp's idiosyncratic gestures take on new meaning, skewering a political fanatic whose rhetoric is so inflammatory that he has to cool off his overheated genitals. The ideas of another famous Austrian, Sigmund Freud, then the rage in sophisticated circles, seem to have influenced Chaplin's thinking about Hitler's power mania.

Chaplin adds another level to the humor of his speech with an unseen radio announcer, who dignifies Hynkel's rantings with his sanitized "official" translation. "Democratia shtunk," declares the dictator. "Democracy is fragrant," says the mild-mannered announcer. "Libertad shtunk," says the dictator. "Liberty is odious," says his more articulate spokesman. "Free sprachen shtunk," insists Hynkel, and the voice tells us, more circumspectly, that "free speech is objectionable." Unlike the Mechanical Salesman monologue in *Modern Times*, which is one-dimensional by comparison, this use of sound greatly enhances the scene we're watching, the measured voice

Chaplin as Hynkel, a study in paranoia.

Crowd control. Hynkel silences the crowd with a flip of his hand.

making Hynkel and his vitriolic blather seem all the more ridiculous.

It is not known whether Chaplin saw Leni Riefenstahl's *Triumph of the Will*, her documentary of the 1934 Nuremberg Rallies, but he did study footage of Hitler, and he certainly saw the frightening images of the automaton-like German soldiers and cheering crowds that were shown repeatedly in newsreels of the period. Chaplin mocks Hitler's mesmerizing effect on the German people with a simple trick of the soundtrack. Whenever he signals for a reaction the crowd erupts in cheers, and when he flips his hand up again the sound stops instantly. An extremely subtle visual bit enhances the effect: In several of the shots the officials behind him are seen in an undercranked rear projection, so they stop applauding with an improbably abrupt "snap" to their movements. The shots of the cheering multitudes also involve trickery, in this case a layered combination of process photography to show the city skyline looming in the background, while a couple of rows of live actors in the foreground are augmented by puppet figures with movable arms that raise to depict the Sieg-Heiling soldiers (with close scrutiny some of the puppets seem a bit wobbly). An apparent mass of humanity behind the live actors and puppets stretches off in the distance. The crowd shot is entirely convincing. Chaplin reports that it required a year to prepare all the miniatures and effects shots.

Returning to his speech, Hynkel praises his loyal henchmen, the pudgy Field Marshall Herring, Minister of War, and the severe-looking Garbitsch, Minister of the Interior. Growing tearful, he says, "Herring shouldn't schmelten fine from Garbitsch und Garbitsch shouldn't schmelten fine from Herring." After his rhapsodic tribute to the beauty of "the Aryan maiden," using the same florid gestures to describe her voluptuous form that he used to describe the "pretty girl" in *Modern Times*, his tirade becomes so violent that the microphones themselves recoil. The translator mildly explains that "His Excellency has just referred to the Jewish people." Hynkel concludes by passionately declaring his intention to conquer the rest of the world, including Europe, France, Finland, and, prophetically, Russia (Hitler didn't attack his ally until July 1941). The narrator blithely mistranslates by saying, "In conclusion, the Phooey (Chaplin's insulting version of "Der Fuhrer") remarks that, for the rest of the world he has nothing but peace in his heart." As the crowd goes wild Chaplin pours water into his ear and at the same time spits a stream from his mouth, a gag he first did at Keystone in 1914.

The sequence is as brilliant as Chaplin's best silent work, a pitch-perfect parody of Hitler's histrionic manner in hilarious gibberish. Chaplin initially shot the scene at an outdoor location, and astonished his associates with his ability to improvise a seemingly endless flow of pseudo-German; the speech was only sketched out vaguely in the final shooting script, so the crew was unprepared for the polish of Chaplin's performance.[5] In the end Chaplin ended up reshooting the sequence in the studio, and no doubt working it out on location helped him to structure the speech, which develops in a very logical fashion in its finished form: Hynkel speaks of Tomania's struggle, criticizes the values of the free world, praises his associates and the Tomanian people, rants about the Jews, and ends with a promise to conquer the world. He punctuates his diatribe with nicely worked-out business with the water, the microphones, and the cheering crowd. Impeccably edited, shot, and performed, the sequence is a no-holds-barred low-comedy assault on Hitler. It's a devastating caricature, as powerful and incisive as the best political cartoon.

The comedy gets broadly physical when Herring, bowing to kiss the hand of a pretty woman, butts Hynkel down the platform steps, as the narrator accurately predicts, "His Excellency is about to descend the stairs." Chaplin films this fall at sound speed, and while his agility is, as always, impressive, it's the first time we see him catching himself and controlling the fall, or hear the realistic clattering sound that accompanies it. It is, for Chaplin, an uncharacteristically awkward-looking moment—but it's also a satisfying comeuppance for the dictator, the first of many in the film for the pompous blowhard.

Hynkel screams gibberish invective at his "bigga booben" war minister, at the same time ripping medals off his chest.[6] The mishap puts Hynkel in a foul mood, so he is sour-faced as he receives bouquets from three adorable little girls in folk costumes, then is handed a baby for a photo opportunity. He smiles tightly as he gingerly supports the child by her bottom, and this time there is no transformation gag as he hands her back to her mother, then wipes off his palm with his handkerchief.

As Hynkel drives down Hynkelstrasse, "the Avenue of Culture," in an open limo with Garbitsch, the narrator explains that they are passing statues of "The Venus of Today," one of her missing arms restored in a Hynkel salute, and "The Thinker of Tomorrow," his arm upraised as well. The use of rear projection is obvious, but the revisionist versions of the classic statues are funny.

Hynkel turns to the patrician Garbitsch, played by Henry Daniell, and asks, "How was it?" When Garbitsch, without looking at him, tells Hynkel his tirade against the Jews was too mild, Hynkel responds in an incredulous "Whaat?" Garbitsch explains that violence against the Jews "might take the public's mind off its stomach." We've already suspected that Garbitsch is the brains behind the throne because of the bored way he looks at his watch during Hynkel's speech. Having Garbitsch act as Iago to Hynkel's Othello allows Chaplin to further skewer Hynkel by portraying him as a dupe to his more sinister and calculating cohort. Hynkel responds by saying, "Perhaps you're right. Things have been quiet in the ghetto lately."

Most of Hynkel's dialogue from this point on will be spoken in plain English. Though delivered in a clipped, authoritarian tone, Hynkel's words will confirm our first impression of him as an arrogant, hot-tempered idiot. He will lapse back into gibberish whenever he's enraged, dictating letters, or making public speeches. It's a neat way of bracketing the mock-German, since the joke would grow tiresome if Chaplin did his entire performance in gibberish. It would also make conversations cumbersome, since almost everyone else in the film speaks in unaccented English.

The scene now shifts to the Jewish ghetto (ironically identified with a picturesque hanging wooden "Ghetto" sign). As noted in a previous chapter, a tonal problem occurs when Chaplin introduces the storm troopers as an uneasy marriage of comic bully and Nazi. In earlier Chaplin films, cops were awesome, humorless figures of authority. These fellows are nasty, but not particularly menacing or impressive looking. On the contrary, they're an old and paunchy lot as they swagger down the street, singing an annoying little ditty about being Aryans. They casually abuse the residents while helping themselves to fresh fruit and vegetables from sidewalk stands. When Hannah, an orphaned Jewish girl played by Paulette Goddard, dares to scold them, they do nothing worse than throw some of their pilfered tomatoes at her, soiling her fresh laundry. Her impassioned response, breaking down and calling them pigs, seems a bit extreme. As we'll see, this film will severely test Chaplin's legendary ability to blend comic and serious material.

Meanwhile, Charlie has been languishing in the hospital for years, a victim of amnesia since his plane crashed. He recovers enough to slip away, but he thinks only a few weeks have passed since his accident. He returns to his barbershop in the ghetto, mystified to find it full of cats and cobwebs. Chaplin's portrayal of the barber's bewilderment is one of several fine dramatic moments in the film. Emerging from the shop, he finds that the troopers have whitewashed the word "Jew" on his shop window, and begins washing it off. Charlie, of course, has no idea of the rise of Hynkel and anti-Semitism in the country.

Charlie's encounter with the Nazi thugs is much more effective than Paulette's, for he can fight back. The tonal problem vanishes as Chaplin forces them into the role of ineffectual Keystone Kops. After some characteristic and skillfully worked-out business with paintbrushes and buckets, with the troopers getting the worst of it, Hannah recovers her spunk and gets into the fray, popping out of a window and conking them with her frying pan. It all comes as a welcome reprise of Charlie's eternal battle with the cops, and it's a pleasure to see the Nazis turned into buffoons, an appropriate goon squad for the buffoonish Hynkel.

When Hannah accidentally conks Charlie he does an inspired, addled little dance along the sidewalk, tripping lightly on and off the curb without breaking his momentum. As in earlier sequences, the undercranking is skillfully integrated with a few well-synched words of dialogue. The ambient sounds, such as the clanging of the frying pan and Charlie's footsteps as he dances along the sidewalk, are also well synchronized, putting us firmly into a sound film reality. In addition, the dance is perfectly accompanied by a tinkling polka on the soundtrack, reinforcing the ersatz Ruritanian charm of the setting. The gag of transforming Charlie's tottering movement into a polka climaxes neatly as one of the stunned troopers, his face a ghostly white from the paint, falls into Charlie's arms. The music slows down as the two stagger a few macabre, lumbering steps. Charlie gently deposits him onto the curb, as though graciously seating his dance partner.

The ensuing sequence, in which the barber is captured by a throng of storm troopers who close in on him from

Invitation to the dance.

every side, is equally well staged. The troopers start to string him up from a lamppost until the aviator Schultz, now a commander, appears and saves him. "Strange," says Schultz, "and I always thought of you as an Aryan." "I'm a vegetarian," Charlie replies innocently.

We now go to Hynkel's palace with a musical fanfare. The newsreel-type voiceover announcer, whom we'll hear on and off throughout the film, extols Hynkel as the "amazing genius" who had built the world's greatest war machine, and "whose ceaseless activity kept him busily occupied every moment of the day." An undercranked camera zooms us rapidly through Hynkel's enormous, barren office as he sits at his enormous desk, signing a letter. In *The Bank* a quarter century earlier Charlie had used a subterfuge to get a man to lick a stamp for him. Now Hynkel merely extends his envelope toward a burly flunky, who bends over and sticks out his tongue so Hynkel can moisten the envelope. The undercranking continues as Hynkel briskly strides into an art studio, where he poses for a painter and sculptor. "Enough," he commands after about three seconds, and dashes out. We quickly get the idea that Hynkel's "ceaseless activity" is largely pointless busywork that serves to bolster his sense of self-importance.

As in *Modern Times* there are Rube Goldberg inventors who tout their dubious wares, this time promoted by the eager-to-please but hopeless Herring. The first one wears a bulletproof uniform, which fails to stop Hynkel's test bullet. Hynkel then steals a few moments away from his onerous schedule to twiddle at the piano keyboard. Jumping up, he sprays his throat in a typically Chaplinesque non sequitur. He returns to his office to dictate a letter, but becomes lustfully distracted by his comely secretary. He takes her in his arms and makes a snorting advance, but she faints in the presence of such overpowering masculinity. He drops her like a sack of potatoes when the phone rings, too busy even to gratify his bestial lust.

It's Herring again, summoning him to another product demo, this time for a ludicrous hat parachute. When the inventor "Heil Hynkels" and jumps backward out the window, Hynkel and Herring watch him fall to his death. Hynkel scowls at his doltish war minister and says, "Herring, *why* do you waste my time like this?" These sequences mark the first time death is played for laughs in a Chaplin feature.[7] Later in the film it will be no laughing matter.

Hynkel dashes into the art studio for another few seconds of undercranked posing, and the artists throw their tools down in frustration when he is summoned within seconds to meet Garbitsch.

With the arrival of Garbitsch, the pace slows and the tone changes. Garbitsch has been imprisoning thousands of dissidents each day, he coldly informs Hynkel, because they have been objecting to poor working conditions. Disgruntled factory workers are complaining of such necessary economies as sawdust added to the bread. "It's from the finest lumber our mills can supply!" exclaims Hynkel in baffled frustration. Chaplin speaks this tongue-twisting phrase well, but he rarely depends on words alone to carry the humor. Instead, he consistently finds amusing and illuminating physical business to underscore the verbal comedy. As this conversation continues, for example, Hynkel opens what appears to be a wall of filing cabinets, but which is actually a three-way mirror. The narcissistic dictator studies his reflection as he speaks, wiggling his mustache and eyebrows and experimenting with various facial expressions.

They need a plan to distract the people from their hardships. Garbitsch, evidently the architect of the anti-Semitic policy of the regime, suggests for the second time that they escalate the violence in the ghetto. Hynkel, however, has an even better idea. "We must do something more dramatic," he says, glowering at himself dramatically. "Now is the time to invade Osterlich."[8] Garbitsch agrees with the plan, but tells him that to fund the invasion they will need a loan from the Jewish banker Epstein, an unlikely prospect given their policy of oppression toward the Jews. Hynkel orders a temporary change of policy as he whisks out of the room. This scene reflects the view, common at the time, that Hitler's foreign and domestic policies were arbitrary tactics devised to keep himself in power by distracting the population. Scapegoating the Jews and other non-Aryan groups simultaneously bolstered German self-esteem and gave them someone to blame for past and present woes, including the loss of ancestral territory.

Back in the ghetto, the barber is moving at a much more leisurely pace. He has cleaned up his barbershop and is finishing cutting the hair of Mr. Jaeckel, Hannah's guardian and the distinguished-looking patriarch of the little courtyard. Charlie distractedly strops his comb like a razor, then opens the cash drawer, but drops the payment into his breast pocket instead.

These absentminded gags, appropriate for the amnesiac barber, continue as Hannah sits in the chair and he prepares her for a shave. He lathers up her face while she jabbers away so rapidly that he can't get a word in edgewise, even to answer her questions. It isn't until he begins shaving her face that they both realize what he's doing and crack up. Charlie gives her a shampoo instead, and she's surprised by how pretty she looks in the mirror. This understated little scene establishes the easy rapport and bashful courtship of these two orphans of the turbulent times.

When Hannah leaves to buy some potatoes, the storm troopers, obeying Hynkel's new directive, are uncharacteristically polite and helpful. This fills her with the hope that finally the persecution has ended, and she delivers a heartfelt speech directly to the camera, a brief prelude to the film's final speech.

The moment is followed by more silliness at the palace, as Chaplin continues exploring the possibilities of sound comedy. Hynkel dictates a lengthy passage in gibberish, which his secretary transcribes with a few pecks at the typewriter. But when he finishes by saying "der fluten," she unleashes a machine-gun volley of rapid typing that goes on and on. When he tries to sign the letter, his pens either get stuck in their holders or are out of ink. He petulantly decides not to mail the letter at all, ripping it up and taking out his frustrations with an insulting (English) diatribe on his innocent secretarial staff.

But Garbitsch soon soothes him by filling him with dreams of world conquest. The blond, blue-eyed multitudes, Garbitsch assures him, "will worship you as a god." "No, no, you mustn't say it," Hynkel exclaims. "You make me afraid of *myself*!" He does a balletic leap across the room and scampers up the drapery. Affecting a Garbo-like ennui, he intones her famous line, "Leave me, I want to be alone." It is Chaplin's only explicit reference onscreen to another film figure, and it heightens the mock-dramatic tension. The ensuing balloon dance, discussed in detail in chapter 7, fulfills Chaplin's vision of the character as a combination of Napoleon and Nijinsky.

Back in the ghetto, the barber shaves a customer in time to music from the radio, Brahms's Hungarian Dance Number 5. This sequence, technically much simpler but just as well choreographed as the balloon dance, contrasts with the dictator's dance of world domination in several ways: in its lively, functional, and pedestrian movements; in the fact that the music comes over the radio instead of from nowhere; and in the nature of the music itself: Brahms's upbeat folk tune versus Wagner's hyperdramatic operatic prelude. These back-to-back scenes are the heart of the film, telling us all we need to know about the contrasting characters of the maniacal dictator and the simple people he victimizes.

Hynkel's invasion plans are thwarted when Epstein refuses to deal with a man he characterizes as "a medieval maniac." "He'll deal with a medieval maniac more than he *thinks*," shouts Hynkel, unaware of the irony of his words. Because Schultz objects to the renewed persecution of the Jews, Hynkel exiles him to a concentration camp. Schultz represents the aristocratic "good German," whose conscience won't let him go along with Hitler's policies. When he is escorted out Hynkel screams, "Traitor! Traitor! You're nothing but a double-die democrat!" Then his shoulders droop and he breaks down. "Schultz, why have you forsaken me?" he says, unconsciously elevating his agony to biblical proportions. An aide drops a cape onto his shoulders, "crowning" his moment of self-pitying glory, and at the same time startling him out of his reverie.

The barber and Hannah, out on their first date, are about to buy Hynkel buttons when the dictator's voice blares over loudspeakers on the street, reversing his short-lived policy of goodwill toward the Jews in a renewed gibberish diatribe. People on the street panic and rush for shelter; Chaplin has the barber and Hannah set off their action simply by standing still and listening. Seeing that the street has emptied, they make haste to get back to their courtyard, but before they can reach it the barber reacts to another of Hynkel's outbursts by diving into a barrel. He extricates himself and they run to the courtyard entrance, but his hat falls off; tiptoeing to escape notice by the omniscient voice, he manages to retrieve it from the sidewalk, only to encounter a hostile storm trooper. Charlie is able to elude him with a few deft moves and a dive through a basement window. Hynkel's rant, rather than music, provides the very effective underscoring for the lively action sequence, and a bit of post-synched dialogue between Charlie and Hannah effectively disguises the undercranking.

There follows more amusing byplay with the troopers, who include droopy-eyed Hank Mann, Chaplin's old boxing nemesis from *City Lights*. The barber is able to hold them off with a display of comic bravado, but when they realize that he is no longer under Schultz's protection they return in force, out for blood. He and Hannah escape to a rooftop just in time to witness the barbershop explode and burn. To cheer him, Hannah speaks optimistically about starting over in Osterlich, unaware, of course, of Hynkel's invasion plans. Again, Chaplin uses stillness effectively as he sits, back to the camera, watching his beloved barbershop going up in smoke. The audience is left to imagine his facial expression as Hannah chatters on, until finally she bursts into tears, her words futile in the face of such senseless violence. With this moving little scene Chaplin once again reasserts the expressive power of the body.

We cut to the palace, where Hynkel again sits at the piano. This time the scene is not played for laughs. As the ghetto is being decimated the complacent dictator

The barbershop goes up in smoke.

plays a tinkling, Chopinesque melody, a candelabra lighting his face dramatically as he sways to the music. The ornate palace wall, with its huge fireplace and marble friezes, looms impressively in the background. For the first time in the film Hynkel looks powerful and hateful rather than simply ridiculous. Just as Chaplin comically juxtaposed his two roles with the globe and shaving scenes a few scenes earlier, with these paired scenes he juxtaposes them dramatically, bringing home the unfunny reality of the oppressor and the oppressed.

The change in tone prepares us for the grim premise of the next scene. Schultz, having escaped to the ghetto, has hatched a plot to assassinate the dictator. To carry it out he calls a midnight meeting with the men of the courtyard. While the unlikely candidates—all elderly Jewish character types,[9] except the barber—are comically skeptical, the patriarchal Jaeckel endorses Schultz's cause, so the men reluctantly agree to go along. The deed must be done by one of them, Jaeckel points out, since Schultz is too well known to pull it off himself. Whoever receives a pudding with a coin in it will be given the task. Unknown to the men, Hannah has sabotaged the proceedings by putting coins in all the puddings, setting up the merry comedy of errors to come. She enters with the tray of puddings, immediately breaking the solemnity of the occasion by accidentally bumping it into Charlie's head.

The delightful, psychologically astute scene that follows is played out at sound speed, but without dialogue. Instead, ambient sounds such as the clack of utensils on plates help to build the suspense, along with a witty musical accompaniment that punctuates the action quite directly. It is rare for Chaplin to use music in this way, and it greatly enhances the comedy.[10]

The plate-passing ballet. The man on the left is Chester Conklin.

Schultz is as concerned about his bags as he is about Charlie. The special-effect photography is very convincing.

The selection process begins with a little plate-passing ballet, as Charlie tries to determine which plate holds the fatal coin by comparing their weights as he distributes them, always holding back the lighter plate for himself. When he discovers that, despite his best efforts, the coin is in his pudding, he promptly and painfully swallows it with some water. Inevitably, he ends up swallowing several of the other men's coins as well, for no one is eager to be martyred for the cause, so they cravenly slip their coins onto their neighbors' plates. Charlie hiccoughs with an embarrassing "clink" several times. When Jaeckel announces that he has been given the fatal coin, Charlie coughs up the three he has swallowed, and Hannah enters and reveals her ruse. Charlie quickly pockets the coins, and the relieved men bid Schultz a hasty simultaneous farewell as he reenters the room.

The next morning the storm troopers return in search of Charlie and Schultz. Schultz's aristocratic background is played for laughs when he insists on bringing his golf clubs and top hat as the duo try to escape. Once again Chaplin stages the action beautifully, including nice bits of business as Charlie hops into a trunk and pops out again, plunges through a skylight, and, in a short thrill sequence, inadvertently walks onto a beam extending from the roof. Charlie not only carries two of Schultz's bags and his golf clubs as he steps over the edge, but he also has an open hatbox covering his head like a bucket. The only false note is struck early in the scene, when the dignified Jaeckel fearfully tries to climb into the trunk along with Charlie.

Chaplin later said that he would never have made the film had he known of the true horrors of the concentration camps.[11] When he and Schultz are sent to a camp after being captured, the worst Charlie has to endure is being repeatedly kicked by the goose-stepping prisoner marching behind him. Chaplin has characteristic fun mocking the mechanistic movement of the goose step, marching to his bed in the barracks and kicking his shoes off before getting in. The sequence is underscored to accent the rhythm and undercranked to enhance the action.

Caught.

Meanwhile, Hannah escapes into Osterlich with Jaeckel and his family, and a montage of their idyllic life on the farm is underscored by the film's most haunting original theme, a beautiful tune heard only here and under the opening cast credits, which was later published and recorded under the title "Falling Star."

Had Chaplin brought the film to a resolution now, it would have been much shorter, running about ninety minutes. But then he would have eliminated the Napaloni subplot, which provides some of the funniest scenes. Jack Oakie as Napaloni is the first actor in a Chaplin film to fully share the comic spotlight, rather than simply acting as a foil to Chaplin's antics. Chaplin would later extend this generosity to Martha Raye in *Monsieur Verdoux* and Buster Keaton in *Limelight*.

Herring's enterprise has somehow made it possible to invade Osterlich without the loan from Epstein, for which Hynkel decorates him during a banquet, attaching a new medal to his crowded chest and offering a tribute in formal gibberish. But when a phone call informs the group that Napaloni is poised to invade Osterlich first, an infuriated Hynkel backs the "pinheaden" Herring around the room, stripping him not only of his many medals, but his coat and suspender buttons as well, before snapping his suspenders and slapping his face.

"Napaloni! The *grosse* peanut, the cheesy ravioli!" screams Hynkel in a rage. But instead of attacking Bacteria he decides to play it cagey, inviting Napaloni to come to Tomania to confer. He will intimidate his rival with a show of Tomanian military might and his own domineering personality.

The plan, of course, backfires from the start, as Napaloni's train car and the Tomanian red carpet never seem to line up properly. This sequence is marred by a too-obvious use of rear projection, but livens up when the ebullient "Il Digadiche" finally disembarks. Hynkel gives the Tomanian salute as Napaloni extends his hand, then they reverse, going back and forth several times until Napaloni, ever the master of the situation, grabs Hynkel's hand.[12] They then try to upstage each other for a photo opportunity, backing ever closer to the train until a blast of hot steam sends them hopping.

Prompted by Garbitsch, Hynkel plans to psychologically intimidate Napaloni at their first private meeting. He will make him walk across his huge office, then seat him in a ridiculously low chair, a bust of Hynkel staring down at him from the desk. Hynkel sits nervously posturing with a flower as the unpredictable Napaloni enters by the back door and slaps him off his chair, causing him to bump his chin painfully on the desk. Napaloni, whose mock-Italian accent sometimes slips inexplicably into a Southern drawl, is seated, but almost immediately hops up and perches on the desk instead, casually stubbing out cigarettes and lighting matches on the bust. Sitting in barber chairs for a shave together, the rivals once again try to one-up each other—literally—by competitively elevating their chairs until, nearing the ceiling, they come crashing down.

A military parade is economically depicted using sound effects and the reactions of the spectators in

Jack Oakie as the pompous Napaloni.

the stand. We hear the rumble of heavy artillery, then nothing when the "light artillery" passes. Far from being cowed, Napaloni keeps Hynkel continuously off balance, bragging about Bacterian superweapons such as flying submarines, and forcing Hynkel to crane toward him to hear what he's saying, when in fact he's just chomping contentedly away on a mouthful of peanuts. Finally a Tomanian plane crashes, and with it Hynkel's plan to intimidate Napaloni.

That night, at a ball in honor of Napaloni, Hynkel is determined to get the upper hand. Garbitsch suggests that if Hynkel were to dance with Madame Napaloni, "it will carry weight." "You mean, *I* will carry weight," says Hynkel, laughing maniacally at his clever quip. He advances on the sad-eyed, heavyset woman. Striking a series of comically debonair poses and smiling wolfishly, he invites the flustered matron to dance. Hynkel's quip about carrying weight becomes literal as he pulls her, with an all too evident effort, out of her chair. As they move across the floor Chaplin skillfully exaggerates her weight by going over backward as she moves forward, losing his balance repeatedly as he is bowled over by her apparently irresistible momentum. He ends the dance and recovers his aplomb, managing to turn a compliment into an insult by telling her that her dancing was "superb . . . excellent . . . very good . . . good." He kisses her hand,

Hynkel puts on the charm . . .

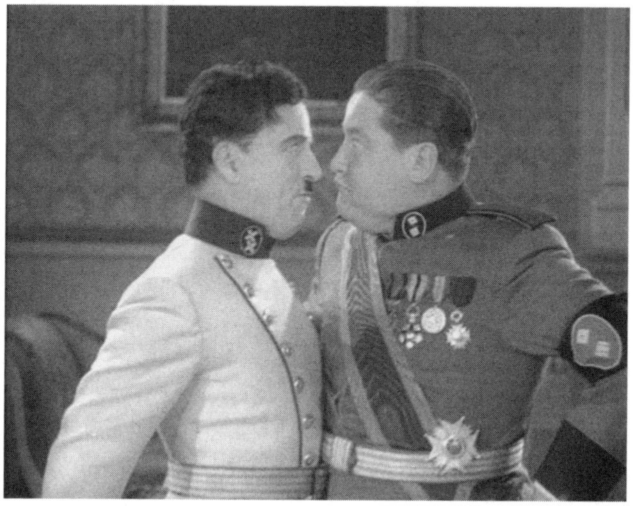

A diplomatic standoff.

. . . but it's Madame Napaloni who bowls him over.

polishes her diamond ring with his sleeve, and, flashing her a torrid look, departs, leaving the poor woman dumbfounded. The sequence is a small comic gem, seamlessly blending verbal and physical humor.

Napaloni, however, isn't so easily won over. The rivals meet in a private buffet room to discuss the Osterlich situation. Napaloni has prepared a treaty declaring that neither country will invade, but Hynkel petulantly refuses to sign until Napaloni removes his troops. Things quickly degenerate into a food fight, with Hynkel "bombing" fruit into a punchbowl to demonstrate the havoc his planes will wreak on Napaloni's artillery. Both men ladle hot English mustard onto their food and writhe in agony on the couch, trying to continue their argument with napkins stuffed in their mouths. A nosy reporter gets a pie in the face. Hynkel picks up a handful of spaghetti and threatens to "tear [the Bacterian people] apart like *that*!"—but finds himself unable to tear the rubbery strands apart. Finally Garbitsch gives Hynkel some practical and cynical counsel—sign the treaty, and then break it by invading as soon as Napaloni removes his troops. This is Tomania, after all, where the swastika has been replaced by the sign of the Double Cross (Chaplin's insulting version of the Nazi insignia).

The Napaloni scenes provide the film with its most exuberant and uncomplicated humor, allowing Chaplin to present the rival dictators as equally pompous and ridiculous, while letting the backslapping Bacterian loudmouth best the easily flustered Hynkel at every turn.

The film now moves quickly to its conclusion. Contrary to the way most doppelgänger stories unfold, the two look-alike characters in *The Great Dictator* never meet, but Chaplin now contrives a neat way for them to switch places. Schultz and the barber have managed to escape from the camp and are trying to be as inconspicuous as possible as they walk along a rural road in stolen military uniforms. Meanwhile, the dictator, duck hunting to avert publicity as the invasion begins, is mistaken for the escaped barber and arrested. Soon enough the barber is mistaken by Tomanian soldiers for Hynkel. He and Schultz are escorted into an open limousine as the invasion of Osterlich begins. These instances mark the first time in the film that anyone has noticed the resemblance between the barber and the dictator, a dramatic convenience that we can easily accept because it's the first time it's mattered. In addition, Chaplin had playfully dismissed the issue of the characters' resemblance in the film's opening subtitle, telling us that any resemblance between the characters "is purely co-incidental."

The tone changes once again as the invasion is shown. The soldiers only rough up Hannah and the Jaeckel family on their idyllic farm, but they brutalize and murder unarmed Jews in the Osterlich ghetto.

The barber is escorted to a platform to address the conquering army following their successful invasion, along with the vast radio audience. There's one last comic bit with collapsing chairs as he's seated, and then the film remains serious until the end. Garbitsch makes a chilling speech about the coming new world order, then introduces Hynkel—or rather, the man he thinks is Hynkel—to the assembled troops as the "future emperor of the world." Schultz tells the barber, "You must speak." "I can't," he replies. "You must," Schultz insists. "It's our only hope." These portentous words, of course, refer not just to the dilemma the characters find themselves in, but to the double dilemma Chaplin faces—how to end his film, and what to do about the looming world crisis. His solution would lead him to perform the most controversial scene of his career.

"Hope," the barber murmurs, getting up. As in *Modern Times*, Charlie must reluctantly speak. But this time Chaplin can't finesse the situation with gibberish and mime. Hynkel's already done that. Nor can he resolve the plot as a wish-fulfillment dream, as he had in *Shoulder Arms*.

So he speaks. He begins softly, his eyes downcast and unfocused, "I'm sorry, but I don't want to be an emperor. I don't want to rule or conquer anyone. I should like to help everyone, if possible—Jew, Gentile—black men—white."

Soon he's looking directly into the camera, as he had so often done before. But this time, instead of a passing comic aside, a knowing wink at the audience, he rivets us with his gaze as he warms to his subject, and proceeds to deliver an eloquent attack on the dehumanizing material and spiritual conditions that have led to fascism. With rising passion he exhorts the soldiers to lay down their arms, to refuse to fight for dictators "who free themselves, but enslave the people," and concludes with a plea for them to unite, in the name of democracy. The speech mirrors Hynkel's opening speech, matching it in intensity, but replacing the hate-filled promise of world domination with a rousing call to universal brotherhood.

The impassioned orator.

As the soldiers cheer he quietly speaks his message of hope directly to Hannah, who has been lying on a field outside the farmhouse and sobbing. The same stirring Wagnerian music that had earlier accompanied the dictator's selfish and infantile dream of world conquest now accompanies his alter ego's inspiring and comforting words to Hannah.

> Hannah, can you here me? Wherever you are, look up. Look up, Hannah. The clouds are lifting. The sun is breaking through. We are coming out of the darkness into the light. We are coming into a new world—a kindlier world, where men will rise above their greed, their hate and brutality. Look up, Hannah! The soul of man has been given wings and at last he is beginning to fly. He is flying into the rainbow—into the light of hope. Look up, Hannah! Look up!

Hannah seems to hear these words not over the radio, but directly, as though they fill the very air. When he stops speaking she rises, still listening intently. Her face, in profile, is outlined dramatically against the cloudy sky. Jaeckel, standing at the door of the farmhouse with his little family, says, "Hannah, did you hear that?" It's unclear whether he means the speech to the soldiers, the message to her, or both. She beckons him to be silent, and says, "Listen." She continues looking into the sky. Then she looks around in a close-up, and her face seems to light up from within. She turns her head so that we see her in profile again, looking slightly upward, and as the film ends she breaks into a radiant smile.

By having Hannah listen for a full minute after the barber stops talking, her face infused with joy as the music swells, Chaplin gives the film a transcendent, even mystical quality that elevates it above the story of its characters. One is reminded of Humphrey Bogart's speech to Ingrid Bergman, a couple of years later, at the end of that other great war film, *Casablanca*—"It doesn't take much to see that the problems of three little people don't amount to a hill of beans in this crazy world." Bogey is telling her that they have to sacrifice their own happiness for the greater good, and the effect is both sad and uplifting.

The final scene of *The Great Dictator* has a similarly sad and uplifting effect, but it's harder to understand, in dramatic terms, how Chaplin achieves it, since there's neither noble self-sacrifice nor a love triangle involved. We're not even sure what, exactly, Hannah is hearing and seeing as she gazes up into the sky. What is perfectly clear is that she's experiencing a revelation, that the better world Charlie has envisioned has become real to her. That's all we really need to know. Everything about the scene—the music, the lighting, and especially Paulette Goddard's luminous performance—combine to create a moving and satisfying finale for the film.

It wasn't very satisfying for critics of the time, however, because they couldn't get past Chaplin's speech, which they condemned almost unanimously as a misguided, confused, poorly written assemblage of platitudes, however well intentioned. They also complained about its length, often cited as six minutes. Actually, the bulk of the speech—the address to the soldiers—takes three-and-a-half minutes. That's still, of course, an extraordinary amount of screen time for a speech, especially a speech that consists of only two shots of Chaplin and one brief cutaway to Hannah. Many characters give speeches in Hollywood films, some of them just as long as Chaplin's. But it was a blatant violation of conventional filmmaking practice to remain on an actor for that long without cutting away repeatedly to show reaction shots of people listening, or some kind of montage.

Critics also pointed out then, and have never tired of pointing out since, that Chaplin seems to step out of character, since the barber has been largely inarticulate until he makes his speech.[13] He also seems to change religion, quoting from the Gospel of St. Luke. Of course, it wasn't the first time Chaplin had stepped out of character at the end of a film. In *The Gold Rush* the man who kisses Georgia at the fade-out doesn't seem in the least like the innocent who's been stumbling his way through the rest of the film. And Charlie's remarkable turn as a cabaret singer would not seem to be in the repertoire of the factory worker in *Modern Times*. No critic on record ever complained about those lapses, however, perhaps because they liked the scenes better, and perhaps because there were no words to get in the way.

More serious than stepping out of character is the fact that Chaplin seems to step out of the film itself, addressing the film audience with his demand that the dictators of the world be defeated, and that a better world be installed than the one we currently have.[14] While hardly anyone disagreed with the sentiment, almost every critic disagreed with Chaplin's way of presenting it. For them, the scene failed both as art and as propaganda, and seriously compromised his film.

Chaplin disagreed, and vigorously defended the speech, most notably in a letter to the *New York Times* a week after the film's premiere.[15] He argued that it was in character, that it was a logical ending to the film, and that he'd earned the right to speak out for a few minutes after two solid hours of comedy. Indeed, he felt he *had* to speak out, and that what he had to say was of critical importance.

He surely wasn't so naive as to believe that he was "our only hope," as Schultz puts it. But the fact that the film community had been almost completely silent about the world crisis impelled Chaplin to break his own filmic silence and Hollywood's at the same time. He was adamant that the film be shown, whether or not he made any money on it. In an interview published just before the film's release, he said, "If they won't give me theaters to show my picture I'll show it myself. In tents. I'd like to do that anyway, so that everyone can go and see it. I have enough money. I don't have to worry about profits."[16]

He did have to worry about profits, of course, so it was worrisome that not just the controversial final speech, but the film as a whole, received decidedly mixed reviews. Many critics felt that the blend of comic and dramatic content, previously one of Chaplin's signal achievements, didn't work in this case. Everyone agreed that his comic lampoon of Hitler was superb, and most felt that if he had stuck to comedy rather than trying to introduce grim reality the film would have been better.[17]

The problem of sticking to comedy, of course, was that grim reality doesn't simply intrude during the few serious moments and the final speech, but hovers over the entire film, providing its sole reason for existing. The veil of fiction disguising world events and figures is gossamer thin, and for many contemporary commentators the unfunny reality was enough to put a damper on the humor, or at least make the film seem wildly uneven.

At this remove, with Hitler a historical villain rather than a looming threat, we can't see the film as they did. Not only do we know the full extent of the catastrophe, but we've since been regaled by a steady stream of comedy treatments of the subject. Nevertheless, judged on its own merits, Chaplin's first venture into verbal comedy has to be counted, for the most part, as a spectacular success. While there are some questionable character choices, such as those ragtag storm troopers, the lapses are precious few. Chaplin deals with the darkest of subjects by using the lightest of humor, filling the film with pun-filled references to bad smells, and keeping up a steady stream of silly but very funny dialogue. The Hynkel scenes are particularly strong and remarkably consistent, driven by Chaplin's fierce performance as the dictator.

Chaplin's great gift was always his ability to intermingle the comic and the serious, rather than simply juxtaposing them as he does at the end. His deft touch is seen in the contrasting characters of the humorless Garbitsch and the cartoonish Herring, who coexist comfortably and embody the film's serious and comic poles. The tightly structured and fast-moving plot maintains the delicate tonal balance as well. In rapidly alternating scenes, we see the way the callous and capricious leaders make life increasingly difficult for the powerless citizens of the ghetto. The ghetto scenes, full of charm and quiet humor, elicit maximum sympathy for the gentle and unjustly persecuted people.

Ironically, some of the film's weakest scenes involve physical comedy, not all of which sits as well as it might in the brave new world of sound film. Parts of the prologue, and later moments such as Napaloni's pie in the face of the reporter, look peculiarly old-fashioned. The last time pies were thrown in a Chaplin film was in 1916's *Behind the Screen*, in which he made fun of how old-fashioned the gag had become by *then*. On the other hand, Chaplin repeatedly and successfully uses slapstick to rob Hynkel of his dignity, counteracting the seriousness inherent in the material and providing a visual equivalent to the many bad-smell puns that punctuate the film. It is also physical comedy that provides what by common consent are the film's two best scenes, the balloon dance and the shaving scene.

These scenes, along with Hynkel's brilliant opening speech, occur before the film is half over, however, which may be a clue to the "viewer fatigue" experienced by some, since Chaplin never tops them. At two hours and five minutes, *The Great Dictator* was by far his longest film to date. Given the scope and enormous range of the material, it was probably inevitable that some scenes work less well than others, or simply go on a bit too long. This is particularly true of the Napaloni scenes. While Jack Oakie is wonderful in the part, four scenes and twenty minutes of the rival dictators begin to wear the viewer down.

The problem isn't simply that we've stayed away from the other characters for too long. The film is perfectly balanced between its two stories, devoting equal time to each, and the preceding ghetto sequence is as long as the Napaloni scenes. But the action—the burning of the barbershop, the assassination plot, the capture of Schultz and the barber, and the escape of the Jaeckel family to Osterlich—is more varied and dramatically interesting than the lengthy battle of wills between the dictators.

With the Olympian wisdom of hindsight it's easy to imagine solving this and the film's other problems with a bit of judicious trimming. The film probably could have been effectively shortened by a half hour. But, as Chaplin informs us, given the wisdom of hindsight he'd never have *made* the film.

Many people at the time wished he hadn't. Understandably, there were vociferous protests from the German and Italian governments. More disturbing to recall are the protests from within America. Chicago, with its large German population, banned it altogether.

Nevertheless, Chaplin's great gamble paid off handsomely. The public loved the film and flocked to it, and it proved to be the biggest box-office hit of his career. Hollywood loves a winner, and the film earned five Academy Awards nominations, for Best Picture, Best Actor, Best Supporting Actor (Oakie), Best Original Screenplay, and Best Original Score. Chaplin also won the award for Best Actor from the New York Film Critics Circle. Two months after its U.S. opening, in December 1940, *The Great Dictator* played in London, heartening people during the dark days of the Blitz. Chaplin's judgment had been vindicated. He remained stubbornly proud of the final speech, reciting it over national radio

Hirschfeld captures Hynkel's dance with Madame Napaloni. From the original press book for the film. Illustration © Al Hirschfeld. Reproduced by arrangement with Hirschfeld's exclusive representative, the Margo Feiden Galleries Ltd., New York, www.alhirschfeld.com.

on January 19, 1941, as part of the commemoration of the third inauguration of Franklin Roosevelt, and printing it in its entirety in his autobiography.

There is a touching autobiographical reference in *The Great Dictator*. Chaplin named the film's spunky heroine after his mother. While few viewers, then or now, would be aware of this, it provides us with a clue as to why the ending—not the speech, but the film's actual ending—is so powerful. While Chaplin's words and the stunning photography speak of hope, we've seen how the storm troopers have brutalized Hannah and her loved ones throughout the film. The ending is a hopeful dream of a better future, as false in its own way as the Tomanian soldiers cheering the barber's speech about embracing democracy. The barber can speak of hope, but he can't save Hannah, any more than the young Charlie Chaplin could save his beloved mother from poverty and insanity, or any more than Chaplin's courageous film could save the world from another catastrophic war. Hannah's glowing optimism at the end defies all reason. It's as quixotic, heartbreaking, and wonderful as trying to stop fascism with a funny film.

Although Chaplin would go on to make four more films, the Tramp's cinematic journey, begun in silence on the eve of the First World War, ends with his heartfelt oration at the dawn of the Second. In effect, Chaplin sacrifices his great character to his great cause. Although the Tramp gets the last word, in speaking it he vanishes before our eyes.

Notes

1. Max Eastman, *Great Companions* (New York: Farrar, Strauss and Cudahy, 1949), 235–36.
2. Charles Chaplin, *My Autobiography* (New York: Simon & Schuster, 1964), 392.
3. Chaplin, *My Autobiography*, 366.
4. A 1932 film roughly along the same zany lines of the Marx Brothers *Duck Soup*, *Million Dollar Legs* is about a mythical kingdom called Klopstokia. It stars W. C. Fields and Jack Oakie, who plays Napaloni in *The Great Dictator*.
5. This according to Dan James, one of Chaplin's assistant directors on the film, as cited by David Robinson in *Chaplin, His Life and Art* (London: Penguin, 2001), 534.
6. Herring is played by Billy Gilbert, a comic actor familiar from his many performances as an apoplectic foil to Laurel and Hardy, notably in *The Music Box*, their Academy Award winning short from 1932.
7. As noted in a previous chapter, he plays it for laughs in two shorter films, *Carmen* and *The Pilgrim*.
8. The term *Osterlich* neatly combines Austria, the head-in-the-sand ostrich, and Austerlitz, the Czech city that was the scene of one of Napoleon's greatest military triumphs. For years Chaplin had contemplated making a film about Napoleon, and he put the preparation to good use in *The Great Dictator*.
9. The man sitting on Chaplin's right is his old cohort Chester Conklin, who appeared earlier as the victim of his musical shaving experiment. Unrecognizable without his walrus mustache, Conklin contributes several nicely played comic takes to the scene.
10. Chaplin liked this music so well that two years later he incorporated it into his sound reissue of *The Gold Rush*. It accompanies Mack Swain's stalking of Charlie when he thinks he's a chicken.
11. Chaplin, *My Autobiography*, 392.
12. This is a variant of a running gag in Buster Keaton's last silent film, *Spite Marriage*, in which Buster keeps encountering a man who extends his hand as Buster tips his hat, and then vice versa, and so on. Keaton liked the gag so much he ended his film with it.
13. Chaplin's friend Max Eastman, in some Monday-morning quarterbacking years later, suggested that if the barber had been shown unsuccessfully attempting to make speeches earlier in the film, then his final speech would have made better dramatic sense. Indeed, it is easy to imagine Charlie being asked to say something to the assembled courtyard residents before his date with Hannah, or, better yet, being delegated to explain to Schultz why the men don't want to become assassins. Failing to speak out a few times would have made the final speech a personal breakthrough for the character, rather than an apparent break *with* the character. See Eastman, *Great Companions*, 231.
14. In yet another blatant violation of conventional Hollywood storytelling, the speech fails to address or resolve the character's immediate problem, which is to prevent himself from being unmasked as an imposter in the midst of his enemies. One can argue that the barber is solving the problem in the best way possible, by converting his listeners to his cause. But it hardly seems likely that his speech—or any speech—would do that. This probably explains why Chaplin doesn't cut to reaction shots by Herring and Garbitsch, for how could they react, other than to be totally baffled, or shoot him on the spot? They certainly wouldn't become converts to the democratic cause.

Chaplin actually shot an alternate ending in which the soldiers dance in celebration after the speech, and he planned a montage showing soldiers around the world throwing down their arms and acting to save rather than destroy lives. He wisely omitted these scenes.

15. "Mr. Chaplin Answers His Critics," *New York Times*, October 16, 1940, sec. 1, p. 29.
16. Cited by Ella Winter, "Charlie Chaplin and 'The Dictator,'" *Friday*, August 30, 1940, 22.

17. The Three Stooges did exactly that. Nine months before *The Great Dictator* came out they released *You Nazty Spy!* in which Moe plays a gibberish-spouting Hitler clone, the dictator of Moronica, and Larry and Curly play thinly veiled versions of Goebbels and Göring. It is somewhat amazing that it was made at a time when Hollywood was under considerable internal and external pressure not to meddle in politics or offend the Axis powers—but the Stooges, minor comedians working for a minor studio, slipped in under the radar with this eighteen-minute short. The film is a funny, silly, and typically rude Stooges romp. While Moe's performance is quite admirable, and he's actually a better Hitler look-alike than Chaplin, the film had little of the satiric bite or moral indictment of the Chaplin film, and caused none of its stir.

CHAPTER TWELVE

Return Engagement

In his biography of his father, Charles Jr. recalls private screenings Chaplin held for him, his brother, and their friends in the 1930s. Before long Chaplin's eyes would be on the kids rather than the screen, intently scrutinizing their reactions.

> Dad, however, couldn't stay quietly watching for long. Presently he was providing a running commentary for us.
>
> "There he is now, there comes the Little Fellow," he would say, rubbing his hands together gleefully.
>
> "Yes, there he is, with the big fellow with the bandaged foot. That means trouble. Watch it, boys."
>
> Our father's eager monologue seemed quite natural to us. We never thought once, then, that we were the only children in the world to enjoy the privilege of Chaplin dialogue with silent Chaplin films.[1]

The rest of the world got that privilege in 1942, when Chaplin reissued *The Gold Rush* and replaced the subtitles with his own spoken narration and musical soundtrack. Like his previous three films, it is a bold experiment in bridging the gap between the silent and sound film worlds.

Comparison of the 1925 and 1942 versions of the film reveals that Chaplin removed more than the subtitles. He also took away much of the epic, almost mythic power of the film, leaving in its place a simplified tale that seems more for children than adults.

The subtitles in the 1925 version are the best Chaplin ever came up with for a silent film. They provide essential expositional information and dialogue, punctuate the film visually by providing well-timed breaks from the action, and are often witty in and of themselves, such as when Big Jim chases Charlie through the dance hall, shouting, in increasingly large letters, "The Cabin!" For the most part they are also poetically brief, introducing the Tramp as "a lone prospector," Big Jim as "another lone prospector," and Black Larson as "a lone man" in "a lone cabin." Whenever possible, Chaplin dispenses with them altogether. For example, we learn the names of Jim and Larson not through subtitles, but in the film itself: Jim's name is seen on his claim stake, and Larson's on a wanted poster that he casually throws onto the flames in his stove.

The "undaunted lone prospector."

When he came to narrate the film Chaplin considerably embellished these character introductions. The Tramp is "an undaunted lone prospector," and later "our little Columbus," "our hero," and, most often, "the little fellow." Black Larson is "an unmitigated predatory scoundrel." Unfortunately, Chaplin continues in this vein throughout the film, often offering more information than is needed or wanted in his thumbnail character sketches, such as this description of the saloon girl Georgia and the loutish Jack:

> Jack was a ladies' man. Georgia was quick and impulsive, proud and independent. Jack had lots of appeal for Georgia . . . perhaps that's why she resented him.

At dramatic moments Chaplin often speaks with a hint of the mock-heroic, as though reciting one of the those epic poems popular in the nineteenth century. The effect is amusing, but sometimes undercuts what we're seeing. For example, when Big Jim discovers that Black Larson has jumped his claim and the two stand glaring at each other, Larson's power and malevolence is hardly enhanced by Chaplin saying that "Big Jim looked deep into the eyes of Black Larson and saw there the soul of a skunk." The serious moment is made less serious.

Chaplin also intrudes into some of the film's romantic moments, such as the delicate scene when Georgia first enters Charlie's borrowed cabin:

> There she stood, her loveliness lighting the room, filling his soul with the music of romance for which he was so ill fitted. And as she introduced her friends his heart began to sing.

Later in the scene, when Georgia discovers that Charlie has saved her torn photograph, keeping it under his pillow, we're informed that

Georgia lighting up the room.

> the girls giggled and laughed, perhaps in order to hide their pity, for in the world of the dance hall it wasn't wise for the girls to reveal their hearts . . . and so she fooled and flirted and stroked his hair. He knew she was fooling but he was happy.

For the record, there's not a trace of pity to be seen in the girls, nor is there a hint that Charlie knows Georgia is fooling. By adding such information Chaplin alters the fundamental content of his film.

Even when he's not contradicting what we're seeing, but merely reinforcing it, a problem arises, because the effect is not mere redundancy. The performances, circumscribed by the spoken word, become less evocative. Unlike his careful blend of verbal and physical comedy in *The Great Dictator*, words and images in the new *Gold Rush* are sometimes perversely at odds with each other.

In addition to offering editorial commentary, Chaplin often lets the characters speak for themselves by voicing their onscreen dialogue, sometimes lip-synching it precisely. The effect is at first disconcerting, because it's *almost* like watching a sound film, except for three things that keep reminding us that we're watching a silent. First, Chaplin speaks all the dialogue himself, framing it, storybook-style, with lots of "he saids" and "she saids." Second, he doesn't try to provide distinctive voices for the various characters. Third, as in *Modern Times*, there is a complete absence of naturalistic ambient sounds. Instead, the orchestral score provides stylized sound effects, which are, in fact, one of the most appealing things about the revised film. For example, when Charlie plucks icicles from the cabin ceiling to cook with, we hear precisely synchronized chimes, as though Charlie is "playing" them.

Substituting dialogue for dialogue subtitles certainly makes the film more accessible to young children, but it also has the effect of subtly shifting the focus to the spoken word. While Chaplin wisely allows many sequences to play out without narration, once begun he has to keep it going, and to do that he ends up supplying many more lines of dialogue than he ever translated into subtitles, such as this, when Larson comes upon the starving Charlie gnawing away at a chicken bone in his cabin:

> "Come here," said Larson. "What are you doing?"
> "Eating, obviously," said the little fellow.
> "Get out! Get out!"

Larson keeps yelling at Charlie to get out, but a strong wind makes that impossible. In 1925 the entire scene played out with the single subtitle "Get out of here!" Hearing the words doesn't utterly destroy the drama and comedy of what we're seeing—after all, he's only saying what we can plainly read on Larson's lips—but the lip-synched dialogue subtly distances us, for the storyteller has interposed himself between us and the film. On the other hand, the musical accompaniment, "The Flight of the Bumblebee," provides a witty and appropriate wind-like sound as Charlie struggles to exit the cabin.

While Chaplin is careful to let most of his visual gags play out without speaking, he occasionally puts a damper on one. For example, after the dance hall girls leave Charlie's cabin,[2] having facetiously agreed to return for New Year's Eve, Charlie joyously swings on a ceiling beam and punches a pillow, causing a feather snowstorm to swirl around him. He is sitting on the floor, exhausted, when Georgia suddenly reappears in the doorway. He looks back at her, then back toward the camera—and twitches his feet. It's a typically inventive Chaplin way of showing emotion. The little foot twitch invariably gets a big laugh—but only in the silent version. In the sound version, just before the twitch Chaplin pipes in with, "And of course, at that moment Georgia would forget her gloves." Our attention is distracted just enough by the comment that we don't see the movement as clearly, and the laugh is lost.

Chaplin speaks through the film's thrill finale as well. The cabin is teetering on the edge of a cliff, and Charlie thinks the swaying sensation he feels is a result of his hangover. This is conveyed solely through his reactions in 1925, but in 1942 Chaplin supplies his inner thoughts: "This is the worst liver attack I've ever had." Back in 1925 only two subtitles accompany the ensuing action climax, as both men struggle to exit the wildly tilting cabin. Big Jim exhorts Charlie to "Take it easy!" and then, "Don't move . . . don't breathe!" Jim speaks throughout the sequence, but we don't see, nor do we need to see, his words in a subtitle. In 1942 Chaplin not only supplies his words, he embellishes them into a comic monologue that isn't precisely lip-synched, for Jim said no such things in 1925:

> "Now," said Big Jim, "don't get excited. Take it easy. Don't move, don't breathe! I said don't breathe, stupid. You can be most annoying at times."
>
> "If you'll only be cool, be calm," said Big Jim, "we have nothing to worry about."
>
> "See what I mean," said Big Jim. "Your mind is chaotic. You have no psychology. You have no control."

Chaplin delivers these lines in a fairly amusing way, but it sets up a parallel world in which Chaplin indulges his verbal wit at the expense of his visual storytelling. Putting funny words in the mouths of his characters pulls us away from the primal simplicity of their actions, and in that apparent simplicity rests the profundity of Chaplin's visual art. It simply can't be improved by words, even Chaplin's words.

Chaplin also did a bit of reediting for the sound version. He eliminated a short scene in which Charlie and Big Jim just miss seeing each other outside the assayer's office. More critically, he reworked the important scene that follows, showing Charlie's encounter with Big Jim and Georgia in the dance hall that night.

What leads up to this encounter is that on the previous night the capricious Georgia had completely forgotten about Charlie's New Year's Eve dinner. Later, when she and her friends discover his elaborate dinner preparations, remorse dampens her festive mood. Jack, her "ladies' man," tells her to forget it, and forces a kiss on her. She slaps him, hard.

In the dance hall the next night she sends Jack a note:

> I'm sorry for what I did last night. Please forgive me—I love you
> Georgia

Georgia watches from the balcony as Jack reads the note, chuckles, and shares it with one of his lady friends. Upset, she turns away. When Charlie enters, Jack callously has a waiter deliver him the note. Charlie, of course, thinks his dream has come true, and that Georgia returns his love. He begins frantically looking around for her.

Just then Big Jim, standing at the bar, sees Charlie for the first time since they parted after being snowbound in Black Larson's cabin. Jim, who's lost part of his memory due to a blow on the head from the villainous Larson, desperately needs Charlie to help him find his way back to the cabin; from there, he's sure, he'll be able to find his lost claim. Jim chases Charlie around the saloon, finally sweeping him off his feet in a bear hug. He promises to make Charlie a millionaire if he will take him to the cabin. Charlie then sees Georgia, pulls away from Jim, scales the wall to the balcony like a proper action hero, and embraces the dumbfounded girl. With melodramatic gestures and two subtitles, he tells her "—Georgia, I got your note—" "—and now I'm going to make good—" whereupon Big Jim unceremoniously yanks him off his feet and drags him away, his illusion of love intact.

In 1942 Chaplin changes the note so that it actually is from Georgia to Charlie:

> Please forgive me for not coming to dinner. I'd like to see you and explain. Georgia

Charlie reacts to this rather noncommittal new note with the same wild enthusiasm he displayed before, but this time we hear his rush of words.

> Ah, Georgia, You don't have to explain, I understand. I love you. I'm going to take you away from this life. I'm going away, but when I return, I shall come back!

Chaplin finesses Charlie's outsized reaction to the new note by removing his passionate embrace of Georgia, which in the original had mirrored Big Jim's embrace of him. He also shortens the chase. The focus of the scene shifts from the tug-of-war action between the three characters to the words—Jim's promise to make Charlie rich, and Charlie's hurried declaration of love to Georgia and his silly joke about returning.

The reworking of the scene doesn't just reduce some of the dramatic tension, it also removes much of the astringent quality from the love story. In the earlier version Georgia, despite her moment of remorse at the cabin, is pretty much completely indifferent to Charlie's feelings; she's only concerned about Jack's. Jack compounds her unkindness with his cruel trick of redirecting the note. All this makes Charlie a more put-upon and sympathetic character in the original version. He is buffeted about by people as cold and merciless as the elements that buffet him in the rest of the film, and he goes forth into the wilderness inspired by a love that's illusory. The revised scene takes the cynical edge off.

It's possible that Chaplin made this alteration because he felt Georgia's indifference made her abrupt change of heart at the end of the film less believable. The final scene, however, worked perfectly well in the 1925 version. Nevertheless, in 1942 Chaplin felt the need to alter that scene as well, making an even more puzzling and disappointing editorial change.

Charlie and Georgia meet again by chance on the voyage home from Alaska. Her brashness seems to have vanished, and she appears genuinely pleased to see him. When she assumes he's a stowaway she comically demonstrates her newfound concern by pushing him into a coil of rope to hide him. Then, when he's apprehended, she pleads to be allowed to pay his fare as Charlie looks on, beaming.

While Georgia's sudden warmth and protectiveness toward Charlie is never explained, the seeds were planted earlier in the film, in the form of her remorse over her earlier treatment of him and her belated recognition (at least in the 1925 version) that her man Jack is a total cad. Then, too, she's also left the harsh gold rush town on her own. For the most part, though, we welcome her dawning love in the same way we accept the storm that blows the cabin right onto Jim's claim, and the coincidence that Georgia just happens to end up on the same boat. These are plot contrivances that make perfect emotional sense. Primal forces of nature and human nature, good and evil, have been set into play in the story, and all must be made right by the end. Georgia's love is the reward Charlie has earned for the resourceful way he's dealt with all the hardships he has endured and for the noble way he's acted toward the woman he adores. In the course of the film he's earned our love and admiration, and it's only fitting that he earns hers as well.

Chaplin shows his dramatic savvy by setting up the scene so that Georgia has no idea he is now a multimillionaire. He thus avoids the slightest hint that Georgia is interested in Charlie's wealth, rather than Charlie himself. The cynical part of the love story is behind us. Georgia is no gold digger. On the contrary, she is the gold that he has sought. He takes her hand and guides her up a shipboard ladder toward the upper deck, as the narration concludes, fairy-tale style, "And so it was—a happy ending."

This is very pleasant, and even moving. But in the original film Charlie and Georgia continue onto the upper deck, where a photographer is waiting to shoot him for a newspaper feature on his life story. Now Georgia becomes part of the photo. The photographer poses them, placing their faces close together and telling them to stand still. Instead, they slowly draw together for a kiss. In the film's final subtitle the photographer says, "Oh, you've spoilt the picture!" Charlie waves him off as they kiss. Neither Chaplin nor anyone else has ever explained why he felt the need to omit what is surely one of the most satisfying kisses in movie history.

Despite all of these caveats, the reissue of *The Gold Rush* makes a fascinating companion piece to the 1925

Posed by the photographer. Original ending for *The Gold Rush.*

The kiss.

version. The music, a new score by Chaplin, is melodic and inventive, effectively underscoring the action, much of which is permitted to unfold without narration. He makes clever use of several well-known classical themes. "The Flight of the Bumblebee," used to depict Charlie's struggle against the wind, returns during the tilting cabin finale. When the Tramp tries to dance gracefully with Georgia, unaware that there is a dog attached to his waist by a rope, the comedy is effectively counterpointed by the famous romantic theme from Tchaikovsky's *Sleeping Beauty* ballet (later used in the Disney film as the song "Once Upon a Dream"). And Chaplin's narration, despite the inherent pitfalls of narrating a silent picture, is well delivered, witty, and mercifully absent from most of the film's celebrated set pieces, including the shoe-eating and roll dance scenes.

Given current attitudes toward the sound version—the responses range from contempt to horror among Chaplin fans—it may come as something of a surprise to find that the revival was a smash hit in 1942. The film came out just a few months after the United States entered the war, and was gratefully received by both critics and audiences. The warm reception proved that, once again, Chaplin had perfectly gauged the temper of the times. Bosley Crowther of the *New York Times* assured his readers that the new version was even better than the original:

> Mr. Chaplin has violated nothing in his modernization of it. In fact, he has rather improved it—for new audiences, certainly. His so-called "descriptive dialogue" is just a pleasant narration, written and spoken by him, in which he somewhat replaces those persons who used to read titles aloud. The effect is surprisingly agreeable and just a shade nostalgic, too. When Mr. Chaplin observes, for instance; "Big Jim looked deep into the eyes of Black Larson and saw there the soul of a skunk," he does so not in tones of menace or hiss-the-villain burlesque; he speaks it straight and crisply. And when he first recognizes the heroine (Georgia Hale), he utters the single name, "Georgia!" with such tenderness and affection that genuine sadness haunts his voice.[3]

The paper listed the film, as it had in 1925, as among the ten best of the year, and it received Oscar nominations for its two new elements, the musical score and the sound. The latter is clearly a nod to Chaplin's narration, the only sound on the film other than the music. *The Gold Rush* became one of the first silent films to have a theatrical afterlife, decades before the major revival of interest in silent films in the 1960s.[4]

Unfortunately for Chaplin, his representatives failed to renew his copyright to the silent version in 1953, embroiling him in endless litigation to protect his rights to the film. Because of this lapse, prints of *The Gold Rush*, many of dubious quality, began to circulate both theatrically and nontheatrically, eventually appearing on television. It thus became the first of his features to be widely seen before the theatrical reissue of his films in the early 1970s and their subsequent release on the home movie and video markets. Partially because of this copyright issue, the narrated edition remains the Chaplin estate's preferred version of the film. However, the estate has made a superb print of the silent version available on the most recent DVD release, with a piano score by Neil Brand. The estate also allows the silent version to be shown with symphony orchestras, using composer Carl Davis's expansion of Chaplin's 1942 score.

Despite the film's success, Chaplin never repeated the experiment of narrating a silent film. In subsequent reissues he simply provided musical soundtracks. Fortunately, he managed to score all of his films made after 1918.

His next reissue was *The Chaplin Revue*, in 1959, a compilation of *A Dog's Life*, *Shoulder Arms*, and *The Pilgrim*, preceded by what appears to be documentary footage of Chaplin at work in his studio. This material, most of which dates from around 1919, was originally intended to be part of a tongue-in-cheek documentary called *How to Make Movies*, but which was never released during Chaplin's lifetime.[5] The portion Chaplin recycled features a photomontage of the studio being built, edited together so that it almost looks like time-lapse photography. There is also a funny scene on the open-air stage in which Chaplin, wearing street clothes, rehearses with company members Edna, Henry Bergman, and the diminutive Loyal Underwood, who suffers abuse as Chaplin instructs another actor how to throttle him. A brief scene of Chaplin in the dressing room completing his makeup concludes the sequence. Chaplin offers a sprightly commentary over the footage, then introduces the films we're about to see as "a sort of comic ballet," and explains that they will be accompanied by music rather than intrusive sound effects "or a lot of yakety-yak talking as I'm doing now." He invites the viewer to return to the "good old days of silent films" as he retires behind his "curtain of silence."

After *A Dog's Life* Chaplin introduces *Shoulder Arms*. Over historical footage of World War I trench warfare, he points out they had no atomic bombs then, so had to fight with primitive weapons such as cannons, bayonets, and poison gas. "Those were the good old days," he says with a wry chuckle. The footage serves to show how authentic the film itself looks. During the end credits of *Shoulder Arms* he briefly introduces *The Pilgrim*. The only other words in the film are the lyrics for a faux-Western song Chaplin composed to begin and end *The Pilgrim*.[6]

Chaplin's new score for *The Chaplin Revue* was superb, but he ran into a technical problem with the film speed. Some of the footage seemed too fly by too fast at twenty-four frames per second. The only solution available at the time was a process called stretch printing, in which every third frame was printed twice, slowing down the action. Unfortunately, this also gives the movement a peculiar hesitant quality, particularly marring the rhythmic scenes of *A Dog's Life*. Chaplin was aware of the problem, but saw no other solution. With the exception of one other First National film, *The Idle Class*, he never again used the process in a rerelease.[7]

In addition to the musical soundtracks, there is a much less apparent change in the reissues. The films themselves differ in varying degrees from their original incarnations. When he began setting his films to music in the late 1950s, a task that occupied him through the early 1970s, Chaplin had the opportunity to reedit according to any second thoughts he might have had over a lifetime of viewing the films. Happily, most of his changes are minor, such as the rewording of titles and elimination of dated references. In *My Life in Pictures* Chaplin published studio documents detailing his original editing continuity and a list of subtitles for *A Day's Pleasure*. Comparison with the current release version reveals that he rearranged the three major sequences in the film. In the original version, Charlie has trouble starting the car for the family excursion, then gets stuck in traffic and in tar on the road, and finally goes on his boat trip. For the reissue, Chaplin places the traffic scene last, a wise change, since it's the comic highlight of this strangely uninspired comedy. It's not enough to rescue the film, but at least it saves the best for last.

More puzzling are changes he made to other films. In *A Dog's Life*, for example, many shots are exactly the same as the silent version, but Chaplin substitutes inferior alternate takes of Charlie confronting the crooks to regain the stolen wallet. In the brief scene in which he pulls the booth curtains closed before knocking Albert Austin out, his performance is less focused. This change is minor, a matter of nuance. But the lengthy arm-substitution scene that follows is a different matter. While the rerelease version is certainly good, the original take is tighter and funnier. Both Chaplin and Austin give better performances, and the angle of Austin's body makes the illusion work better. The climax of the sequence, in which the crooks fire away at Charlie and Sydney as the brothers duck behind the lunch wagon counter, is also much better in the original. In the rerelease their heads pop up together just a couple of times before Charlie does the gag in which he shields his face with a plate. In the original their heads pop up together, then alternately, better nailing the illusion that they are mechanical figures in a shooting gallery. The plate gag is also better executed.

It is now a matter of some speculation as to why Chaplin made these and other changes to his film, but it's possible that he had little choice. The original release negatives were thirty to forty years old, may well have been damaged from overuse, and possibly also suffered the nitrate deterioration that afflicted so many silent films. In the 1940s Chaplin had his cameraman, Rollie Totheroh, prepare pristine new backup versions of the films from outtake negatives, and it appears that Chaplin had little or no involvement in this process.[8] In the early 1950s he ordered Rollie to destroy all his remaining outtakes. So by the time he began preparing his rereleases, Chaplin may have had little to work with other than Rollie's backup versions, along with what he could salvage from the original release negatives.[9]

But at least some of the changes appear to reflect changing sensibilities. For example, in the 1918 version of *A Dog's Life*, Scraps is frantically digging in the empty lot, and when Charlie peers through her back legs he gets a faceful of dirt. In the reissue he looks, winces at the smell of her rear end, and pushes her tail down with his hand. Perhaps he deemed the gag too explicit or vulgar in 1918, but the original was better performed and funnier. Similarly, when he reissued *The Kid* in 1971, Chaplin edited out some of the more melodramatic and dated material in Edna's performance. Nor were the changes limited to Chaplin's silent films. He also fiddled—to a lesser degree—with rereleases of his sound films, including *Modern Times*, *Limelight*, and *A King in New York*.[10]

Even at the time of their original release there were various versions of Chaplin's films. Like other major stars of the day, Chaplin shot every scene with two side-by-side cameras operating simultaneously.[11] This was necessary because the sprocket holes of film negatives would eventually be damaged by the printing process, and the images themselves could easily be scratched. Repair options were limited, and making duplicate negatives would significantly degrade the image. The footage from the "B" camera was used to make a European negative. Because of the great popularity of Chaplin's films, hundreds of prints had to be struck, so in some cases three or even four versions of the films were prepared, using the best alternate takes from each of the two cameras. Prints of some of these alternate versions are housed in film archives in various countries, while others are in the hands of private collectors, reflecting the lively black market in pirated Chaplin prints that began in the 1920s. As the copyrights to Chaplin's silent films expired, some of these unauthorized prints found their way onto the market, and a number are currently available on budget video and DVD brands.

Watching some of these variant versions can be painful—the image quality is often excruciatingly bad, and the music—when there is music—is almost invariably so. But for a Chaplin aficionado it can be an extraordinary experience to see alternate takes of familiar scenes, like having a favorite performer return for an unexpected encore.[12]

Notes

1. Charles Chaplin Jr., *My Father, Charlie Chaplin* (New York: Random House, 1960), 92–93.

2. As most readers will be aware, there are two cabins in the film: Black Larson's, out in the wilderness, where Charlie and Big Jim seek refuge during a storm; and another just outside of town belonging to Hank, a kindly mining engineer (played by Henry Bergman), which Charlie is taking care of. All the scenes with the girls take place in Hank's cabin.

3. Bosley Crowther, "Charlie Chaplin's Memorable 'Gold Rush,' Made in 1925, With Modern Renovations by Mr. Chaplin, Opens at Globe," *New York Times*, April 20, 1942.

4. There were others. *The Birth of a Nation* was occasionally revived. William S. Hart reissued his 1925 film *Tumbleweeds* in 1939, introducing the film with an eight-minute on-camera prologue, after which the film was accompanied by a musical soundtrack.

As noted in an earlier chapter, the popular Chaplin Mutuals were reissued theatrically in 1932, with cartoon-like music and effects. Theatrical reissues of Chaplin's Keystone and Essanay films followed, including several questionable attempts to string old films together into "new" Chaplin features. In addition, 16mm and later 8mm films, some of them merely a single scene or two, were produced for the burgeoning collectors' market starting in the 1920s. Several distributors began renting the early films to clubs, schools, and other groups for nontheatrical showings. For a good account of the tangled history of these reissues see Ted Okuda and David Maska, *Charlie Chaplin at Keystone and Essanay: Dawn of the Tramp* (Lincoln, NE: iUniverse, 2005).

5. The footage was discovered and edited together by Kevin Brownlow and David Gill when they were working on their *Unknown Chaplin* documentary. *How to Make Movies*, with a score by Carl Davis, debuted in a live orchestral performance, along with *City Lights*, during Chaplin's centenary celebration at the Dominion Theatre in London in 1989. *City Lights* opened at the theatre in 1931, with Chaplin in attendance along with George Bernard Shaw and Winston Churchill. The 1989 gala was hardly less glamorous, with a star-studded audience that included Princess Diana, Dustin Hoffman, and Daniel Day-Lewis. *How to Make Movies*, without the Davis score, has been released on the MK2 DVD editions of *The Chaplin Revue* and *The Kid*.

6. When he reissued *The Circus* in 1970, Chaplin also added a song over the opening credits, this time singing it himself. His old-man's voice and superb diction gives the lovely "Swing, Little Girl" the nostalgic sound of a music hall ballad.

7. Film preservationist David Shepard produced versions of *The Chaplin Revue* films using video technology to slow up the image and match it to Chaplin's soundtrack. These were released on DVD by Image Entertainment, and, as of this writing, are the best available versions of these films.

8. See David Robinson, *Chaplin, His Life and Art* (London: Penguin, 2001), 564–65.

9. As it turned out, most of the outtakes were not destroyed at all, but stolen from the studio in the middle of the night by the notorious film pirate and silent-film promoter Raymond Rohauer. The Mutual outtakes were part of this cache and became the basis for the extraordinary documentary *Unknown Chaplin* by Kevin Brownlow and David Gill. For an account of the fascinating detective work that went into the recovery of the Mutual outtakes, see Kevin Brownlow, *The Search for Charlie Chaplin* (Bologna: Le Mani/Cineteca de Bologna, 2005). The surviving Mutual outtakes now reside at the British Film Institute. The rest remain in private hands; one can only hope that they are being well cared for and will surface eventually.

10. The Image Entertainment versions of *Modern Times*, *Limelight*, *Chaplin Revue*, and other films contain material that Chaplin cut before rereleasing these films. A good essay on the variant versions and present availability of Chaplin's post-1918 output is Hooman Mehran's "New DVD Releases of Chaplin Films" in *Chaplin's "Limelight" and the Music Hall Tradition*, ed.

Hooman Mehran and Frank Scheide (Jefferson, NC: McFarland, 2006) 198–205.

11. He apparently began the practice as early as 1916, with the Mutual series.

12. The Chaplin estate has done an admirable job of preserving Chaplin's archives and filmic legacy, and one hopes that eventually it will make definitive, original-release versions of his silent masterworks available as well—ideally with their original pastiche musical scores, which Chaplin is reported to have supervised closely from 1923 on. That way, film scholars and interested individuals can see the films as their original audiences saw them. The evidence suggests they will stand the test of time.

CHAPTER THIRTEEN

Monster Movie: *Monsieur Verdoux*

Part of the satisfying sense of continuity in Chaplin's work comes from watching the seeds he planted in one film blossom in another. Thus, just as the "fallen woman" subplot of *The Kid* seems to beget *A Woman of Paris*, so the oration that ends *The Great Dictator* seems to beget the talkative Monsieur Verdoux, the serial killer who lectures his accusers about morality.

Once Chaplin became world famous, many observers were surprised to find that the comedian liked to hold forth on the social issues of the day. Reactions ranged from the awestruck admiration of many of his early interviewers, like Waldo Frank and Frank Harris, to the skeptical bemusement of friends and kindred spirits like Max Eastman and Thomas Burke, to the outright ridicule of some of his intimates and professional associates, such as Paulette Goddard and Buster Keaton. Chaplin had a marked preference for associating with world-class intellectuals rather than his professional colleagues. Virginia Cherrill commented dryly on his tendency to assume for a time the personality of whoever impressed him, noting that at one point during the making of *City Lights*, "overnight Charlie became Waldo Frank, and it was a terrible bore until he got it out of his system."[1]

The enormous popular success of both *Modern Times* and *The Great Dictator* could only have reinforced Chaplin's belief that social commentary and political satire were the natural next stage of his art. He had, it seemed, escaped George S. Kaufman's dictum that "satire is what closes on Saturday night." Yet while the new film would be Chaplin's postwar response to a world gone mad, it would also, like all his films, reflect his ongoing aesthetic and personal preoccupations—and particularly, in this case, the personal ones. No other Chaplin film raised such disturbing questions about Chaplin himself.

As Chaplin's Tramp character evolved and became more three-dimensional, public respect for Chaplin as an artist deepened, along with affection for his creation. But that affection was sorely tested by publicity about his offscreen life. At first, the stark contrast between the funny man onscreen and the handsome, thoughtful artist who created him elicited fascination and admiration. However, two marriages to teenage girls that flamed into spectacular divorces complicated those feelings. The second divorce, with its lurid allegations of cruelty, infidelity, and sexual perversion, would almost certainly have ended the career of a less beloved star. But the films themselves kept getting better, and the public ultimately sided with Chaplin. His troubled personal life was idealized as the quest of a brooding romantic genius for a perfect mate, a story that was endlessly rehashed in fan magazines of the 1920s and 1930s. Chaplin managed to keep a lower profile through the 1930s, though his decade-long relationship with Paulette Goddard occasioned public speculation, since the two lived together openly but refused to confirm whether they were married.

During the early 1940s Chaplin's public image was further complicated by his outspoken political activism. After *The Great Dictator* Chaplin found that he had a taste for public speaking, and he tried to contribute to the war effort by making several nationally broadcast speeches in support of opening a second front to protect Russia. But as Jane Fonda would find a quarter century later, taking a controversial stand, however well-intentioned, could backfire. As the Red scare intensified he was branded a Communist, or at best a Communist sympathizer, which contributed to the steep decline in his popularity in America in the 1940s. *The Great Dicta-*

tor itself was cited as evidence because of its "premature" antifascism.

While he consistently denied being a Communist, Chaplin adamantly defended his right to think as he chose and associate with whom he pleased. Those associates included film composer Hanns Eisler and playwright Bertolt Brecht, refugees from Nazi Germany who were blacklisted by Hollywood. Eisler was deported in 1948, but not before Chaplin and other prominent American artists rose to his defense. Chaplin, of course, couldn't be blacklisted, since he owned his own studio, but his reputation could be smeared. Although he was never called to testify before the notorious House Un-American Activities Committee, he was publicly criticized in Congress. Suddenly his failure to become a U.S. citizen was called into question, although it never became an issue with other famous expatriates like Alfred Hitchcock—but then, no one knew or cared about Hitchcock's political views.

At least as damning were new revelations about Chaplin's sex life. In 1943 he married yet another teenager, Oona O'Neill, daughter of the famous playwright Eugene O'Neill. The extreme difference in their ages—she was eighteen and he was fifty-four—was duly noted, but the marriage was nothing compared to the public relations disaster that followed. Accusations of sexual misconduct by a promiscuous and mentally unstable young woman named Joan Barry led to the most damaging scandal of Chaplin's career, and the resulting two trials kept him in the news throughout 1944 and 1945. The first invoked an archaic law that prohibited transporting a woman across state lines for "immoral purposes," meaning prostitution, and the second was a paternity suit.

While the case was later exposed as a shamelessly orchestrated attack on Chaplin by the FBI, which was also behind much of the negative publicity he received over his allegedly anti-American political views, that carefully guarded information wasn't revealed for another four decades. To stoke the flames of public outrage, the FBI found willing help from press gossipmongers like Hedda Hopper and Ed Sullivan, along with columnists such as the right-wing, Commie-hating Westbrook Pegler. The FBI also successfully enlisted the aid of patriotic organizations such as the American Legion and the Catholic War Veterans.

Chaplin was found innocent of the prostitution charges, but guilty of fathering Barry's child, the latter verdict a blatant miscarriage of justice, since well-publicized blood tests proved Chaplin's paternity to be a medical impossibility.[2] However, the damage to his reputation had been done, and the punitive verdict was embraced by large segments of the American public as nothing more than his due. He had, after all, admitted to having sex with the twenty-two-year old Barry, even if nearly a year and a half before the birth of her child. That was enough to condemn him as the monstrous, immoral libertine the prosecution painted him as being. By the time *Monsieur Verdoux* came out two years later, Chaplin's image as an aged womanizer coincided all too neatly with his new screen incarnation.

Which, of course, was exactly the point. Having gone though the legal ordeal and public humiliation of the trials, it must have given Chaplin tremendous sardonic satisfaction to create a black comedy in which he mocked his notorious "lady killer" image by becoming an actual lady killer, then mocked the legal system itself by having his character blithely defend his actions as insignificant in a world of mass-murdering nations, a world in which moral standards have devolved to hypocritical pieties. Chaplin used his comic art to strike back at his attackers, but few in 1947 America appreciated the joke.

While Verdoux at first glance might seem to be the polar opposite of the Tramp character, he is in plain view in Chaplin's work right from the beginning, in the cruel-though-suave skirt-chasing Charlie of the early films, and especially in all those drunken toffs Chaplin played into the early 1920s; he has all their insolence and aristocratic airs, only now he's lost his money and sobered up. Like the Tramp, he has to find a means of making a living, and it's not going well; he's as desperately trapped in the middle class as Charlie ever was in the lower.

While the callous and sexually aggressive Charlie largely disappears from the feature films, Chaplin doesn't wait for *Monsieur Verdoux* to reintroduce him: He reappears in a burst of glory in the person of Adenoid Hynkel. For his new film Chaplin resurrects two key aspects of his multifaceted portrayal of the dictator: the way he acts with Napaloni and the way he acts with Napaloni's wife.

Like Hynkel, Verdoux was inspired by a real-life character who was anything but comic. Henri Landru was a notorious French "Bluebeard" who, between 1914 and 1918, seduced and murdered ten wealthy widows for their money, only to be captured, tried, and executed for his crimes. As he had with *The Gold Rush* years earlier, Chaplin saw comic possibilities in the macabre tale.

If *The Great Dictator* is Chaplin's first real sound film, *Monsieur Verdoux* is his first real talkie. Although in the previous film he found numerous excuses to launch into passages of straight physical comedy, in *Monsieur Verdoux* he finds very few. Chaplin had greatly expanded his range while making *The Great Dictator*, experimenting with many kinds of verbal comedy, and also working out how to support it with physical comedy. In *Monsieur Verdoux* he capitalizes on his discoveries but narrows his focus. The new strategy is formally appropriate for its time; the wilder flights of physical invention drop off, so many vestigial remnants of an earlier era. *Monsieur Verdoux* is the first Chaplin film one can imagine being performed by another company of actors. Not that the film is devoid of physical comedy; there are delightful, well-executed moments of it sprinkled throughout the film. And, given his mimetic eloquence, it is doubtful that another actor could have turned in a performance as magnetic and engrossing as Chaplin's. Yet the focus of the film is on the dialogue.

Chaplin establishes the mood at the outset with an ominous crescendo of music over the main title, which consists of stark white letters on a black background edged by floral artwork. It's like an invitation to a wedding, except that instead of an RSVP at the bottom, we see the subtitle "A Comedy of Murders." Verdoux begins the film with a postmortem narration over a shot of his own gravestone. As he speaks, the camera pans across the peaceful graveyard. Unlike the brisk and formal narration in *The Gold Rush*, this time the voice is soft and intimate, as Verdoux succinctly introduces himself and summarizes both the plot and theme of his film:

> Good evening. As you can see, my real name is Henri Verdoux, and for thirty years I was an honest bank clerk, until the Depression of 1930, in which year I found myself unemployed. It was then I became occupied in liquidating members of the opposite sex. This I did as a strictly business enterprise, to support a home and family. But let me assure you that the career of a Bluebeard is by no means profitable. Only a person of undaunted optimism would embark on such a venture. Unfortunately, I did. What follows is history.

What follows actually is the weakest scene in the film, and the weakest opening of any mature Chaplin film, as we meet the obnoxious, bickering family of Verdoux's first victim, Thelma Couvais. Chaplin, of course, is shrewdly stacking the deck from the outset by showing us how unappealing his first victim's family is. But the actors seem ill at ease, and despite several decently choreographed physical gags, the scene is stagy and stilted. It's an uncharacteristic lapse for Chaplin, but one that will unfortunately be repeated in several later scenes.

The family members are supposed to be French wine merchants, but they speak and act more like they stepped out of a Ma and Pa Kettle film. When not snarling at each other, they're worried about the fate of Thelma Couvais, who hasn't been heard from since she married

The dapper Monsieur Verdoux.

a mysterious stranger named Varnay. This exposition dispensed with, the film's first good visual gag is the frozen visage of Varnay in a photo. For the first time we see Chaplin in his new incarnation. As the family comments, he's a "funny-looking bird," a dandy in smock and beret with a supercilious expression on his face.

Things perk up once we join Varnay, the first of three aliases under which Verdoux will conduct his murderous affairs. For his first major film appearance without his iconic square mustache, Chaplin sports a dapper, upturned, pointed one instead, like those of the many false French counts that populate his earliest films. But this mustache is naturalistic, and for the first time so is his facial makeup. He also allows his salt-and-pepper hair to show his age.

The smock, it turns out, is for gardening, not painting, and Verdoux is placidly snipping roses in his garden. The only thing that disturbs the idyllic atmosphere are ominous clouds of black smoke that rise from an incinerator in the back of the yard, revealing the fate of the unfortunate Thelma.[3] Two neighbor ladies complain that it's been going for three days, ruining their laundry.

A mailman arrives with a package that must be signed for by Thelma, and Verdoux nimbly mounts the stairs and signs the receipt himself, all the while keeping up a running conversation with his now-defunct wife. Chaplin has found a dialogue equivalent of his familiar "camouflage" gag, covering his tracks just as deftly as he had years before in *The Circus*, when he filched bites from a baby's hot dog and then wiped its mouth affectionately to fool the father.

In one of the film's wittiest visual bits, he opens the package of Thelma's money and counts it out with undercranked speed and dexterity. It's a perfect defining movement for the former bank teller who spent thirty years counting other people's money, and Chaplin will repeat it as a running gag throughout the film, flipping through cash, financial ledgers, and telephone directories. Other parts of this first sequence are also subtly undercranked, though Chaplin makes much less use of the device here than he did in *The Great Dictator*.

The stately Madame Grosnay calls to look at the house with a real estate agent, and Verdoux immediately pegs her as his next victim. He shows her around the house, twirling gracefully as he keeps up a steady flow of flattering chatter. Suddenly we recognize the character, for we've seen him before, in Hynkel's brief but hilariously seductive assault on Madame Napaloni in the ballroom. Chaplin was wise to recycle this aspect of his Hynkel performance, for Verdoux's encounters with Madame Grosnay are among the funniest scenes in the film. Isobel Elsom's dignified and knowing portrayal perfectly counterbalances Verdoux's outrageous flirting, much as Margaret Dumont balanced Groucho's.

When the real estate agent comes in as Verdoux is pursuing the astonished matron around the room, Verdoux instantly covers by pretending that he's been trying to swat a bee. Clasping his hands together in front of himself and wiggling his shoulders, he takes a neat backward tumble out the window. These familiar gestures lend the sinister figure some of Tramp's childlike appeal, as well as his acrobatic aplomb.

Verdoux, however, is anything but childlike about romance, as we see again when he visits a café. A pretty woman's huge diamond bracelet catches his eye, and when she turns and smiles at him, he gives her a big, unctuous smile, tipping his hat invitingly—but she is actually greeting someone behind him, so he turns away with a sigh. The same gag that was so touching in *The Gold Rush* has soured. Romance, as Verdoux informed us at the outset, is strictly business for him.

In *The Great Dictator* Chaplin had a field day with puns, but in *Verdoux* the few puns are sardonic rather than silly. He is joined at his table by an old bank colleague, who is impressed by the big roll of bills Verdoux pulls out to settle his check. "You must have made a killing," he remarks. Momentarily taken aback, Verdoux recovers and gives him a meaningful smile and a curt "yes." After Verdoux leaves the man reiterates what we heard in the prologue, telling his companion how unjust it was that "poor old Verdoux" was one of the first to be fired after thirty years of loyal service.

But Verdoux has no time for self-pity. His deadly game must continue, for he needs cash to protect his stock market investments. So he becomes Monsieur Floray[4] and visits another wife, the prune-faced Lydia. She is such an embittered old crone that Chaplin ensures that she gets no more audience sympathy than the unseen but presumably equally dreadful Thelma (we never see Thelma, but her ample girth is amusingly shown by her dress dummy, which appears in several scenes).

Verdoux with Lydia (Margaret Hoffman).

After he tricks the unlovely Lydia into withdrawing her money from the bank, they retire to bed. The scene gave Chaplin considerable trouble with the censors, who didn't want it implied that he actually had sex with his victims. In the end it's left ambiguous. Pausing at the hall balcony window before entering the bedroom, Verdoux poetically extols the beauty of the moon. Lydia snarls at him to come to bed. When he enters the bedroom, the camera remains fixed on the balcony, and ominous music tells us what's happening within. A simple lighting change shows us the passage of time to the next morning, and Verdoux briskly emerges in his shirt sleeves after another job well done. The ambiguity about whether they had sex before he killed her works very well in a film in which sex is equated with death.

Verdoux counts Lydia's money with his usual dexterity, then absentmindedly confirms her fate by briskly setting the breakfast table for two, before recollecting himself and removing one of the settings. As he had in *A Woman of Paris*, Chaplin uses props to convey the essential information swiftly and subtly, yet with unmistakable clarity and droll humor.

Having established Verdoux's proficiency at his diabolical trade, the film now provides him with the most conventional of reasons for pursuing it. As we hear a musical theme reminiscent of "Smile" from *Modern Times*, he retreats to his refuge, a modest country home. There he lovingly greets his pretty wife and towheaded young son. Verdoux's wife is concerned that he's working himself too hard, but has no idea how he actually makes his living in the "jungle" he alludes to. He is every inch the loving bourgeois husband as he proudly presents her with the deed to their house as a tenth anniversary present. "*That* they'll never take away from us," he tells her fervently. She doesn't seem to care as much about it as he does, even commenting that their former life wasn't so bad, but he firmly assures her they will never live in poverty again.

A number of critics have pointed out that the depiction of Verdoux's home life is strangely bland and perfunctory compared to the scenes of his exciting criminal career. While Chaplin's interest is obviously excited more by Verdoux's cat-and-mouse games with his victims than with the family for whom he is committing his crimes, the scenes of Verdoux at home not only dramatically justify his behavior, but link the film with one of Chaplin's lifetime preoccupations: his horror of poverty. In the scene Verdoux makes it abundantly clear that his fear and hatred of poverty has forced him into his present circumstances. And, lest we be tempted to question why his wife can't help with the family finances, Chaplin puts her in a wheelchair, with prominent braces on her legs, and makes a point of wheeling her around so that we're in no doubt about her condition. Yet her disability also makes for a disturbing, if unexamined, undercurrent in the film, since her presumed sexual incapacity is in such stark contrast to his professional skill as a seducer.

The scene is necessarily serious, setting the stage for the serious scenes to come. But there is no mistaking the irony when Verdoux explains to his son that they don't eat meat because they're vegetarians, and upbraids the lad for pulling the cat's tail. "You have a cruel streak in you. I don't know where you get it. . . . Remember, violence begets violence." The scene's only other glimmer of humor occurs when two friends, a balding little druggist with funny, upturned side panels on his hair, joins them for dinner, along with his hefty wife, who is comically eager to get to the dinner table. These halfhearted comic bits are reminiscent of the earlier moments with the Couvais family, but with Chaplin present the scene is much better staged and played.[5]

However, discovering that Verdoux is a decent family man hardly persuades us of the legitimacy of his work or makes us think better of him. Ironically, his triumphs and travails as a killer are what earn him our sympathy. Up to this point we have been invited to appreciate his banker's efficiency in dispatching his victims, and for the rest of the film we will enjoy seeing him repeatedly thwarted by his intended next victim, the indomitable Annabella.

The indestructible Annabella (Martha Raye) with her dashing sea captain.

For Annabella, wife number three, Verdoux becomes the dashing Captain Bonheur (Captain Happiness). Along with his scenes with Madame Grosnay, these are the funniest scenes in the film. Although Chaplin would later say that Martha Raye's performance was "in a different key from the rest of the film,"[6] it actually complements the Madame Grosnay scenes splendidly. Once again, Chaplin draws on his work in *The Great Dictator*, this time recapitulating the comic clash between Hynkel and Napaloni. Like Napaloni, the boisterous Annabella effortlessly bests him at every turn, and like Jack Oakie, Martha Raye virtually turns Chaplin into a brooding straight man.

There is amusing verbal business as Verdoux contemptuously exposes the phony business schemes the gullible, lowbrow Annabella falls for, including the Pacific Ocean Power Company, which will generate electricity from the movement of waves, and the Salt Water Fuel Company, which claims to transform salt water into gasoline. They go to a nightclub, where Annabella energetically bounces the dignified Verdoux around on the dance floor, but Chaplin doesn't develop the comic possibilities. Instead, Verdoux leaves her dancing simultaneously with two old men while he goes to purchase some chloroform. But his nefarious plans for the evening are foiled when he realizes the maid is still in the house.

Returning to his real home, Verdoux learns the formula for an undetectable poison from his druggist friend.[7] This is the last time we will see his family. However, both Verdoux's humanity and his philosophy are explored in the next scene, in which he picks up a girl he thinks is a prostitute to test his poison. But he is surprised to find in her a kindred spirit; she, like him, has come to her present desperate circumstances because she was providing for an invalid spouse. It is, in fact, her first night out of jail; she hasn't begun working as a prostitute yet.

The serious ten-minute scene is thematically important in the film, for the girl embodies the optimism Verdoux refers to in his opening graveside narration. She is his alter ego, another example of the fierce embrace of life necessary to do unpleasant or illegal things to protect one's loved ones. But unlike him, she's relatively innocent, having committed only petty theft to get by so far. Nor has she become cynical, despite all her hardships and losses. She reminds him of a happier time in his own life, and he finds himself touched. So instead of poisoning her he feeds her, gives her some money, and sends her on her way—an act of kindness that earns him her gratitude and our sympathy.

The scene is exceptionally well written and staged, and Chaplin's performance is excellent, aided greatly by sensitive musical underscoring. Unfortunately, Marilyn Nash, the inexperienced actress playing the part, is not up to the task, and seriously mars the scene. When Verdoux offers her money as she's leaving, for example, it's very much like that long-ago moment when Charlie offered Edna money to replace her stolen cash in *The Immigrant*; but Nash's reaction when she breaks down isn't believable, making what should be touching seem merely mawkish. It is extremely puzzling that Chaplin did not recast the role. In his last book he admits how inadequate Nash's performance was, but for some reason he evidently didn't recognize it at the time.[8] Nash is equally wooden in their subsequent scenes, almost making one wish Verdoux hadn't changed his mind about the poison.

He gets the opportunity to test it soon enough, however, when he is visited by a detective who has tracked him down as the killer of fourteen missing women. Once again he suavely proves himself the master of the situation, testing the deadly potion while simultaneously ridding himself of the troublesome detective. This cold-blooded murder accomplished, Verdoux's hardening heart is demonstrated in a second encounter with Nash. He doesn't even recognize her at first; then he harshly brushes her off with another gift of cash.

Then it's back to fun and games as he tries to use the poison on Annabella, unaware that the maid has put a bottle of peroxide in its place. Setting up this switch in a logical manner takes Chaplin some time, but it's worth it for the resulting series of comic payoffs. Verdoux spikes Annabella's wine with the peroxide, and meanwhile the maid brushes the poison into her hair. To his consternation Annabella savors the wine ("nice and dry"). In a nicely choreographed bit she inadvertently switches her wine for his sarsaparilla. When he thinks he has accidentally downed the poison his hilarious imagined death throes are topped by the arrival of the distraught maid, her hair coming out in clumps and standing up like a fright wig.

After having his stomach pumped, he makes one final attempt on Annabella in a rowboat the next day. This is the most sustained comic scene in the film, an effortless blend of verbal and visual humor. Raye gives the performance of her career, perfectly using her voluptuous figure and clownish face as she contemptuously tries to get Verdoux to help her catch a fish. Chaplin sets off her pitch-perfect work by underplaying very effectively.

At first Verdoux explains away his murder weapon—a rope with a noose on one end and a rock on the other—as an anchor. He suffers a number of indignities, catching the fishhook in his pants leg and then on his hat, which Annabella promptly "casts" into the water. As he readies the noose, she looks back, and we're treated to some characteristic "peek-a-boo" action; much to Annabelle's disgust, Verdoux minces coyly each time he's caught in the act. These are the same ingratiating gestures that Charlie did in the dressing room in *City Lights*, which boxer Hank Mann misinterpreted as a come-on. Annabella just thinks he's acting like an idiot.

Verdoux next tries the chloroform, inevitably chloroforming himself instead of her. This earns him even more contempt from Annabella, who assumes he's a secret tippler when she finds him lying helpless on the floor of the boat. Finally he simply approaches her with the noose, explaining that he intends to "lassoo" the fish. He demonstrates by slipping it around her neck, but a distant yodeler, watching them with binoculars, saves the day yet again for the indestructible Annabella. Struggling with a fish, she manages to throw Verdoux overboard, drowning his murderous ambitions for another day.

Moving on to greener pastures, Verdoux turns his attentions back to Madame Grosnay. Since their first encounter he has been persistently bombarding her with flowers. The flower shop is another reminder of *City Lights*, complete with a pretty flower seller (Barbara Slater), but this time, of course, Chaplin is the man of means rather than the lowly Tramp. Verdoux is delighted to find that Madame Grosnay has at last succumbed to his entreaties, and has sent a letter to the shop agreeing to see him again. The shop girl listens attentively when he borrows the phone; she turns discreetly away from him, but faces the camera so that we can see her reactions. Once again Verdoux exudes all of Hynkel's wolfish charm as he speaks passionate endearments to the now-receptive matron, some of which he addresses directly to the pretty girl. When he finishes the call and gives her a brisk, purse-lipped nod, she stares at him open-mouthed, and when he asks to settle his account she can barely speak. All three players are excellent in this scene, one of the small comic gems of the film.

But Verdoux's wedding plans are thwarted when the irrepressible Annabella shows up as one of the guests. At one point she and Verdoux back into each other, but, in another neatly choreographed bit, they turn around alternately to apologize and fail to recognize one another. A little later, though, Verdoux hears her unmistakable bray of a laugh, and he panics and crawls into the greenhouse. He explains his doubled-over posture to guest William Frawley (soon to earn fame as Fred Mertz from the *I Love Lucy* show) as an attack of stomach cramps. It's a Chaplin transformation gag as of old, but now words are part of it, an appropriate evolution of one of his best comic motifs. Verdoux escapes, letting both of his unknowing victims off the hook.

Chaplin next fudges with the chronology of his film. We've been told several times that he was fired in 1930. However, a montage of newspaper headlines now depicts the stock market crash of 1929; clips show businessmen committing suicide and a distraught Verdoux being wiped out financially. This doesn't appear to have been simply a careless mistake, since Chaplin actually puts the year 1932 on the newspapers. Evidently, he wanted to link both Verdoux's firing and his subsequent financial ruin with the crash, so he just fakes it. It's a minor glitch that most viewers won't notice, but it has confused or put off some commentators. The montage takes us into the late 1930s, showing rioting crowds and the rise of Hitler and Mussolini, along with their marching armies. This time the images, unlike those in *The Great Dictator*'s newsreels, are all too real.

As at the end of *City Lights*, Chaplin makes an eloquent physical transformation to show his character the worse for wear. Having lost both his fortune and his family, Verdoux is bent, deflated, and walks with a limp. The change is also vocal; he speaks in a breathy, raspy tone. Chaplin the actor was never better.

He encounters the Nash character for the third time. This time she's in a limo, for she's found professional "success" as the mistress of a wealthy munitions manufacturer. "That's the business I should've been in," he remarks. "Yes," she says bitterly. "It'll be paying big dividends soon." She takes him to an expensive restaurant, where, without going into the gory details, he tells her about the life he's lived.

> Since the loss of my family I seem to have awakened from a dream. . . . I was a bank clerk once, my existence a monotonous rhythm, day in and day out, counting other people's money. Then something happened. The rhythm was broken, I lost my position. What followed was a numbed confusion, a nightmare, in which I lived in a half-dream world, a horrible world. Now I've awakened. Sometimes I wonder if that world ever existed.

Without trying to justify his past behavior, Verdoux separates himself from it. We greet this news with mixed feelings, given that the horrible world he describes has been presented in the funniest way possible throughout the film, and has in fact given us considerable pleasure. It's exactly the same dilemma Chaplin faced by turning serious at the end of *The Great Dictator*. Unlike the Chaplin of old, who effortlessly blends the comic and serious, he juxtaposes them, and, as in the previous film, he runs into trouble doing it.

It's not that the serious passage comes out of the blue. Chaplin is very savvy about how he incorporates serious material into *Verdoux*. In *The Great Dictator* there are only a few serious moments before the final speech, most notably the burning of the barbershop. But in *Verdoux* there are serious scenes throughout the film—with the family, Nash, and the cop, as well as various shorter scenes of him conducting his financial transactions on the phone. These dovetail smoothly with the comic scenes, because both the serious and comic scenes show Verdoux busily plying his trade as the plot moves briskly along. But the restaurant scene is different. While it makes perfectly good dramatic sense for Verdoux to express genuine self-loathing for his life of crime, unlike the previous serious scenes, it contradicts the comedy. Chaplin wants it both ways: disavowing his gleeful celebration of misogyny as a nightmare of depravity. This causes a serious disjunction between the film's comic and serious sections. It's not immediately obvious, because the scene works well on its own (aside from Nash's usual stiff performance). But, like the wife's disability, it makes for a disturbing undercurrent.

The girl tries to give him a pep talk, returning the kindness he had paid her years earlier. She encourages him to regain his zest for life, to go on living so that he can fulfill his unknown destiny. It's a bit like the pep talk Charlie gave the gamine at the end of *Modern Times*. But the times have changed; Nash isn't his girl, and his destiny doesn't include a road leading to further adventures. His destiny is death, and he gets the opportunity to embrace it at that very moment, when the flibbertigibbet sister of Thelma Couvais happens by and recognizes him.

In the film's last burst of broad physical comedy, Verdoux proves that he can still play the game, and Chaplin proves that he can still flip effortlessly from drama to comedy. After saying goodbye to Nash—in effect, protecting her once again from himself—he leads the Couvais woman and her brother on a short chase, eluding them easily. He elects, however, to allow the police to capture him, staging his surrender with characteristic élan, master of the situation to the very end.

Throughout the film, rapidly moving train wheels, accompanied by a rising violin theme, have indicated Verdoux's busy travel schedule. During the trial the train wheels appear again, but now they are metaphorical, dissolving into newspaper headlines to show the rapidly approaching end of his journey. In the courtroom we see only the last moments of the prosecutor's summation. "You have before you a cruel and cynical monster," he tells the jury. "Look at him." Verdoux turns his head to look, like everyone else. The little physical gag makes its point: Verdoux is no monster—at least, not to himself.

He soon makes that clear in words as well. In a moment that must have sent a shiver down the spine of everyone who deplored *The Great Dictator*'s last speech, Verdoux is asked if he has any last words before he is sentenced. Chaplin, perhaps still smarting from his critical drubbing over the *Dictator* speech, is brief—his comments last just over a minute. He says nothing about his family, instead calling into question the moral authority of the court to judge him. Without belaboring the issue, he states that he is only an "amateur" in a world that encourages mass killing, a world that blows up women and little children "very scientifically," and is preparing to do so yet again. "However," he says, "I do not wish to lose my temper because very shortly I shall lose my head." The only one who gets misty-eyed over this information is Marilyn Nash, sitting in the gallery. To everyone else Verdoux is the cruel and cynical monster the prosecutor accuses him of being, his argument simply a bit of glib sophistry.

Verdoux's speech in the courtroom allows Chaplin the master actor to convey a rich palette of emotions—resignation, touches of self-pity and pride, irony, outrage, and accusation. Like Chaplin's speech in *The Great Dictator*, the words elevate the film to more than the story of its characters, but without requiring Chaplin to break character to deliver them. Verdoux takes his leave with dignity and intelligence, and at the same time Chaplin is able to lash out at a society he felt had lost its moral compass.

Unfortunately, he can't leave well enough alone. In his jail cell on the morning of his execution, Verdoux ratchets the discourse up a notch, addressing larger issues of moral responsibility and spiritual guilt. This time there is less emotional variety as he holds forth; he seems only weary and resigned, and his cosmic pronouncements come off as smug and sententious.

He first expands upon his ideas to a reporter, insisting that, by the standards of the time, murder is simply a business, and that his problem is that he was working on too small a scale: "One murder makes a villain, millions a hero. Numbers sanctify, my good fellow." When a priest enters, Verdoux is characteristically polite, but uninterested in religious solace. His problem, he tells the priest, is with man, not God. "May God have mercy on your soul," says the priest. "Why not? After all, it belongs to Him," replies Verdoux.

But Chaplin is too savvy to end his film with these verbal sallies. Offered rum before his walk to the guillotine, he refuses, then decides, "Just a minute. I've never tasted rum." The master actor stiffens slightly as he drains the glass, as the final music begins and the camera zooms closer. In this way Chaplin subtly suggests that Verdoux's philosophizing might be nothing more than a brave front. All too human, he feels the need for a stiff belt to face the end. We can see how he still savors life by the way he reacts to the bright sunlight and takes a deep breath as the door is opened.

He walks slowly away from the camera toward the guillotine. For those who have not been alienated by the film up to this point, the ending is moving—Chaplin's ironic last walk down the road. He even limps just a bit.

Unlike *The Great Dictator*, which became a major world event both cinematically and historically, *Monsieur Verdoux* is more of a landmark in the life and career of Charlie Chaplin. Discussions of the film invariably focus on the autobiographical questions it raises—Chaplin's questionable intellectual pretensions, his egotism, his relationships with women, his politics, and his strained relationship with his adopted country.

The film was initially greeted with a distressing combination of hostility from the press and indifference from the public. The New York press conference became legendary for the way it degenerated into a personal attack.[9] The reporters dealt little with the film, but grilled Chaplin about his supposed Communist leanings and lack of patriotism. James Agee was one of the few in the room disposed to defend Chaplin and his film, and he continued to do so in influential reviews, both in *Time* and the *Nation*, for which he wrote an unprecedented three-issue paean to the film. Unfortunately for Chaplin, these reviews, which attacked other critics and the general public for their blindness to the film's virtues and importance, did little to generate public interest in actually seeing the film. The New York run lasted a disappointing five weeks; the film was then withdrawn so a new publicity campaign could be crafted for a national release. While the film did well, interestingly, in Washington, DC, it flopped resoundingly everywhere else.[10] Though it fared much better abroad, in the States it was Chaplin's biggest flop since 1923's *A Woman of Paris*—bigger, in fact, for critics almost unanimously praised the earlier film. Chaplin's message linking capitalism with murder simply didn't play to a weary public that had just fought and won "a never-ending battle for truth, justice, and the American way," to quote the flag-waving words of television's *Adventures of Superman*.

Remarkably, when Chaplin's films were revived in a theater in New York in 1964, a complete reversal of critical and public opinion occurred, and the film garnered better reviews and did better business than any of the others. Times had changed; a new war was looming, and *Dr. Strangelove* was ushering in a new era of absurdist cinematic social satire. Chaplin's film was celebrated as being years ahead of its time, and reviewers used the occasion as an excuse to bash the American government and the public that had so turned against him.

Monsieur Verdoux continues to elicit sharply divided critical responses, but with the passage of time they tend to be based more on issues of aesthetics rather than personality or politics. For some, Chaplin's sound films simply don't measure up to his earlier work. This view was even expressed at the notorious New York press conference, where some of the questions revealed nostalgia for the old, funny Charlie of the silent films. As one writer later put it,

> Everyone recognizes Charlie Chaplin's genius as a pantomime actor; everyone equally recognizes that his skill evaporates when he turns to dialogue.[11]

But *Monsieur Verdoux*, whatever its shortcomings, is a triumph for Chaplin as an actor—so much so that it almost makes up for the absence of a single sustained flight of magical Chaplin mime, his first major film to be without one. This deficiency, in tandem with the film's other failings—its uneasy mix of comic and serious material, and several substandard performances—make *Monsieur Verdoux*, if not quite a monster, at least something of a mutant. There is little doubt that it will remain the most controversial of his films.

In his autobiography Chaplin vigorously defends the film, devoting more space to it than any other. He quotes pages of script, rehashes his battles with the censors, and asserts that it is "the cleverest and most brilliant film I have yet made."[12]

But ten years later, in *My Life in Pictures*, he writes its epitaph:

> There was some clever dialogue in *Monsieur Verdoux* but now I think it was too cerebral and should have had more business. If you have a bit of a message it's better to put it over through business than through words—better for me, anyhow.[13]

Notes

1. Virginia Cherrill, author interview, 1978.

2. The Kafkaesque nature of both trials is well recounted by David Robinson in *Chaplin, His Life and Art* (London: Penguin, 2001) 565–72. The FBI records reveal that the first trial judge had once enjoyed an "afternoon date" with Barry. J. Edgar Hoover not only covered up this compromising information, but made use of it to ensure the judge's cooperation.

3. As Julian Smith points out, Chaplin clearly intends this image to suggest the infamous concentration camp ovens; after he's done in the garden, Verdoux plays the piano, exactly like Hynkel while the ghetto is burning. Verdoux's comment in the spoken prologue about "liquidating" women also links his activities to the mass exterminations.

Smith also notes a more subtle reflexive reference: When Verdoux says to a caterpillar, "Ooh la la, you'll be stepped on, my little fellow, if you're not careful," he's referring to the Tramp. The new film is Chaplin's definitive break with the character, so the Tramp is, in effect, Verdoux's first victim. See Smith, *Chaplin* (Boston: Twayne, 1984), 121.

4. The name is a tip of the hat to Chaplin's associate director Robert Florey. Already a well-established director (*The Cocoanuts*, *The Beast with Five Fingers*), Florey had long idolized Chaplin and was a member of his social circle. Initially, Chaplin asked him to direct the film, but Florey was thrilled to accept the lesser position of assistant director for the chance to work with Chaplin. Among his contributions was helping to ensure the authenticity of the French settings.

The naming gesture was not enough, however, to prevent Florey from writing scathingly about his experience on the film. He was baffled by Chaplin's apparent ignorance of the rudiments of filmmaking technique, along with his unwillingness to accept even the slightest directorial input. Chaplin also infuriated Florey by violating their contractual agreement, demoting him from assistant to associate director, then making him share even that credit with Chaplin's half-brother Wheeler Dryden, who was essentially a glorified secretary at the studio.

5. Many critics see the family scenes as a Brechtian dismissal of the need for conventional motivation. Julian Smith, for one, claims they are a faux-sentimental dodge that clears the way for Chaplin's polemical speeches at the end. Smith defends his position by noting that the home and Verdoux's family are unattractive. I don't agree. The kid is a typical Hollywood moppet, and while the clothing and hairstyle of the actress playing

the wife are rather dowdy, she is a pretty woman, and anything but embittered by her fate. While Chaplin minimizes their screen time, and bumps them off conveniently when their dramatic function has been fulfilled, the heartfelt emotion in his comments about poverty is palpable. Smith also finds virtue in the awkward opening scene with the Couvais family, asserting that it is "so bad that it is good," but again his argument is unconvincing. See Smith, *Chaplin*, 21.

6. Charles Chaplin, *My Life in Pictures* (New York: Grosset & Dunlap, 1975), 290.

7. This scene may have been suggested by a similar exchange in Hitchcock's *Shadow of a Doubt*, released in 1943 when Chaplin was beginning work on *Verdoux*.

8. Chaplin, *My Life in Pictures*, 290.

9. The press conference was reprinted in Charles Wallach, "Charlie Chaplin's *Monsieur Verdoux* Press Conference," *Film Comment* (Winter 1969): 34–42.

10. See Charles Maland's *Chaplin and American Culture* (Princeton, NJ: Princeton University Press, 1989) for an exhaustive account of the film's reception in the United States.

11. Allardyce Nicoll, *The World of Harlequin* (London: Cambridge University Press, 1963), 18.

12. Charles Chaplin, *My Autobiography* (New York: Simon & Schuster, 1964), 454.

13. Chaplin, *My Life in Pictures*, 34.

CHAPTER FOURTEEN

Full Circle: *Limelight*

In the last film of his Hollywood career Chaplin solves the problem of how to integrate physical comedy into a sound film by the simple expedient of putting it into a series of stage acts that he performs. For the first time, he brackets the comedy in a film as something his character *does*, rather than something his character *is*. The result is that the comic and dramatic poles are pushed further apart than in any previous Chaplin film.

Chaplin's hallmark had always been fusing comedy and drama, such as the life-or-death comedy sequences that fill *The Gold Rush*. Even *The Great Dictator* and *Monsieur Verdoux* had put across their serious points—until the endings—with comedy. In *Limelight* the comedy scenes seem lighter, because they are less obviously a part of the dramatic action. In addition, there's a lot less comedy than drama; although the film is about a professional comedian, drama predominates. Even so, the comedy is essential to the film, intertwining with the dramatic story and illuminating it.

Limelight begins with a subtitle that tells us we are in London in 1914, neatly joining the place of Chaplin's birth with the year of his birth as a film artist. Such dizzying autobiographical references permeate the film. Although on some level all of Chaplin's films are thinly disguised autobiography, in *Limelight* the crossovers between art and life are vertiginous. The more familiar a viewer is with Chaplin's life and career, the more the dialogue, the situations, and even the casting resonate with meaning (five of his children and one half-brother appear in the film). Even to those unfamiliar with Chaplin, however, it is clear that he is basically playing himself.

In his autobiography Chaplin deflects this somewhat by claiming that his character, Calvero, was inspired by Frank Tinney, a Broadway comedian who became self-conscious onstage and lost touch with his audience. But Chaplin himself, like most comedians, had lived in dread of losing his talent and his audience, and, of course, in *Monsieur Verdoux* he did lose that audience, and in the eyes of many he lost his talent as well. While he initially attributed *Verdoux*'s commercial failure to poor marketing, he could hardly ignore scathing reviews like the following:

> Only in passages of rather irrelevant pantomime does a great clown of our day remind one of his artistry. . . . It is a pity to see so gifted a motion picture craftsman taking leave of his audience.[1]

In the face of such reactions it is understandable that Chaplin would imagine himself into the skin of a washed-up comedian who has grown reflective about his craft. *Limelight* would be all about craft, celebrating Chaplin's pantomimic and other performing skills, as well as his skills as a storyteller and filmmaker. In making it he pulled back from the social commentary that had infused his films for the past two decades, instead presenting a complex, Victorian-style story of redemption, doomed love, and the fickle spotlight of fame.

Yet despite its historical setting and many references to Chaplin's past, *Limelight* is no nostalgic paean to a lost golden age. Like *Verdoux*, it boldly addresses Chaplin's problematic public image, then at its nadir in America. For the second time in four years he presents himself as an aging womanizer. This time, however, his behavior is exemplary. While his keen interest in sex is indicated by the five prior marriages he mentions, as well as the mildly racy songs and skits he performs onstage, he firmly rejects the young heroine's repeated declarations of love, for he knows that the age difference between them is insurmountable. This noble self-denial, of course, was blatantly contradicted by Chaplin's well-publicized domestic happiness with his much-younger bride, Oona. Adding further to the confusion of art and life, Claire Bloom, the film's heroine, is a virtual look-alike for Oona, who actually doubles for her in one shot.

For those disposed to dislike Chaplin—and their numbers were legion in the United States at the time the film came out—the disparities between Chaplin and his new screen incarnation rankled. That the most successful comedian of the century chose to present himself as an alcoholic, broken-down has-been who resists the overtures of a beautiful younger woman was viewed in some quarters as rank hypocrisy, a grotesque exercise in self-pity, or a disingenuous attempt to curry favor with a public that had rightly rejected the comedian for his personal and political misdeeds. Half a century later these feelings have largely dissipated, and the film emerges as a flawed but remarkable capstone to Chaplin's career, recapitulating his primary artistic concerns and breaking new artistic ground as well.

The parallels to his earlier films are striking. As in both *City Lights* and *Monsieur Verdoux*, Chaplin helps a physically handicapped woman, and suffers greatly by doing so. As in *City Lights*, the heroine's love is compromised by feelings of pity and gratitude. As in *The Kid*, he reluctantly "adopts" a dependent who subsequently becomes his alter ego. As in *The Circus* and *Modern Times*, he is presented in the role of a professional entertainer.

Limelight is most often compared to *City Lights* because they both feature afflicted heroines and doomed love stories, but it can also be viewed as a superior working out of the unresolved problems in *The Circus*. While Chaplin's last film of the silent era has comedy sequences as good as anything he ever created, the reflection on what it is to be an entertainer is only partially realized, and the romantic plot is superficial compared to the films that bookend it, *The Gold Rush* and *City Lights*. In *Limelight* Chaplin addresses both issues in a more satisfying way, and at the same time he finally brings his nemesis, the sound film, under full control, offering a dazzling display of his full range of verbal and physical skills. He is by turns wry, witty, silly, and self-indulgent; he acts, he sings, he dances, and, best of all, he does pantomime. In his autobiography Chaplin writes that he was certain of his achievement: "I had fewer qualms about its success than any picture I had ever made."[2]

One of the keys to the success of *Limelight* is Chaplin's deep understanding of both his character, an aging music hall entertainer, and the film's theatrical milieu. The juggling act of characterization that caused him problems in his other sound films is here handled with aplomb; in *Limelight* all the characters are well rounded and realistic. The overall casting is more sure than in *Verdoux*, without any conspicuously weak performances. Claire Bloom, in her first film role, was only twenty when the film was shot, but, already an experienced stage actress, she gives a most sensitive performance. Chaplin is also well supported by his son Sydney, Nigel Bruce of Dr. Watson fame, and, in a casting decision both brilliant and moving, Buster Keaton, to share Calvero's final moments of triumph on the stage.

The achievement of *Limelight* stems from Chaplin's separation of the stylized, presentational performance of the onstage acts and the offstage life of the character. As Calvero in real life, he gives a strong dramatic performance, building on his similar work in the serious scenes in *Monsieur Verdoux*. Onstage he is at his flamboyant best: singing, dancing, miming, and delivering rapid patter routines with comic abandon. Dividing the serious and comic poles of his performance this way allows Chaplin to relax into each; without the burden of being constantly funny, he is able to explore new depths in his serious characterization while indulging his flair for comic invention when he goes onstage.

Backstage films have always fascinated moviegoers, but frequently the theatrical performances in them are presented in a ludicrous or unrealistic manner. As noted earlier, it is difficult to translate the qualities of theatre into cinema. One film that succeeds spectacularly well in this regard is the 1945 French masterwork *Children of Paradise (Les Enfants du Paradis)*, a biography of Baptiste Deburau, a celebrated nineteenth-century French mime. Chaplin had seen and admired the French epic when it became an international sensation in the mid-1940s.

Its opening contrasts life with art as the dreamy Deburau, sitting listlessly on a barrel in front of his theatre, snaps to alertness to reenact a scene he has just witnessed, in which a fat man ogles a pretty girl as a thief picks his pocket. To get the girl off the hook when the fat man calls for a policeman to arrest her, the mime acts out the scene for the assembled crowd. Deburau (played by the great French mime Jean-Louis Barrault) fluidly portrays all the characters, much as Chaplin had done in the song-mime of *Modern Times*. At one point he becomes the fat man and the thief simultaneously, showing the thief's hand creeping around the fat man's body to lift the watch from his pocket; it's an ingenious one-person variation on Chaplin's body part transformation gag.

As Deburau rises to theatrical success, *Children of Paradise* continues to contrast the real lives of the characters with their onstage performances. The mime sequences, which total about fifteen minutes of the nearly three-and-a-quarter-hour film, are seen on two levels: as beautiful, highly stylized mime, accompanied effectively by music; and as artistic transmutations of the real-life relationships between the characters. By this device the film succeeds in bringing the stage performances to life in a way that is totally engrossing.

Limelight's four music hall performances are well worked into the story of the film because each of them demonstrates the old comedian's multifaceted art stirring back into existence. While they have a less direct relationship to the offstage lives of the characters than the mime sequences in *Children of Paradise*, they are strongly connected thematically. Three of them are about the power and wonder of love and sex, which is a subtext of the scenes between Calvero and the ballerina he takes in.

The film begins outside Calvero's apartment building. Three young children (Chaplin's first three children with Oona: Geraldine, Michael, and Josephine) listen to an organ grinder cranking out a tune on the street. In a series of dissolves the camera tracks swiftly through the building into a room, where a girl lies sprawled unconscious on her bed. She holds a pill bottle in her hand; the oven door is open, the window closed, and the opening under the door is sealed with a rolled-up towel.

Chaplin makes his entrance stumbling down the street, and hops nimbly, if a little unsteadily, up the steps. He has great difficulty inserting his key into the door lock, evoking his countless incarnations as a comic drunk—except that now there's no square black mustache on his face, and instead of the familiar inebriated swell we see a white-haired sixty-year-old man. For any viewer familiar with Chaplin's work, this first appearance is at once a nostalgic evocation of times past and a bracing reminder of just how much time has passed—it's been nearly four decades since this comic drunk first staggered onto the screen. Chaplin can't resist a drunken gag or two as of old, holding onto the door as if he's steadying *it* instead of the other way around. But the girl dying inside the building robs the scene of its comedy, and so does the fact that Chaplin shoots the scene at sound speed. If he fell, this comical drunk might hurt himself, and we'd hear the thudding sound.

Inside, Calvero pauses on the stairs to light his cigar. Looking directly at the camera—something he will do more in *Limelight* than in any of his other sound films—he unsuccessfully tries to strike his match on the seat of his pants. He smells something unpleasant and, in yet another Chaplin transformation gag, sniffs his cigar and checks the bottom of his shoe. Noticing the rolled up towel under Terry's door, he breaks in and discovers the unconscious girl. He struggles against his inebriated state to drag her from the room, then trots off to find a doctor.

In both *The Kid* and *Limelight*, Chaplin's character is reluctantly drawn into caring for a helpless person, but the intervening years have wrought a major change in Chaplin's filmmaking. In the silent film, the situation is established in a few brief scenes of eloquent and funny mime. In a nicely choreographed round robin, the Tramp unsuccessfully tries to foist the Kid off by slipping it into a perambulator with another baby. The other baby's indignant mother doesn't go for that, however, so he tricks a doddering old man into holding it and runs off. The oldster, in turn, slips the baby back into the perambulator when the mother isn't watching. She discovers it just as the Tramp passes by, and thrashes him soundly with her umbrella and makes him take it back. All too human, he momentarily considers dropping the child down a sewer, but gives in to the inevitable when he finds a note begging the recipient to love and care for the child.

In *Limelight* there is considerably less choreography and many more words required to establish the situation. Chaplin adds what humor he can, but he doesn't find much, other than a few mild gags that result from the way he plays the scene drunk, and even these are mostly verbal. For example, to explain Terry's presence in his apartment to the scandalized landlady, he says, "You have a leaking gas pipe . . . I mean, that room has a leaking gas pipe." Unfortunately, the humor of this and later exchanges with the landlady is dampened by the reactions of the actress, Marjorie Bennett, who gives the weakest supporting performance in the film. Later, when he's late with the rent money, she confronts him sternly as he enters the building. "Just the man I want to see," she exclaims. "How thrilling!" he replies with a lascivious grin. He continues flirting, with Verdoux's wolfish charm, but because her responses are pallid the exchange remains more expositional than charming.

Many critics who were longtime Chaplin fans, notably Walter Kerr,[3] deplored Chaplin's capitulation to verbal rather than visual storytelling. For Kerr, the wrongheaded development that began with *The Great Dictator*'s final speech continued into the thesis-driven *Monsieur Verdoux* and climaxed in the melodramatic *Limelight*. His disappointment is understandable; it would have been wonderful had Chaplin seen fit to crank out a few more stunningly brilliant physical comedies. The stage scenes in *Limelight* demonstrate that he still had the chops to pull it off. But writing two dialogue-driven scripts had evidently whetted Chaplin's appetite for telling stories in words; before he even began on the screenplay he made unusually elaborate preparations, in the form of a lengthy treatment in the form of a novel that gives extensive background stories for the main characters.

In addition, in the late 1940s Chaplin had gotten involved with an upstart theatre company in Los Angeles begun by two young men, his son Sydney and Jerry Epstein. Chaplin started bringing his celebrity friends to their productions, and before long the Circle Theatre attracted national publicity and became a hot ticket. Chaplin couldn't stay on the sidelines for long, however, and soon enough he was helping to direct—or, more accurately, redirect, since he tended to come in late in the rehearsal process to add his input. He worked on period comedies like Richard Brinsley Sheridan's *The School for Scandal*, modern melodramas like Somerset Maugham's *Rain*, and avant-garde pieces like Albert Camus's *Caligula*. Epstein later fondly recalled Chaplin's directorial methods, which consisted, as always, of acting out all the parts himself while keeping up a running monologue about underlying principles, occasionally stopping to illustrate his points with dead-on impersonations of the actors of his youth.[4] Working in live theatre again stirred Chaplin's theatrical memories, and helping the actors to bring stage dialogue to life surely influenced both the literate script he wrote for *Limelight* and his own richly nuanced performance.

Theatricality infuses *Limelight*. While Kerr and others criticized Chaplin for falling in love with the sound of his own voice and wanting to be a sage rather than a comedian, almost every word in *Limelight* is dramatically justified by the interwoven story of Calvero the failed comedian and Terry the failed ballerina. Having trapped them in a room together, a suitably theatrical conceit, the plot begins unfolding as Calvero must do psychological detective work to uncover the cause of her hysterical paralysis. This takes the form of a series of bedside chats. In the first of them he upbraids her for trying to do away with herself, holding forth rather pompously about the value of life, but Chaplin mocks his own verbosity when Terry, still groggy from her suicide attempt, simply falls asleep on him. Later, Calvero holds a pair of large raw fish he's just gotten from the market as Terry tearfully reveals that she can't walk. As they talk Calvero walks around trying to get the smell off his fingers, defusing another potentially melodramatic scene.[5] And so it goes, the story unfolding through canny, plot-driven dialogue enlivened by bits of business. Though he occasionally seems a bit smug, Calvero's tendency to spout pithy little homilies about life and art is perfectly in character for a down-on-his-luck former headliner whose life seems to have passed him by.

Fish and philosophy. Calvero with Terry (Claire Bloom).

Drink plays a unique role in this film. With the exception of *City Lights*, in which the millionaire recognizes Charlie only when drunk, it's the first time in a Chaplin film that alcohol has been more than simply an excuse for physical comedy. There's a bit of that, as we've seen, but the various drunken scenes in *Limelight* aren't played for laugh-out-loud comedy. Calvero remains drunk during the whole afternoon and evening of the first day to lighten the exposition, then stops drinking to properly care for the girl. At first it appears that his drunkenness is a symptom of his disengagement and anesthesia; much as Barrault shakes off his dreamy state at the beginning of *Children of Paradise*, Calvero sobers up and enters the stream of life, opening himself once again to the possibilities of love and loss.

But drink plays a deeper role than that, as we soon discover. When Terry asks Calvero about his drinking, he explains that he started because as he grew older he acquired a feeling of "sad dignity" that was fatal for his comedy; he lost touch with his audience, but found that when he got drunk he was funny again. The trouble is, this resulted in a heart attack, placing Calvero in a neat double bind: If he drinks to be funny he'll weaken his heart, which might kill him; if he doesn't, he'll die a failure.

This situation is another good example of the convoluted way the film both reflects and refracts reality. Chaplin, who never touched a drop to play the comic drunk, turns into Calvero, who has to be drunk to be funny, a fun-house mirror reversal. On the other hand, the drunken Calvero also summons up the shade of Chaplin's father. Chaplin was convinced that his father's alcoholism and early death resulted from his profession, which required performers to mingle with the audience at the music hall. The film reverberates with such overlapping echoes of Chaplin's personal and artistic past.

It is when Calvero speaks about the theatre that he seems to merge most directly with his creator:

> Terry: But you're not the great comedian?
> Calvero: I was.
> (later)
> Terry: To hear you talk no one would ever think you were a comedian.
> Calvero: I'm beginning to realize that. I can't get a job.
> Terry: What a sad business, being funny.
> Calvero: Very sad, if they won't laugh. But it's a thrill when they do. To look out there, see them all laughing. To hear that roar go up, waves of laughter coming at you . . .

And so on, telling of his love of his craft, his ambivalence toward his audience, and his despair over his failure.

The first two times Calvero performs in the film are in his dreams. As he drifts off to sleep, three street musicians play a haunting melody.[6] Calvero strides onto the stage dressed as a lion tamer, complete with top hat, tails, checkered vest, jodhpurs, thigh-high boots, and a whip, which he snaps smartly as he sings "The Animal Trainer," describing his fortuitous discovery "while searching through my underwear" of a pair of fleas, who have become his latest attraction. The song is another reminder of Chaplin's father, the music hall singer of funny, risqué songs. When Calvero finishes singing the song he brings a small table forward, labeled "Phyllis and Henry/Performing Fleas." Lifting the lid from a small pillbox, he cracks his whip, peers in, and says:

The Flea Trainer, 1952.

> Phyllis! Henry! Stop that! What do you think you're doing? You ought to be ashamed of yourself—fighting like that.

Chaplin's appalled expression as he looks into the box makes it clear that the fleas aren't just fighting, and the sexual reference reinforces the song's lyrics, which allude to Calvero's troubles with women and drink, and describe the intimate relationship between him and his little performers. The camera zooms in closer as he commands them to hop from the back of one hand to another. Inevitably he has obedience problems; Phyllis jumps onto his eye several times, and, despite his threat to squeeze her between his fingers, disappears up his sleeve and down his pants. "Come out at once! You go too far! Crazy little creature you!" When he finally fishes her out, he exclaims, "That's not Phyllis!" But Phyllis makes herself known, biting him in the rear end and "forcing" him to make his exit. As Calvero returns for his bow, the camera closes in on his shocked face, and we see that the auditorium he faces is empty. Dissolve to Calvero, sitting up in bed with the same haunted expression.

In addition to deploring Chaplin's abandonment of visual storytelling, Kerr was dismayed by the fact that he devoted three of his four music hall acts to songs, dance, and comic patter rather than mime. In fact, Chaplin's movements provide an eloquent mimetic accompaniment to all the songs. The problem with the flea number, strangely enough, isn't with the song—which is amusing and well performed,—but with the flea mime routine that follows, which is uncharacteristically lackluster for Chaplin. This must be ascribed partly to the verbal humor he incorporates into the routine, which requires him to shoot at sound speed. As a result, the bit seems rather sluggish, and the fleas don't come to life as well as they might. It's not that it's bad; it's just not as good as it might be.

We know this because Chaplin filmed a silent version of the routine in 1919 for an unreleased film called *The*

Professor.[7] There, Chaplin's invisible fleas seem much more real because the "act" takes place in a setting where we would expect to find fleas—a grimy doss-house. Chaplin's character, the foul-tempered Professor Bosco, enters with his precious flea circus in a box. Before bedding down he feels one of the company members crawling around under his jacket. He commands it to come down his sleeve, and we follow its progress down his arm through his supple motions. He decides to put it through its paces before returning it to its box. The snap in Chaplin's undercranked head movements and his characteristic precision bring the little creature vividly to life as it leaps from hand to hand.

But the routine is just beginning. As soon as Bosco beds down his errant insect, the man in the bed next to him (Henry Bergman) starts scratching his huge beard. Bosco quickly counts his troupe and discovers that none of the precious beasts are missing; nevertheless, he plucks the flea from Bergman's beard just to double-check, and returns it when it proves to be a stranger. But as he stretches out on the bed he accidentally kicks his box onto the floor, knocking the lid open. All the sleeping derelicts suddenly erupt in furious scratching as the fleas turn the place into an itchy bedlam.

All at once Bosco becomes a real circus performer, snapping his whip furiously as though he's in a cage full of snarling lions. He rounds up his fleas and orders them back into the box with threats and menacing gestures. The residents sit up and gape at the impromptu spectacle. Bosco coaxes the last one out from under a bed, and when the stubborn thing refuses to obey his instructions he brutally kicks it along the floor, then decides to recap a "death-defying" portion of his act by stepping over it in the manner of a tightrope walker, as the presumably

The Flea Trainer, 1919. Professor Bosco commands his flea to jump through the hoop. *The Professor.*

cowed flea hops back and forth across his feet. He then commands it to hop from the back of his hand into the box, but it hops onto Bergman's beard instead. He plucks it back, makes it hop into the box, then gives the glaring Bergman a "zip it up" gesture to preclude him from making any comments about the fleas. Bosco goes to sleep, but a mangy dog enters, noses into the box, and exits scratching, the company of performers in tow, as the hapless professor chases them down the alley.[8]

It is a beautifully realized routine, rich in gags and incident, and Chaplin's later version pales in comparison. As a solo stage routine, with verbal humor substituting for the visual, it's artificial and much less funny. The only time it even approaches its earlier incarnation is when Calvero exits spasmodically, as though he's being bitten, introducing the broader physicality that made the 1919 version so effective.

The following day Calvero learns more about Terry, including the fact that she was a dancer. That night he dreams up an entirely new routine that includes her. Her presence better grounds the dream—and the act—in filmic reality. He begins again with a music hall song, "Spring Is Here," against a backdrop of a forest scene. Like the flea song and patter, the spring song deals with sex, but this time much more explicitly. It describes the various creatures, from birds to whales to worms, who are all "wagging their tails for love." Chaplin carries the Tramp's flexible cane and wears comedic tramp clothes, but he's not the Tramp. He sports a straw boater and wears an upturned, split comic mustache and the heavy theatrical makeup of the stock unshaven tramp. After the verse of his song he sings the chorus, consisting entirely of the word *love* repeated again and again, and at the same time he executes a lightning series of kick steps. He then goes into a little dance break, including the backward glide from *Modern Times* and a nifty vaudeville fan kick that Buster Keaton had done in *The Playhouse* in 1921. The action is so brisk during the "lovelovelove" chorus and dance that it appears to be slightly undercranked, although it's hard to be certain.

Calvero then does a soft-shoe shuffle along the stage until he is interrupted by Terry, also heavily made-up. She wears a ballet costume and carries a parasol. They launch into a delightful quick-patter routine. Calvero begins reciting his "Ode to a Worm," but is stopped short by the realistic Terry, who explains that a worm, contrary to his poem, cannot smile. "How do you know?" he asks her, "Have you ever appealed to its sense of humor?" When he sneezes, she says, "Gesundheit." "Certainly does," he snaps." Terry is confused by this response. "The dress," he says with a leer. "It certainly

As a comedy tramp, but not *the* Tramp—although the familiar cane and big shoes are a reminder.

goes on tight." While these jokes seem rather tame in print, Chaplin's fierce comic brio makes them work well. She postures prettily as he archly banters away, grinning at her lasciviously.

The routine parodies all the serious talk in the film by bringing the discourse decidedly down to earth. Calvero puts his arm around her waist and solemnly intones, "I'm beginning to grasp the meaning of life." "You're sensitive, you feel things," she declares, which prompts him to hop backward, slapping his leg with his cane. "Now, don't encourage me!" "So few people have the capacity to feel," she informs him. "Or the opportunity!" he quips, beating a tattoo with his feet and stamping like a bull.

Calvero regally presents her with his feather duster as a bouquet, then escorts her off with a grand, high-stepping exit, a moment of bold theatricality that is unexpectedly quite moving. The two characters, so thwarted in real life, not only become whole in Calvero's stage routine, they become a romantic couple as well, making light of their sexual attraction at the same time as they celebrate it. The lovely musical theme quietly underscoring the routine adds to its emotional quality,[9] and this time the audience applause doesn't dissolve into a shot of an empty house.

Calvero and Terry make their grand exit.

Inspired by his dreams and encouraged by his own pep talks, Calvero responds to a long-awaited summons by his agent. There his fragile confidence is battered by the agent's well-intended but cruel reality check. He informs Calvero in no uncertain terms that he's a has-been who should be grateful for any work at all. When Calvero sarcastically suggests that perhaps he should perform under a different name, the agent readily agrees, to Calvero's dismay.

For the first time we see Calvero before a real audience in the film, and his performance is a disaster. He halfheartedly sings the ending of his "Sardine Song," which deals with reincarnation, reinforcing the film's theme of rejuvenation and the passing of the torch to a younger generation. But the song and his tired jokes are met with indifference by the audience, and he gives up and leaves the stage as the audience itself begins leaving. It's a nightmare scenario familiar to any performer. Removing his makeup as the other performers leave the dressing room, Calvero is so close to tears that he can barely mutter his good-byes. As he lowers the makeup towel from his face we see the same shocked expression he wore at the end of his first dream, when he realized that his audience had vanished; now it really has.

Lest the reader think that, aside from *Verdoux*, failure was outside the experience of the eminently successful comedian, in his autobiography Chaplin himself cites a number of disasters from his stage career that he found amusing—in retrospect. Charles Jr. recounts another that occurred closer to the time of *Limelight*:

> For my father, who was at his best among a circle of close friends, to come out cold before a strange audience and be funny was excruciating torture, with the dread of almost certain failure.

After his disastrous performance.

> He tried it once at the request of the head of the personnel division of one of the big aircraft corporations near Los Angeles. One noon in the company's open-air theatre where all the workers were gathered with their lunches, he laid, I think, the biggest egg of his career. No one laughed, no one clapped, apparently no one was even watching him. Everyone was too busy eating. My father came out of the experience unnerved and shaking.
>
> "I'll never do it again, never," he said. "I can't. It's not my kind of entertaining."[10]

Returning to the apartment, Calvero breaks down as he tells Terry, "They walked out on me. They haven't done that since I was a beginner. The cycle is complete . . . I'm finished, through." As he sits sobbing at the table he and Terry switch roles. Unable to bear seeing him accept defeat, she rises from her chair to give *him* a pep talk, then suddenly realizes what she's done. "Calvero . . . look . . . I'm walking . . . I'm walking!" she cries. The melodramatic moment is well played by Bloom, and the camera moves away from Calvero and in on her, laughing and crying at the same time.

Terry soon obtains a job in the corps de ballet of a prominent theatre. Earlier in the film we learned that the root of her psychological problem was discovering that her sister supported her by working as a prostitute. The guilt and shame Terry felt resulted in her depression and hysterical paralysis. Now, in the opulent theatre where she dances, a prostitute circulates among the well-dressed gentlemen, offering her services. It reinforces the theme—implicit in many Chaplin films, but most prominent in *Verdoux* and *Limelight*—that protecting one's loved ones sometimes involves not only sacrifice, but personal humiliation and degradation.

Calvero keeps house while Terry works at the ballet, but one night she returns home to find him having a drunken party with his musician friends, the same picturesque trio that accompanied his dreams; the landlady staggers in with more beer, and Marjorie Bennett acquits herself well this time—evidently she, too, has to be drunk to be funny. Terry tolerates Calvero's lapse with good grace.

He goes with her when she auditions for a lead role in a new ballet, and she turns out to be a brilliant dancer (her dancing is doubled by Melissa Hayden, a principal with the New York City Ballet). Calvero sits alone backstage as everyone leaves. The lights are turned out, leaving him in deep shadow. The lighting, here and elsewhere in *Limelight*, is appropriately theatrical and highly effective. Calvero is moved to tears by Terry's artistry, and she chooses the moment to declare her love. He laughs it off but doesn't refuse her offer to set him up with a clown job in the new ballet *The Death of Columbine*.

The romantic plot thickens as Terry runs into the ballet's composer, Neville, played by Chaplin's son Sydney, at lunch. They have met each other before; before her breakdown Terry worked at a stationers, and she was fired for giving the impoverished young composer extra blank music sheets and extra change. They fell in love, but their quiet affection was unspoken. She had spoken of this relationship to Calvero during her recuperation, and he predicted that they were destined for each other. But now, over lunch, Terry informs the crestfallen composer that she intends to marry Calvero.[11]

At the first rehearsal for the ballet Calvero is skeptical about his role, which is to do funny clown tricks for the dying Columbine. The old comedian knows it is impossible to be funny in such a situation. Of course, in any other Chaplin film this would be a perfect setup for a riotous comedy in which he turns the ballet into a shambles, much as he upset the ritualized performances in *The Circus* with his spontaneous behavior. But this isn't a comedy, and the ballet can't become a shambles. The plot requires that Terry have a chance for stardom, and that Calvero endure one last professional humiliation, completing their role reversal. So, as the ballet begins, Chaplin simply performs several halfhearted bits with two clown foils (one of them, a clown cop, is played by Charles Jr.). It's one thing to see him fail as a comic singer, but seeing him do boring clown comedy is more distressing.[12] The premise, of course, allows Bloom, who lies decorously dying as the clowns go through their motions, to appear in the ballet without actually having to dance.

The ballet corps enters as the toe-dancing spirit of Columbine. She's the only one who can see them, and she longs to join their dance. Since a parody of ballet dancing was central to Chaplin's conception of his Tramp character, and since he so often lampooned pretension in all its forms, it is strange to see this sort of melodramatic ballet action played totally straight in one of his films. The corps sequence is short, though, and when they depart Terry is mercifully allowed to expire.

The curtain closes, and a spectacular overhead shot shows the stage being reset as a graveyard. There Harlequin, played by New York City Ballet dancer André Eglevsky, does an athletic solo, which features an impressive series of entrechats, and falls on Columbine's grave. The corps returns, whereupon Columbine is supposed to reenter in a burst of glory for a triumphant postmortem solo and duet with Harlequin. However, before her entrance Terry has a panic attack in the wings. Calvero, the seasoned professional, slaps her soundly across the face and orders her onto the stage. "Whoever you are, whatever it is," he prays behind a flat, "just keep her going—that's all." When a burly stagehand discovers him on his knees he mutters an excuse about losing his button. Predictably, Terry is a triumph, and so is the ballet.

The Death of Columbine recapitulates the key elements in the film: Calvero's inability to be funny in front of an audience and Terry's near death and resurrection, which is replayed both onstage and in the wings, when she has to be "resuscitated" yet again by Calvero. It also benefits from Chaplin's beautiful score, the main theme of which became the perennial song hit "Eternally." But what works in theatres for a specialized audience of ballet fans tends not to work very well on film, and this film is no exception, even with the excellent dancing of Eglevsky and Hayden. However much it may connect with the film thematically, at ten minutes the scene begins to drag, despite cutaways to the offstage drama in the wings and several handsome overhead shots. The steps and gestures, while executed with bravura technique, are drawn from the standard cookie-cutter ballet repertoire, and are dramatically inert in this context. Chaplin, who was a master at making stage skills work cinematically, ought to have known better.

Calvero is thrilled by Terry's success but depressed over his own predictable failure in the ill-conceived role. He leaves the after-show reception early and gets so drunk that he collapses just inside the front door of his apartment building. There he suffers further humiliation as he overhears Terry talking with Neville outside. Neville professes his love—their love. Neville says what Calvero already knows—that Terry's love for Calvero is really pity and a sense of obligation. But she insists that it's more. She loves his soul, "his sweetness, his sadness—nothing will ever separate me from that." Nothing, that is, except Calvero himself, who knows that Terry and Neville belong together, for it is the natural order of things referred to in the film's opening subtitle, "The glamour of limelight, from which age must pass as youth enters."

The next morning the reviews come out, confirming Terry's stardom. Chaplin could be speaking to his younger self as he asks her how it feels to wake up famous—he actually *is* speaking to his younger self, in the form of a photo of the young Chaplin displayed prominently on the wall behind him. "Have a good cry and enjoy it. It only happens once." But Terry is crying because she understands that her success has created a barrier between them. She begs him to marry her. Calvero, unconsciously mirroring his pose in the photo, tells her again that it's out of the question because of their age difference, and reiterates that she is destined for Neville. He berates himself for not having summoned up the courage to leave her before it came to this.

Calvero's performance is deemed inadequate by the ballet's producer, Postant (Nigel Bruce).[13] When informed that the clown is actually Calvero, and that Terry intends to marry him, Postant delivers the film's funniest line: "What, that old reprobate? Bless my soul, there's hope for me yet." He immediately reverses his decision to fire Calvero, but it's too late; outside the theatre Calvero meets the man who's been sent to be his replacement. This is the final straw, and he finally summons up the courage to pack up and leave.

Time passes. Terry (in a dancing montage featuring Melissa Hayden) becomes an international sensation. We next come upon Calvero outside a pub, dressed in multicolored patchwork jacket and large top hat, strumming a banjo and singing his "lovelovelove" song with his three musician friends. Going inside to pass the hat, he runs into Neville, who tells him that Terry is still longing for his return. Sydney plays very well against his father, his deep voice expressive as the two men talk with feeling about the woman they love. Postant shows up and is appalled to find the former star busking, but Calvero professes to be happy with his new life:

> All the world's a stage, and this one's the most legitimate. . . . There's something about working the streets I like. It's the tramp in me, I suppose.

Indeed, he looks healthy, happy, and quite spiffy in his ridiculous outfit. The scene is skillfully staged to minimize the portentous line about the tramp—just as Calvero says it, Postant jumps up to offer him work, an offer

Calvero cheerfully brushes off. He is no pathetic wreck, thank you very much.

Neville, of course, tells Terry about Calvero's return, and it doesn't take her long to spot him from a passing cab as he enters another pub. He seems genuinely delighted to see her and invites her to sit down. But when she speaks of her love for him, his cheery facade crumbles, and we see again how easy it would be for him to fall into the arms of this adoring woman. "Calvero, come back. You've got to come back," she pleads. "I can't—I've got to go forward. That's progress." For the second time he breaks down in front of her. Chaplin's acting in this scene is gut wrenching.

With an effort he pulls himself together when Terry explains that a benefit performance has been arranged for him by Postant. Such benefits were common in music hall, the only form of social security for aged or infirm performers. Calvero doesn't want charity. What he wants is to prove himself after his years of failure and obscurity: "I would like the chance just to show them I'm not through yet." He tells her about "a comedy act for myself and my friend. It's a sort of musical satire . . . it's very funny, got a lot of funny business."

And so it is. But before we get to it we're treated to the film's most extraordinary backstage scene, as Calvero sits sharing the dressing room with his friend, who turns out to be Buster Keaton. Seeing the two silent film greats together is an electrifying moment for anyone who loves film comedy, and Chaplin capitalizes on it by giving Buster a great opening line, "I never thought we'd come to this." Buster immediately pulls us back to filmic reality by continuing on in his gravelly voice, "Here we have the star dressing room without a dresser. Oh, well, I guess we can put up with it for one night." Calvero smiles indulgently and continues making up. The stage manager comes in and says it's just like old times, and when he leaves Buster says, "If anyone else says it's like the old times I'll jump out the window." Whereupon Postant pops in says just that. Buster simply excuses himself and walks out of the room, leaving the old impresario and the old comedian to talk over the old times.

Postant: In those days you were drunk instead of sober.
Calvero: I'm supposed to be funnier when I'm drunk.
Postant: You were killing yourself.
Calvero: You know what they say—anything for a laugh.

When Postant leaves and he's left alone, Calvero seals his fate by taking a drink. Terry enters and knows instantly. She expresses no disapproval, only concern. But Calvero is determined that his performance be a success, whatever the risk to his health: "Not that I care for success—but I don't want another failure."

His melancholy mood deepens as Terry tells him they'll soon have a home in the country together.

Calvero: This is my home. . . . I don't like it. Everyone's so kind to me. It makes me feel isolated. Even you make me feel isolated.
Terry: Why do you say that?
Calvero: I don't know. I really don't know.
Terry: Remember, I love you.
Calvero: (cynically) Really?
Terry: Really! With all my heart.

Calvero strides onstage for his flea act. We see it begin and end, and it is indeed a great success—but we also learn that the audience has been padded with professional "appreciators" to ensure a good response, and that Terry has gone so far as to rehearse them in the appropriate places to laugh. As we will find out later, Calvero is well aware of the claque as well. How can he prove himself when he can't trust the audience response? Chaplin paints himself into a corner, and the only way out is for Calvero to top himself with a show-stopping act so outstanding that it blows everyone away. Much as *Modern Times* builds inexorably to the moment when Chaplin breaks his long cinematic silence, so *Limelight* builds to the moment when Calvero must show his two audiences—the audience within the film and the live audience in the movie theater—that he still has the stuff.

After a proper, high-energy rendition of his full "Sardine Song"[14] Calvero exits with a theatrical flourish that sets the stage for his final routine: He executes a dance step, somersaults into a split, "squeezes" himself back up to a standing position, and trots off. The sequence seems impossibly nimble, and it is; in actuality, Chaplin does these movements in reverse—he trots onstage backward, slides down into a split, turns a backward somersault, rises, and does his dance step—and then reverses the film in the lab. Because of Chaplin's careful reverse-action choreography, the artifice is not apparent (although his jacket gives it away slightly when it defies gravity and flaps in the wrong direction during his somersault). As he had done in his similarly reversed bricklaying routine in *Payday* thirty years earlier, Chaplin merges simple film technology with cleverly conceived movement to lend himself comically improbable skill. He undercranks the shot as well, so that he moves with the silken grace of old. Chaplin slyly precedes his stunt with a second undercranked shot of the audience applauding his act. The applause on the soundtrack, along with the uninterrupted music, provides naturalistic sounds and continuity that help the two undercranked shots blend into the larger sound sequence. All the elements combine to make the transition from the sound to the silent film world virtually undetectable.

When Calvero is called back for an encore, he has to switch into a different costume while the audience waits. For his quick change Chaplin resorts to the oldest trick in film history: Calvero and Buster walk behind a screen, only to emerge a moment later with Calvero fully costumed. This little bit of film magic sets the stage for the routine, a series of "magical" gags that will be accomplished, as ever, with a combination of physical skill and filmic trickery.

As they walk onstage, Buster, wearing thick spectacles, myopically bumps into the piano. The first chord he plays brings his thick sheaf of sheet music cascading down into his lap. Calvero is having problems of his own. When he lifts the violin to play, his high collar covers the lower half of his face, and he rips it off impatiently.

As Buster continues to struggle with his cascading music sheets, Calvero walks back to the piano and taps the lid impatiently with his bow. But when he walks forward again he trips over his own foot, and for some reason this causes his right leg to shrink upward into his pants leg. To accomplish this illusion, Chaplin contrived a pot-bellied costume that holds his pants far enough in front of him that we don't see his knee bending as he draws his leg up. The illusion is startling, convincing and very funny.

Calvero is able to kick his leg back out to its normal length, but when he turns around to admonish the still-struggling Buster, he trips again, causing his leg to shorten once more. Calvero puts his violin and bow down on the piano lid and holds his hand against the

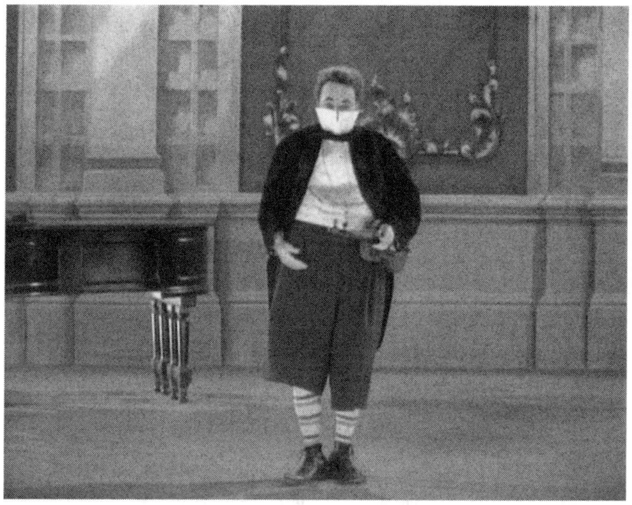

A high-collar shirt.

The vanishing leg.

Buster struggles with his sheet music.

Both legs shorten.

piano, enabling him to keep his balance as he kicks his leg out to its normal length, only to watch it slowly retract again up his pants leg. He looks around in alarm and tries again, then walks forward with a lopsided gait. He's able to pull the leg out by crouching down, stepping on his right foot with his left, and unbending, stretching the stubborn leg out to its full length again.

When Calvero walks back to the piano to retrieve his violin, he trips once again, and once again his leg shortens. After a couple of futile attempts to kick it out, he gives up and picks up his violin and bow—but now *both* his legs have shortened! He walks forward, appalled by this latest development. No matter—he puts his violin on the floor and passes his bow between his legs, then pulls himself upward by the crotch (a trick he first did—less effectively—in *The Circus*).

The costume is a brilliant comic contraption on a par with the hall of mirrors in *The Circus* or the feeding machine in *Modern Times* and would have made the reputation of any music hall comedian. But comic perfection didn't come easily—Chaplin reshot the leg-shortening sequence several weeks after the initial shoot with Keaton, and then again several months later. Some of these retakes were undercranked, and possibly remain in the film, although it is difficult to verify this from either the existing studio records or the film itself.

The "tuning" sequence that follows relies on comic sound effects, and it's not as strong. Buster's "A" mysteriously rises in pitch, causing Calvero to break his strings noisily as he tries to tune his violin. Calvero then tries to tune the piano, and ends up snapping the piano wires as well. Snipping and discarding the tangled mess solves the problem with Harpo-like logic, and Calvero magically plays an arpeggio down the keyboard.

The missing violin.

The mad fiddler.

During all this, Buster has accidentally stepped on the violin, which attaches to his foot like a snowshoe. In searching around for the instrument, Chaplin and Keaton "speak" to each other with uncharacteristically overemphatic gestures, a curious lapse into clichéd pantomime that is reminiscent of the bad circus clown routines in *The Circus*; it's the one false note in the act. They finally discover the violin on Buster's foot when he crosses his legs. Calvero braces his foot on Buster's chest and yanks the violin off, knocking Buster off his piano stool in the process. Disgusted to find his instrument destroyed, Calvero tosses it away and whips a "fresh" one from behind his back (a cutaway to Buster allows Chaplin to preset the extra violin behind his back). Finally, the duo begins their musical number.

With an expression of maniacal glee, Calvero tears into a furious, gypsy-like dance tune. His playing motions, in a medium close-up shot, are so perfectly synchronized with the music that only a trained musician can detect that he's not actually playing what we're hearing.

Calvero suddenly segues into a touching, slow melody, pausing to murmur "You darling" (the only spoken words in the routine) and kiss his violin. Both he and Buster are so overcome that they break down sobbing against the piano. Abruptly, Calvero whips around and tears into the fast theme again. It's so fast that Buster spins his stool out from under him, but he falls to the floor without missing a note.[15] We cut to a longer shot showing both of them playing even more furiously, courtesy of more well-masked undercranking: Calvero finishes his violin theme with a flourish, his perfectly synchronized final bow stroke so violent that it causes him to spin around and somersault into the orchestra pit. As clearly indicated in the shooting log, Chaplin shoots this "payoff" shot at twenty frames per second, a 20 percent speedup of his action.

As Calvero vanishes from sight, we hear him crashing into the bass drum, only to resume playing immediately. He continues fiddling away as he is lifted from the pit in the drum and is carried triumphantly offstage as the audience goes wild. Like the reverse-action exit shot that preceded the routine, the undercranked shot of Chaplin falling fits seamlessly into the sequence.

Apart from a welcoming round of applause at the beginning, this is the first time we hear the audience reacting during the act. Instead, up until the moment when Calvero and Keaton play their duet, we hear only a lilting tune playing very softly in the background and the ambient sounds of the two comedians as they go about their funny business. By omitting the sounds of the theatre audience, Chaplin brilliantly insinuates his real audience—the live audience in the movie theatre—into his film. The "blank space" on the soundtrack is filled in by the spontaneous laughter of the movie audience, rather than by the prompted laughter of the audience within the film. *We* are the audience that confirms Calvero's triumph.

But Chaplin's triumph is even greater. Exploding the common critical myth that his direction is static and stagy, he gives us a carefully constructed cinematic illusion of a stage act that could never have been performed on a stage. Skillful "invisible" editing, coupled with inspired use of synchronized music and sound effects, conspire to convince us that the stage act we're watching is real. To resurrect the vanished world of music hall, Chaplin fuses the charmed world of silent-film movement with the naturalistic world of talking-picture sound. In so doing, he conjures up his three ages of comedy before our amazed and delighted eyes.

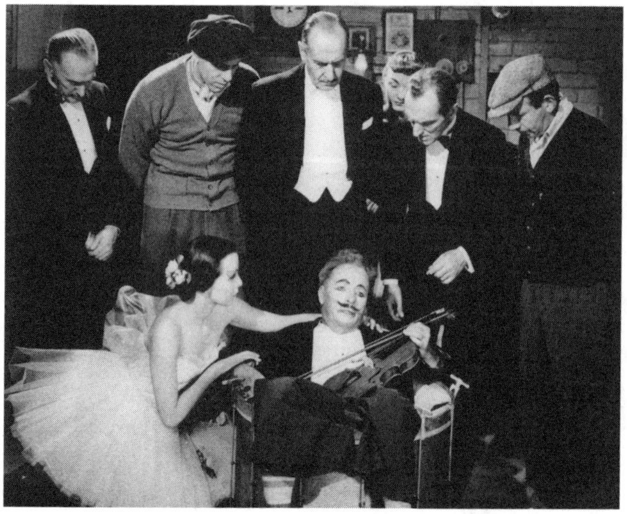

Death in the wings.

Calvero's triumph is short lived, for he has suffered a heart attack during his fall. Carried back out in the drum, he summons his strength and says, "On behalf of my partner and myself I'd like to continue—but I'm stuck." Backstage, Terry rushes to him, and he bravely assures her that they will be together, touring the world with her ballet and his comedy. He insists she go on with her act.

"I believe I'm dying, doctor," he says. "But then I don't know. I've died so many times." It's a beautiful exit line, and with his last bit of strength he asks to be moved so that he can see his protégé.

Watching Terry dance, his great colleague Keaton behind him, he finally dies as the spotlight—the limelight—follows the new dancer on her journey across the stage.

It is fitting that Chaplin's Hollywood career ends with a tribute to the music hall of his youth, a humble form of popular entertainment that gave birth to Chaplin's art, his joyful comedy of movement tinged with sadness.

Notes

1. Howard Barnes, in the *New York Herald Tribune*, cited by Gerald D. McDonald, Michael Conway, and Mark Ricci, eds., *The Complete Films of Charlie Chaplin* (Secaucus, NJ: Citadel, 1988), 215.

2. Charles Chaplin, *My Autobiography* (New York: Simon & Shuster, 1964), 459.

3. Walter Kerr, "The Lineage of *Limelight*," *Theatre Arts* 36 (November 1952): 73–75. Kerr's beautifully written article serves as a coda to his perceptive analysis of Chaplin in *The Silent Clowns* (New York: Knopf, 1975), even though it was written nearly a quarter century before.

4. Jerry Epstein, *Remembering Charlie* (New York: Doubleday, 1989). Chaplin brought Epstein on to assist him on *Limelight* and all his subsequent films.

5. As Bloom smiles before breaking into tears in this scene, she looks remarkably like Jackie Coogan in *The Kid*. She has described the process of working with Chaplin as simply one of mechanically executing his choreography.

6. One of these is Keystone comic Snub Pollard, one of Chaplin's few remaining colleagues from the early days. These musicians, incidentally, are clearly the inspiration for many such characters in Fellini's films, notably in *La Strada* and *Amarcord*.

7. This can be seen on the M2K version of *Limelight* and in the documentary *Unknown Chaplin*.

8. This six-minute sequence is so brilliant that it is a major disappointment that apparently nothing else survives from *The Professor*. In *Chaplin, His Life and Art* (London: Penguin,

2002), 314–16, David Robinson reprints a series of telegrams that the Chaplin brothers exchanged in 1922, indicating that Charlie had completed *The Professor* as a two-reel film, which the brothers used as a bargaining chip with First National when negotiating terms for *The Pilgrim*. When Chaplin got the terms he wanted, he refused to allow First National to distribute *The Professor*, even though they offered to do so. Adding to the mystery is the fact that studio records don't indicate that he ever shot anything for the film *except* this scene, which was shot over three days in 1919 and edited together by Chaplin. Yet the telegrams are clear that the film was finished and ready to be presented to First National in lieu of *The Pilgrim*. Robinson speculates that Chaplin might have assembled the film with outtakes from other productions, but it's hard to imagine how, given the new character. It's also hard to imagine what further adventures Chaplin might have dreamed up for Professor Bosco, given that he surely used up the possibilities of flea humor in the self-contained doss-house sequence.

In an interview with Margaret Hinxman for *Sight and Sound* (vol. 27, no. 2 [Autumn 1957]), Chaplin described the routine in loving detail, saying that he'd tried to work it into *The Kid* and regretting that he'd only been able to work part of it into *Limelight*. This interview is reprinted in Andrew Sarris, *Interviews with Film Directors* (New York: Avon, 1967) 86–91.

9. The slow, sad melody begins playing softly under the banter and swells as the couple exits, lending the scene an achingly melancholy quality.

10. Charles Chaplin Jr., My *Father, Charlie Chaplin* (New York: Random House, 1960), 347.

11. It is somewhat disconcerting to watch Sydney, who strongly resembles his father as a young man, play Calvero's romantic rival in the film. Add to the film's down-the-rabbit-hole crossovers of art and life the fact that Charlie met Oona when she was dating Sydney, and that Sydney and Bloom had an affair during the making of *Limelight*!

12. The most interesting thing about the scene is that Chaplin's costume and makeup evoke Joseph Grimaldi, the early nineteenth-century performer who virtually defined the clown role for English pantomimes and circuses, at the same time as Deburau was redefining the Pierrot role for French audiences. The two bits Chaplin does, squirting water into the cop's face with a plunger and stealing eggs, are typical Grimaldi gags, but Chaplin's performance deliberately fails to re-create Grimaldi's raucous comedy style.

13. The character is named for William Postance, the kindly stage manager of the Duke of York's Theatre when Chaplin played in *Sherlock Holmes* there in 1905.

14. Robinson says Chaplin does a perfect vocal parody of music hall star George Bastow in this song. Robinson, *Chaplin, His Life and Art*, 619.

15. For this stunt a rigged piano stool was substituted, with a center post that extended about eight inches into the stage floor, anchoring the stool for Buster's spin. It is tempting to think that Keaton worked out this technical detail.

CHAPTER FIFTEEN

The Banished Monarch

"I suppose I shall always be a bit of film."[1]

In the quarter century left to him after *Limelight*, Chaplin worked incessantly. He wrote his best-selling *My Autobiography* in 1964; a decade later he produced a lavishly illustrated coffee-table book entitled *My Life in Pictures*, an annotated scrapbook of his life and career. Artistically, his most enduring project was to create musical scores for ten of his silent films, all eight First Nationals plus *A Woman of Paris* and *The Circus*.

Having done away with himself in *Limelight*, Chaplin had every intention of retiring from the screen. Certainly *Limelight* would have been the perfect film with which to end his remarkable career, a valedictory work in which he reflected on being a famous comedian and exited with a knockout comedy routine. But he couldn't resist returning for two encores. And why not? By all accounts he still retained his power to delight and mesmerize those around him with his impromptu storytelling and mimicry. Robert Payne spent time with the comedian in the early 1950s while writing his adulatory book, *The Great God Pan*. Watching him at work on *Limelight* and at play in social situations, Payne wrote a portrait of an artist at the height of his powers:

> There are a hundred comic characters Chaplin could have played, if he had ever allowed himself to dwell for more than a few moments on the imps which crowd in his brain. I have seen him do things which I thought only Indian fakirs could do. His deep blue smoky eyes can change color. In a moment his splendidly arched brow can become low and mean. His face and neck can swell out until he resembles to perfection the latest news photograph of Winston Churchill, or he can suck in his cheeks until he resembles some poor devil in a prison camp, and by some unwarranted process of magic he can speak the very words they would utter. . . . The perfection of his technique is bewildering; he is over sixty, but the casual sureness of gesture and mime remains, increasing in brilliance with every day that passes.[2]

Payne went on to describe how Chaplin would keep party guests breathless with laughter with his portrayals of disastrous fishing expeditions, Russian noblewomen, Japanese bathhouse girls, and anything else that took his fancy. Unfortunately, little of this comic zest would come through in his final two films.

Long after his fortune permitted him to retire at the height of an unparalleled career; long after the technical revolution of sound movies ended the era of pure mime in movies and popular entertainment; long after his own preoccupations and choices of subject matter ceased coinciding with popular taste; long after increasing age decreased the physical vitality and resilience that were so much a part of his performances; long after reviews went from unanimous raves to cautious appreciations to outright pans; long after the public that idolized him in the United States turned against him; long after the government of the United States selected him as a political and moral enemy of the people and ultimately harassed him into exile—long after all these inducements to quit, Chaplin kept making films. He explained why succinctly when interviewed by *Life* magazine during the making of his last film, *A Countess from Hong Kong*:

> What has always sustained me—the place where I have really existed—has been my work. . . . I care about my work. It's the best thing I do.[3]

A King in New York, which came out in 1957, concludes Chaplin's filmic autobiography by telling the story of King Shahdov, a deposed monarch who seeks refuge in America. He brings with him a plan for world peace through the responsible use of nuclear power. Before long the dignified king is swindled of his fortune by his prime minister and exploited by the American advertising industry, which first tricks him into appearing on TV to promote products, then hires him to do so. When the king's altruistic plan for world peace falls on deaf ears, he leaves the country for another place of exile, Paris, to reconcile with his estranged queen.

It requires little imagination to transpose King Shahdov into King Shadow—Chaplin, King of Moving Shadows, former King of Comedy—and to see the parallels between the two exiled monarchs, both of whom find their humane political messages unheeded by an America in the grip of political, commercial, and even artistic hysteria.

Like *Limelight*, *A King in New York* resonates with allusions to Chaplin's cinematic and personal past. As in *The Circus*, he becomes a star by being unintentionally funny, in this case by accidentally ruining a TV commercial. As in *The Kid*, he takes in a young child. As in *The Gold Rush* and *Limelight*, he reflects on the capricious nature of fame and fortune. He also derives a good deal of material from his lifetime of experience as a celebrity. He re-creates one of his legendary party performances, gets mobbed repeatedly by autograph hunters, suffers mistreatment by the government, and is chased by process servers. While all this is self-referential, it also serves Chaplin's primary purpose, which is to gently chide the country that rejected him. As in *The Immigrant*, he presents a deeply ironic take on the "land of opportunity."

The film was not shown in America until 1973, but upon its original release it was widely attacked in the American press as a vicious satire of American values, the unfunny product of an embittered man who wanted to strike back at the country that had first enriched and then abandoned him. While there is both political and social criticism in the film, it is hardly vicious. Unlike *Verdoux*, which was a blanket indictment of capitalism, almost all of the political satire in *A King in New York* is directed toward McCarthyism, already on the wane by the time the film came out. The political story, however, serves mainly as a framing device. Most of the film is taken up with making fun of other aspects of American culture.

Chaplin's comic targets are the same ones lampooned on television variety shows of the period—inane TV commercials, depressing film-noir dramas, loud rock-and-roll music and the crazy behavior of the screaming female fans, plastic surgery, and whiplash-inducing wide-screen movies. This gives the film a dated quality quite absent from most of his earlier work. Worse, except for a couple of outstanding sequences, very little of it is funny.

Chaplin includes moments of physical comedy, as he had done in all of his sound films, and there are a few sequences with undercranked action, notably a pantomime nightclub act reminiscent of the clowns' shaving cream routine in *The Circus*. But Chaplin doesn't perform in the act, he just watches it, and it doesn't justify the riotous reaction of the nightclub audience. Nor are his own physical bits in the film particularly inspired. They include a brief miming of his order in a noisy restaurant and a fully clothed leap into his hotel bathtub after he's gotten sexually excited by an encounter with the young woman in the adjoining bathroom. Forgetting his old editing principles of showing such moments in single shots, he divides the leap into several—Shahdov jumping balletically into his bathroom, an awkward-looking medium shot as he twirls around and throws his bathrobe away, and another full-figure shot showing him taking the plunge. Nevertheless, it's impressive to see the sixty-eight-year-old comedian still so spry, obviously the shot's intention.

Despite these misses, Chaplin does manage to score a few comic bull's-eyes. In one of the film's best sequences, Shahdov rehearses for a live television whiskey commercial, but the dialogue of the actor playing his butler implies that the king is a lush.

> Shahdov: Thank you, Melrose. Royal Crown whiskey I always enjoy.
> Melrose: I know it, sir. Your gracious majesty is never without it.
> Shahdov: I don't like that last line.

They cut the line, but the butler keeps saying, "I know it, sir" in an insinuating way (Nicholas Tannar is the very funny actor playing Melrose). Finally, they eliminate the butler's line altogether and start the broadcast—but Shahdov chokes on the whiskey. This bit of unintentional comedy unaccountably makes him a huge star, and billboards of the apoplectic monarch are plastered all over Times Square. He is soon able to replenish his depleted bank account by endorsing other products.

One of the surprises of the film is the realistic manner in which Chaplin deals with the king's sex life. In *Limelight*, he had finessed the sexual theme by putting it into the stylized music hall numbers, while offstage he resisted the heroine's repeated offers of marriage. In *A King in New York*, he's not interested in marriage either,

The king is captivated by Dawn Addams, who's about to astound him by launching into a deodorant commercial.

The king is not pleased by his new look.

but he is comically eager for sex. Chaplin introduces a type of heroine new to his films, though common to films of the period—a sexpot who uses her charms to get her way. Dawn Addams plays a beautiful advertising executive who wangles an introduction to Shahdov by taking the hotel room next to his. As she bathes she is perfectly aware that Shahdov and his aide are taking turns peeking at her through the keyhole. The king is enchanted by her, and when they meet at a society party that's being secretly broadcast on television, she tricks him into helping her promote toothpaste and deodorant. After that, they quite casually begin an affair. It's the first such naturalistic treatment of sex in a Chaplin film since 1923's *A Woman of Paris*.

Chaplin was well aware that the sight of such May-December sex play would be offensive to some, but he was one step ahead of his audience, so he included a lengthy sequence in which he dealt with the issue comically, and at the same time skewered America's obsession with youth and beauty. After his whiskey commercial has made Shahdov famous, Addams photographs him for more ads, and she offhandedly remarks on how much his commercial prospects would improve if he got a face-lift. To his growing distress, she describes his sagging physiognomy with clinical precision. He reluctantly agrees to the surgery, which raises his nose and pulls up his upper lip, making him look a cross between a pig and Lon Chaney Sr. in *Phantom of the Opera*. It is the film's best visual gag, grotesque and very funny, and Chaplin capitalizes upon it through the startled cries and horrified expressions of everyone who sees him, including Addams. After he bursts his stitches watching the nightclub comedians, his face is mercifully restored to its former aging glory.

There are other visual pleasures in *A King in New York*, including a bathroom-wall TV screen complete with windshield wipers, as well as a few well-executed visual-verbal gags. When Shahdov arrives in America, a reporter shoves a microphone in his face and demands a comment about America. Shahdov graciously says:

> I am deeply moved by your warm friendship and hospitality. This bighearted nation has already demonstrated its noble generosity to those who come to seek a refuge from tyranny.

Of course, the fact that he is being fingerprinted at the same time by the immigration authorities completely undercuts the sentiment. During the Joan Barry trial, Chaplin had been humiliated by being fingerprinted with reporters present, and now he gleefully strikes back at both the press and the government. But even those unaware of his prior treatment can't fail to get the satirical point.

There are also a few pleasures in the dialogue. During the party scene the rich but gauche host shows his cultural ignorance when Shahdov asks him about a painting on the wall. But his host thinks Shahdov is referring to a servant:

> Shahdov: Oh, by the by, is that an El Greco?
> Host: Oh, no sir. He's a Filipino.
> Shahdov: I meant the picture opposite.
> Host: Well, I'm not sure. My wife bought it at an auction sale.

The social and political planes of the film intersect when Shahdov visits a progressive school. Child-centered education that allowed for self-expression was much in the news at the time, and Chaplin makes his opinion clear by populating the school with precocious spoiled brats. A boy kneads pastry while picking his nose, a young sculptor complains about having to censor his nude statue with a fig leaf, and several children torment Shahdov as he tries to argue with a young radical, played by Chaplin's ten-year-old son Michael. Michael spouts leftist jargon as though he's on a soapbox. The other children torment the king as he tries to get a word in edgewise, but their business is no more believable than Michael's dialogue, and the scene falls flat.

It does, however, set the plot spinning toward its conclusion. Michael's parents, it turns out, are Communists, and he runs away from school because they have been brought before the notorious House Un-American Activities Committee (HUAC). Shahdov takes him in and they form an affectionate bond, two outsiders who don't fit into the prevailing culture. Before long the boy is taken into custody by governmental authorities. To save his parents, he implicates their Communist friends, which breaks his spirit.

Because of his act of kindness toward the boy, the king finds that he's going to be called to testify before the dreaded committee as well. There's a bit of a chase through the lobby as he tries to avoid a man he thinks is a process server, something Chaplin himself had done during his first divorce. The man turns out to be just another autograph hound, and soon Shahdov is surrounded by them. Inevitably, one turns out to be the real process server.

Before he left the United States, Chaplin was repeatedly threatened with being called up before HUAC. Though he was never actually called to testify, it must have given him great pleasure to stage a scene in which he accidentally douses the committee with a water hose. Such anarchic fun takes us back to the very beginning of Chaplin's film career, but unfortunately he executes the gag with little of the old comic brio. While HUAC may have loomed large in Chaplin's life, in the world of the film the committee doesn't loom large enough for us to care about their comeuppance. Ironically, though, Shahdov's "testimony" makes him a bigger celebrity than ever.

But he's had enough. When his utopian plans are met with indifference by government officials, he decides to leave. Like Chaplin himself, the king feels ill-used by his adopted country, however much it has enriched him. Despite Dawn Addams's assurances that the present craziness is just a passing phase, he decides to "sit it out in Europe."

On his way to the airport, he visits the boy, but can offer him little solace. As his plane flies out of New York, Shahdov sits reading the paper, a neutral expression on his face as we watch the city pass below through the window. It's a flat ending for a flat film.

The most interesting thing about *A King in New York* is the way the Tramp shadows Shahdov; every now and then we catch sight of him in a familiar gesture or facial expression. Though Chaplin has grown stouter, his performing technique remains crisp and clear, and in many scenes he demonstrates his characteristic fluidity of movement. But his comic inspiration has flagged. At his best, Chaplin was able to turn even expository scenes into rich comedy. Here most of the comedy seems to turn into exposition. In *My Life in Pictures* he admits as much:

> I was disappointed in the picture. I meant it to be so up-to-date and modern but perhaps I didn't quite understand it. It started out to be very good and then it got complicated and I'm not sure about the end. There are funny gags in it . . . yet even these seem too elaborate to me now, and I feel a little uneasy about the whole film.[4]

But even with its pervasive dullness, *A King in New York* is a veritable laugh riot compared to Chaplin's final film, *A Countess from Hong Kong*. Chaplin wrote the script in the 1930s as a light comedy vehicle for Paulette Goddard and Gary Cooper, and it's intriguing to think what he might have made of it back then. When he decided to dust off his script, a shipboard bedroom farce with much slamming of doors and peek-a-boo slapstick hijinks, his first choice for the male lead was Sean Connery, then at his intrepid best as the star of the James Bond films. Connery would surely have made more of the role than Marlon Brando, who is so stolid that he robs his scenes of every vestige of humor. But Chaplin is also unable to make effective use of the considerable comic talents of Margaret Rutherford as a dowager and Patrick Cargill as Brando's valet.

Sophia Loren, playing an impoverished stowaway countess, is given the most physical business, and she gamely goes through her Chaplinesque motions. Chaplin makes much of her voluptuous beauty with clothing that is sometimes provocatively revealing and at other times ridiculously large or small. But while the camera lingers lovingly over her extraordinary face and figure, there's little life in the proceedings. This sad postscript to Chaplin's career livens up only momentarily when Chaplin does a brief cameo as a seasick steward. Appropriately, he exits films as he began, in eloquent silence.

Notes

1. Charles Chaplin, "Does the Public Know What It Wants?" *Adelphi*, January 1924.
2. Robert Payne, *The Great God Pan* (New York: Hermitage House, 1952), 289–92.
3. Chaplin, cited in Richard Meryman, "Chaplin: Ageless Master's Anatomy of Comedy," *Life*, March 10, 1967, 94.
4. Charles Chaplin, *My Life in Pictures* (New York: Grosset & Dunlap, 1975), 306.

POSTSCRIPT

Teaching Charlie Chaplin How to Walk

I was in Pittsburgh, preparing for the debut of my new solo show, when the call came from Hollywood. Robert Downey Jr., researching his role as Charlie Chaplin for Richard Attenborough's upcoming film, had come across my first book, *Charlie Chaplin's One-Man Show.* "I think you may be the only person in the world who can help me pull this off," he said. This was flattering, but since parts of the book read like an instruction manual on how to play Chaplin, it was understandable that he would think that. The trouble was, I had never taught anyone to act like Chaplin, nor had I ever learned to do any of his routines myself. But I was willing to give it a try; after all, seeing Chaplin's films had inspired me to become a performer, so I was glad to return the favor by contributing in any way possible to his film portrait.

Facing the daunting challenge of portraying the man who was arguably the greatest comedian, filmmaker, and, some would say, *actor* of the twentieth century, Robert, even then notorious in Hollywood as a brilliant but undisciplined bad boy, realized that for once he couldn't get by on chutzpah and native ability. This time he needed a number of highly specific physical acting skills, many of them discussed in my book. Playing Chaplin in a major motion picture was the opportunity of his lifetime; to succeed would move his career to a new level, and to fail would confirm many industry people's worst opinion of him. Within a couple of weeks he flew to Pittsburgh, and we began the task of preparing him for his role. Our work went well, and I was hired by the production to train Robert and create several of the film's comedy sequences.

Hollywood, 1991

"I want you to correct me when I'm eating. How would he hold a *fork*?" Thus began Robert Downey Jr.'s short but intense course in becoming Charlie Chaplin.

Robert, although he bears a striking facial resemblance to Chaplin, is physically quite unlike him. Taller than Chaplin and less wiry, he has the squarish build and strong musculature of the typical male movie hero.[1] His movement defines him as a typical product of the late twentieth century. When I first met him he wouldn't so much sit down as slump down; he would stab at his food, and chew with his mouth open; his motions were tense, coarse, bound. It would be a challenge to get him to move with Chaplin's distinctive choreographic grace and fluidity. Luckily, Robert proved to be an eager and hard-working student. He had to be, as we had only a few weeks to effect his transformation.

Given Chapin's excellent posture both onscreen and off, we began by changing Robert's with daily postural alignment exercises.[2] He was struck by the powerful effect the subtle exercises had on him, and how directly they applied to the task at hand. In such work breathing is an important conceptual and physical tool to move the body toward the desired alignment, and soon the phrase "breathe up your line" became our daily mantra. For Robert, achieving an acute awareness of his centerline was critical; not only did he have to alter his own slouchy posture to become the regal offscreen Chaplin, he also had to learn the Tramp's deft, quicksilver postural changes.

Even though I'm a lot taller than Chaplin was, I'm the same basic body type, so certain of his movement qualities come naturally to me, including a kind of loose-limbed relaxation. As soon as I began working with Robert, this loomed as a central issue, for he found it hellishly difficult to achieve. Like most people, he confused a collapsed with a relaxed body. Robert, who could fall asleep at the drop of a hat, found the idea of maintaining a relaxed state while standing in an aligned posture paradoxical.

The problem became even more apparent when he attempted to walk like Chaplin. While Chaplin's walk is often caricatured as a penguinlike, stiff-legged gait, in fact it's an extraordinarily centered and flowing movement. Trying to walk like Chaplin, Robert looked like he was encased in a suit of armor. To break down that armor we made relaxation an important part of our daily regimen. I used every technique I knew to loosen him up, and made up more. We did endless physical improvisations.

I began adding to our daily relaxation and alignment work exercises that isolated key Chaplin movements. I was determined that Robert resemble Chaplin more than superficially, that he move with Chaplin's characteristic fluid precision. These qualities were apparently automatic with Chaplin at all times, as we could see from newsreel footage we acquired of Chaplin out of character. I studied these films intently, finding moments to review and work through with Robert. Soon I *was* correcting the way he held his fork. At the same time, I began working out the various comedy scenes and incorporating them into our regimen. The amount of repetition required to master some of these movements surprised and discouraged Robert, an excellent but instinctive actor. I encouraged him to persist by stressing that his acting had to be "on top of automatic."

I spent hours breaking down the dance of the rolls from *The Gold Rush*. It was fascinating to delve into the mechanics of this fabulous sequence, even though it turned out to be only a throwaway bit in the film. But the work wasn't wasted, because I later taught the routine to Johnny Depp for *Benny and Joon*. It was the only physical comedy bit in that film I didn't make up myself—if you're going to steal, steal from the best. Depp and I rehearsed the routine endlessly, and it shows in his fine performance.

Robert and I put in endless hours on Chaplin's drunk act. In his autobiography Chaplin recorded Sennett's disappointment when he met Chaplin for the first time out of makeup. Chaplin was twenty-four and looked about eighteen, and Sennett wondered if this solemn youth could possibly be the funny drunk he'd seen on stage. In the film version Chaplin demonstrates his identity and comic virtuosity to Sennett by launching into a drunken improvisation. Because Robert repeatedly fell into my arms during rehearsals for this scene, I ended up playing the part of the Keystone Kop he draws into the action; he knew I wouldn't drop him, so it made it easier for him to focus on simply playing the drunk like Chaplin. Although Robert proved fearless and adept at falling, it was much more difficult for him to achieve the delicate disorientation of Chaplin's drunken movement. But the effort was well worth it, because by focusing on the wavering centerline of the drunk, Robert became better at sensing his own centerline, and this helped him to assume Chaplin's upright yet relaxed bearing.

We needed every moment of our five weeks of preproduction time, for Attenborough wanted Robert to inspire both cast and crew by becoming the familiar Tramp character at the outset. Accordingly, one of the first things we shot was Chaplin putting on his costume for the first time, then "discovering" his walk as he strides toward the set. The walking scene was shot about a dozen times, and Robert nailed it just once. Luckily, that was enough.

Then Charlie/Robert continues onto the set, where he proceeds to improvise the first Tramp comedy scene. The three-minute sequence, in which Charlie disrupts a wedding party, is not based on an actual Chaplin film. For our purposes, Chaplin's early years of artistic development had to be compressed into this single scene. I created it, as much as I could, in Chaplin's style, quoting specific gags here and there.

A bit later in the shoot we also filmed a montage of scenes that traced Charlie's artistic development and his burgeoning romantic relationship with Edna Purviance, his leading lady from 1915 until 1923. Unfortunately, this montage, which included some of Robert's best work, was cut from the final film. I particularly recall a nice bit on the set of *The Cure*, and a twilight tango across the empty stage, during which Edna pulls off Charlie's mustache and they kiss.

Once shooting began, Robert's schedule was grueling, for he appeared in virtually every scene shot for the next several months. Whenever possible we would begin the day with warm-ups, then steal moments during lunch breaks and setup changes. But our primary work now had to be accomplished during the shooting itself. Luckily, Robert and I had established an excellent rapport, and much could be communicated nonverbally. I would shift my head slightly backward, and he would nod and make a postural change that affected his whole body;

I'd shake my arms, and he would relax into a more fluid movement. Inevitably, from time to time my presence on the set as movement-acting coach and comedy choreographer put me at odds with the director, but by and large things went smoothly.

For the scene in which Chaplin put together his iconic costume, the script called for a series of magical special effects, as Chaplin, describing the moment much later, ironically mythologizes it. I persuaded the director to let Robert do part of the sequence with a Chaplinesque combination of skill and film technology. Instead of the derby hat flying onto his head, it seems to roll of its own accord up Robert's arm. In reality, Robert learned to roll the hat down his arm and the film was reversed—of course, he had to think and act backward, beginning the movement at the end with his eyes looking upward at the hat before he rolled it down his arm. The end effect was, I thought, very pleasing.

Attenborough wisely undercranked some of the action at twenty-two frames per second, an undetectable speedup that gives Robert's movement a little extra snap. This worked particularly well during the wedding party scene. The speedup had to be quite subtle, because, from the point of view of the movie, we aren't watching a film, but the shooting of a film; it had to be slipped in, much as Chaplin slipped undercranked sequences into all his sound films.

To my mind, one of the most successful moments in the film was our re-creation of a scene from *The Immigrant*, in black-and-white footage that skillfully replicated the photographic quality of the original.[3] When it was shown to Chaplin's daughter Geraldine, who played her own grandmother in the film, she thought she was seeing an actual clip from *The Immigrant*. This was heady praise indeed.

But the most satisfying part of the experience was the chance to travel back to the days of silent movies. The Keystone Studio, where Chaplin made his first films, had been reconstructed with scrupulous accuracy in the middle of an orange grove in Fillmore, California, about two hours from the snarled traffic of the movie capital. It was almost laughably Spartan, consisting of a huge open-air stage, a row of dressing rooms, and a tower, from which Mack Sennett kept watch over the multiple films in production. The sunlight on the stage, filtered through large muslin diffusers high overhead, was soft and watery, a shimmering light unlike anything I'd ever seen. I spent hours on that stage rehearsing with Robert and the other actors, and more hours alone, basking in that magical light of early cinema. The October air was filled with the pungent smells of fall and the newly constructed sets. Near me, antique hand-cranked movie cameras sat poised upon their tripods, waiting for the action to begin again.

Notes

1. Bodies can be classified as roughly rectangular, linear, or circular in shape. Robert is the first type, the blocky mesomorph. Most leading men in movies have been mesomorphs, from Rudolph Valentino to Clark Gable to Keanu Reeves. Ectomorphs are linear—skinny or stringy-looking people, like Chaplin, Woody Allen, Marty Feldman, and Basil Rathbone. When you watch them, your eyes are often drawn to their extremities, their hands or feet; their movements tend to be either delicate or nervous-looking. Their opposites are endomorphs, people like John Candy or Oliver Hardy, who are fleshy and rounder. Their movements seem to emanate from deeper inside their bodies, and they can look powerful, lumbering, or sluggish. When an endormorph moves delicately, like an ectomorph, it has an incongruous, comic effect—think of Hardy's signature tie-twiddle or the balletic hippos in *Fantasia*.

2. The work we did was based on a system of postural alignment called Structural Awareness, developed by Dr. Dorothy Law Nolte, whose name is more familiar as the author of the poem "Children Learn What They Live." Dorothy learned her approach to alignment as an early disciple of Dr. Ida Rolf, whose "rolfing" system of deep tissue massage has the same effect as Dorothy's system, the difference being that Structural Awareness can be done without the pain of the rolfing process. Early in my career I sought Dorothy out because of a whiplash neck injury that for a year had made my life a daily ordeal. Within two weeks of beginning her exercises, the pain of the injury lifted, and a new disciple was born. Eventually, Dorothy certified me as a teacher of the technique, which was critical to my work with Robert.

A related and better-known method of postural alignment through exercise, often incorporated into theatre and dance training programs, is the Alexander Technique. This is a powerful and effective method, but it takes much longer than Structural Awareness to achieve its effects.

3. The film was shot by Sven Nykvist, Ingmar Bergman's cinematographer.

Index

Note: Listings of film titles other than Chaplin's are accompanied by the name of the film's director. Since Harold Lloyd and Buster Keaton often directed their own films without taking credit, this index lists their names with their films.

About the Author

Dan Kamin created the physical comedy sequences for both *Chaplin* and *Benny and Joon* and trained Robert Downey Jr. and Johnny Depp for their acclaimed starring performances. He also played the wooden Indian that came to life in the cult classic *Creepshow 2* and created the Martian girl's weird movement for Tim Burton's horror spoof *Mars Attacks!* Dan performs his one-man shows internationally. A frequent guest artist with symphony orchestras, his popular series of "Comedy Concertos" combine movement, comedy, and classical music. You can find out more about Dan and see some of his antics at www.dankamin.com.